BREXIT
What the Hell Ha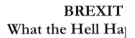

By
Christopher Bartram BA Hons, Diplom.-Betriebsw.

Copyright Christopher Bartram 2019

Acknowledgements

My thoughts and concerns about Brexit began as soon as the result was declared in 2016 and have been fermented in the proceeding years leading to this book being completed.

I would like to thank many people for their input opinions and support in creating this work including author Martin J Cobb for his design and style of the book, Klavs Henriksen MSc for his editing and content input / critique, and Graham Windram MSc for his input. Also, Toby Bartram for his design input to the book cover and input, as well as my business Partner Tony Large and his understanding with my focus being elsewhere (i.e. with this book) sometimes because of the time needed to finish such an endeavour.

Finally, thank you to my wife Natalie who has been very understanding regarding the time this book has taken up affecting our social life and weekends, as well as getting used to me burning the midnight oil frequently trying to hit set deadlines and trying to keep up with the rapid Brexit developments in the last 3 years.

"All your dreams are made when you're chained to the mirror and the razor blade."
Oasis

"The most important thing is not to fool yourself and you are the easiest person to fool."

Feynman

"If a democracy cannot change its mind, it ceases to be a democracy!"

David Davis

Applicable to Brexit?

Preface

Introduction

Why this book was written

<u>**The Past**</u>
- How did we get here? Important events in history that brought us to the 2016 Referendum

<u>**EU Specific**</u>

- The origins of the EU

- Why the EU?

- How is the EU made up, and who makes the laws?

- Why did the United Kingdom join the EU?

- Qualified majority voting (QMV)

- Unanimity of votes and the power of the UK

- Article 7 of the EU Treaty

- Light bulbs, fridges other way around

- Interpol

- Some myths of the EU debunked

<u>**Some benefits of the EU**</u>
- **Freedom**

- Consumer protection (and protecting your rights)

- Foreign affairs

- Sovereignty and opt-outs

- **Economic and Monetary Union (EMU)**

- The UK opted-out of mandatory EU refugee quotas
- Security
- Business & trade

The referendum and the campaigns

- The problem of the Referendum in the first place!
- What became clear during the referendum campaign
- The old against the Young?
- The worst political campaign (on both sides) of all time?
- But Leave.EU was not the official leave campaign?
- Leave Campaign never defined a destination!
- Who was to blame for the poor Campaigns?
- Lies and the EU referendum campaigns
- A project by the rich for the Rich?

Brexiteer Amnesia Ignorance or Duplicity?

- Customs Union
- Irish Border

Brexit Hard or Soft Boiled?

- The Brexit Process
- What is hard and soft Brexit?
- What was the Leave position – Soft or Hard?

Brexiteer and leave arguments

- We have too many immigrants!
- We just need to be tougher in the negotiations

- We must carry out the "WILL OF THE PEOPLE"

- "EU Migrants are Benefit Scroungers"

- "Charity begins at home"

- "The German Car makers will tell the EU to give us a great deal!"

- "We can trade with the rest of the world when we leave!"

- "We want to Take back control of our Trade"

- "Why should Germany, France etc. have input in our laws?"

- "Churchill would never have allowed us to be swallowed up by Europe!"

- "It's our money argument"

- "I hate the EU Laws and regulations imposed upon us!"

- The "Crystal Ball" argument

- "It will be alright, eventually"

- The "we just need to be stronger" argument

- The "Abolish all Tariffs" argument

- "Job Losses and Depreciation of Sterling is Project Fear"

- "It's OK we are preparing for a no-deal Brexit"

- "We voted to Leave but still have high employment and low unemployment!"

- "They need us more than we need them!"

- "It's not all about money"

The MEDIA

- The British Media is largely right wing AND very powerful

- The Lies of the Press & political intent

- The Press and Tax avoidance

- What did the media focus on during the Referendum Campaign?

- Immigration - Prominence, volume and persistence

- Deliberate and horrendous Language

- The deceitful use of images by the Press

- Summary to Press

Brexit Options

- In Out shake it all about

    - What is the Canada Option, and would it work for the UK post Brexit?

    - Is the "Norway" solution and Option for the UK?

    - Could we be like Switzerland?

    - Would a No-deal Brexit be so bad?

The potential and probable cost of Brexit to the UK

- Future Trade with the EU?

- Future of the EU Galileo project

- Universities and students

- Money Money Money - EU money around the corner from you!

- Every club has rules, get used to it!

- Our rules and only our rules!

- Increased costs disproportionately affect the poor!

Social

- Multiculturalism
- "We are losing our identity!"
- Economic wastelands
  - Would people buy a house in the same way as they voted for Brexit?
- Leavers and Machos and football factories.
- Housing.

Immigration

- Shock horror - There are racists and racism!
- When does an Immigrant cease to be an immigrant?
- "Most immigrants don't speak English"
- NHS gastric bands and Immigrants
- Don't forget our animals and pets!
- Areas of low immigration voted Leave, why?
- Has political correctness contributed towards the racism we see?
- "We cannot stop EU immigrants coming in"
- Australian points-based system
  - Will those that voted Leave because of Immigration end up being more disappointed than anyone?
- "We must control our borders!"
- Are immigrants really the greatest threat to jobs in the UK?
- Have the lies about race gone since the Referendum?

An age of ignorance, simplicity and 'Alternative facts'?

- No more experts please!
- Give them simplicity
- Brexit debate is not easy

Digital and Social Media

- DIGITAL SOCIAL Media was HUGE
- Right-wing social Media Groups on Facebook, etc.
- AggrecateIQ and Cambridge Analytica
- 'Echo Chambers' and Social Media
- My personal experience of Brexit on Social Media
- The Nazis, the EU and Brexiteers?

Nostalgia, Imperialism, sovereignty and the illusion of Independence

- Nostalgia and Imperialism
- Sovereignty & Independence
- Other countries have sovereignty too you know!
- Taking back control has costs!
- Could Leaving the EU make us less Free?

Economics

- Money NOT economics
- The single market and its value
- The Single Market
- The European Union Customs Union (EUCU)

- The EU and services

- Lessons of Japan?

- The success of UK financial services

- The Financial Markets are important

- Did the Bank Of England bail out the UK economy?

- The Brexiteers Economist even told us the problems of Brexit!

Trade

- Trade is not a simple Profit and Loss account

- It will all be so easy, quick and painless!

- Percentage of World Trade and the EU

- Trade Deals are NOT that easy

- Will the UK always be a rule taker in the big world?

- Frictionless Trade and Lorries at Dover

- 'Forgotten' or 'hidden' industries

- Independent Trade Policy

- British waters and fishing

- Will the planes be halted and grounded?

Brexit and Foreign Direct Investment into the UK

- How could Brexit affect Foreign Direct Investment into the United Kingdom?

- The EU has helped open global markets to UK firms on strong terms

- Jobs

- Free movement of labour has brought benefits to the UK economy

- Do not underestimate the Long-term effect of investment!

- Cost versus Investment

- Future of Jobs and pensions

World Trade Organisation (WTO)

- What simply is the WTO?

- What would it mean for us to crash out of the EU on WTO rules?

- "UK can simply scrap all tariffs with the EU and the rest of the world"

- "No problem as the average EU import Duty is only 3.2%!"

- "We can become like the Singapore of Europe with Zero Tariffs"

- WTO and Services

- "WTO rules will solve the Irish hard border"

- "Agriculture and fisheries will be much better off under WTO terms"

- Summary of WTO and Brexit

Future Trade Deals and the big wide world

- Problem with a trade deal with India

- A free Trade Agreement with the USA?

- Problem with a trade deal with the USA

- Problem of a trade deal with China

- What about Chemicals?

- Other EU countries will exploit our Myopic Brexit decision

Politics

- Article 50 and the timing

- Lies, damn lies and statistics

- Remember £350 million and the Big Red Bus?

- A plethora of lies (claims and reality)

- Deselection of MPs just for their opinion of Brexit? Really!

- Did Angela Merkel help the Leave vote?

- Teresa May's 'deal'

- How could Brexit have ever been delivered effectively?

- Are we really 'Lions' and are we really led by 'Donkeys'?

  - Is the European Research Group (ERG) a most unpatriotic group?

The confusion between referendum and general elections

- A Referendum and general elections ARE different

The march of the right, the angry and the disaffected

- The rise of national populism
- Don't underestimate the populist right!
- Is the Right wing really that dangerous?
- Is the Brexit Party UKIP repackaged?
- Does the Brexit party have a long-term future?

The politics of Personality

- Nigel Farage
- Boris Johnson
- Arron Banks
- Dominic Cummings
- John Redwood
- Hypocrites, tricksters or opportunists?
- The people against the Elites!

The Government and broken promises

- 11 broken promises?
  - The Leave campaign and its pack of lies during and since the referendum.
- Boris Johnson, the new Prime Minister.

Personal Experience of myself and others

- When is an idiot not an idiot or just idiotic?

- "WE believe in Democracy"

- The People's vote - Can there be Too much Democracy?

- Did Leavers really want Democracy or a simple OUT result?

- The Prevention of War in Europe

- The "Condescension complex" (or Patronising Paradox)

Recent developments and the future

- Before and after

- What will happen with Boris and Brexit?

- What happens when we leave?

- Leavers – Will you genuinely get what you wanted?

- The cost of Brexit?

- Other Possible Costs and inconveniences post Brexit

- Roaming Fees

- New Driving Licenses

- Cost to families

The winners?

- What have the Leavers won?

- What voters did not vote for!

- Why no second referendum?

The End?

- Brexit – will it actually happen?

- Government research report Project Yellowhammer (July 2019)

- Why not Revoke and Stay?

- Summary and conclusion

- Final thought

- References

- Resources

- Bibliography

- Glossary

- **Appendices**

1. The Quick-Fire replies to Brexiteer arguments / reasoning

2. The Quick-Fire overview of potential issues of a no-deal Brexit

3. Quick Fire guide to the advantages of being a member of the EU

4. Lies or just Misinformation

Chapter 1
Preface

Brexit has generated the most important political and economic series of events in decades. It will change everything in our political, economic and trading relationships with the European Union and with the rest of the world, and how did we actually even get here?

This acclaimed book is insightful with the facts, the issues, the rumours and lies combined with the impassioned arguments and the equally passionate counter arguments are carefully documented. It looks at the flawed EU referendum campaigns by all parties failed to properly inform the voting public plus reports of illegal activities and foreign influence all contributed to the misinformation aided hugely by social Media. Also, the ignorance of the public about the EU and its role within the UK were all reasons for voting leave based on false information and lies.

The British peoples fear of losing their identity, their NHS and social care, their monetary system and their ability to legally govern themselves all played into the hands of the referendum result and the chaos that ensued.

What of sovereignty and independence? What is democracy and how has it changed? Who are the personalities and what lies / alternative facts have been promulgated? What is going to be the cost of Brexit? How will families and communities heal the internal rifts that have been created by Brexit? What role did racism, the impact of immigration and multiculturalism play? Hard and soft Brexit, what will the UK stand to lose or gain?

What exactly did voters vote for and vote against?
AND
who are the **winners and losers?**

With Britain moving towards the European Union (EU) exit door, I have approached this project with a passion and energy that was sadly lacking in the Remain EU referendum campaign where arrogance, lies, hate, intimidation and misinformation reared their ugly heads in a repugnant manner. David Cameron opened Pandora's Box to protect his own backside but unleashed the most horrid and illogical feelings and philosophies that were always there beneath the surface, but he could not control those forces and they ultimately destroyed him. This act will always haunt him and reflect his premiership into history.

The referendum shattered the equilibrium of British politics by bringing down political leaders such as David Cameron and Teresa May it also created a new segregation on Leave and Remain lines, as opposed to the traditional right and left divide, and it is not clear whether that will ever return in the form we knew it.

That was Mr Cameron's decision and I lose no sleep over him or his political and advisory teams as that is the business they are (were!) in, but felt for the poorer less fortunate in our society, many of whom were lied to and conned by rich public figures into voting to leave with a vision of a completely different United Kingdom with sunny uplands that will never visit them in their lifetime. It will most probably make them poorer and they will feel the sharp end of any downturn, loss of jobs and any subsequent recession.

Too many Brexit books are written by political figures, advisers, economists or political commentators whereas this is a book written by a 'normal' bloke who could not, and still cannot, understand why the UK and 17.4 million people had decided on the greatest act of self-harm in the UK's history when anything logical or factual pointed towards it being an absolutely atrocious decision when the UK already has a good deal with the EU. As this book was started after the EU referendum result amid the chaos and uncertainty that ensued it is being written about events going on around you and I have attempted to understand the roots of what happened in 2016 and is still going on in 2019 to help us grasp an understanding of what will happen moving forward and its implications on what will happen in the future.

I look into and cover all the real issues people were concerned about, the implications of this momentous decision, the disgusting duplicitous actions of the country's biased right wing press, some of the personalities and cheats who were front and centre, how did we ever get to making such a simple question out of an extremely complex interwoven political and economic system built up over 40+

years, the racist underbelly that showed its true side and dragged people with it that do not believe they are racists. The total lack of understanding of the EU of us all including some of the politicians promoting Leave, how can only 37% of the electorate be the "will of the people", why can Leavers not see the dangers and damage 3 years on, the split in our society, the difficulty Leavers now have justifying their decision so try to shut down dialogue or debate, the battle of the ages as well as many more critical aspects of what has turned out in some quarters and families to be all out 'Brexit war'.

If you want to know the background to Brexit, the arguments, witness the lies, see the passion, witness the hate, analyse the implications of the vote, as well as consider the probable future including the risks and opportunities as the rise of the deceitful and dishonest Boris Johnson now in Number 10, then this is the book for you. Written in a simple easy-to-understand manner and not entering into high convoluted language it gets to the real heart of "The war of Brexit"! Were the arguments in favour of Brexit sound and certain enough to justify the risk the UK is taking and exposing our children and our children's children to an unknown future with no plan or strategy?

Some aspects are repeated deliberately as many people may not want to read a whole book from cover to cover but rather focus upon certain subjects depending on their particular interest at that specific time, but also some aspects of the Brexit story cut across Social, EU Specific, and economics, etc. So, for example, you may want to look at the WTO as a whole or may be only the fisheries aspect of Brexit in which case fisheries has its own section, And this applies to many subjects linked to the Brexit debate and arguments. The book uses the United Kingdom (UK) and (Great) Britain interchangeably for reasons of style and flow but although technically not correct when talking about (great) Britain it does include Northern Ireland. The same applies when referring to the British people as well.

Michael Gove and the new Boris Johnson Government speak of preparing as if it will cure all the ills and demons of Brexit, but it will not, although it may soften the blow? But as it was explained to me "prepare for me to punch you in the face, you may be prepared but it will still bloody hurt!" This is the unfortunate reality.

The last word in this section I will leave to the title which is intended deliberately to be provocative but also the eyes refer to the surprise, shock and exasperation of people that are sick of Brexit but also are astounded and disillusioned as to why the country (or more accurately 37% of the electorate) arrived at such a decision in the first place and where are all those benefits and advantages they were regularly promised?

Chapter 2
Introduction

To get some context I have been attacked for my arguments and attitude linked to Brexit having been called condescending, arrogant, demeaning, aloof, patronising, treating people as idiots (more of that later), narcissistic, and a passive aggressive, which I must admit to not knowing what it meant at the time. But now I am quietly angry about it!

I am fascinated by people and how they think, how they are influenced, how some succeed and how some do not, how some are happy and how some commit acts of self-harm. I suppose I just love the good and the dark side of human nature and their thinking but was never intelligent enough to be a professional psychologist. But when seeing Brexit form itself in front of my eyes and the dark hatred and racism that reared its ugly head I was in my element as it really captured my imagination as it became a psycho drama very quickly with the most extreme, bizarre, ill-informed and downright dishonest opinions / positions coming to the fore. I could not understand why my fellow Brits could not see Brexit was an obvious act of self-harm with no discernible point or upside but probably a lot of downsides, both short and long term.

As I spoke to Leavers, or before the actual vote potential Leavers, the more confused I became when they spoke about 'Independence' but could not name any laws imposed on the UK by the EU they did not like. The same applied to 'sovereignty', but when challenged they did not even know what it really meant!

Even after the result people spoke of the "Will of the People" deliberately forgetting or dismissing almost half the people that voted the other way. I didn't understand how 37% of the eligible electorate (yes it was 52% of those that actually voted) can vote for a hypothetical easy pain free Brexit with a great deal (as some of them genuinely believed) could become an unbreakable mandate to Leave whatever the cost. It just seemed wrong and bizarre. But it got worse not better as more time passed since the referendum when we witnessed the UK stockpiling food, medicine and industrial products / components and the former British Prime Minister Teresa May trying to blackmail MPs into supporting her deal which made Brexit look even more senseless than it appeared in the beginning. But still people thought it was and still is a good idea which fascinated me, what made them think this?

I was very pro-Remain as it just seemed sensible, logical and an absolute 'no brainer' for me but whilst sitting beside a swimming pool on holiday in Turkey (more of Turkey later!) the 2016 EU referendum result came through and hit me like a tidal wave. I was genuinely astounded at the result and what I perceived to be the greatest act of self-harm our country had committed in my lifetime. So probably that was when the seed of a book was sown as I was clearly missing something or many things to understand why 17.4 Million people voted to leave an organisation within which we had been economically very successful, especially as we were not flourishing as an economy in the 70s and effectively the "Sick man of Europe".

Why do people keep saying it is the "Will of the people" when it was 52-48%? This makes no sense, unless you think it is democratically legitimate to forget 48% of voters or 63% of the electorate that did not vote to leave. Imagine if only less than 5% had changed their vote and we would have been in a completely different place with none of the hate, uncertainty and chaos that the EU referendum vote unleashed.

Therefore, I set myself on a journey to better understand the history of our relationship with the EU, what reasons people had for leaving, what they expected from leaving and how they believed it would improve their lives and more importantly the lives of their children and their children's children. I interacted with as many Leavers and Brexiteers as possible rather than being stuck in the usual Remainer bubble or echo chamber to better understand the other side of the arguments and where they were coming from and what I was missing. And it was these interactions plus the almost 3 years of chaos in Westminster that eventually made me put pen to paper (well fingers to Laptop!) to collate and organise my thoughts and what I had learned from my Leaver and Brexiteer friends and connections.

There are obviously a lot of books about Brexit in the bookstores and online but I found most of them were written by political hacks, literary authors, political commentators or indeed politicians which were highly convoluted, not always easy to follow, and only suitable for people that are extremely interested in the EU referendum, politics and everything associated with it. This book I hope will reach a wider audience that are looking for a Brexit related book that is written by an everyday person that does not use unnecessarily complicated words and theories and tries to stick to the important issues and those that have affected individuals over the years but more importantly those that will affect individuals and their children in the future.

At the time of writing this book all the stated positions, stances, opinions, laws, regulations cited were correct but may have changed in the interim and at the time of publication and / or reading. Many of the books mentioned above and those I have read are based on interviews or positions of politicians, political journalists and other experts which are useful, but I always longed for a book that was based on facts and well thought out arguments and logic. BUT written by an everyday person that is not actively involved in party politics or writes for the media or press and how they saw the Brexit developments, build up and aftermath to the chaos we see today. This is the view from the ground based on conversations, arguments, and correspondence with everyday Brexiteers and Remainers who were very strong and honest in their opinions and positions.

The basis of this book came after many arguments, debates and discussions with friends, colleagues, and acquaintances both on Social Media (Facebook, Twitter etc.) as well as face-to-face discussions and debates. You see my genuine amazement (and disappointment) that after the referendum result Leavers could vote to leave, as it seemed to be the greatest act of self-punishment and damage the UK had carried out in my living history. But I was genuinely passionate to try and understand why people acted as they did and began a focused research programme, a series of conversations, Facebook posts and discussions / debates to better understand the EU and what happened and why. Only people that voted leave could tell me that. Once I began this journey what became clear was there were several key influential issues that I had never, before the referendum, considered. I will go into more details on these and pose many other questions to you the reader, but these were the main ones that came to mind when starting this journey:

1. People's understanding of the EU and its relationship with the UK was very poor.
2. MY understanding of the EU and its relationship with the UK was Poor (I just didn't know it).
3. The Leave vote was much more passionate than that of remain.

4.   Emotion can trump logic and facts.

5.   People become rooted in their positions and will not or cannot move, as they became entrenched with their 'tribes'.

6.   The anti-EU feeling had clearly been built up over many years and did not suddenly raise its ugly head at the referendum in 2016.

7.   Simple solutions on either side are not satisfactory as many issues are interrelated, interconnected and historical.

8.   The older generations have not forgotten what they perceive to be their Great British imperialistic past.

When you read the following pages you will see the journey I have been on, the twists and turns of opinions and actions of many people and organisations before and since the referendum, highlighting some lesser known facts, extreme positions on both sides, the efforts to kill free speech and discussion, plus many other interrelated issues. What you will get here is quite simply a no bullshit thought provoking analysis and personal investigation into what happened before, during and after the EU referendum from a person (unconnected to the Westminster bubble) who has taken it upon himself to delve as deeply into the important Brexit issues that affect most people's everyday lives, whether they realise it or not.

Ultimately we have to ask ourselves some basic questions and answer them honestly and directly, and not like politicians or political individuals with a vested interest or an obsession with leaving the EU giving biased, vague or sometimes deliberate misinformation. Any decisions and answers should be based on logic, fact, and observable reality rather than emotion and fear. I had to ask myself whether I am as bad as those rabid Brexiteers that will not listen to logical arguments or the dismantling of the fabrications they have listened to as they have this blind belief in their ideal. I have asked so many Leavers their reasons for leaving trying to understand their logic, reasoning, fears and desire to see a different type of country outside the EU and what that country will look like, and at times this has been almost impossible as many lack a clear logical thought process often preferring stereotypes, sound bites and absolute inaccuracies which is not a great way to make an informed decision. But how could we be surprised when that is exactly what Nigel Farage et al. have done for years?

The 50% +1 vote system decided upon for the referendum was dumb from the outset, and with hindsight now seems more foolish for such a critical far-reaching constitutional change with no reasonable accurate idea of how it would affect the UK going forward. Such a change should have reasonably been carried a required 70% + vote for change. This was not the case and what resulted was only 37% of the eligible voters voting for such a change. Even those that voted was

23

51.89-48.11% showing the country was split, so to make such a momentous leap into the dark was logical madness and politically crazy. Even the Brexiteers who had lied and fed the electorate with misinformation seemed shocked at the result and once questioned after the result were devoid of any ideas or plan to take the mess forward, apart from repeating "Out means Out", "we have our Freedom" or "today is Independence Day" and other such empty slogans. They were like rabbits in the headlights making many bizarre statements and contradicting each other such as Nigel Farage claiming he would never have made such a claim as '£350 million per week for the NHS', although he never questioned it during the referendum campaign for obvious reasons. The bar of truth and honesty was at an all-time low.

The EU is not and will never be a perfect organisation as no huge corporation or organisation like the NHS or the Indian Railways system etc. can be, but Brexit is a blind leap of faith, based on so much false information comparable to throwing the baby out with the bathwater rather than working intensely with our partners from the inside to help reform it. The shame is that history (which is what Brexit is) must be lived forward and learnt backwards. It has also been cited by family close to the author that they knew of an Italian company that did not follow Health & Safety rules and was not punished and felt that was a justified reason some could consider for leaving the EU. But again, these are isolated anecdotal cases and even if there are several of them, they in no way justify a huge decision to leave the EU and damage our country as a few companies flout the rules. There will also be companies in the UK that do not follow the letter of the law and try to cut corners.

Many of my peers, admittedly white males and females between 40 and 65 ish, were mostly Leavers and some passionate aggressive Leavers at that. So, I questioned myself, "Am I strange?" "Why do I think so differently from them?" "Why do they dislike or are scared of foreigners so much when those very same foreigners do not seem to impact those people's lives in any negative way?", "Why do they seem to hate the EU so much when I have never heard one mention the EU before the referendum campaign started, and immigration was front and centre?" So many questions and so few answers, which led me to look more deeply and dig into the psyche of those 'friends' and their beliefs, fears, and prejudices.

When I questioned these beliefs and positions and dissected their arguments with facts and logic, they got angry and would get angrier at me for highlighting the misinformed positions they took rather than getting angry with the likes of Jacob Rees-Mogg, Nigel Farage, and Boris Johnson etc. that had told them such lies. Were they embarrassed they had been hoodwinked, or did they not care because they were so entrenched in their position and disliked immigrants so much that they didn't care as long as they got the result they wanted? These are intelligent people, but why did they make such an ill-advised decision for the UK? What was I missing? These encounters resulted in unfriendly, aggressive responses and arguments with one guy even calling me a complete "knob" (colloquial for penis for our foreign readers) as I would not agree with the 'tribe'[(IL.)]. I will address many issues and implications in the following pages but also ask YOU the reader some pressing questions! This is not a one-way book but hopefully an interaction between people with a genuine interest in the phenomenon that is Brexit and the psyche of the English and British people (yes they can be different) whether you be for remain, leave or sitting on the fence smack in the middle.

It was interesting when asking people (and I asked a lot!) why they voted leave and they obviously tried to avoid saying "immigrants" after the result, although this was the focus during the campaign as we all experienced. After the result they changed and chose words like 'Sovereignty', 'freedom', 'taking back control', 'independence', etc. I also asked who they would normally vote for and why which resulted in different parties as I tried to get a good variation, but the main reason was "whatever party made my life better" or words to that effect, which is understandable (although I should state that the majority by far of my peer group and friends are Conservative voters). I then proceeded to ask them based on that same logic how the EU negatively affected their lives or that of their families? This tended to stump people as they struggled to give examples and even got many things totally wrong as regards the EU such as longer sentences for Terrorists or Boris's good old bendy Bananas, which set off alarm bells at the beginning of this project as ignorance could have played a significant part. This is when it became clear when you peeled back the onion it all seemed to boil down so often to immigration in some shape or form as that was visual to them, even though several other complaints such as fewer police, unacceptable minimum wage, and higher pensions in Germany had absolutely nothing to do with the EU, and we will return to these later.

One question kept ringing around my head when thinking of my teenage kids that I could not rid myself of, which was this:

Q. Were the arguments in favour of Brexit sound and certain enough to justify the risk we are taking and exposing our children and our children's children to?

And so, my journey began to try to understand why Leavers voted Leave and was it a sensible logical decision for our country, our children and our children's children?

Right enough 'waffle' and come with me on our Brexit Journey where we are about to discover many interesting and some shocking things that I, and maybe you, never knew which will open your eyes as it did mine!

I will just leave you with one question for consideration and will return to it at the end of the book to see whether you have changed your mind or have a different perspective:

Q. How will your life and that of your friends and family will improve post Brexit, and what benefits will you see personally?

Chapter 3
The Past

How did we get here?

Important events in history that brought us to the 2016 Referendum

Just to add some context to where we are now and where we came from I thought highlighting these historical events would help, especially to those who are not as informed of where we have come from because as you will see when reading this book this situation we find ourselves in 2019 did not begin in 2016 but way before that.

- Early 70s – the UK was economically performing very badly, especially in comparison with France and Germany, And was referred to as the 'sick man of Europe'.
- 1973 – Ted Heath takes Britain into the EEC, or often referred to as the 'common market'.
- 1975 – British public backs EEC membership in Referendum with 67% voting to remain in.
- 1992 – Maastricht Treaty was signed.

- 1992 – Wednesday 16th September Britain crashed out of the Exchange Rate Mechanism (ERM) causing interest rates to rise to an inconceivable 15%.
- 2007 (September) – David Cameron gives a 'cast-Iron guarantee' to hold a Referendum on the Lisbon Treaty if he becomes PM (as a part of his Leadership pitch appealing to the right wing of the Conservative party)
- 2015 (May) – David Cameron wins the first Conservative majority since 1992 at the general election and vows to hold a Referendum before the end of 2017.
- 2015 (June) – Dominic Cummings charged with setting up the 'OUT' campaign.
- 23rd June 2016 – EU Referendum Day.
- 24th June 2016 - at 4.39am Leave is announced as the winner.
- 24th June 2016 - at 8.15am David Cameron resigns as Prime Minister.
- 11th July 2016 – Teresa May becomes Conservative party leader unopposed as Andrea Leadsom withdraws from the race.
- 13th July 2016 – Teresa May, after visiting the Queen at Buckingham palace, becomes Prime Minister.
- June 2019 – Teresa May resigns as Prime Minister, not being able to get her 'deal' for the withdrawal agreement voted through parliament.
- July 2019 – The Conservative party elects a new Party Leader, Boris Johnson, and therefore Prime Minister.

There are of course many other events and dates that are important between and after these specific dates which will be covered in this book but we hope these set the scene for you as the chaos begins and indecision, lack of clarity and the true meaning of democracy (abused by many) comes into question and the future of the UK and constitution are thrown in the balance.

Chapter 4
EU Specific

The origins of the EU

I believe it was worth highlighting where the EU came from and why it exists as I have never seen this in any of the newspapers although have seen bizarre headlines such as 'EU to ban zipper trousers' – The Sun, or 'Bosses to be told what colour carpets to buy by EU' – The Daily Star and some people will have believed these.

The origin of the EU began between the time of the two world wars by some visionaries with the ideal of trying to stop the result of wars and world wars. But we should add that the developments of the EU have gone further than was first envisioned resulting in a much more interdependent union we have now.

At the time there were only a few supranational organisations and bodies and before the time of the World Bank and the IMF (International Monetary Fund) and the League of nations was impotent and achieved very little (it really dies in the ashes of WW2). Trade at this stage was largely carried out on a country to country basis that had not really changed for hundreds of years. The General Agreement on Tariffs and Trade (GATT) was founded and signed in 1947 which is a legal agreement between many countries, whose overall purpose was to promote international trade by reducing or eliminating trade barriers such as tariffs or quotas. According to its preamble, its purpose was the "substantial reduction of tariffs and other trade barriers and the elimination of preferences, on

29

a reciprocal and mutually advantageous basis." It stayed in effect until 1994 when the World Trade Organisation (WTO) was formed and covered in more detail later in the book.

The aim of a French diplomat Jean Monnet and others were to look to create a body that had actual teeth and would be able to achieve set goals including making wars less probable between EU States due to the interdependent nature of the relationships so reducing the chances of them beginning and then escalating potentially to world wars and nation states could not be trusted to do this on their own. The logic was that if you bring countries closer together with common goals and interests to achieve peace and prosperity. Fast forward to 1953 and 'closer union' was enshrined in the Treaty of Rome which had the original goals and more including making the commencement of wars difficult and almost impossible to the benefit of all countries and populations concerned. The benefit a free trade agreement and the creation of the largest free trade area in the world has benefited all countries in the EU, despite seeing such serious issues with Greece, although one of their major issues for them was not effectively collecting taxes and weakness in the economy that should have may be meant Greece should never have joined in the first place?

Those that say they never expected the EU to be a political as well as an economic one was not paying attention as since its very inception the EU was always going to be more than an economic Union. The political dimension was explicit from the moment it was founded in 1957. It was born out of war and conceived as a way of finding a better future for Europe than fighting and how then was that not going to be political? To misunderstand this fact is to miss the point completely of the goals and aspirations of the 'founding fathers' of the European Union, and the attempt for Europe to Learn that only interdependence and not Nationalism could bring about peace.

We have seen so many memes of Churchill and how he would have hated the UK being a part of the EU, but this is just not true. On 19 September 1946, Churchill went to the University of Zurich to speak. 'We must create the European family in a regional structure' he declared, 'it may be, the United States of Europe'. Core to his vision was that there can be no revival of Europe, without a spiritually great Germany'. Churchill was ambivalent about the extent to which he saw Britain playing an integral part in any United States of Europe. But there was no doubting the tonic his speech gave leaders across Europe in the face of Stalin's increasingly belligerent Soviet Union, so recently an ally in the Second World War, was a further attraction. [10]

Why the EU?

The EU aimed to set rules and regulations to try to avoid the market being flooded by shoddy goods and even dangerous goods!

How is the EU made up, and who makes the laws?

As with any major or multinational organisation the EU is a complex structure made up of a number of presidents including the following. It should be qualified that the use of the word president for English speakers can sound 'loaded' as they are not true presidents as the EU is not a country, but rather 'heads of' specific parts of the European Union machine.

1. President of the European Council of ministers
2. President of the European Commission
3. President of the European Parliament

It is indeed complex how the individuals of the various bodies including representatives on the Council, the commission (consisting of appointed officials), the parliament and other bodies interact and work with nation states.

Behind the scenes you have a team of officials beavering away in 24 different languages to produce draft laws with the aim of improving and protecting the people's lives in the EU. These are processed by the Brussels machine and, if approved, emerge as regulations, which apply across the EU without further ado or directives, which also have to be made into law, but in the form of legislation by the parliaments of each member state. This is policed by the European Court of Justice (ECJ). If a country fails to correctly comply with what it is told by a directive, it can be stamped on by the ECJ. [8]

As with any law-making organisation and process it is never perfect including our own and the complexities of making laws applicable to 27 different countries is not easy. But our own British law-making machines has the same complexities, albeit it on a smaller scale as making laws that are evenly applicable and appropriate for all regions and cities including Cornwall & Devon, small Northern towns and the colossus that is London, all of whom have their own issues and challenges. So, when people criticise the law-making process, we should also look closer to home rather than just using it to bash the EU again. I challenge you to ask any of your Leave friends what Laws made by the EU they would change and why or which EU laws have negatively impacted on their lives? You will find very few that can answer those questions sensibly (I mean without mentioning Boris Johnson's bendy bananas). Yes, he invented that lie!) but they still dislike or in some cases hate the EU. The claim of the EU being undemocratic is somewhat weak from British perspective when part of the UK legislature, i.e. our upper house, can be appointed for life and also unelected.

Why did the United Kingdom join the EU?

The actual history of the UK's membership of the EU is that we went from the sick man of Europe in 1973 to the world's 5th largest economy in the world in 2016. That is the reality when you strip away the arguments from both sides. Now in a normal world surely one would say well that is a great result and we should be pleased with that but during the campaign the EU was accused by Brexiteers such as Boris Johnson that the EU is holding us back (even though the chance of us becoming the 4th largest economy in the world was unrealistic so what he expected was unclear as usual) including calling it a 'a job destroyer engine, you can see it all across Southern Europe and you can see it alas in this country as well' even though we had the highest employment numbers for decades when he made that statement! Still Boris never let facts get in the way of a sound bite. So, he was either ignorant of the reality of our position or he was again being economical with the truth.

Michael Gove, also an arch Brexiteer claimed 'the majority of people are suffering as a result of our membership of the European Union' although he did not clarify how and whenever I asked people that agreed with him they could not explain how either. Then from John Redwood we hear 'the economy would get a boost, our public services would be better funded, and some hated taxes could be removed' although no guarantees and no clarification as to how that was going to actually happen, especially in light of most economists claiming quite logically that leaving the EU with no deal would shrink the economy for years. In 'defence' of Mr Redwood he is obsessed with the EU and has been a veteran of Eurosceptic sentiment even going back to John Major when he was thought to be one of those that the Prime Minister referred to as "Bastards". So, we have to have some sympathy for his desperation. What linked all the above and their anti-EU membership comments is that they offered no clarity, clarification or a sense of a plan, for obvious reasons.

Now over those years we had influence (despite what the British Media would have you think) because as a large member state the UK had weighted votes in the Council, votes in the European parliament, and has been active in lobbying Brussels. But once we leave, we will lose that influence and voting power, but will still have to meet several EU rules / regulations and obligations if we want to openly trade with them, and it is vital we do. We will still have shared interests and goals with the EU including foreign policy, the Iran nuclear deal, standing up to Russian aggression and influence as well as many other international issues. Once we leave, we will lose that ability to work as a part of the EU to amplify our voice and that could be significant.

It was quite clear that British leaders were looking at how they could mitigate the UK's long-term decline and joining the European common market was the obvious and only realistic option, and history has shown it to be a good one. Now potentially the baby is going out with the bathwater!

Qualified majority voting (QMV)

The telegraph in its article entitled '20 reasons you should vote to leave the European Union' from the 22nd June 2016 placed at number 5 'We wouldn't have to accept decisions forced on us by other countries' and then goes forth highlighting the QMV implying how badly we are served by such a system. But in such a large club the only way to get the amount of legislation though is with QMV otherwise nothing would get done, and because we were the 2nd largest economy in the EU, we received a disproportionate number of votes as does Germany and France, etc. The Telegraph highlights the UK was on the losing side of 12% of QMV votes whereas France was on the wrong side of only 1% with the implication the EU is against the United Kingdom rather than may be France better understands the meaning of cooperation and team and doesn't try vote against everything that doesn't give them everything they want, i.e. they compromise. This is the difference between a staunch Brexiteer and an EU member state and partner. The bottom line is it is a requirement that even the local Tennis club committee may use as otherwise that club like the EU would achieve nothing if every decision had to be voted for with unanimity.

In fact, their list goes downhill pretty quickly even citing a number 8 'We would have proper vacuum cleaners' whatever a proper vacuum cleaner is? But this is linked to Dyson being pissed off with the EU and campaigning against it when he lost his case against the ruling where the EU was trying to save energy and encourage more efficient devices, they banned motors of 1600 watts and above. He claimed it was skewed in favour of German vacuum cleaners over his products. This could demonstrate Dyson being one of the very few high-profile companies promoting Brexit with very little reasoning compared to other major businessmen and their organisations. He very much pushed Britain and Britain being great again outside the EU and was very persuasive and the power of his name would have convinced many people. But then moved his Headquarters to Singapore. Make of that what you will, but the timing and the principle seemed strange in light of his pro-British stance.

Unanimity of votes and the power of the UK

Certain policy fields still remain subject to unanimity in whole or in part. These include:
- Taxation;

- the finances of the Union (own resources, the multi-annual financial framework);
- membership of the Union (opening of accession negotiations, association, serious violations of the Union's values, etc.);
- change the status of an overseas country or territory (OCT) to an outermost region (OMR) or vice versa.
- harmonisation in the field of social security and social protection;
- certain provisions in the field of justice and home affairs (the European prosecutor, family law, operational police cooperation, etc.);
- the flexibility clause (352 TFEU) allowing the Union to act to achieve one of its objectives in the absence of a specific legal basis in the treaties;
- the common foreign and security policy, except for certain clearly defined cases;
- the common security and defence policy, except for the establishment of permanent structured cooperation;
- citizenship (the granting of new rights to European citizens, anti-discrimination measures);
- certain institutional issues (the electoral system and composition of the Parliament, certain appointments, the composition of the Committee of the Regions and the European Economic and Social Committee, the seats of the institutions, the language regime, the revision of the treaties, including the bridging clauses, etc.).

Article 7 of the EU Treaty

Don' worry I am not going to get technical (basically because I can't!) but this is an example of what the EU is trying to achieve when setting a set of common rules and laws and in this case attempting to stop countries introducing laws that could be detrimental and potentially dangerous to the rest of the community and its citizens.

Article 7 is a mechanism within the Lisbon Treaty that ensures as it states, "all EU countries respect the common values of the EU" and was devised as a way to prevent member states backsliding on the principles and values of the EU laws, to keep the standards and expectation high. The measure came into force in the Treaty of Amsterdam in 1999 but had not been triggered until December 2017. This was when the European Commission launched Article 7 against Poland and the European parliament who sanctioned proceedings against Hungary in September 2018 for controversial judicial reforms. The mechanism is triggered when the EU feels there is a "Clear risk" of an EU member state breaching the bloc's fundamental values which include "human dignity, freedom, democracy, equality, the rule of law for human rights, including the rights of persons belonging to minorities." Note this was enacted against Hungary and Poland, but Brexiteers would have you (falsely) believe it is only the UK that suffers at the hands of the EU, which is either misplaced Paranoia or deliberate misrepresentation.

Article 7 is an important piece of legislation and could be used to halt ultra-right-wing governments or governments introducing ultra-right-wing laws against minorities for example and that should be applauded but is rarely mentioned in the scope of the EU. The question is, and it is only now being tested, as to how effectively it can be implemented and enacted against a member state against its will? Only time will tell.

Light bulbs, fridges and Blue Passports

In an article entitled '20 reasons you need to leave the European Union' The Telegraph was struggling so much to come up with credible reasons why you should leave that it resorted to the following:

- proper light bulbs (number 20) when the EU is trying to reduce power consumption and help the environment!
- No more stupid recycling bins', (number 18) when the EU is promoting sensible recycling schemes to help the future generations!
- 'It would be easier to get rid of fridges' (number 17), when the EU is trying to promote sensible disposal of white goods and dangerous substances and not just filling landfills with poisons!
- 'We could have blue passports again' (number14), well less said about that the better when we think about the cost and the fact that the company that won the bid to produce the UK's new passports was a French company as they offered the best value proposition in the tendering process! Author: In truth, we could have blue passports within the EU, but until the EU referendum it was never felt important!
- We could get rid of wind farms' (number 13), when it is proven that we need to use fewer fossil fuels to help protect our environment and planet and wind power offers and an excellent opportunity for us as a windy Island! Author: In reality, wind farms are NOT mandated by the EU!
- Plus, others......

So, we can see how desperate the Eurosceptic press becomes when trying to prove we are better served outside the EU and by doing this they ignore the huge benefits of free trade with 44% of our exports going to the EU and counter this major benefit for the UK with Fridges, recycling bins and blue passports. This is Dogma and Myopia in action. Many of the EU decisions are aimed at and trying to create a better world. No, it is not perfect and never will be, but these are positive well-intentioned developments for mankind.

Interpol

It would appear that despite its importance for the UK for enforcing law across the EU such as finding and bringing to account British criminals who escape to Europe, or protecting our Isle against terrorism we will have limited access to Interpol of not more than non-members such as Norway or the USA for example. According to the Institute of Government: "The countries with the closest security co-operation with the EU... do not have access to all EU databases (i.e. critical information), cannot take part fully in the operations of Europol, the EU's police agency, and have more complicated extradition arrangements with the EU." It should be added that because of an opt out from earlier treaties even Denmark as an EU member has had difficulties with access, so it is not always so clear cut.

Some myths of the EU debunked

1. The EU makes member states vote and vote again until they get the result they want. - The Eurosceptic rhetoric from the likes of Daniel Hannan has been built up to give this impression, but it does not hold up to scrutiny. France and the Netherlands were never ignored as the thing they voted against, the EU constitution, was actually dropped!

2. As for Ireland and Denmark being made to vote twice over the things that were rejected the first time went back to the drawing board and were changed significant concessions and opt-outs achieved and a NEW proposal went back to the public in each of those countries and were voted through with a high percentage acceptance and higher turnout in both occasions. I am sure you will agree this looks like a good form of democracy and not a dictatorship as some would have you believe! Perhaps this is why the Brexiteers do not want a second referendum as citizens learn and understand more the second time around and the same lies which have now been debunked are less effective, although some people will still swallow them as they have a fixed mindset.

3. We will have more control when we leave: We are currently one of Europe's leaders which helps us punch above our weight on the global

stage where we can impose tough sanctions that brought Iran to heel and checked Putin's war in Ukraine; combating climate change, fighting terrorism, and creating jobs for example. If we leave Europe, we won't be in the room when the other 27 nations decide what to do, rather we'd follow and as a follower, becoming a rule-taker rather than a rule-maker. Our former partners and other allies would listen to us less and our government would have less power to do the things we want. This is just a simple reality.

4.   Eurosceptics say the UK always get bossed around by the EU and Brussels because we kept getting outvoted but lost only 56 votes in the EU's Council since 1999 whilst being on the winning side 2,466 times. 2,466 to 56 is not a bad return when we are polling sovereignty and achieving many other benefits for our economy and citizens via our EU membership.

5.   The UK's Rebate will be scrapped – realistically if the EU wanted to scrap, reduce or otherwise change the rebate, there would need to be a unanimous Council vote which means in other words, the United Kingdom could veto it, so is a ridiculous argument. EU economy is shrinking while the rest of the world grows - the reality is that the EU grew 1.9% in 2018, while the Eurozone grew 1.8%. Yes, it has slowed but as export is very important for many EU economies such as Germany the global slowdown is bound to have an effect. But in summary at the time of writing it is growing and the claims it is not are just bogus, and clearly political.

The above are just some examples of the abuse of the truth and misinformation about the EU the UK has become used to and unless one is willing to check these facts they will be believed, and we can then see how the anti-EU feeling mushrooms and resentment rears its ugly head. We saw and still see comments about other countries being subservient to the EU without really understanding or appreciating that these countries are in fact a part of the EU, but also it rings with a sense of superiority that many Brexiteers still think Great Britain is better than other countries for some reason. But also, this attitude allows racist tendencies to creep in due to that same perception of superiority that is an illusion. Nevertheless, a powerful emotion that can cloud their judgement.

Chapter 5
Some of the Benefits of the EU

The following list is by no means extensive but gives you a good overview of the real benefits and will destroy the fiction and misinformation that has been circulated for years about the EU.

Freedom
The EU gives you and your children the freedom to live, work and retire anywhere in Europe with little administrative issues compared to being a non-EU citizen. Even your holiday is much easier - and safer, for example, when visiting other European countries British citizens have the right to receive emergency healthcare!

The forgotten millions!
Although there are circa. 3.5 million EU nationals living in the UK there are also an estimated 1 million UK nationals living in the EU whose freedom of movement and freedom to live where they want within the EU will be curtailed. Did those voting Leave even consider those fellow Brits (after all it was patriotic to vote Leave right?) or were they never even considered as people focused on this perceived swarming of EU immigrants to our shores? This just proved that the simplistic rhetoric of Farage et al. is not as simple as portrayed and presented these 1 million Brits with a lot of problems to consider including potentially non-EU

citizen taxes, property taxes for non-EU citizens, Visa requirements and any other legislation that may be added / amended for non-EU citizens. It seems Brits are all equal, but some are more equal than others. For those million we have not taken back control we have handed control of their lives to the state in which they reside with all the inherent complexities, and their future is unsure and confused currently and may be for a long while to come.

Some rule changes could affect Brits returning to the UK, their homeland, with their spouses as the couple may not meet the minimum income requirement (which may change) so effectively a Brit could leave the country for a few years and the rules of the game have changed and they cannot return to their homeland with their wife or husband. This is just one of the intricacies of Brexit that are rarely spoken of but could dramatically affect people's lives and split families up. Was that what people voted for? Where is those people's control? Have they taken back control or lost it?

Consumer Protection (and protecting YOUR rights)

This is a very underrated benefit of the EU and in simple terms means you're less likely to get ripped off. Consumer protection is a key benefit of the EU's single market and ensures members of the British public to receive equal consumer rights when shopping anywhere in Europe. The EU's consumer rights ensure transparency from sellers themselves, and the quality and safety of their products. A two-year guarantee on all products, and the introduction of a ceiling for roaming charges across member states, are just two examples of things the EU has done to improve the rights of its customers. You may not think this affects you much or even at all but look, for example, on the packaging of all children's toys etc. and they have the CE mark which helps ensure the safety of these products your children will play with so they are safe and not that they receive dangerous non-Tested products from the Far east! This all for you and your children.

Foreign Affairs

As part of a 500 million-strong community, the United Kingdom has greater influence over international matters as a member of the EU. Yes, we are strong economy on our own but as a part of the largest free trade and political block in the world we punch above our weight as all EU Members do, and this influence should not be underestimated when standing up to major powers such as USA, China and India, etc. We will only know this and miss it when it is gone.

Sovereignty and Opt-Outs

Firstly, it must be said that there has been so much misinformation about sovereignty before and since the EU Referendum in 2016 as we have ALWAYS been a sovereign state, which is why we can and have said to the EU "We are Leaving". But we have always had that sovereign ability, and that has never gone away. The difference was that consecutive governments since the 1970s knew it was in our interest to pool resources with other EU countries to create a win-win scenario which has helped lead to the growth and prosperity of the UK whilst a member of the EU!

The United Kingdom has proved that it can opt out of some EU policies which it considers are not in our favour, such as the Euro but also the following (to name just a couple):

Opted out of Schengen agreement (with Ireland)

The United Kingdom is not a member of the Schengen area. Unlike when travelling across the rest of the EU, passports must still be checked when crossing the UK border. This establishes we have controls of our borders to help stop illegal immigration, which some Brexiteers try to (incorrectly) question.

Charter of Fundamental Human Rights (with Poland)

The UK obtained a "clarifying protocol" which states the Charter "does not extend" the ability of the European Court of Justice to find UK law inconsistent with the Charter.

Basically, this "clarifying protocol" was obtained because of fears the Charter would infringe on UK labour law, or more accurately it could interpret stricter criteria that the UK wants.

Freedom, security and justice (with Denmark and Ireland)

The UK has the right to opt-out of legislation relating to what is known as justice and home affairs. Without getting too technical Protocol 36 of the Lisbon Treaty grants the UK may opt-in/out of individual pieces of legislation coming under a Title V legal base. There has been recent controversy over exactly what the UK deems JHA and what the EU does. For example, upcoming legislation on legal highs, which are an area dealt with domestically by the UK Home Office will not be under Title V. Instead they will come under rules governing the single market.

When talking of sovereignty let me just remind you of what Teresa May said in April 2016,

"International multilateral institutions invite nations to make a trade off to pool and therefore to cede some Sovereignty in a controlled way to prevent a greater loss of sovereignty in an uncontrolled way through, for example military conflict or economic decline."

Sounds very sensible, logical and realistic in today's global world, but once Mrs May was put under pressure from the ERG and the right wing of her party, as well as the likes of Farage and the British press, sense was lost in the rabid world that became Brexit. Was this the story of Brexit in a nutshell?

Economic and Monetary Union (EMU)

Protocol 25 of the Maastricht treaty cleared the UK and Denmark from the chapters related to the Economic and Monetary Union, exempting them from using the Euro currency. For both countries, this means monetary policy remains a domestic issue. When the financial crisis broke out in 2008, this allowed the UK to introduce quantitative easing much earlier than the Eurozone. The UK is also allowed to run a much higher budget deficit than other member states, as it not subject to the Stability and Growth Pact, which caps public deficits at 3% of GDP.

The UK opted-out of mandatory EU refugee quotas

We have what's often referred to as an opt-out, although strictly speaking EU laws on the likes of asylum and border control don't apply to the UK **unless we choose to opt in**. So, we do have control of this!

In summary, we have excellent flexibility that most EU states don't have so just illustrates we have some great benefits but limit the potential downsides of, for example, Euro membership. We have all these opt outs plus our rebate but Brexiteers still try to say it is a terrible deal which it is not. It is more their obsession to leave that muddies the waters and prevents them from acknowledging the benefits.

Security

Another example of a not so well-known benefit of our membership of the EU is that of cross border coordination and cooperation in the fight against crime. As many security issues are global now rather than just nationally and the EU better protects the UK to tackle threats to security, including terrorism, paedophiles and cross-border crime such as people smuggling, cyber-crime and drug trafficking. All these crimes are cross border and cannot be controlled purely on a national basis, so cooperation is key.

Business & Trade

EU membership gives the UK access to the European single market, which is invaluable for trade and enables the easy movement of goods, services and people across member states and dramatically reduces the cost of doing business which means more money / profits for our UK companies that can be invested in the business including job creation. In the Times newspaper on 23rd February

2016 two hundred business leaders, 36 of them from FTSE 100 companies (including Asda, British Telecom, Vodafone, and Marks & Spencer), put their names to a letter arguing that 'leaving the EU would deter investment and threaten jobs. It would put the economy at risk'.

There will be many hidden costs to companies once we leave the EU including having to change and develop new more agile supply chains, adjusting product portfolios, changing sourcing strategies, and reviewing inventory strategies. All these costs and resources needed would have been unnecessary had the UK stayed a member of the European Union.

■ **Free trade within the EU**

Reduces barriers and enables UK companies – particularly small ones – to grow and develop their export businesses in Europe or even source excellent EU produced products such as highly engineered German products. It should also be highlighted that the EU has been very successful (much more than the USA for example) of developing a framework for mutual recognition of professional qualifications. This has resulted in many industries finding it easier for their professionals to work pan-European than even the comparison of Americans working across state in the USA. This EU development has proved vital for the UK where 80% of our trade is in services.

■ **Membership has increased significant flows of investment into the UK**

Investment flows across borders inside the EU have roughly doubled following the introduction of the Single Market. The UK is the EU's leading investment destination, which makes the UK a major beneficiary of such investments. the EU accounted for 47% of the UK's stock of inward FDI at the end of 2011, with investments worth over $1.2 trillion! But will the UK still be as enticing once we leave the EU as this changes the dynamic significantly?

It seemed simple and obvious that thousands of foreign companies including car manufacturers, Aerospace companies and component distribution organisations came to the UK for easy access and free trade into the huge EU market. But have some forgotten this or did not understand the implications of that as an advantage for foreign investment? One of the ironies of Brexit was Sunderland voting leave when the biggest employer in the area is Nissan and one of the major reasons they set up in the UK because of that easy access to the EU market. Yes, government incentives probably also helped but they would have received them also from other EU states had Nissan pushed to set up in Spain, Portugal or Eastern Europe. But many of these industries are reliant on high quality supply chains including Just In Time (JIT) delivery and once we leave the EU, they may be faced by friction (i.e. delay) at the UK border both to and from the EU which means the highly developed systems will no longer work. This means a second major reason for such Foreign companies to invest in the UK will disappear as well as the lack of a free trade agreement. This obviously bodes the questions why should such companies 1. Remain here or if the re-investment costs are too high and they must stay at least for a few years. 2. Why invest in the future where 2 of its most important selling points no longer exist?

It was clear after the referendum result when UK businesses were asking the Government for clear direction and understanding of how they intended to ensure UK business could trade smoothly with no downsides. But it became clear, despite the rhetoric, that the Conservative Government had very little understanding of business or was so wrapped up in the politics of Brexit and holding the Tory party together. This was highlighted when Dominic Raab the Brexit minister admitted that he had not understood how important the Calais Dover crossing was to our trade as we are, as he stated, "... a peculiar, frankly, geographic economic entity that is the United Kingdom." So basically, Dominic Raab had discovered we are an Island, and this incompetence was what business had to battle with before and after the Referendum in 2016. This is the same Dominic Raab that claimed he doesn't support the Human Rights Act or believe in economic and social rights! Not for this book but what would then happen to sick and disabled people? This is the type of people we are having to deal with in this era of selfish politicians. Many business groups had slightly different focus points, but the common thread was that the government should focus on making it as easy as possible for business to do business as business was the economic engine for the UK and its future.

The Federation of Small Businesses (FSB) said its top priority is to secure a full, time-limited transition period. Other organisations say that businesses are optimistic but apprehensive, want clarity about the transition, and suggest a full or partial customs union with the EU, or for tariffs to be kept to a minimum. A survey carried out by Moore Stephens, an accountancy and advisory firm, on behalf of the FSB asked owner-managed businesses whether they felt the Government is considering the concerns of small and medium businesses in their negotiations with the EU. Moore Stephens told us that 649 responded to this question. The result was that 94% of small and medium-size businesses highlighted that they were not happy with the attitude of the Government towards their concerns with some highlighting the Government was ignoring their concerns about how we leave the EU! But if Dominic Raab was anything to go by, it was not the Government's fault as they really did not have a clue and were more focused on trying to avoid the break-up of the Conservative party. This was a prime example of where economics meets politics to the detriment of business and potentially the electorate.

But it was not just the FSB that showed concerns, the British Chambers of Commerce (BCC) set out the key priorities on trade negotiations which included keeping tariffs with the EU to a minimum and easing other barriers to trade with the EU and the rest of the world. The Institute of Directors (IoD) went further suggesting a partial customs union for industrial goods and processed agricultural products. The manufacturers' organisation the **Engineering Employers' Federation (**EEF) stressed they need more details on Government Trade plans post Brexit highlighting the future relationship with the EU must ensure frictionless trade.

The Electronics Components Supply Network (ECSN) in 2019 highlighted that the run of twelve consecutive periods of twelve consecutive periods of 'quarter-on-same-quarter-the previous-year' growth was abruptly halted by an unexpected decline in billings (shipped and invoiced amounts) in April 2019. Compared to billings from the same period from 2018 it showed a 1.3% decline which is very concerning, and clearly Brexit is causing issues in many diverse industries and markets. The risk of a no-deal Brexit and all the uncertainty concerning Brexit and the Government's lack of a plan will continue to be a drag on investment and trade until there is some clarity as well as hopefully positive trading conditions. Businesses are largely unprepared for a no-deal cliff edge Brexit as how does one prepare for something that has not been clarified? It is just guesswork and potential wasted cost such as the stockpiling that happened before the planned March exit that did not happen.

Chapter 6
The Referendum & The Campaigns

The problem of the Referendum in the first place!

We should not forget Brexit and democracy are processes not isolated events, the UK is a parliamentary democracy with MPs having the time and salaries to examine complicated political and economic issues thoroughly and in-depth which most people do not have. With another referendum capable of naming a ship 'Boaty McBoatface' despite wanting serious suggestions, should warn us to the issues of simple referendums let alone one of such complexity.

The referendum was meant to be purely about the UK's membership of the EU i.e. with a simple (way too simple as we will see in this book) question 'IN' or 'OUT'. But after a financial crisis in 2008 followed by years of austerity, many people had been economically marginalised or 'left behind' and this was very important to them and would filter very powerfully into the referendum campaign and vote. Why? Basically, because this would work indirectly for them to see Brexit as a risk, as they perceived their situation couldn't get any worse, plus gave them a chance to kick Cameron's Government (and by default the Remain campaign) and the establishment as they perceived it, even though Boris Johnson and Jacob Rees-Mogg led the leave campaigns and are very much the establishment. The Brexit vote we will see was not caused by one factor i.e. the EU membership rather the vote reflected a much more complex mix of emotions, and frustrations with the voters feelings on immigration and national identity already baked into their psyche a long time before June 2016. There were many drivers behind the Brexit vote and not just the one that it should have been about in the first place. Welcome to referendums!

It was quite clear that the referendum came to fruition because David Cameron was being pressured by the right wing of his party as well as the pressure from the UK Independence party (UKIP) with the obvious aim of strengthening his position within the Conservative party and as Prime Minister. Also, he thought he would win comfortably, which blew up in his face.

He was in fact advised by William Hague that he needed to do this as he personally got killed by Europe (the Bain of most Conservative Prime Minister's lives) and that one Tory leader needs to lance this boil and end this once and for all. Although his Chancellor George Osborne was fervently against and perhaps shows he had better political judgement and strategic forethought than his Boss. Perhaps he should have thought about his hero McMillan's words about the most dangerous thing for politicians when he wisely replied, "events dear boy events". Michael Gove, even though he went against his good friend by taking up arms with the Leavers, did not want a referendum at the time either.

But the main problem with it for such a critical and important potential constitutional upheaval was the 50% +1 system whereas it should have been, for example, 70% but definitely a minimum 60% to change it so the result was clear and not contested. As we have now seen with a 51.89% to 48.11% i.e. only a 3.78% difference. After the referendum a lot of new information and facts have been revealed about the EU, the UK economy and how everything was highly interwoven so would not be as easy to make a smooth exit as many of the Brexiteer leaders had claimed. Other issues such as the divorce Bill, the Irish backstop (who even discussed Ireland in the referendum campaign?), border checks, difficulties trading on WTO, Just in Time supply chains, Inward investment of the future, plus many others.

But the Leavers quite legitimately as they believed it, despite all the new information and developments, claimed "they knew exactly what they were voting for" and as a Remainer if you disputed that you were calling them stupid or misinformed and expected to back off from the debate and just accept the result. Now I discovered many people who were misinformed about the EU and I do not blame them as most people including politicians, civil servants, journalists and TV stations were also in the dark about many issues. Plus, for many I spoke to or communicated with it would not have made a jot of a difference as they just wanted fewer foreigners in the country, period and believed they would definitely get that.

I found it frustrating that people were ill informed including one Lady who justified leaving the EU (apart from the immigrants) was that the Germans had higher pensions than us! (L.W.) I did try to point out that has nothing to do with the EU but more the fact the Germans pay more tax, have a more successful economy, and save more not being obsessed with getting on the housing ladder and ploughing a large percentage of their income into buying a house but rather renting. Unfortunately, this fell on deaf ears. But this demonstrates quite clearly why such a referendum was misplaced on many levels.

But still the frustration stayed with me until I discovered the following: 'the most searched EU questions on Google on 24th June, the day after the referendum result, were "What does it mean to leave the EU?" and even more striking "What is the EU?"'! It was not people's fault, which at that stage was firmly at David Cameron's doorstep, but it quite clearly exposes the British ignorance of the EU. So, how in fact were they to make an intelligent informed decision unless they had one strong overriding passion such as being anti-immigrant. In that case they do not care how the EU works or what it adds to the UK as they are totally focused on their dislike of immigration. The fact they will be extremely disappointed in their aim is another aspect we will cover later in the book. Although some may claim it was not only David Cameron's fault that the Referendum took place with a number of others playing a role it was Prime Minister Cameron that opened 'Pandora's Box'.

Although the vote was technically advisory to the government and carried no legal weight it took on a life of its own with Brexiteers pushing a strong moral angle creating so much pressure for politicians that their sense of self-preservation kicked in rapidly so even if they thought the result was a catastrophe for the UK, with many not having the strength or courage to go against their Leave voting constituents. The result is a country unable to reconcile its traditional and very successful parliamentary democracy with its experimentation with the direct type of democracy like the EU referendum where complex issues are being asked of unprepared and ill informed (in such complex inter-related issues) citizens. But even if not advisory Mr Cameron and his Government or any future Government would never have had the mandate or the power to deliver the result because there were many acts of Parliament contained which only Parliament can change, as that is our democratic Parliamentary system.

It appears many are asking MPs to close their eyes and vote for something (especially a no-deal!) that damages mine and their country, but surely that cannot be right? The government in 2019 had largely given up seriously claiming Brexit is good for the country (as they know it is not) but rather are hiding behind it's the 'will of the people' (covered elsewhere in the book) rhetoric which looks like a dereliction of duty and possibly cowardice to save their own skins. If it is the will of the people ask them about what you are actually going to do, even if that is a no-deal Brexit.

At the end of the Referendum and Leave had won, the government and was left with making policy for this 'new world order' for which nobody had planned as nobody expected it to ever happen. Nobody seemed to recognise or admit the complexity of withdrawing from 45 years of pooled sovereignty and intertwined laws and standards or in fact the obvious longevity of the withdrawal and transition processes due in part to those intertwined complexities, even if we could get an alternative deal with the EU. At this stage crashing out on a no-deal WTO basis had not even been calculated as everything was going to be so simple.

It was said by the Leave campaign having won the vote that everyone knew exactly what they were voting for, which obviously they would as who in their right mind would say the people that voted for their side of the argument did NOT know what they were voting for. If this is in fact true surely, they must have known exactly what they would get, what they would lose, what they had already (i.e. the truth what the EU gave and offered them as British citizens), as well as what advantages leaving the EU would give them, their families and the fellow UK citizens, but my experience both personally, listening to interviews and online this was clearly not the case. If they were to genuinely and fully understand what they were voting for they would surely have at least known about the following: The single market, the customs union, as well as the probable impact on Sterling exchange rate, shrinking of the economy, inflation, etc.

The Dominic Cummings character as shown in 'Brexit – an uncivil war' stated 'The Referendum is a really dumb idea. Referendums are literally the worst way to decide anything, they are divisive they pretend that complex choices are simple binaries red or blue, black or white but we know there are more nuanced and sophisticated ways how to make political change and reform, or that we live in a more nuanced and political world. Discourse has become absolutely moronic thanks to the morons who run it.' Some may argue that is exaggerated, and that was not realistic or feasible and a lot people did feel they knew what they were getting (or at least they knew that they wanted) such as reduction or stopping of immigration for example. But if that was to be true then they would understand the following: the shortage of qualified, nurses, Doctors and other NHS staff, the lack of low-skilled workers to pick fruit and the horrendous lack of social care workers, Veterinary surgeons etc.

How many people did not in fact bother to vote for Remain even though that was their position as it appeared Remain would win anyway and therefore complacency set in? If we look back sensibly and logically nobody should ever do (and may never have every done anywhere in the world) a referendum by asking a simply YES or NO question for such a critical constitutional change, also with a simple 50% +1 system for the reason we now see as the result was not clear cut enough regardless of the fact there was no plan or strategy for in this case a Leave result. It borders on stupidity, although may have been decided that way as Cameron was so confident in his own abilities and the likelihood of winning.

As a final thought on the referendum we should not underestimate the impacts, both short and long term, of the significance of a vote that rejected the Status quo and all its comforts in favour of an unknowable future, and that the seeds of the UK's decision were sown over a far longer period than just the referendum campaigns.

What became clear during the referendum campaign

There were certain things that became clear during the Referendum campaign and in fact in the result's aftermath also, including that people were willing to say almost anything including plain lies to get the result they desired. But also, one thing that became irrefutable and underpinned the developments in the campaign and quite possibly the Leave result was the lack of knowledge and understanding of the EU. There was a clear general lack of knowledge and information and willingness to learn about and understand the issues and the implications of those issues which led to people keeping their already formed opinions based on 20-30 years of a lot of false information published and then shared by many sources including the British Press. More of that later. These firm almost unmovable opinions were exacerbated after the result with clear unwillingness to move from a position despite the changes in circumstances, facts and the additional information available.

Clearly that this campaign was much different from any before it with Digital media and fake social media accounts playing major influential roles but also the usual wealthy men talking about the "will of the people" which on the surface seemed strange as I looked at Jacob Rees-Mogg and 'will of the people' was not the first thing that came to mind but rather 'extreme privilege' yet he was having success in getting his message out there. Certain individuals always want to win elections, but this was different as several prominent anti-EU campaigners such as Nigel Farage, Arron Banks, John Redwood, Bill Cash and Jacob Rees-Mogg had made leaving the EU a lifelong aim and were little known for much else and were desperate for us to leave. It was this desperation that made this campaign different from any general election campaign we had seen. Arron Banks made the largest ever donation, £8 million ($11 million) to a British political campaign which indicates the level of desperation for the result they wanted. More of Mr Banks later but this donation was in fact being investigated as to the allegations that it was indeed illegal. It has been alleged that Mr Banks' dislike of the EU is because the EU is very hot and focused on stamping out tax avoidance (and Tax evasion schemes) and this tax avoidance could have an effect of his complicated and extensive use of tax havens and shell companies. This was the alleged issue with the donation as it was not clear where all the money came from, or even whether it originated from him.

In fact the quality of debate of how valuable the EU was to the UK and vice versa was extremely poor with the British Press constantly attacking the EU including many headlines that were absolutely untrue which led to most of our Prime Ministers and political leaders for 40 years failing to stand up for the advantages of the EU due to the fear that the Press would target them with their vilification and attacks. There was clearly a case for a positive position of the EU, and it's benefits to the UK, but this was rarely argued by our major political leaders, yet constantly attacked by specific MPs and political leaders who were obsessed by the EU including John Redwood, Norman Tebbit, Bill Cash, Mark Francois and Nigel Farage to name but a few.

The Leave campaign was successful in manipulating a number of concerns people had, whether it be the economy, jobs, public spending or most important immigration. But at the same time, they managed very skilfully to garner an anti-establishment feeling amongst those fed up with what they perceived to be the political elite. This despite having the likes of Boris Johnson and Jacob Rees-Mogg on their side, but they achieved it which created a real issue for the Remain campaign that they never came to grips with.

Everything had been so internally focused but what had this ugly, nasty referendum campaign made us become or were we these type of people beforehand and the Referendum had simply exaggerated or intensified our personalities? Plus, how did we look as a race of people to the outside world and the International community? Does the vote tell us what sort of society we are and what is important to us?

It certainly appeared to anyone willing to take an open look that we were and still are a divided society and it was split in so many ways:

- Old against Young;
- Old economy against new;
- Big City against country / provincial;
- Liberal against conservative;
- South East against the North;
- Isolationists / imperialists against globalists.

Etc.

As we can see from the word clouds below the results of research by www.thebritishelectionstudy.com the focus of Leavers differed greatly from Remainers, some may describe as heart versus head, but we know that the emotion

50

of the heart can be a more powerful emotion and in this case a motivator to get out and vote than simple economic numbers. The first word cloud shows very clearly that a key concern for leave voters was immigration. The issue dominates the leave voter word cloud and other words like 'borders' also feature. Other words that feature prominently concern issues surrounding sovereignty, including the word 'sovereignty' itself and 'control', and 'laws'. [53]

Leave focus:

The remain word cloud illustrates clearly that the primary concern of remain voters was the economy, which again dominates the word cloud along with related words like 'trade' and 'jobs'. Other words that feature prominently for Remainers are 'rights', 'security', 'stability' and 'future'. [53]

Remain focus:

These very stark differences display how voters of the respective sides were not just divided in terms of geography and demographic characteristics. They were fundamentally divided in what they considered important and relevant to how they were intending to cast their vote.

In some ways undecided voters were a mix of leave and remain voters – 'economy' and 'immigration' both feature prominently in the undecided word cloud, along with other words that pop up in the other clouds like 'future', 'security', 'rights, and 'control'. Neither side had an obvious advantage among these respondents if we examine only those issues respondents thought would be important in deciding how to vote. However, something that characterises the responses of the undecided voters is the number of words relating to uncertainty about the effect of Brexit, like 'facts', 'information' 'affect', and 'impact'. [53]

It should be highlighted that these results show that while the single largest word that Leavers say is "immigration", they were actually more likely to mention sovereignty related issues overall. The clear picture we get from this analysis is that Leavers are concerned primarily about sovereignty and immigration. In fact, reading responses shows that many respondents mention both sovereignty and immigration together, showing that these two issues were closely linked in the minds of British voters.

When talking to people and since the result it appeared that rather than weighing up the prospective costs and benefits of leaving comparing all the competing claims made by both sides of the argument, many had decided beforehand. And would be very difficult to change. It was clear on the day that Vote Leave mobilised its supporters with a passion and their voters to come out and did exactly that and that made a difference. But also, they managed to undermine the remain position that membership of the EU would mean stability for the country and turned this into a distrust of the political establishments and gave many unhappy people the opportunity to kick the government but also the political elites at the same time.

One thing was clear and differentiated the two sides, was that the remain side was basically the Government that had to stick together and not attack fellow Tories so were somewhat limited on what they could say and how they could target specific groups. The Leave side on the other hand did not have that limitation so Vote Leave could concentrate on the messages of take back control and fear of potential changes to the EU whilst the more extreme Leave.EU (note they both lied!) could be more visceral and direct to attract the more extreme parts of society that were bordering on or had entered into the realms of racism. The two main Leave groups did not get on, but it benefited them as in some ways they tried to outdo each other plus had the advantage of two lots of funding streams. Their guerrilla warfare was much more successful and won them the referendum.

The old against the Young?

As we saw in conversations and social media interaction and then the statistics backed this up that the referendum was not fought on traditional Left versus Right lines, the first time this had happened in my lifetime. It was not even the case when we joined the Common market in 1973 where the older generation held more sway over their youth when it came to politics but now with the expansion of the Internet and Social Media younger people were being more vocal, proactive and engaged.

The old and the young vote was very clear with the young very much voting to remain and the old overwhelmingly voting to Leave. This may be because the younger people are more comfortable with immigration and a multi-cultural country where they have grown up in school etc. with people from many countries and cultures whereas the older white generation have not had this experience and maybe more nervous about what they do not understand. Certainly, on social media you see the older generation making references to the second world war or our imperialistic past, and even comparing the EU to the Nazis, etc. This in itself is bizarre but you can see their longing and where a lot of them are coming from, even if mis founded. Facts and logic can be trumped by emotion and the dislike for an organisation such as the EU plus the immigration they perceive it to bring results in such strange decisions, attitudes and beliefs.

These war related comments are strange and so often incorrect or misplaced by people that should know better. It was recorded by the Telegraph that D-Day veteran and former head of the Army Lord Brammall condemned Sir Bill Cash (conservative MP and Eurosceptic to his core) for using the Normandy landings to boost the Leave campaigns. He said: "As a veteran of D-Day I'm disgusted at the use of this battle by the Leave campaign. We fought to bring World War II to an end; and greater European cooperation [rather than British isolationism] has helped keep peace in Europe. We should stay in Europe to solve common problems not scapegoat foreigners in the way Vote Leave is doing." [44] Who would you listen to an actual D-Day veteran and expert or Bill Cash MP, who has been an MP for decades and can you remember one thing he has actually achieved?

But we should not put all 'old' people into one homogeneous group as the London School of Economics (LSE) did some research and found that Britain's wartime generation were almost as pro-EU as millennials and post millennials. It was found that in the over 65s group those that lived through the Second World War were far more likely to oppose Brexit, associating the EU more with peace, and thus have a more positive attitude towards integration. [47] These are the people that actually lived through and experienced Wars and didn't sit in front of the TV watching The Great Escape or the Dirty Dozen!

Many highlight how more motivated the older generations were to leave the EU rather than the younger generation was to remain which showed in the percentage turnout which was much higher for the older generations. Now this could be for many reasons such as the older were desperate to leave the EU which gives focus and purpose whereas the young thought Remain would win anyway, or were just not engaged enough, etc. But it is quite clear that if the younger voters had turned out in the same numbers as the old the result could very well have been different. Some claim still that as it was such a major long-term decision that 16-year-olds should have been given the vote especially as any outcome would affect them more than any other generation, and that could have made a significant difference to the result.

It should be noted that on the remain side, through their arrogance of thinking they would win, believed they did not necessarily need the young vote.

Age and generation clearly played a role but the older generation would agree with that, claiming the youth have not had the experience and wise heads of the more mature voter, which to a certain extent should be true, unless of course their decisions were based on a dogmatic dislike of the EU and based not on facts and logic but rather emotion and prejudice. The Youth would counter that the older generations were out of touch, did not understand or want to understand what the EU did for us as a country and that we thrived within their club and partnership. Also, it is patronising to say 16- and 17-year-olds cannot make an informed decision.

As stated the statistics show that basically the referendum result was essentially the over 55-year-olds wanting to change the future lives of the under 55s against their wishes, which created a clear split. When reading these stats and reports Herbert Hoover's war quote came to mind when he said "Older men declare war. But it is the youth that must fight and die." Now admittedly the older generations will suffer from any detrimental effects of say a no-deal Brexit, but it would obviously impact the younger and their children and their children's children for potentially decades to come. Successive polls consistently found there was a relationship between age and likelihood to support leaving or remaining in the EU with a survey by Lord Ashcroft polls (a very respected polling company) of 12,369 referendum voters after they had cast their ballot suggested that the older people were more likely to have voted Leave. This is clearly not a science but when you speak or communicate with people of different of generations, it is clear this is the case and certain like-minded 'tribes' grew up around many lines.

How different age groups voted

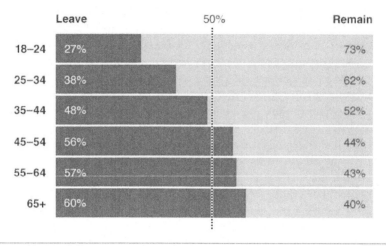

	Leave	50%	**Remain**
18–24	27%		73%
25–34	38%		62%
35–44	48%		52%
45–54	56%		44%
55–64	57%		43%
65+	60%		40%

Source: Lord Ashcroft Polls

B B C

We can see from the above graphic from Lord Ashcroft Polls almost three quarters (73%) of 18 to 24-year-olds said they had voted to stay in the EU, compared with 62% of 25 to 34s and 52% of 35 to 44s. Of the 45s and above it appears Brexit was the preferred route with the highest percentage with 60% of those aged 65+. It's very clear that areas with many older voters voted for Brexit while places with a higher number of younger voters voted Remain. [63]

Plus, as indicated age is not a guarantee of good experience or prudence and it is patronising to assume because of age a younger person cannot vote and decide as well as a more mature individual. This sometimes arrogant attitude of the older towards the younger generation was stark but also reflected some hypocrisy as they did not like to be talked to in a similar way when Remainers disputed and dissected their arguments for Leave, and we cove this more in the "Condescension Complex" later in the book. No matter what our position and people's views everybody's vote has the same value and although many could point out many people they feel are ill-informed of specific issues about the EU or the referendum as a whole, this is the only way democracy can and should work. So, education is the key.

I am clearly a minority in my peer Group being a Remainer and it has made been an interesting, albeit frustrating experience, trying to understand where Leavers are coming from, their arguments or beliefs, their logic if there was any (as at times there simply was not), how they reacted to arguments being dissected including untruths they had been told or revealed to them, as well as misinformation highlighted to them. What was astounding was the lack of understanding of the EU and what it actually did for them Despite their age and experience it was as if the EU had played very little part in their lives but suddenly the referendum campaign and references to Maggie Thatcher and Churchill etc. had opened Pandora's Box and had brought them to life and into action, but without the knowledge.

One such example of the above is whilst at a boxing event and talking to a colleague he categorically swore that we did not vote for anyone (i.e. MEPs) in the EU and it was all jobs for the boys even though the European Election was only weeks away. Unfortunately, I could not get an Internet connection on my phone to prove it to him, although even then I question whether he would have still thought it was Fake News, so could not move him from his entrenched position. But at the same time, he confirmed he was a definite leaver, and nothing would ever change his mind and we need to be out as soon as possible with or without a deal. Now he was 70+ but it did illustrate the lack of understanding of the EU even down to the real tangible stuff like voting for MEPs in this country that would represent us in Brussels and Strasbourg. This disconnect was frightening and highlighted the massive issue of the EU referendum.

The debate and banter of going back and forth which got heated at times with my peer group, especially on Facebook was enlightening but I did not expect to change people's minds as some of them were never going to change no matter how circumstances and facts change, and that is their prerogative. But it was more to try to even up the misinformation and lies we witnessed during the referendum to try to bring some balance to the discussions and as I had spent a lot of time finding out the facts to try to educate those that want to learn what is really going on rather than the images of the sunny uplands they were painted. I wanted to do my little bit if you like. If they take it on board, then fine and if not well my research and time spent has educated me if not anyone else. Pride was very prevalent both before and since the Referendum with many people young and old suddenly realising that we had all been significantly lied to and some had voted on the basis of those fabrications (for examples of the untruths please see the separate section in the book) and that pride was not going to allow them to admit face to face, online or on Social Media that they were wrong or know they had been duped. But in quiet moments or in private messages the penny had clearly dropped with many realising where we genuinely are as a country, the madness of a no-deal Brexit and maybe when in the privacy of the voting booth would change their mind and vote Remain in a second Referendum.

As one person [JB] wrote to me when I recommended more research into facts *"Chris why would anyone research to try to prove the other side right? You have been highlighting all the Remainer arguments to me and others for 2 years + and still haven't moved me an inch. Just goes to prove just how insignificant your arguments are when stacked up against freedom."* Now this is in some respects an intelligent individual but despite having had all the facts laid before him he was incapable of moving "even an inch" so entrenched he was in his position and could not even admit some obvious results of the Brexit vote such as plummeting Pound, loss of jobs, loss of foreign Direct investment and huge uncertainty were now a reality. This was a regular occurrence with Brexiteers in that they felt too proud to admit even a move in their position as they believed their Brexit position was built on such a weak foundation and could not afford to "give an inch", otherwise potentially the whole 'pyramid scheme' comes tumbling down. To say the logic is based on sand would be an understatement.

They have done nothing special to be fair, but they will listen and learn to recognise the difference between promises, lies and reality and not remain like many in an entrenched position they struggle to defend apart from hope and belief that the sunny uplands and unicorns are just over the horizon. They realised we need more immigrants to do specific jobs and fulfil specific skills and that it was the lack of houses that was the root cause of the problem of housing and not immigration. Watching Parliament tussle with the issues of Brexit and 40 years of cooperation with the EU they realised we actually have sovereignty as that was what was actually happening now. We had voted to leave, and our parliament was democratically trying to agree a withdrawal deal, which IS sovereignty! But we just chose to pool sovereignty for the common good of the UK and cooperation. They also saw the swashbuckling British past and independence was a pipe dream as countries now have to work together very closely and the world is now INTER-dependent NOT independent and that was fine. Due to the withdrawal agreement extension Teresa May negotiated / agreed to in March 2019 many were suddenly faced with the European Elections having been told by numerous Brexiteers that there was no democracy in Brussels? See how once one picks away at the arguments they start to fall apart like a cheap suit. So, figure that irony! So, although I seem to have more in common with my more youthful citizens I have great faith in my older peers to reflect and change for the better future of the UK. With some I have to admit defeat but only mushrooms grow in the dark.

The lower turnout of the young and the subsequent result would in the future, and certainly if there was a second referendum, tell them they really can make a difference and if they do not the result could work against their interests. Will they rise to the occasion or seep back into apathy? Should a second Referendum ever be called?

Would it have made a big difference if 16- and 17-year-olds had been able to vote? It would be easy for Remainers to say it would and Remain would have won had this indeed been the rule, but we should be sceptical. Remember many 16 and 17-year-olds, unlike 18-24, are still very influenced and to some extent controlled by their parents and so may have voted the way of their parents or the way their parents told them.

Clearly, an interesting aspect of a second referendum in 2019 or 2020 would be the fact up to 2 Million of the older generation would have died which by default would have changed the numbers. Consequently, any second Referendum would not be the same as the first as a number of older generation would have passed, it would be on a specific deal that can be better analysed and calculated, plus the Government may give 16 to17-Year-olds the vote as well. These changes are huge and could make a significant impact!

http://chainsawsuit.com/comic/2014/09/16/on-research/

The other clear aspect of the campaigns and 3 years since the vote also and that was the clear confirmation Bias where individuals, and exacerbated by MPs, see the Brexit debate purely through the prism of whether or not it supports their favoured outcome. Obviously with this at the forefront of people's minds sensible debate or compromise becomes virtually impossible. I have personally seen this when one puts forward an obvious checkable fact the other side claims it is fake news, and that is without even checking as they do not want to know the truth but feel more comfortable in their confirmation bias position and comfort zone, surrounded by like-minded people in their own tribe. It is quite clear that some people were saying things through lack of knowledge and information and others such as Nigel Farage or Jacob Rees-Mogg it is more deliberately false as they have a vested interest and a dogmatic obsession with leaving the EU.

The worst political campaign (on both sides) of all time?

I am not referring here to the unimaginable number of deceptions on the Leave side and at the time of writing unknown source of a large amount of Leave Campaign funds (rumoured to be Russian money and being the subject of a criminal investigation by the police) but rather the Cameron and Osbourne led Remain campaign.

However, you look at it, the Remain or 'Stronger In' and peripheral campaigns were so poor one must ask oneself why? Were they too arrogant thinking they would win whatever? Did they not understand the issues with real people? If they did know the key issues did they not know how to defend them? Did they ever have a chance of winning when one looks back at how things panned out?

It is always easier with hindsight, but one could say that 3 strategic errors lost Remain the referendum:
1. The wrong message (which is key);
2. The wrong people (which are key to communicating that message);
3. The wrong Tactics (which allow the right people to deliver the right message effectively)

Andrew Marr commented it was 'the biggest establishment cock-up in my lifetime'. (2)

We must appreciate that the Remain campaign was up against an aggressive volatile anti-EU right-wing media, but Cameron did not challenge their lies and half-truths and was very passive towards the press may be hoping they would come around to his thinking or position but looking back in history this would be very naïve. Alternatively, he was playing the political long game knowing he needed their support thinking he would win the referendum any way and did not need the right-wing press on his back like they did with John Major in the 90s? Or he was just too timid and not brave enough to take the risk of fighting back against that wing of the Press and effectively pandered to their every whim. He even claimed he could renegotiate the Free Movement of People that was totally unrealistic, but he knew that would go down well with these Eurosceptic publications.

It should be noted here for clarification that the EU states do not see EU Free movement of people as the issue some of the British population and right-wing press do as they are focused on and more concerned about external migration from outside the EU, particularly in Southern European countries like Italy and Greece that bear the brunt of such migration movements. It is quite amazing that some of the British political class still think the EU 27 are as obsessed by Free Movement within EU that we are, but again may an example of how our politicians and civil servants do not really understand the EU, or our press is more extreme and fans the flames of fear. Added to this is the conflation of refugees, non-EU immigrants, EU immigrants, and illegal immigrants which are totally separate and different groups all covered by different laws and regulations which creates confusion and leads to ignorance and understanding of the law and the implications of each.

Remainers got too passionate too late, but it was exactly that and the lack of passion compared to the tub-thumping speeches of the likes of Nigel Farage and Boris Johnson. Often at such speeches and rallies it is not what is said, but how it is delivered, and they knew that. One only must look into history to see that the likes of Hitler or Goebbels knew how to work and motivate a crowd (or in this case an electorate) to go with them on their journey even if they have no idea where they are going or what it will mean. it is possible all Remainers did not think the UK would commit such a great act of self-harm and only got passionate AFTER the result, which was obviously too late. This sudden passion in defeat was reminiscent of a boxer that had been very negative and did not engage in the fight and then having lost the decision went berserk complaining and accusing the judges for robbing him. Too late mate!

There are many reasons why people voted to leave and not all the shouting, and screaming was necessarily even about the EU as many felt left behind by globalisation, de-industrialisation, austerity, and the technical revolution where they do not have the skills to grow and were looking for someone to blame. Now immigrants, as history has exhibited, are an easy cheap target as they are visible and their benefit to the UK cannot be explained in an easy slogan and friends and family are keen to join in and agree with you (group think) being very polite and do not want to 'rock the boat'. But as well as immigrants many looked to the Government as those that had let them down and someone to blame. So, to have David Cameron, the Eton educated posh boy as the face of the campaign was a huge mistake and on reflection a joke as it would never work, apart from against the Remain campaign. It just gave the Leavers another reason to vote against Remain as they perceived David Cameron and George Osborne the chancellor, as the root of many of their problems.

Yes, Boris Johnson and JRM were Eton educated posh boys of great privilege with Boris known as a serial liar and Nigel Farage was a City Trader and politician for 20+ years and a clear part of the establishment, they had the ability to cut through with strong rhetoric or in Johnson's case a bumbling likability that cuts across people of different backgrounds. An ability Cameron did not have, and which would be needed to win votes in the Northern Labour heartlands as he would get no help from Corbyn, who was playing (some would say) a clever game of politics and allow the Tories to take part in Blue on Blue attacks and allow themselves to tear themselves apart so labour could pick up the pieces afterwards. What Cameron underestimated was senior Conservatives such as Priti Patel attacking her own Government with deliberately targeted attacks such as lack of primary school places to help strengthen the Leave arguments and her Brexiteer credentials. His position of stopping any attacks on Conservative Brexiteers to protect his party had helped put the UK in jeopardy of a Leave win. He wanted and expected loyalty, but he did not get it which reminds one of the saying "Want loyalty, get a dog!"

Cameron had started the demise himself but had this put the final nail in the coffin when the fabrications and lies espoused by Boris Johnson. could have been exposed regularly by his colleagues and several false arguments nipped in the bud very easily! His policy of no 'blue on blue' attacks no doubt hampered the remain communications team from hitting back quickly and effectively and made it totally impotent against such blue on Blue attacks from the Leave side. Therefore, it was ineffective.

George Osborne saw this issue but rather than biting the bullet he said they could let loose on those people but NOT on Gove of Johnson! What sort of strategy is that, a halfway house cowardly decision or protecting his Eton friends to keep some future brownie points? Whatever it was it was totally insufficient and unsatisfactory. At one-point Peter Mandelson told George 'we feel like sometimes we're taking a spoon to a knife-fight'. (38) Clearly, this was bonkers when Grove and Johnson got the majority of the headlines.

History shows that this did not work and many Labour voters as well as many other voters hold Corbyn also responsible for the vote being lost as he did very little to motivate the Labour voters to vote Remain, even though many economists and experts were telling him that these poorer Northern constituencies would suffer most from Leaving the EU, even more so now with hindsight and a potential poor FTA or no deal withdrawal. What the EU referendum showed was that outside his core vote Corbyn cannot or does not know how to appeal to a wider society and lacked the Leadership skills that he will need to win a large majority in the UK like Blair did. It highlighted that the skills and politics of protest on the back benches no matter how well intentioned left him sadly wanting when on the international stage.

The lack of passion and involvement from Corbyn and his front bench (to the real frustration of many of his more moderate Labour MPs) left the Remain campaign to be led by David Cameron who presided over a catalogue of errors.

Firstly, they seemed to think that just pitting the economic benefits against Immigration was logical and would be obvious for all to see, but they underestimated the power and visibility of Immigration which the everyday men and woman could see and the abstract economic benefits that often, if they even understood them, they knew did not trickle down to them. So why not take a risk with the Leave vote? Why did the Remain campaign not be honest and admit there is a current problem with immigration but not exclusively the fault of the EU (so a Leave vote would not address the whole issue, with more immigrants coming to the UK from outside the EU) work on a temporary cap and outline future measures? At least that would have looked like taking action and a semblance of a plan!

We now see that the EU also sees the issues with immigration from outside the EU and will be working on reforms to improve this. It may have been enough to convince people going forward their concerns would be addressed.

Other advantages, benefits and reality such as the following never broke through in the face of the simple focused LEAVE campaign:

- The fact the EU had helped generate / increase jobs and trade and therefore UK jobs would be lost or was never highlighted enough by the Remain campaign.
- What about the cheaper mobile data roaming charges across Europe?
- Cheaper safe airline travels available for everyone.
- Better employment rights.
- Freer trade (and it's direct benefits to British people).
- The energy union benefits.
- The fact we had been at peace since its inception rather than at war as had been the case on regular occasions for the preceding 200 years. As Churchill so famously said "Better War War than Jaw Jaw!"
- Or when we joined the EU one of the reasons was because Britain was at the time "The sick man of Europe" and this was turned around whilst a member of the EU to become the 5th largest economy in the world.

But not only highlighting the benefits they did little to counter the Leave claims and fiction that areas such as Education, health and housing were controlled in some obscure way by the evil empire of the EU which in reality does not have much impact in these areas. Why not make it clear the EU did not run major parts of the UK economy and hammer that home? But then I reflected and posed the question to myself (but it must be said without a definitive answer!) - Can emotion with a message (no matter if true or not or possessing logic) Donald Trump style trump on (no pun intended!) a sensible one consisting of logic and facts in a political campaign? This certainly appeared to happen in the EU referendum when Nigel Farage got up to speak and spouted many empty slogans many of which were just plainly incorrect. It's feasible there is an academic study on this question, but my simple brain looks at the election of the 45th President Donald Trump in the US and the Vote Leave result in the 2016 referendum the answer is a resounding YES. For both campaigns there was so much false rhetoric, lies, and hyperbole to motivate enough people (albeit in close decisions) to win both those votes. The problem is not just a current one but also longer term when campaign teams learn from this and utilise a lot of the tactics used with a scant disregard for facts, truth, or morality which are superseded by Win at all costs, regardless of the consequences and that is indeed very dangerous.

As regards a misplaced strategy, you only have to look at George Osborne's claim that each family would be £4,300 worse off which seemed to do more harm than good, even if it was well intentioned and his economic calculations well founded. The problem was that the average man on the street does not follow economics or politics programs and did not understand where Osbourne even got those numbers from, as he did not explain them very well so they could not see how that could be true and so ignored it! The same with the threat of an emergency budget which was a complete waste of time, after all how many people actually listen to or read about the Budget apart from the headline features newspapers and TV stations highlight such as has the price of cigarettes and beer going up, etc?

The Remain campaign and Andrew cooper's polling consistently claimed that the economy would trump immigration in the end and Cameron and team believed this and went with it, but this was not the message people were hearing on the doorsteps, on social media or in interviews on TV etc. Still they did not heed these warnings and looked like posh boys in the clichéd ivory tower analysing spreadsheets without having that finger on the pulse or that common touch that Tony Blair seemed to master winning three general elections. Many hold this approach to blame for their loss in that it was too data driven and lacked any context or nuance that you can get on the doorstep or town centres, etc. Out of touch comes to mind.

It seemed like Remain saw immigration and the economy as 2 separate issues whereas Cummings and Leave saw them as inextricably linked i.e. "I am earning less money than 5 years ago not because of a global banking crisis or austerity but because of immigrants!" It does not matter that that may be factually inaccurate, but they believed it, and many were never going to be swayed from that position and they believed the best way to rectify that would be to vote Leave and 'make Britain great again'.

This version of project Fear and the focus on economics and numbers with no explanation did not work and was actually foolish as it was so easy to oppose and bat back and claim effectively that it was all exaggerated and will never happen. It appeared that the focused Leave campaign concentrated on emotion and easily trumped the more logical approach that lacked emotion and connection to the public. But also there was a perceived problem that the Remain campaign was very much a Tory dominated campaign, especially as Jeremy Corbyn went missing during the campaign doing as little as possible, which would always be a problem motivating and enthusing Northern Labour voters to vote Remain, as they may be saw it as an opportunity to kick the Tories. But it went a bit deeper in that this Tory dominance did not know how to pitch their messages to those Labour supporters, or what vision of the future either.

'The refusal to listen to and understand Labour and Lib Dem voters was a major strategic error', says one campaign official. 'Our message-carriers were not the right ones to win in the areas we needed to. The number ten grid had three PM-Led days per week. Number 10 genuinely didn't seem to understand that he doesn't have universal appeal, and his credibility had been impacted by his decision to call this referendum and his inability to keep his party together'. [36]

A prime example of where Cameron and Osbourne did not get it was when David Cameron tweeted in February 2016 'The IMF is right – leaving the EU would pose major risks for the economy' Now to miss the point would be an understatement as I challenge anyone to ask 10 people on their high street to tell you who the IMF are and what they do! And before people accuse me of saying everyday people are stupid, it is more the fact that this International organisation has no tangible effect on their life so why should they care about them? Still the fact Cameron thought this was a vote winner shows how disengaged he was from the normal public, but can we blame him with his background, upbringing and circle of friends and colleagues? This is more a question of the weaknesses in our political system and the advantages the rich and connected have over the majority, but that is a whole new book on its own. The point linked to Brexit is that Cameron et al. did not have a clue as they had no emotional or social link to the people that were going to win or lose the vote for them. It seemed like they tried a Bill Clinton "It's the economy stupid" tactic but not realising it was in a completely different setting and context with a completely different focus for the public, as well as not reacting to or understanding how the Leave campaign was going to approach their campaign with a more emotional narrow focused (albeit untruthful) campaign. Cameron knew they were lying but was so weak and indecisive as to how he dealt with it, even when he did actually do something it got lost in the 'Ether' and more 'exciting' news. 'Call me Dave' was a nice bloke from a very privileged background never really having to get down and dirty to get what he wants as that could normally be done with a pleasant manner, good contacts and financial backing and in the scenario of the EU referendum he instigated he could not cope with Dominic Cummings, Nigel Farage, Arron Banks and their unrepentant disinformation machine. He was a lamb to the slaughter, and 3 years later he is still irrelevant, well apart from the man that split the country and instigated the biggest constitutional crisis since Charles 1 - some Historians may disagree and I bow to their better judgement, but you get the point.

Even when the Leave campaign presented their Big red bus and the lies, they added to the side of that bus about 350 million per week to go to the NHS, but David Cameron and Osbourne were very weak in attacking and disproving such claims. Cameron felt that he did not want to attack Boris or Michael Gove directly for fear of it being reported as a Blue on Blue conservative war and so put party before country and his lack of vigour in disproving these claims was perceived as if he must agree with them. This was disastrous as he made no attempt to nip it in the bud and allowed it to take on a life of its own.

The idea of having Cameron and Osbourne lead the Remain campaign where they were quite clearly a part of the despised Eton and Oxford upper class establishment was a bad one, but moreover his approval rating was lower than Jeremy Corbyn's only 8 weeks before the vote! Why did nobody in the Remain campaign mention this or suggest alternatives to head up the campaign, may be supported by Cameron and Osbourne? Too many yes men without a strategic brain or an idea of what was needed in the whole team. Yes Dominic Cummings, chief strategist, was an enigmatic difficult character and you may question his morals as to his tactics for the Leave campaign, but he knew exactly what he was doing and what he wanted to achieve and did so effectively.

It must be said that Dominic Cummings who became campaign Director at Vote Leave's operation knew from a very early stage what needed to be done to win and he wasn't going to take any prisoners and did not have the same concern as Cameron for avoiding conflict. In an interview with the Economist on 21st January 2016 he was clear that a simple campaign message about cost and control that could be digested by ordinary voters rather than constitutional abstractions: 'He has thousands of books and zillions of pamphlets and has been talking about this for many decades. The challenge is not to say more things. The challenge is to focus and simplify things'. [34] We can see here the pinpoint focus and simplicity Cummings had compared to the more generalist approach of the Remain campaign.

Steve Baker sums up what happened best: 'Dominic Cummings is like political special forces. If you do not care about collateral damage you sustain, he is the weapon of choice. He operates with the minimum of civil restraint. He is a barbarian. Dominic has undoubted mastery of leadership and strategy and political warfare. But he will not let himself be held to account by anybody. And that is basically what that attempt to sack him was about'. [35]

There is no other way than saying the level of debate and the number of lies was lamentable and I could actually see that business / marketing / PR degree courses will use David Cameron and his team's Remain campaign as an excellent case study of how things should NOT be done, learn from the mistakes and come to an alternative strategy and plan to win the vote. It will not be pretty! On the other hand, not sure Universities will use the Leave campaigns' win at all costs case study unless questioning the use of lies, misinformation, lack of morals, no plans or strategy once a campaign / vote is won.

In the general election of 2015 the tactics used successfully to undermine Ed Miliband were not used against Johnson and Gove despite enough material there from their pasts to go viral on Social Media as Cameron wanted to avoid such Blue On Blue attacks which is very admirable BUT he lost, and must be seen as a mistake and a fatal one. What became clear was that Stronger In did not have the strong focused experienced campaigner like Dominic Cummings at Vote Leave where someone like Lynton Crosby the Tory strategist could have played a significant role in making it clear to the Prime minister where he was going wrong, and what to do. Perhaps he could have even changed the result so good a campaigner he is. Maybe a start would have been Cameron saying quite clearly the Turkey would not join the EU as long as he was PM and probably not after that, but instead he played the diplomat and did not want to offend Turkey, the result being his silence put one extra nail in his own coffin! Without such a figure the team was quite inexperienced in such campaigns and did not want to utilise the skills of Peter Mandelson more considering he was the most experienced campaigner on the team. It is clear they did not want a Blairite (despite his electoral successes) to be one of the heads of the campaigns for political reasons but on reflection it is another mistake to not use all the skills and talents you have to hand to win the referendum. Another nail in his political coffin. To put it in context as to how seriously the Vote Leave was taking the campaign they sent out half a million texts in the last 24 hours of the campaign as they had accrued such a huge database of contacts that they were right on ensuring all their voters got out and voted.

The Dominic Cummings character as shown in Brexit – an uncivil war stated, 'I will get us across the line whatever way I can but to do that we have to re-stack the odds in our favour, we have to hack the political system, a cyber hack to get in through the back door, re-programme the system so it works for us. You are talking about posters and flyers I am talking about re-ordering the matrix of politics.' May be that was the difference?

Ultimately, we will never know exactly what people voted for or why but many were unhappy with their lot, the deep austerity they faced and felt the status quo was not acceptable so voted for change, in many cases not knowing what the implications of that were and as we now see in 2019 they include job losses, higher costs, uncertainty etc. But their lives have not improved and show no sign of improving in the foreseeable future. Some will say they were conned some will say they knew exactly what they voted for, but we cannot seriously think that people voted to be poorer!

But Leave.EU was not the official leave campaign?
No they were not but without going into details there was originally a battle to be the official campaign and how big characters like Arron Banks, Nigel Farage and Dominic Cummings were involved but could not cooperate or work together effectively as everybody wanted to be number one dog and had different ideas of campaigning or what was needed to win the EU Referendum vote. But the fact Leave.EU was not designated the official campaign was not going to stop Banks and Farage and their egos who had a lot of money from various sources and a high profile through the UKIP machine.

Arron Banks allegedly spent more than £11 million on social media campaigning from the summer of 2015 until polling day with a strategy of targeting the voters they wanted such as working-class people in Labour areas who seldom voted with deliberately provocative adverts they knew would make people sit up and take notice, but also received lots of free publicity which was priceless. They had learned a lot from the Trump presidential campaign with outrageous statements aimed at a specific demographic which also generated masses of free publicity.

Leave Campaign never defined a destination!
Dominic Cummings the 'brains' and chairman of the Vote Leave campaign deliberately avoided any detail of what life would be post Brexit or where we would be etc. but instead focused on what it didn't want, and the logic was clear. Why highlight in detail something that can then be scrutinised and dissected it would become clear they had absolutely no clue how to efficiently remove ourselves exiting an organisation that we have been a member of forty years and all the complex interlinked way it was a part of our legal and economic fabric. This is why the campaign was full of empty slogans and negative fear slogans as there was no plan, but there never was any intention of compiling a plan. It was not incompetence it was a clever focused campaign to keep telling the public what they

didn't want rather than what would actually happen should we leave.

This was no accident as Cummings wrote in 2015 when looking at how the people could be convinced of the unicorns and Narnia many of the Levers painted when he wrote "there is much to be gained from swerving the whole issue," Opponents of the EU "have been divided for years". In any case, "the sheer complexity of leaving would involve endless questions of detail that cannot be answered".[13] You may question Cummings morals but you cannot question his focus on getting the result that he and his team wanted and was never going to get into detailed conversations about what the future would look like or the details of how that would be created. Rather, he focused on taking people on a magical mystery tour with a 'Narniaesque' vision and praying on people's fears and prejudices to create an imaginary world that many voters bought into, without ever knowing what they were getting.

But what alternatives did they have (and Cummings understood this) as there were no tangibles to hang their hat on and so hyping up nationalistic fear and fervour worked. Had they come with something like "let's go for a Norway+ (whatever that means in detail?) solution" – do you think people would have been clamouring for their pencil at the ballot boxes? Some would of as anything that said we are leaving the EU, they would have signed up to, but it would not have got 17.4 million votes. The 'Promise everything, guarantee nothing' was the only way to go.

But it was not just the destination they promised but also on 3rd June 2016 Vote Leave promised to spend £100 million of the £350 million that they claim goes to Brussels on the NHS, but the people promising this had no authority or ability to promise or even deliver this. But it didn't seem to matter in the fervour of the referendum campaign as Leavers were willing to believe anything to get the result they desired. It was the same two days earlier when Gove AND Johnson claimed a Brexit government would introduce an Australian points based system to control immigration but again with no authority to offer this, no costings, no details and no idea of how it would actually work in practice compared to how Australia actually run their system. Also failing to mention that Australia has more immigrants per head of the indigenous population than we do and have to set up holding centres in various locations within Australia and outside its borders at great expense. But this so-called perfect solution actually admits more immigrants per head of population than the current British system for non-EU immigrants – was that what Brexiteers meant with a perfect solution?

In summary, it was Cummings' job to WIN, nothing else! Not to define anything, and it would be for others to sort out the shit which is exactly what transpired. In a word chaos, which all began in earnest in 2015.

Who was to blame for the poor Campaigns?

Here there are many people in the firing line as it would be easy to blame Dominic Cummings, Boris Johnson, Nigel Farage and several others on the Leave side who were economical with the truth as well as David Cameron and George Osborne who were incompetent on the remain side. But we should not forget all those MPs that voted for the referendum (a number assuming Remain would win), or prominent businessmen that should have made it clear the huge damage Brexit could do to people's jobs and standard of living. But also culpable are the TV / Radio interviewers and journalists that let so many people get away with the lies, misdirection and misinformation (perhaps as they themselves were not well versed in the workings or advantages of the EU?) as this allowed the misinformation to seep into the fabric of our society. Very few held the relevant people to account so the voters never knew what form of Brexit they were actually voting for. Hence this was one of the root causes of the chaos that followed the 3+ years after the referendum vote. John Major made his feelings clear on Boris Johnson and the Leave campaign claiming a 'squalid', 'deceitful' and 'depressing' campaign!

David Cameron called a referendum about something most people did not understand about and nor should they have as they never really saw or knew how the EU affected their lives and suddenly had it thrust upon them and they had to make a decision within a few weeks. With that in mind Cameron never successfully explained what the benefits of the EU are including especially membership of the single market and the benefits the UK has from that membership.

It would be easy to blame Cameron for everything and there is a long list, but he was limited as he could not just make government policy up during the campaign but Gove and Johnson could say what they wanted, promise what they wanted and were effectively making future government policy on the back of a fag packet in a very cavalier manner. Gove and Johnson did not win the referendum, but they gave the Leave vote legitimacy which may not have been the case if it had only been the right-wing media, Nigel Farage and a few Conservatives largely irrelevant old boy MPs like Bill Cash and John Redwood that have had an obsession with the EU for decades. These two meant Cameron avoided blue on blue attacks and Osbourne tried as hard as he could to protect his friendship with Gove which helped nullify their attacks or exposure of Leave lies. He almost became complicit in his inaction.

What became clear as the campaign progressed was that Farage and co. were willing to push the envelope as much as possible, for example, with their Breaking point poster which was getting him a lot of publicity. Now everybody knows that Farage is on the far right of politics, but Gove and Johnson are not seen in such a position but if they were shocked at the racist nature of Leave.EU's poster and messages, they did not say so and therefore must be held complicit in such messages. But their silence added validity to these messages whether they meant to or not as Farage's populism and shock tactics combined with Boris Johnson's voice (ironically through his silence) gave these messages more impact. We must remember that the average voter did not really know or care who was sending the message whether it was Leave.EU, Vote Leave or any of the other less prominent campaigns all they were looking at was the simple message and the fear and concern it created.

Christopher Bruni-Lowe (Nigel Farage's campaign specialist) was clear that he and Nigel Farage knew that they were pushing the limits (of acceptability), but they felt it was the only way to win the referendum. Again, we see another example of 'win at all costs' which follows Nigel Farage around as he seems impervious to critique or having any sense of morals or what is acceptable. Even Dominic Cummings who wanted to win at almost all costs texted Chris Grayling on the day of Jo Cox's death to ask him if there was any way he could stop Nigel from publishing any more of these posters? This is how bad his own side thought they were, although looking at it strategically Cummings was probably thinking they were counterproductive for the campaign rather than any moral judgement, especially as he was pushing the Turkey fabrication at every opportunity. Boris Johnson and Iain Duncan Smith also spoke to the UKIP leader about these posters for the same reasons.

The leave campaign clearly played on English nationalism and uncovered latent racism which helped result in immigration becoming the main issue in the referendum campaign and Stronger Ins lack of action to counteract or explain this and show the positive side of immigration they allowed it to become entrenched and unchallenged. Yes, they did this to avoid bringing more attention to it hoping it would possibly go away but the Vote Leave and Leave.EU campaigns were not going to allow that and kept it on the front pages of Newspapers and a digital Media including Facebook groups and feeds. Clearly, another mistake by the remain campaigns as they did not offer better answers or counteract untruths about immigration to reduce its inflammatory affect and almost added to the impression they were out of touch and did not understand people's concerns. He may not have been able to win the campaign on immigration, but he may have been able to add value to the pro-immigration argument and pour some water on the anti-foreigner flames to have reduced its effects.

The Referendum did not create divisions within the country because they were already there as people were not happy with their lives and the fact they felt poorer with little or no light at the end of the tunnel for the improvement of their lives or that of their families with low and middle incomes not rising. If we then add inflation their lives were going backwards. Areas of the country had suffered

71

more than others and they could not attack Austerity or zero-hour contracts as they were outside their control, but they could give the government a kick at the ballot box and blame foreigners for all the ills in their lives. It made them feel good that they believed they were making a difference but incited the patriotism leading to nationalism leading to some hate and were actually blaming the wrong thing as it was not Igor from Bulgaria taking their houses but rather the aftershock of a global banking crisis and austerity introduced by the Coalition government and continued by the Conservatives which has had a major impact on people's lives and their living standards.

It seemed that either through arrogance or a misreading of the country David Cameron and George Osborne ran the same economics-based argument referendum as they did in the Scottish referendum campaign which was clearly different and had much less complexity and issues that were more apparent than the EU referendum. It was like an unsophisticated corporation carrying out exactly the same advertising campaign for a different product to a different target audience expecting to get the same positive wining result

The question is when they realise that the EU was not the root cause of their problems and is not this horrendous organisation it was characterised as, and we still have the same levels of immigration as we need those people and skills who will these Leavers then blame after that? And we have seen that many of the Leave arguments need someone to blame, whether or not legitimately and once those scapegoats are removed what then? The emperor will be shown to have no clothes and people had in fact been tricked by the Leave campaigns. There will be a number of people you could blame but how many Leave voters will blame themselves for having made a decision that makes the country poorer. If the leave voters did in fact know what they were voting for then they should be treated as informed adults and held responsible for a poor decision, but how many people are honest enough to say 'this is not what I voted for' or 'I was told something completely different from what we now have' etc? Could we genuinely feel sorry for a Leave voter in Swindon who worked at Honda and lost their job because Honda set up there in the first place for a number of reasons but one of the main ones was being inside the EU due to free and frictionless trade? Surely, it's basically bad luck my friend, however harsh that may sound. You voted for it, so pick up your unemployment cheque.

One issue the Stronger In campaign faced with social media or even with the traditional way of campaigning was finding the Remain supporters, whereas Leave had all the circa. 4 million plus UKIP supporters that were obviously Leavers, and that gave them a focused base (and then expand to their friends and family) from where to begin and the remain campaign was always playing catch up and never did actually ever catch up.

The comment from the Stronger In campaign leader Will Straw should concern us when he said, 'The thing I'm proudest of is that we did create this cross-party culture, which is hard in our very adversarial political environment.' It sounded like a plucky British loser with a sporting cliché who was happy to lose and therefore probably didn't do enough to win or was not willing to go that extra mile like Dominic Cummings clearly was. Could you imagine Cummings doing that!

One of the clear issues different from a general election was that, for example, as soon as Vote Leave won the vote it effectively did not exist anymore and was disbanded so did not have to deliver on anything at all. So we are left with a government and a parliament that has to deliver a complex interrelated solution to a simple IN or OUT question, with organisations like Leave.EU inflaming attitudes and fanning the flames of hate with its posts and messages which has resulted in absolute chaos and an impasse at Westminster as it is much more complex than the ideologies at the referendum indicated.

Lies and the EU referendum campaigns

As stated previously and we will cover these more throughout the book but misinformation was an integral part of the Leave campaign (some say the Remain campaign also but these were more warnings about the dire consequences of a Leave vote, many of which came true such as a plummeting pound), but how did this originate? May be the fact the 2015 Presidential election included so many lies and untruths which resulted in a positive result for Donald Trump was a light bulb moment for the Leave campaigns? Why would they not get together and discuss the idea of making up any lie possible that would get them the result they desired knowing that after the vote those campaigns would be closed down and nobody could be held responsible for the lies. So, what is the downside for them in doing that? In some ways they were just continuing the misrepresentations of the right-wing British press that had been espoused for 40 years often without any foundation at all.

The campaign became clear that it was not the traditional Left versus Right politics but rather true versus false, much of which we realised more with hindsight, unfortunately after the horse had bolted. It was amazing how such verifiable truths were waved away as misinformation on so many occasions and people's willingness to accept that explanation was horrifying as these are the same people that would decide the future of the UK.

When did provable facts come under such attack? It was clear that an age of "tribal epistemology" which is basically where an individual accepts the truth or falsity of a statement or article etc. based on which tribe it belongs to or that tribe's values and goals they agree with. So, it has nothing to do with the truth or accuracy of the statements but their already preconceived ideas and philosophies. Yes we all have our own confirmation bias i.e. we listen more to our friends than enemies and we see this when President Trump tweets and regardless of it being based on fact his fans and voters accept that as "Truth" which is frightening as regards the development and education of a population and the world in general. Obviously if people like Donald Trump wish to spread such untruths, then social media is their weapon of choice as the algorithms can share that 'lie' so quickly and target like-minded people already who also share it resulting in a potentially dangerous lie spreading around the world in seconds which cannot be recalled and will be there for posterity. Pandora's box of fraud has been opened and cannot be put away or seemingly controlled now. But it goes one step further where it appears many people now appear to only believe information from THEIR group and if it comes from other groups, it is seen as fake News and this causes a real problem when it comes to education and people changing their positions or opinions rather than sitting in their own tribe's silo and never surfacing from it.

It was clear in my interactions on social media and even face to face with ardent Leavers that you could propose a fairly simple verifiable fact they would refuse to believe anything and anyone that contradicts their already preconceived beliefs and that of their tribe. An example of which was when they would tell me "we have too many immigrants". But when I pointed out we have the highest employment for decades as well as the lowest unemployment for decades whilst still needing to fulfil hundreds of thousands of jobs including 97,000 in the NHS, I receive the simplistic answer of "oh you are full of shit!" This is the development we are all seeing which is concerning as how do citizens develop and learn if they are so entrenched in this tribal epistemology, as well as the fact that the words "Alternative facts" have entered the English language from the highest levels in society including the White House?

We will cover the impact on Sterling elsewhere in the book but for context between the polls closing and the announcement of the result, the pound fell 10% against the Dollar – a slide larger than those that had accompanied both the financial crisis of 2008 and Sterling's departure from the ERM (Exchange Rate Mechanism) in 1992!

A project by the rich for the Rich

What do Boris Johnson, Jacob Rees-Mogg, Nigel Farage, Richard Tice, Rupert Murdoch, Conrad Black, Paul Dacre, Richard Desmond, John Redwood, the Barclay brothers and their friends and family have in common? – Money, Connections, Offshore bank accounts, and businesses operating in foreign territories? Or all of the above? The anti-EU sentiment as we have highlighted elsewhere in this book had been going on for years in the Media as well as with the right wing of the Tory party in parliament. The Brexit party, the so-called party of the people, had no manifesto with policies but claimed it would scrap inheritance tax if elected into government, and who would that most benefit? The Brexit party is financed by donations from the super-rich and elites linked to tax havens, Think Tanks and private members clubs, and such a cessation of inheritance tax would mean circa. £5 billion of income lost to the exchequer.

As Rupert Murdoch was reported to have once said, the reason he is opposed to the European Union is because when he goes to Downing Street they do what he says: when he goes to Brussels they take no notice! That is what size, and power does and not having a biased media with vested interest severely influencing a nation. Will the UK be forced to become a low-tax, low-regulation economy to attract inward investment and who in the UK would benefit from a low-tax, low-regulation economy? Have the British public been played by the super-rich in this movement that benefits the super-rich, but they have sold it to the less fortunate in the country that it is all for them? Once one digs deeper it does resemble a project defined by the rich for well..... the rich!

David Cameron claimed in April 2017 *"The lack of referendum was poisoning British politics, and I put that right"*. [46] Really David? History tells us differently, and it is still rumbling on!

75

Chapter 7
Brexiteer Amnesia - Ignorance or Duplicity?

Perhaps all of the above is possible but what critical information or items did Brexiteers forget to tell us during the Referendum Campaign and for some time after, only for it to be dragged out of them? But what did the Brexiteer leaders 'accidentally forget to tell the electorate during the EU referendum campaigns?

The Customs Union

This was hardly mentioned as focus was on immigration and sovereignty etc. even though it is at the heart of the EU project, but we cover this in more detail elsewhere in the book, but it makes very interesting reading and has huge impacts to the UK.

The Irish Border

Do you remember anyone in the campaign talking about the Irish border or mentioning anything resembling a Backstop? No of course not as those pushing Brexit had not even considered the issue or with the normal arrogance of Westminster towards Ireland it didn't really care. The campaign was so Anglo-centric. But it does bode the question after the violent history of the Irish conflict and the Good Friday agreement, what will happen to the Irish border when we leave the EU? Certainly, ex-Prime Ministers Tony Blair and John Major believed it is needed to protect the 1998 Good Friday agreements which drew the line under the sectarian troubles and the more than 3,600 lives it claimed. How many times was Ireland, or its border mentioned in the EU campaigns? Was Dominic Cummings and Vote Leave sensitive to the implications and the horrors of the recent Irish history? Of course, not as they did not care. Cummings was interested in winning and nothing else and to do that he had to keep saying "1 million immigrants from Turkey" and "Taking back control". If the Northern Irish suffered in the process, then so be it. It was so English centric with the proverbial St George's cross flags being flown literally and metaphorically that the other parts of the union were forgotten and thought almost insignificant! A huge oversight and the leave campaign must be held responsible for that mistake with the chickens now coming home to roost.

Currently there are no tariffs or customs checks or goods crossing the Irish border in either direction but what will happen once we leave? The honest answer is nobody knows as no realistic feasible solution has been proposed despite all the rhetoric from Brexiteer MPs. Ireland has to observe the EU's rules on both customs and on protecting the single market, which would normally require checks at the border with a third country which the UK will be once we leave. However, the head of Ireland's Office of the Revenue Commissioners said in January 2019 that in the event of a no-deal Brexit, it is "not planning for customs posts" as avoiding a hard border is the Irish government's "overriding objective". But it does not say what it is planning.

We could go in-depth into the theoretical possibilities the technologies that could be used but as this would be so hypothetical it was not felt appropriate for this simple book, although it should not be underestimated how important an issue both politically and economically as well as from a security point of view this is. Just another issue the Brexiteers did not know about or discuss but insist people knew exactly what they were voting for, well the people of Northern Ireland certainly did not.

It may be some time in the future that technology can help with making borders more efficient but that is currently not the case and despite the protestations from Brexiteers they cannot point to one single example when the technologies they talk of are being used in the way they describe. It is again worrying that they are still 3 years later trying to dupe and lie to their voters.

Just finally for clarity (and for those who don't understand this (as I didn't at the beginning), the Irish backstop is:

The "Irish backstop" is effectively an insurance policy in UK-EU Brexit negotiations. It's meant to make sure that the Irish border remains open (as it is today) whatever the outcome of the UK and the EU's future relationship negotiations. It would keep the UK very closely aligned to EU customs rules, with some regulatory differences between Northern Ireland and the rest of the UK. The idea was that the backstop would kick in at the end of the transition period if the UK and EU failed to finalise a future trade deal that kept the Irish border open as it is today.

The EU and UK have both said they don't want the backstop to be used and will attempt to negotiate a future relationship that means the backstop won't be necessary before it's due to come into effect at the end of 2020.[26] But as a part of Brexit with the UK intending to leave both the single market and customs union and the UK does not have to be a part of these for the Good Friday Agreement to be upheld but customs and regulatory checks on goods WILL have to be carried out in some form or other, possibly away from the border.

As the Irish backstop had become such an issue, it was felt we should spend a bit more time explaining that but the following points were also very much overlooked by Brexiteers during the campaigns and after the result, only now to discover the general public are realising it is not simple and these following disadvantages will hit the UK hard. Some of these issues include:

- What Brexit will actually mean!
- We may leave without a deal (yes "NO-DEAL")!
- Exclusion from the Erasmus programme for scientific research and collaboration
- No certain future for farmers and due to high Tariffs they may go out of business and we may have to destroy animals
- Loss of over 40 different EU agencies including the European Medicines Agency (EMA), European Chemicals Agency (ECHA), and European Aviation Safety Agency (EASA) resulting in the likelihood that the UK will probably have to set up its own systems of regulating and authorising pharmaceuticals, medical devices and procedures etc. i.e. duplication and unnecessary additional cost.

- Leaving the Euratom treaty which is crucial to the transportation of nuclear fuel for power stations and isotopes for life-saving medical use in the UK
- Loss of the designation for UK laboratories appointed AND PART EU FUNDED as authorised EU reference laboratories for many diseases of agricultural importance. For example, the Pirbright Laboratory and the Animal and plant health Agency. Again, more duplication and cost needed.
- Withdrawal of the mutual defence commitment with other European democracies, resulting in a major advantage / coup for Russia.
- The loss of parts of the financial sector to EU competitors which has already started as Paris and Frankfurt entice people away from the City of London. We have the luck that people still want to work in London and do not necessarily want to learn French or German, if indeed they actually have to when in these International companies the language used is English due to the international nature of its staff and global nature.
- No more EU regional funding
- No more EU permanent safeguards for workers as the conservative UK government looks to deregulate the economy.
- Withdrawal from the customs union and all its benefits to the UK trade.
- Losing the economic, democratic, and political privileges of being an EU citizen.

Such a long list must bode the question whether the Brexiteers were ignorant of such issues and implications in which case they were selling something they did not understand, like any spiv snake oil salesman, OR they knew the implications all the time and chose to keep the public in the dark and not be truthful with the facts. In which case it was it was either incompetence or deceit and that is unacceptable from public figures, politicians and those posing as experts.

Linked to this the absence of checks on the border have also obviously fuelled fears of a smugglers charter allowing criminals to supply Britain with tariff-free EU goods through the back door of Northern Ireland. But just think that a huge selling point of the leave campaigns was take back control of our borders, but they are now considering no border controls of people on the Island of Ireland so how do they square that circle, and how do the leave voters think that immigrants get into the country?

Boris Johnson in his so-called great deal had basically resurrected something that Teresa May's government had rejected as it did not include the whole of the UK and set Northern Ireland apart from the rest of the UK. Mr. Johnson did not seem to bother about treating Northern Ireland differently if he could get what he wanted I.e. any deal to take back to Westminster. But only days after his deal had been agreed with the EU Mr. Johnson and his Brexit minister Steve Barclay were at odds offering conflicting evidence as to how this new so-called Front stop with the Border in the Irish Sea would actually work! Mr. Johnson said absolutely no checks or paperwork when products crossed the border, but Mr. Barclay said exactly the same, both claiming they were right! This is how confused and fascicle the whole Brexit debacle had become, but the public were being deceived yet again.

Chapter 8
Brexit - Hard or Soft Boiled?

The Brexit Process

We need to just clarify how this is planned to go forward as there has been a lot of rubbish written about the whole process from both sides, normally twisted to their own benefit.

Stage 1

The UK government triggered Article 50 which basically notified the EU of our intention to leave the European Union, which was agreed by parliament and became law in March 2017.

Stage 2

This is working out the arrangements for withdrawing from the EU. This had been agreed between negotiators for the UK government and the EU in the form of the draft withdrawal agreement. But before this could be initiated it had to be agreed by the UK parliament and other EU institutions, and at the time of writing the UK parliament cannot get it through the parliament with a majority.

This is largely because there are many variations of Brexit, none of which has a majority in the UK parliament. At the time of writing Boris Johnson got the deal he had agreed with the EU voted through Parliament with the help of some Labour votes but only once the December 2019 election has been concluded and the make-up of the Houses of Parliament known will this be moved forward. Also, despite the withdrawal agreement being agreed it is still possible a no deal exit is the end result if a Free Trade Agreement cannot be concluded. So, Brexit will be with us for a few years to come.

The withdrawal agreement is a very important document and contains many items and issues to be addressed some more important ones are as follows:

1.   The "Divorce Bill" which is basically what the UK will pay to settle its obligations for future investments on a 7-year cycle it committed to.

2.   The "Transition period" which will go on until the end of 2020 unless extended. During that time, we remain in the single market and the customs union and continue to trade freely with the EU. But the plan was that we leave EU institutions, for example, we will have no members in the European Parliament (MEPs). The fly in the ointment here was that due to the extension agreed between the EU and Teresa May until October 2019 to allow her to try to get an agreement through the UK parliament, the UK will have European elections and send MEPs to Brussels, even if for only a few months, which most people find farcical of course, but then this is Brexit!

3.   The rights of UK and EU citizens post-Brexit. For example, UK citizens who have been living in an EU country for 5 years by the end of the transition period will have the right to live there permanently and vice versa for EU citizens living in the UK.

4.   Then the issue proving most difficult the Irish "Backstop" (who spoke about Ireland in the Referendum campaign?) which is an arrangement to try to avoid a hard border in Northern Ireland. We will cover this in more detail elsewhere in the book as it is proving a real stumbling block with no obvious solution.

Stage 3

This is where we negotiate our future trade relationship and hopefully agreement with the EU, which is set to happen during the transition period, but obviously we still have an issue with Stage 2 and the withdrawal agreement. But this should be addressed after the 2019 general election and before the end of January 31st which was the latest extension.

What is hard and soft Brexit?

What became very clear after the result was that many people have many ideas and understanding of what OUT would mean, whether there would be a deal or no deal, as well as the number of variations on what Brexit could really mean. We will cover some of these options later but what was crystal clear was the simplistic "Out Means Out" slogan meant nothing whatsoever apart from to a number of MPs with an extreme entrenched position. They had often been built up for decades in the case of MPs such as John Redwood and Bill cash, or political figures such as Nigel Farage who are known for little else than Europe and have been obsessed about the EU for years. In fact, it has kept them in front of the cameras and microphones and in the limelight for years whereas without the EU they would most probably have sunk into obscurity.

But we often heard about Hard and soft Brexit which are not exact positions but do show two different ends on the spectrum and let us just clarify what these positions literally mean.

Hard Brexit

This is basically about the UK moving further away from the European Union and cutting the main formal ties that have been built up over years with the main areas being:

1.   Freedom of Movement
2.   Money paid to the EU in our 'membership fee'
3.   EU law overriding UK law.
4.   Some decisions being made in Brussels and Strasbourg and not Westminster.

Soft Brexit

At the other end of the spectrum is the soft Brexit where we still continue to have close ties with the EU. An example of that could be the Norway solution (although there are others) where, for example, they are still a member of the Single Market which means they pay money in (albeit less than if they were a full member), and citizens can move between EU countries freely as we do as a full member of the EU with closer trade links to non-EU countries. More of Norway later but they are technically NOT a member of the EU so this would fit the "out means out" and "leave means leave" mantra, but as we will see it is not that simple for Brexiteers, and many would never accept such a solution.

As mentioned above there are other options, sometimes referred to as middle ways and we will touch on these later but wanted to begin by outlining the extreme of the spectrum as this sets the tone and picture of where people have positioned themselves and what implications those positions have for the UK moving forward.

Most economists analyse the closer we get to a hard Brexit the worse it will be for the UK economy. Clearly, geographical position relative to or distance from your trading partners do have a direct effect which is why we have been successful in growing our trade with the EU plus the shared rules and regulations with the EU. Economists and experts also highlight that the UK may have greater control over its own affairs but may mean we have to pay Tariffs, have different product standards and regulations making trade much more difficult which would most probably negatively affect the UK economy due to, for example, higher costs.

The above does establish that there are so many versions of "OUT" or "Soft" Brexit where we see extreme no-deal Brexiteers claiming Norwegian and Swiss-style (more of them later) deals are "Brexit in name only" and a betrayal of the "Will of the people" even though these solutions are in fact outside the EU, even if Brexiteers won't accept this fact. They run loose and free with facts, and reality, to match their simplistic view of the world and how they had been sold the post Brexit Britain.

What was the Leave position – Soft or Hard?

Their position was never clear and may be as they never thought they would win they didn't feel they had to but it was far from clear and with different Leave factions having different priorities and ideas it reduced into a list of empty slogans (albeit effective empty slogans!) and platitudes rather than any sense of plan or destination. If one looks back, it was a mish mash of up to 25 different countries the UK could emulate including as bizarre as it sounds the Pacific island of Vanuatu! In any other situation in life this would be unthinkable but Leave sold a dream and an illusion that enough people bought into.

Chapter 9
Brexiteer & Leave Arguments

Brexiteer and leave arguments

In this section we just briefly touch on several Leave / Brexiteer arguments we heard before, during and since the referendum with alternative ways of looking at those arguments or retorts to them. Many won't contain great detail as they are covered in separate sections in the book but the author felt having them in one section would be good for someone that may just want to read that section and only go to the more detailed sections of the book where they have a greater interest. Alternatively, some people may want to email me (details at the back of this book) to contest every point and tell me how wrong I am, and that is also fine.

It should be noted that all those proposed arguments or justifications for Brexit could not be included as they were vast and literally stretched from the sublime to the ridiculous, one gentleman[JB] claiming that after the vote all 27 of the EU countries should come to the UK immediately for us to tell them what we want as this could lead to a quick resolution of the issues faced! And yes, he was serious. Unfortunately, he didn't understand how the EU and negotiations works, but this was a common theme throughout the 3 years post the leave vote with such ideas put forward with the utmost confidence. JBs attitude was quite clear cut and as long as "we" (i.e. UK nationals) make all the decisions the outcome doesn't matter he believed! It was a nationalist position plain and simple.

To set the tone vote Leave made a statement two weeks before the Referendum stating *"After we vote Leave, we could immediately start negotiating new trade deals with emerging economies and the world's biggest economies (the US, China and Japan, as well as Canada, Australia, South Korea, New Zealand and so on), which could enter into force immediately after the UK leaves the EU."* This obviously sounded great, but the reality is we have achieved very little in this regard and Japan, for example, concluded one of the world's biggest trade agreements with the EU which they said cannot be rolled over to the UK. This is where hyperbole and reality clash to the detriment of the UK voters that believed such statements and the simplicity of the transition out of the EU.

"We have too many immigrants!"

This is obviously something we heard a lot of time during the referendum debates put in a more politically correct manner by politicians and Leave personalities or using a more direct language by people favouring Leave in the referendum. We cover aspects of this in this book as it cuts across economics and social policy as well as many other areas including the NHS and Housing, etc. Without over complicating this thought process of some citizens I look at it as simply as this: "In this country we have the lowest unemployment in decades, the highest employment (i.e. the number of people actually in work) in decades but still have many jobs to fill (e.g. 97,000 in the NHS) where the British public do not want to do those jobs or we do not have the skills in the indigenous people to fulfil those required positions. Yes, you can argue about the types of jobs, low pay and zero-hour contracts, etc. But they are different arguments and have nothing to do with the EU and are things our own independent sovereign Government could change tomorrow by, for example having stricter rules on zero-hour contracts and increasing the minimum wage if they wanted to.

Linked to controlling immigration the government claimed in 2019 that it will enforce a minimum £30,000 salary threshold for immigrants, but this is seen as purely a sound bite to take a hard line on immigration and to quell the right-wing protests against 'unskilled' labour. But Make UK claim that 90% of the migrant manufacturing workforce would fail to qualify for that threshold as would many other workers including nurses (90% of nurses from outside the EU earned less than £30,000 in 2018) and social workers, et al.

In the 2019 general election campaign Home Secretary Priti Patel and her Conservative government had deliberately avoided guaranteeing reducing numbers of immigration as they know they cannot guarantee it but they will not come out and confirm that as they know many Brexiteers voted for that as they were led to believe that would happen. The reality is we need those immigrants, but the deceit of the Government towards the electorate is palpable.

Therefore, this is just simple maths as regards 'we have too many immigrants' and then we can address increasing house building and supplying more social housing by Governments taking a longer-term view and investing in the future of house building. But immigrants are not the root cause of that issue consecutive governments are.

"We just need to be tougher in the negotiations."

This argument pushed by Brexiteers had no basis and lacks a real understanding of the political and economic impacts of us being outside the EU but expecting to get the same benefits. It almost sounds like the joke about foreigners not understanding so the English bloke shouts the same words just louder and expects the foreigner to understand. Or even when our national football team fails to perform and fans shout "they must show more passion" which sounds good but just like this Brexiteer argument it is based on false logic. To a large extent the football issue has been down to foreign footballers being better technically, may be playing fewer matches, and a lot of our players not playing regularly in the Premier league or not being as tactically aware which are the REAL reasons and not the lack of passion. Using the same logic the 'we need to be tougher' argument falls down as it just ignores the fact that the club of 27 countries have set rules and pay to be in that club to get the benefits, and anyone outside, no matter how much they shout or try to be 'tough', will NOT get the same benefits for obvious reasons.

"We must carry out the 'WILL OF THE PEOPLE'."

This is a misnomer pushed by Brexiteers that there was one will of the people i.e. everybody that voted leave in the Referendum had exactly the same ideas and vision of what that meant to them. Clearly, this was not the case when so many versions were put forward to them during the Referendum campaign such as soft Brexit, Hard Brexit, Norway, Switzerland, Canada+ etc. All different models with different plans ideals, and implications. The problem was not just the lack of understanding of each or even the confusion of what they wanted but rather the arguments espoused by each different Brexiteer that their version and only their version was the "Will of the People". But how could it be with so many versions and not one nailed down as the version that would be "Brexit"?

The "will of the people" I often see rather like "The referendum was an unconditional vote to Leave" in that it has a built in desperation to get it over the line whatever the cost to our people as it had become such a dogmatic matter of principle for many, that they were unable to see the wood for the trees. How can people not see that things change, people's opinions change, especially when their original decision was based on lies, misinformation and deception. Imagine we made a decision that would lead to a recession, high unemployment, or incomes slashed – how could that be the unconditional solution? How could that still be the will of the people, etc? The worrying thing is I know people that would still vote in the same way despite such a disaster as they are entrenched, and their pride becomes more important to them. This also highlights a major weakness in such a binary question to an uninformed electorate about complex inter-related global and domestic issues. The only thing I have heard that gets anywhere as near to being as bizarre is when Leavers say "having another Referendum would be undemocratic" i.e. more democracy is less democracy! Yes, go and figure that! Well I did, and this is obvious Leavers have a real fear despite the rhetoric of the result being overturned as for some that would literally be the end of the world, even though when challenged they cannot say how their life would be better outside the EU. Some it appears would find that more traumatic than losing a relative!

The 2016 referendum was not some kind of contract, where all those voting to leave committed to support any vote to leave for all time. It is highly likely that some people voted for a particular kind of Brexit and would prefer Remain to other types of Brexit, which is crucial given the narrow victory (which is also why claims that Remain cannot be on any second referendum ballot are nonsense.). Some may have voted Leave to give more money to the NHS and to stop Turkish immigrants, in which case they may have changed their minds now knowing they were both lies. It does not say "we should leave whatever the form of leave at whatever cost" on the ballot and there is no small print. [25]

If an individual's decision to vote Leave was based on or conditional on some fiction and misinformation told they cannot legitimately be counted as committed "Leavers" and therein we find another issue with this so called "Will of the People" especially as it is impossible to say there is a unified people with a unified will. It is just nonsense. Many have changed their minds since the referendum but even if they had not we have a completely different electorate 3+ years on with 2 million newly eligible young voters whilst many older voters have died. Why should that make a difference? Well basically voting was highly correlated to age, and more than 80% of the young reported as favouring staying in the EU and this demographic change alone could move the overall balance of opinion. This bodes the question of whether it is logical to bind the British people to a marginal vote based on a lot of misinformation without allowing them to vote again, ideally on a specific deal or even no deal if that is all the government can muster?

How could a more transparently fair vote, allowing the British people to use the information available and knowledge gained since 2016, plausibly be indicated as "undemocratic"? Although it is clear why adamant Leavers would not want that second vote, as a lot of them including Gove and Johnson felt they got lucky the first time around, if they did win again there would be no doubt and no arguments against leaving. We would have to leave.

There was a distinct change of focus or positivity from Brexiteers post referendum especially 3 years on when it changed from the 2016 'This is going to be a great move for the UK everything will be positive, no problems and all upsides as well as the EU will be desperate for a deal with us' to realising the reality of the situation and replacing the positivity with 'well we voted leave so we have to leave'. No strong reasons and positivity why, just we must leave as quickly as possible! Reality had destroyed their comfortable illusion that they had been sold and had melted before their faces in the 3 years since their great victory. This poses the question that I have posted elsewhere in the book – "what did the Leavers in reality win? As it seems like we are all going to lose!"

"EU Migrants are Benefit Scroungers."

Now many of the people that state this know that most immigrants come to the UK for work, and so they accuse immigrants at the same time of taking all the British jobs, but if they don't they have just come to the UK to get benefits. Some even go so far as to say they do this to save money and take it home to live a life of luxury, one even claiming to me that they could build a house in Bulgaria with the money they save from their benefits! Now clearly, anyone with sense or who knows how much benefits an individual receives know that that is not possible, but this is where such rumours and propaganda begin – from literally a nonsensical idea that becomes an urban myth. In fact, EU citizens are not eligible for UK benefits from the outset of their stay in the UK. If EU citizens haven't found work or can in some other way provide for themselves (legally of course) within three months the UK is obliged not to let that person remain let alone pay them benefits. There is a relatively well-known case called the Dano case where the European Court of Justice (ECJ) found in favour of the German government against a Romanian citizen, and we cover this in more detail in the section "We cannot stop EU immigrants coming in" that follows, but basically they found she had not moved for work so did not qualify.

What was interesting with the above attitude towards immigrants was that at one stage the public were focused on UK benefit scroungers and a number of TV programmes popping up focusing on this social issue highlighting benefit cheats wherever they could. But when the Free movement of Labour included Bulgaria and Romania those benefit cheats must have thought their prayers had been answered as the focus suddenly changed and it was the Eastern Europeans that were suddenly the spawn of Satan. The focus had clearly moved from the lazy British benefit scroungers to immigrants, and the right-Wing press made the most of it. The discrimination was clear and not all scroungers were born equal!

One person [1A] tells me that he knew of many Romanians and Bulgarians that worked for his company saved up lots of money (presumably as they had worked hard, paid British taxes and contributed to British society?) and then apparently went home and built themselves a house. Now you could see that as a focused hard-working individual, but he saw it as some kind of abuse as if they should never have been here in the first place, forgetting he had employed them in the first place! But they had gone home, so he got what he appeared to want. So sometimes the British logic towards immigrants is very muddled almost as if they do not really know what they want or how to deal with it and tend to begin shouting then about "you are not a real patriot" when challenged on their thinking or ideas for immigration. It looks like they hear these accusations about immigrants without any proof, run with them and they become urban myths that spiral out of control and are to them "The Truth". This claim that you are not a true patriot if you believed in immigration ran through many Brexiteer stances.

"Charity begins at home."

This was seen and heard more and more during and after the Referendum as many of the UK population became more inward looking as the anti-foreigner rhetoric was increased by the likes of UKIP, Nigel Farage and many right-wing MPs as they tried to increase that Leave vote and get the result they wanted. But the negative and almost aggressive dislike of us spending only 0.7% of our GDP to help the poorest and less fortunate people in the world did shock me, although the inflammatory language of the likes of Farage in the referendum campaign had heated people up so much that almost anything foreign was unacceptable, and I am not sure many appreciate that it is our government's decision to give that amount of money and not an EU decision, but it did show how the waters had been muddied.

As regards refugees, the UK is genuinely a fortunate beneficiary of an EU agreement where it was agreed that the first country the refugee enters has to process that applicant. That means the UK can send a boat back to France after they have crossed the English channel, and the French know and accept that. What would happen once we leave the EU is anyone's guess.   A letter from well-known Non-Government Organisations (NGOs) or charities including Oxfam, Action Aid, Christian Aid, and Save the Children wrote a letter to the Guardian newspaper arguing that EU funding helped efforts to tackle the 'humanitarian emergency in Syria' and poverty in Africa. Again, it shows that cooperation and economies of scale benefit many operations including that of International charities that were never mentioned during the Referendum.

My shock was I found it so harsh that they do not want to help such people in need despite being relatively privileged, yes privileged compared to 95% of the population in the world through no Skill or talent themselves but rather a pure accident of birth. Just think they could have been born in Syria or Sierra Leone for example, but they seem to prefer spending more money at home on say meals on wheels or physiotherapy in hospitals to make people's lives more comfortable (which is complementary) but compared to saving lives or supplying children clean water etc? Really! How can British people be so callous or have a lack of compassion? In the same vain we saw comments such as "Let them drown in their boats" when talking about refugees fleeing war and poverty which I find shameful as a British citizen especially compared to when we see Brits phoning the 999-emergency services telephone line when KFC ran out of Chicken! One must look at this and think the world has gone mad and hiding behind a slogan such as

'Charity begins at home' is a cheap and moronic statement in the scheme of things, and certain members of the British populous should take a long hard look in the mirror.

The reality is that Sweden, Austria, France and Germany grant asylum to more refugees (2017 figures) that the UK despite the cries of Brexiteers as if we are the only or main recipient of refugees. It's a shame that such disregard and in some cases hate for foreigners in dire straits and in need are dismissed by some British folk when they think that Mr. Jones getting seen by the Doctor within 3 days for her varicose veins rather than a week is more important than saving a life of a starving child in Africa or one who has had their whole family killed in Syria. Where do such attitudes start and finish?

Some UK based refugee charities have raised concerns about losing out on EU funding from 'The Asylum, migration and Integration Fund' (Amif) which is a pot used by EU member states to support integration on non-EU national, including newly recognised refugees. Some charities have been told by central government that the remaining allocations would cease immediately the UK left the EU with no deal. The Refugee Council for example was awarded £2.6 Million of Amif funds via the Home Office to support 3500 refugees, said the withdrawal of funding was a "disgraceful U-turn" after the British Government had assured it and other charities when it first awarded the Grants that funding would be secure post-Brexit. What other victims will we see post Brexit as the law of unintended consequences takes a hold?

"The German Car makers will tell the EU and Angela Merkel to give us a great deal!"

I would love to have had a pound for every time I heard or read that, and like all Leaver slogans it sounds very powerful. But like many other leave slogans when you investigate them more closely it is most unlikely this could ever happen despite the automotive industry being a high-profile industry as it consists of major brands such as Volkswagen, BMW, Mercedes Benz and Porsche. If 20% of the German workforce for example was working for these automotive companies then yes, I would understand that argument but in fact it is only 1/20th of 1% of the German population is employed in the German automotive market – so don't bet on that making a major difference! It is not such brands that are driving the German economy but rather the thousands of successful SMEs (Small Medium

Enterprises) often engineering or technical new technology companies known as the German <u>Mittelstand</u>, i.e. "Made in Germany". If it was ever going to happen, it would have happened by now, but it was / is just Brexiteers clutching at straws or repeating what they read on some Facebook group parrot fashion rather than doing some investigation and truly understanding the facts.

The German car industry benefits greatly from a well-functioning, internal market which is of much greater benefit than a deal with the UK, if the deal compromises the internal market. So again, the Brexiteer argument is so oversimplified it becomes almost meaningless.

"We can trade with the rest of the world when we leave!"

This was the narrative of the Leave arguments during and after the referendum campaign as our trade with the EU is falling as a percentage of our global trade, which sounded great and music to the ears of the Brexiteers. But as with a lot of these arguments it is only once we delve into the details that a clearer picture becomes apparent. So, who are the rest of the world that they are talking about? Basically, any country that is not in the EU and obviously the larger countries such as USA, India, and China are often cited.

From a business point of view, I always found this 'benefit' highlighted to be a strange one, although I admit the leave congregation lapped this up as it gave them the impression of control and telling the rest of the world what to do and may be an air of the imperialistic past. But for me it was always posed 2 main questions:

1.   Why, when we already have 65 trade agreements via the EU with other Countries around the world including major countries like Canada, Japan and South Korea? And;

2.   With whom will we trade to make a significant difference and improvement to our economy if 44% of our exports are already with the EU our closest trading partner and they will get worse?

If one looks at point 1 logically without the "Britannia Rules the Waves" type nostalgia it is pie in the sky idea that the UK with a 60 million population can negotiate a significantly better deal with any country than the EU with a single market of around 520 million and all the economic power they have. But also, we do not have enough people to negotiate all these potential deals and the complexities involved especially when we will be negotiating with the EU at the same time. Such complicated trade agreements can take years but when we are trying to negotiate with many countries at the same time with limited resources and people, these could take many years. Again, this thread running through the Brexiteer arguments implies negotiating and more importantly completing these agreements is much easier than it genuinely is, and they are painting a very simplified vision of the future without considering the complexities or basic reality. Concerns are that it is not due to lack of understanding but from many corners it is a deliberate misinformation simply to leave the EU as quickly as possible and then to work out all the problems after that day, with little or no detailed planning. It is concerning how intelligent people can think this way but so deep does the Brexit obsession run, that anything is possible no matter how illogical.

On point 2 I asked myself with whom if we leave the EU with no good FTA and can negotiate all these other countries, who are they and what are the implications? One of the arguments was for being fairer and trading more with Africa and our former colonies etc. which sounds great especially when one looks at the size of Africa on a map of the world. But when one looks at the facts and peels back the onion, the issues become evident. Firstly, if one looks at the pure GDP numbers we discover that the GDP for the whole of Africa, yes the whole of Arica including the Gold of South Africa and the Nigerian Oil and all the huge natural resources still accounts for only the same GDP as that of France, which is on our doorstep and anyone that knows trade knows distance between the two trading partners of goods plays a significant role.

The other point on who we could sign trade deals with is to look at the big beasts of world trade who we do not currently have trade deals with, and they are quite obviously the USA, China and India all of whom are now hugely protectionist with the USA under president Trump becoming even more so over time. Yes, we would hope he is no longer president in a few years but is that really a way to plan a trading strategy and who knows who would become President and their policies after him? China is extremely protectionist and make it very hard for foreign companies to set up and operate effectively on the mainland and have more of an influence now in Hong Kong and are only really interested in our niche luxury goods such as Land Rover vehicles, etc. We could also see an even greater influx of cheap Chinese products or even lower cost engineered products to compete with our own home-made and designed products which could negatively affect our competitive position and further increase our balance of payments deficit with China.

As we have now added a bit of context to this trading dilemma to highlight the challenge, the UK faces when we leave the EU on worse terms than we have currently. And to highlight this further There are 193 member of the United Nations only 39 seen by the IMF as advance economies like our own and of those 33 are wholly or partly in Europe (27 are EU members)! [15] There are none in Africa, none in Latin America, none in the Caribbean and only a few in the whole of the continent of Asia. But with this in mind (if they indeed know this and with the likes of Nadine Dorries I doubt it very much as she had to be told the differences between the Customs Union and the Single market a year after she had been campaigning for it!) Brexiteers were claiming we would be fine as 80% of the world trades under WTO rules. The problem is 80% of the world is POOR, and to reiterate again the GDP of all the countries in Africa including all the diamonds, Gold, Oil and valuable minerals and raw materials they produce is only about the same as that of France, who is on our doorstep. So, this 80% of countries argument is literally bogus when it comes to real value of trade. The UK produces largely advanced or luxury products and goods for advance economies and affluent people like our own which is why we export a large majority of our manufactured products and financial services to those countries. Not many farmers in Africa will have a need for any complicated debt instruments embedding a derivative instrument or high end complex medical equipment designed and manufactured in Cambridge. And this is where the dishonesty or misunderstanding fall down. Yet again the electorate were sold a statistic i.e. we can trade with 80% of the world no problem as they all trade on WTO rules, but the reality (yes that word again) is there are not all these huge trading opportunities that the Brexiteers would have you believe for the reasons cited above. It's a smokescreen, a charade.

"We want to Take back control of our Trade."

The bizarre situation here is that we have so-called Free Trade Brexiteers like John Redwood and Jacob Rees-Mogg etc. claim to be free traders but at the same time wish to take back control so they can rig markets and competitions in favour of British suppliers and producers. You cannot have it both ways as it is simple hypocrisy and they know this as they are intelligent gentlemen, but the problem is that they are so obsessed and have been for decades, about leaving the EU they espouse such things knowing they are not compatible. Blind obsession can be very dangerous and can make people say and do strange things.

"Why should Germany, France etc. have input in our laws?" [JB]

This was a question proposed to me by a connection on Facebook.

The question is easy to answer in that the pooling of cooperation and decision making for the benefit of the whole EU participating countries to help create level playing fields, the same rules, laws and regulations to help benefit the ease of trade, health standards, product standards, environmental issues /anti-pollution human rights etc. e.g. Working time Directive to avoid abuse of workers etc. which I am sure you will agree is a good thing? Therefore, raising and keeping standards at a high level and avoid individual countries using low wages or standards at the expense of others and workers, which I assume you also think is a good thing? Plus remember it is the UK ALSO that has input to the EU law as it is a seat at the table and is not just an 'us against them' as many seem to imply. We partake in these decisions.

It is not about isolationism but rather positive cooperation as countries work together. This idea some form of perceived 'power' is exactly that 'perceived' in an interdependent world where trade deals etc. are a reduction in power in certain areas for the better good for both parties, but you do not seem to appreciate the concept of compromise or collaboration, or at least that is how it comes across, as they try to justify their strong Leave tendencies. Just a bit of history in that Margaret Thatcher is often portrayed as this extreme anti-EU figure, but she signed agreements with the EU as, unlike say Enoch Powell, she did not see Sovereignty as an absolute and some diminution of sovereignty / power was a price worth paying for the economic benefits to the UK that she believed would arise from the creation of the single market, and so it proved once she signed the Single European Act in 1986.

But I go back to the original question when questioning their passionate desire to Leave – "how does the EU negatively affect your life or that of your family that makes you want to leave so much?", or "Once we leave how will your life and that of your family improve?". These are the realities of life and not some abstract fear or losing some perceived power you think we should have or what we would do differently with it. This is real life and not waving union Jacks or posting St. George cross Emojis on Facebook.

"Churchill would never have allowed us to be swallowed up by Europe!"

Obviously we have not been swallowed up by Europe but rather pooled sovereignty and resources and as the second largest economy in the EU (until France overtook us post-Brexit) we had more influence than most if we were willing to cooperate and use that influence in a positive manner.. But as we saw so often from Brexiteers like Mark Francois references to the Wars and Churchill were cited verbatim, and if you listened to such characters, you would think Churchill was the most Eurosceptic you had ever come across. But to nip that myth in the bud please just read the quotes from Winston Churchill below and you be the judge.

Britain should promote *"every practical step which the nations of Europe may take to reduce the barriers which divide them and to nourish their common interests and their common welfare."*

Winston Churchill, News of the World 1938.

"We hope to see a Europe where every man of every country will think as much of being European as of belonging to their own native land, and that without losing any of their love and loyalty for their birthplace. We hope wherever they go they will truly feel 'here I am at home. I am a citizen of this country too."

Winston Churchill 1948.

Sounds rather like a man that understand the advantages of closer cooperation with one's neighbours especially as he had seen the horrors of war first-hand but also understood the benefits to the UK of ever closer trade and political ties. He was not afraid so why are Brexiteers?

98

"It's our money argument"

Yes it is true as the 3rd largest economy in the EU (we were 2nd before 2016, now having been overtaken by France) we are a net contributor to the EU which means we pay more in directly than we receive back directly. But this does not consider the huge increase in trade we have benefited from as a full member of the EU, but that goes slightly off tangent for this particular Brexiteer argument.

Currently the UK receives about £2.2 billion a year from EU structural funds, a stream of money that will disappear after Brexit. An example of how this money can benefit areas of the UK is a drilling project 4.5 kilometres under the ground in Redruth Cornwall that benefited from a £10 million grant from the EU. If successful it could create a new renewable energy source and create jobs to one of the UK's under-developed regions.

But it is our money anyway I hear the Brexiteers cry which isn't strictly true as all countries pay into the pot and it is distributed based on the need and validity of the projects, but we get there point, i.e. don't give it to the EU distribute it in the UK. This sounds simplistic and easy and the government agreed claiming in their 2017 manifesto they will create an UKSPF or UK Shared Prosperity Fund which will "reduce inequalities between communities in our four nations". Excellent crack on. Well 2 years later and nothing, no further details about what the UKSPF will even look like. When asked about these in June 2019 Brexit Minister Kwasi Kwarteng admitted the details that were due to be published by the end of 2018 will not be released until 2020. And this is just another problem of Brexit when our regions need the money now and especially when we leave to help create growth and prosperity but we haven't even got the basic information of who will decide how the money is spent, what activities / projects will be eligible for support / grants, how will the money be divided across the regions and countries, but also the actual monetary value of the fund.

This is what happens when empty promises meet with reality and the fact the EU is delivering on these projects for the UK development, but our government cannot in 2+ years give us the basic information. Is this a sign of things to come?

As a part of this we often heard "We will take back control of our MONEY our LAWS and our BORDERS" etc. but let's have a look at "our money" and the EU a bit closer. It appears that we already have control over all but a very small percentage of our money (at 4.5%) - look at UK annual tax and spend graphic below that shows this stark reality. We are creating all this worry, hurt and increased poverty for 4.5%?

Whilst we are on the subject of our money it is also claimed that the EU dictates the VAT rate we must charge, but this is not true as the EU sets a floor of 15% BUT it is the UK government that decided on the 20% we now pay, Not the EU. Also, there is a logic to the 15% floor as it stops EU states going not ridiculous levels to compete with each other and create a race to the bottom. The base was set out in the agreement with all countries and exceptions were accepted for the for the de facto lower VAT rate on some products at the time of the agreement. The UK, for example, does not pay VAT on printed books but in Denmark they pay 25%.

The graphic below shows just how small the EU input and influence is as to where the UK raises its money, and this is largely due to the pooled sovereignty as all other EU member states do for the better good and to increase the international power and influence of the EU and therefore its member states. Customs duties are just a small part of the UK income but is often misrepresented by Brexiteers and not based on any facts, which we have seen is a regular occurrence.

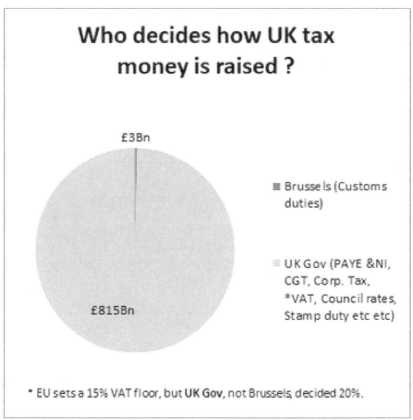

Who decides how UK tax money is raised ?

£3Bn

■ Brussels (Customs duties)

■ UK Gov (PAYE &NI, CGT, Corp. Tax, *VAT, Council rates, Stamp duty etc etc)

£815Bn

* EU sets a 15% VAT floor, but UK Gov, not Brussels, decided 20%.

Source: Jim Grace @mac_puck

"I hate the EU Laws and regulations imposed upon us!"

I hear this and many variations of it from many Brexiteers, admittedly sometimes looking to hide their anti-immigrant tendencies but when asked what those laws were that were being imposed on them or making their life a lot worse than it would be without the EU nobody seems to be able to tell me. I would get replies such as "Lots" so I would push "then name a couple" but again no forthcoming flashes of enlightenment. Occasionally I got a nervous laugh and a half joking reference to bendy bananas (a lie and rumour started by Boris Johnson!) and I say half-jokingly as I think a couple of them secretly still thought this was true and were hoping I could confirm indeed it was. Some may disagree but it would be a matter of conjecture how Britain, with its weak economy at the time, might have weathered the economically turbulent 1970s if outside the EEC?

It appeared that they, like the 'normal man' on the street had no idea what laws were originated in the EU and what were decided by our own British courts which is amazing when you think a total of 52,741 laws [5] have been introduced in the UK as a result of EU legislation since 1990, according to the Legal business of Thomson Reuters, the world's leading source of intelligent information for businesses and professionals.

Surely if there have been that many it would be easy for any Brit or especially a Leaver to highlight several them that are so bad? At the end of any of these discussions I concluded that the argument about the EU laws was a red herring and a distraction from other real reasons for the dislike of the EU project or just a plain dislike of the EU, may be influenced by the constant barrage of Eurosceptic propaganda from the British Press?

The Telegraph in its article on 22nd June 2016 entitled '20 reasons you should vote to leave the European Union' number 3 was 'we can make our own laws again' but does not highlight that our representatives at the EU level have significant input into those laws, but also does not cite one that is so bad for the UK that they would change it tomorrow. Laws are not perfect whether made at the EU level or the UK level, but the EU has a good record of developing laws to improve the lives of its citizens and organisations.

The above article continues with number 4 being 'Our courts would have the final say over those laws', but the UK has opted out of all but 35 of the 135 areas of the criminal justice policy utilising its opt-outs to give it the best deal in the European Union. We participate in the European arrest warrant scheme so EU nationals can be arrested and extradited to other EU countries which is a very practical and effective EU wide tool for crime prevention and justice. Beforehand it was very difficult, and people escaped justice. But also, as previously stated again no example of a Law they would change tomorrow as it is so bad that is negatively affects the UK within the EU.

The irony of this position about the EU laws that were so bad that the UK government in planning for Brexit decided that all EU laws were to be passed into UK law so our day after the departure from the EU we had a set of laws in place. This was over 19,000 provisions and hundreds of thousands of pages, which was basically a very expensive unravelling of 40 years of EU and UK cooperation. So, when Leavers say we will be saving £39 Billion we will not as we would have spent billions on many aspects of exiting the EU whether it be those type of changes to the law or the immense cost implication to our whole new trading system, preparations, loss of trade, etc. But even the much talked about £39 billion* 'divorce bill' Brexiteers claim we do not have to pay it despite us committing to this or a similar calculated figure for future commitments before we voted to Leave. If we default on this payment our reliability as an international ally would be shot and the EU could probably pursue the UK government through the courts to collect the money we owe. But this is how desperate Brexiteers have become to get somewhere near their Nirvana, but this 'default' compared to how our economy and Sterling are struggling with Brexit on the horizon our credit rating and international reputation could take a massive hit again.

Boris Johnson in his November 2019 deal with the EU conceded we would pay the divorce bill which was always going to be paid no matter how often Brexiteers like to tell us the EU could go whistle for it!

* Brexiteers kept quoting this figure, but it had been reducing by the month and with the further extensions it had reduced and as of September 2019 it had reduced already to £33 Billion and may drop further if there was a further extension after October 2019. The figure of £1 Billion per month Dominic Raab and Prime minister Johnson claimed it was costing the UK for further delay didn't factor in payments received from the EU, so was again a false figure the Government was espousing to deceive the public in its propaganda war.

If one looks at the House of commons library, it states just 4,514 out of 34,105 laws have been influenced by the EU, of which just 72 of them were forced on us that we do not agree with.

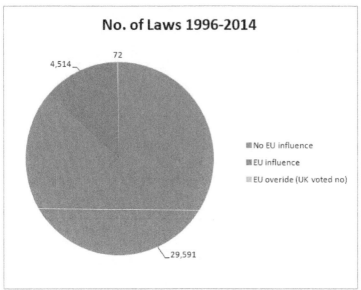

No. of Laws 1996-2014

72
4,514
29,591

- No EU influence
- EU influence
- EU overide (UK voted no)

Source = Jim Grace on Twitter @mac_puck

These included regulations such as making sure food labels say if Aspartine is present, which has been linked to cancer, headaches and seizures, and banning carcinogenic residue in meat! So, you would be correct in asking yourself why on earth would the UK not want such information printed on products we consume, but we can like other governments be influenced by lobbyists for certain Pharma companies, etc. Linked to this labelling is any trade deal with the USA (when we are desperate to get a deal) may not include such labelling, and as a Danish friend of mine sarcastically said "Good luck with that!"

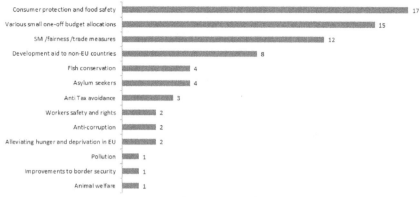

Breakdown of all 72 EC Directives implemented against UK wishes

Category	Value
Consumer protection and food safety	17
Various small one-off budget allocations	15
SM /fairness /trade measures	12
Development aid to non-EU countries	8
Fish conservation	4
Asylum seekers	4
Anti Tax avoidance	3
Workers safety and rights	2
Anti-corruption	2
Alleviating hunger and deprivation in EU	2
Pollution	1
Improvements to border security	1
Animal welfare	1

Courtesy of Jim Grace #FBPE @mac_puck [21]

If we scan the directives implemented against our will, we will notice very quickly that they are mainly items that protect our citizens, workers, animals, fish, unacceptable pollution, and tax avoidance which are surely all surely good intentions and aims, which is why our public cannot find issues that make their lives worse rather than better than in the actual real-life examples above. The lack of understanding and appreciation of the EU is huge in the UK, but largely down to a Eurosceptic press and propaganda.

For more information you can go to the London Economic website which shows some great information on those aforementioned EU laws: https://www.thelondoneconomic.com/news/rationalist-destroys-leavers-with-list-of-all-eu-laws-that-have-been-forced-on-us-against-our-will/22/01/

The "Crystal Ball" argument

This argument I came across many times from Leavers with the basic logic of 'well nobody has a crystal Ball so let's go for it and Leave the EU and see what happens!' At first this was very frustrating when debating as it was almost the cricket adage of offering a dead bat and not entering into a factual or logical argument. But from that point of view it was effective, even if it lacked substance.

It often occurred when the other party ran out of arguments for Leaving (often without any deal) and then offered up "well you haven't got a crystal Ball so you don't know what the future will hold", and that is obviously true as nobody can know exactly what the future holds. But it is a cop out as in any other important area or areas in their life they would not use such a lack of logic or argument, for example, moving to a new house. Would they say to their wife, "right love we are moving tomorrow but I am not sure where we are going, how much we will get for our house, whether we will be buying or renting, not sure where we are going etc. (I could go on, but you get the point) BUT you do not have a crystal ball, so you do not know any better, so we are just going for it!" It's just not sensible or logical is it?

So why do people think and talk that way? Is it just sheer frustration that the Leave dream is melting before their eyes and people like Jacob Rees-Mogg and Boris Johnson have moved their positions and changed their minds since the referendum, but the people are not allowed to change their mind with a Second referendum / People's Vote? Both the aforementioned politicians described Teresa May's proposed deal with the EU as "Vassalage" and a "Suicidal vest" but then in March 2019 they voted for it as they had no better option, i.e. they had changed their mind! Dominic Raab voted for it as well. The Brexiteers despite three years since the referendum were split and could still not agree on what Brexit actually was and the hypocrisy was rife.

But perhaps it was a simple way of closing down the argument they were losing when it started to become reality that we probably would not have fewer Immigrants once we leave the EU as we need them. We always had sovereignty, so that was found to be false, OR we would not be totally independent as they were told as we would have to work closely and 'INTER-dependently' with other countries on any trade deal or any aspect of cooperation around the world. The days of Great Britain sailing around the world on our big ships telling other countries what to do or we will invade and enslave them are long gone but talking to a number of the older generation one gets the feeling they still hark after such a world when we were that naval power. Obviously they forget the raping and pillaging part, but it is there and is quite concerning and somewhat saddening.

Then obviously pride plays a major role as they were told so many myths (although one must say at the time sounded realistic to many people) and they had innocently shared these myths and misinformation from the likes of Nigel Farage etc. and could not now admit they were wrong but also it would hit them quite hard if they had to admit yes we do need more immigrant workers, we had our sovereignty all the time but decided to pool that sovereignty with 27 other countries for the better good (including Trade, prosperity and security), it is going to make the UK poorer, it is not going to be easy and we will have 40 trade deals completed the day when we leave, or that when we leave, we will not be totally independent and we have to cooperate and work closely with many other countries and organisations who will have a say and their input i.e. their sovereignty to the end result – that is interdependence NOT independence.

"It will be alright eventually."

How could many of the 17.4 million people admit to either having been conned and swallowed the deceptions they were fed, or they still believe in such nonsense when to any sensible person the 3+ years since the referendum has proved this to be totally untrue? Many Leavers were put in a very unenviable position, but it was those at the top leading the Vote Leave, Leave.EU, the ERG, and the right-wing press that peddled falsehoods that had led them there with it being very difficult to turn 180 degrees. But the interesting aspect of this frustration was that much of their anger was targeted at Remainers that had told the truth and continued to highlight these aspects and not the elites such as Jacob Rees-Mogg and Boris Johnson that had taken them on this journey and abandoned them for dogmatic reasons and obsession with the EU or personal gain. They were literally 'shooting the messenger'. The Brexiteer and Conservative Member of the European Parliament Daniel Hannan was born in Peru and privately educated at Marlborough stated he was radicalised about the EU in his first term at Oxford University basically because of the Maastricht Treaty. As an undergraduate, he established the Oxford Campaign for an Independent Britain when most first-year students are getting off their faces. So, you can see this obsession at a young age and have to ask whether this is a healthy obsession or does it cloud his judgement that he cannot see how people less well-off than himself will suffer more than he ever will with say a no-deal Brexit.

It is clear that the anti-EU sentiment in many people runs illogically deep and whatever he (or any Brexiteer) says or does as long as it is anti-EU or anti-foreigner some will lap it up and follow the likes of Nigel Farage him like the messiah, but messiah of what? He has never demonstrated a shred of a plan and only numerous empty slogans and platitudes to appeal to his small right wing thinking older demographic which massages his ego to make him carry on and lead a very privileged life with support from the likes of Arron Banks.

The "we just need to be stronger" argument

We heard many people including former Foreign secretaries and former Conservative leaders claim we were not strong enough with the EU and just had to be stronger with them to get what we want. They were either being unrealistic, disingenuous or still failed to understand that in a negotiation with 27 other countries we are at the short end of the stick. Was it arrogance, desperation or were they just too dense to grasp this simple fact? It wasn't as if they just whispered this in the dark corridors of Westminster they also wrote it in articles, obviously with no meat on the bones of how, showing their ignorance for posterity. It reminds one of the old joke about the Brit abroad and if a foreigner does not understand you, just shout a bit louder and he will! Did they genuinely think if we shouted and threatened the EU 27 would just roll over have their tummy tickled and give us all we want?! Stronger for what? What did they want? The EU had already given the UK much of what they wanted. It's an easy albeit lazy argument.

The "Abolish all Tariffs" argument

This was the argument that cropped up about 2 years <u>after</u> the referendum result once the complexities of international trade and its implications to the UK once outside the EU became clear, which were not made clear during the campaigns. The basic logic is that if we reduce all tariffs to zero, it will reduce the costs of things like imported food etc. and many Brexiteers such as Jacob Rees-Mogg were proposing this as a realistic option, although it should be noted that JRM is so desperate to leave the EU he may agree to almost anything and then hope we can work it out afterwards somehow. Not a great strategy, but then when has it ever been? Do you remember anyone talking about this as a serious option during the referendum?

This idea of unilaterally abolishing tariffs some Brexiteers felt would soften the blow of a no-deal Brexit or even leave the UK better off than it is now. As John Longworth, who runs Leave Means Leave a pro-Brexit lobby group says, "Brexit means cheaper food". They use the example of Singapore (no there are not many other examples!) who charge practically no Tariffs on their imports, BUT they hardly produce anything locally so do not have anything to protect or suppliers that could suffer from this tariff free competition. Therefore, nothing like the UK, and therefore somewhat irrelevant.

It is true that outside the EU the UK could devise its own trade policy including setting its own import tariffs, but under World Trade Organisation (WTO) rules the UK would have to charge the same tariffs on EU imports as on non-EU ones, which is where it starts to get more complex than many Brexiteers would have you think. Also have you noticed that we are having to follow rules, albeit WTO rules which is what a lot of Brexiteers didn't want as we had to be independent and totally sovereign in this new free world. So, the first move is we have to obey some rules that we did not set which makes a farce of the independent argument when we live in an interdependent world. This is the reality.

In theory the UK could receive Sweetcorn from Thailand 10% cheaper than it otherwise would be, but this is only if the importer, wholesaler and retail establishments do not put their margins up as they know people paid 10% extra for it before so will pay the same price for it now and they can pocket the extra profit. So, there is no guarantee.

Abolishing tariffs could detrimentally expose domestic manufacturers and sectors such as UK farming which is why Michael Gove suggested that tariffs would be applied to food imports in the event of no deal to protect farmers from ruin. The same is said to being considered on finished cars otherwise the auto manufacturers in the UK could no longer be competitive. But in summary the Brexiteers could not agree and had no plan.

Note that if these industries suffer or companies close so to do the suppliers to those industries including tractor or feed suppliers, or in the case of automobiles component and sub-assembly suppliers could disappear. Never forget the knock-on effects as companies are not isolated islands immune from these disastrous events in related or interlinked industries and vertical markets.

Some say that Farming needs to adapt or die but one of the strategic reasons farming and domestic food sources are important is that if in the future if there is ever a war or a global shortage of food, the country can sustain itself, whereas if most food is imported they may keep that food for their domestic use as they need it. So, without good farming and food producing industries we do not have a secure supply of food for our population. Another reason as to why this is not a great argument, (but rather one used by Brexiteers desperate to leave and will worry about the consequences later), if farmers and other companies go into liquidation.

The other thing that people often forget linked to this is that with a no-deal Brexit Sterling will almost definitely depreciate and therefore causing import price rises so the combination of this and the issue for farmers etc. of abolishing Tariffs shows how it is complete folly, following just behind the elusive Unicorns.

Remember also that trade in goods only accounts for 20% of our economic trade and services are much more important where reducing non-Tariff barriers, such as harmonising regulations and standards are much more complex.

But a lot of these ideas are bandied around by Politicians with limited commercial experience without consulting business or looking at specific industries in any detail. Carolyn Fairburn, the CBI Director General was quoted on the BBCs Radio 4 Today programme saying, "what we are hearing is the biggest change in terms of trade this country has faced since the mid-19th century being imposed on this country with no consultation with business, no time to prepare." Surely this is unacceptable in such critical times when the future of our trading relationships and corporations is at stake.

Finally, the idea of leaving the largest trading Block in the world but claiming to aspire to be the leading light in free trade is Brexiteer nonsense and clearly incompatible goals.

"Job Losses and Depreciation of Sterling is Project Fear"

Well the 12% drop in Sterling which would increase the cost of imports happened straight after the Leave result as forecasted by Mark Carney and the Bank Of England but this may take time to filter through to the high Street for people to see the impact in their pockets, although when it comes some may not make the link and the die-hard Brexiteers will just ignore it or claim as usual it has nothing to do with Brexit.

In July 2019 Sterling took another tumble in light of soon to be Prime Minister Boris Johnson claiming he will take the UK out of the European Union on 31st October "Do or die". Although in true Boris fashion later stated there is a "Million to one" chance we will not get a deal". Clearly, the two are incompatible, but get used to this with Mr. Johnson as his will not be the only example.

The jobs angle is an interesting but complex one which we can only touch on here in this book but clearly for companies trading internationally or with the EU specifically the Leave vote and our imminent departure from the EU is a major concern. But the government is making preparations for us leaving even if with no deal so everything will be OK right? No, as no matter how many preparations you make if I do not know exactly what tariff rates will I have to pay as an importer or my customers as an exporter of products and services, or what and how much paperwork and red tape will be required, or how much longer products will take to get to and from a company's customers and suppliers.

The depreciation of Sterling we have seen since the referendum result has already disproportionately affected the lowest paid by pushing up food and fuel prices. When combined with low pay growth and benefit cuts the impact could be worse for the poorest third of households than even after the financial crisis. But we should also remember that the financial crisis was not a vote for our lowest paid to be poorer as the referendum result has become. So, a significant difference.

The reality of the threat to jobs is where companies are dis-investing, moving staff / facilities, and moving future investments offshore and not in the UK. A worrying example of this is Airbus saying it was contemplating relocating UK sites (14,000 jobs) for strategic reasons, and even if that does not happen short term the risk will always be there as long as we are outside the EU and have no free trade deal or have the benefits of free movement of labour.

How can a customer make accurate costings and make proposals? What if products such as sub-assemblies go across borders multiple times how does that affect my costings and delivery times? Even once a company can do all that which will only be after we leave, how can that company prepare for its EU customers not accepting the company's now higher prices, longer lead-times and unknown amount of increased paperwork when they can more easily source the products from another EU state where they do not have such concerns? The UK has just made trade a lot more complicated and uncertain, not the customers and suppliers in our EU partner sates.

The result of the above could be loss of business and profits and therefore taxes to the exchequer, but also less money means fewer opportunities for growth and employing more people. This is the reality to business and our economy.

111

"It's OK we are preparing for a no-deal Brexit"

The impression given by the government ministers and Brexiteers in 2019 was that as long as we prepare for a no-deal exit everything will be OK. But this is not correct as even preparations would not eradicate the sort of problems highlighted above. As a friend of mine in rather brutal terms put it "If I went up to one of those ministers and told them to prepare for me to punch him in the face and then punched him in the face would it still hurt and would there still be pain afterwards? Of course, there would!" I would have prepared a less graphic analogy, but I am sure you will agree it serves its purpose and may be establishes the seriousness of the issues at hand and the fact is preparations do not avert the pain even if they can reduce it.

On day 1 of a no-deal scenario a good percentage of HGVs travelling via Dover etc. may not be ready for French customs, despite the government spending £100 million of taxpayers on an advertising campaign, influenced also by the fact companies were faced with the first false dawn in March 2019. This issue could cause significant delays and backlogs in Kent sometimes resulting in an estimated 1 to 3-day delays. The obvious concern here is regarding the supply of products that cannot be stockpiled due to short shelf lives, particularly medicines and medical supplies for both humans and vetinary services.

Jacob Rees-Mogg as a member of the Boris Johnson government said that measures were in place for flights to be used should there be any issues with supply post Brexit but air freight capacity (especially short notice requirements) and special import schemes are not a financially viable way to mitigate risks associated with such requirements, unless the government is going to subsidise these industry requirements with more of the taxpayers money. This would make a nonsense of the Brexiteer claims during the campaigns that the move / transition to a post EU life would be easy and smooth with no additional costs.

"We voted to Leave but still have high employment and low unemployment!"

Now I am sure you will agree this is a bizarre argument considering we are still at the time of writing a member of the European Union when these arguments were made forgetting that job creation takes some time and all those jobs were created whilst a member of the EU and must point towards the fact that it was not too bad was it for the UK but some still want to crash out. The impact on jobs has been seen already albeit we have not even left yet, and nobody knows how the UK will leave yet the impact has been muted. But also, we should not forget that the UK has one of the lowest productivity rates (defined as the efficiency of a worker or group of workers) in the EU and due to the uncertainty and risks of Brexit industry is cautious regarding or does not want to invest in capital such as automation, as it is easier to offload staff in the event of hard times and a recession as opposed to expensive capital equipment which is often a fixed asset of the business and cannot be liquidated very easily or quickly.

"They need us more than we need them!" [BH]

This was so often espoused before and after the Referendum based basically on the fact that Germany exports a lot of cars to the UK and we import more from the EU than we export to them. But there are some serious floors in these arguments as firstly, any pain suffered by the EU would be spread across 27 countries whereas our pain will be borne by just ourselves one country, so the pain is much more serious. For us also those 27 countries can look to buy and sell more products from each other which they may have purchased from the UK previously when we were in the Single European market and customs union either to make it easier as regards paperwork, border checks etc. but also potentially price as Tariffs start to come into play when we leave the EU.

The amount of trade between the two entities is really meaningless but rather size matters when we consider the UK exports to the EU is 13% of our total economy but the EU exports to the UK amount to only about 3% of their total economies. 27 countries losing one of their most important trading partners is much less important to them than it is to the UK losing its 27 closest trading partners, especially when it is not self-sufficient. Plus, we must not forget the total legal framework under which it does that trade. This idea that as the EU 27 buys

113

more from the UK than vice versa does not mean they need us but rather they have just chosen to purchase from the UK up to now. I buy more from the Sainsbury's supermarket than it does from me, but that does not mean I can waltz into the shop and start telling them we have to now work together under my rules, and then complain they are bullying me as they do not accept my terms and conditions.

So, they have much more flexibility with suppliers and customers on their doorstep whereas we are talking about trade deals with Canada, USA, India etc. who are quite far away and will impact trade due to the distances and cost of shipping, etc. involved. That is even if we finalise agreements in the first place and what we have to forgo or sacrifice in those arguments.

Yes, it will negatively affect other EU member states, which is why they want us to remain. But this Leaver attitude to a no-deal Brexit shows either a lack of understanding or they do not care that this would create a Lose Lose Scenario with no apparent winners. Who wins in this no-deal Brexit scenario? My Grandmother would often say "He would cut off his nose to spite his face!" and that is what it appears like when one takes a rational cool calm and collected consideration of the no-deal Brexit some crave.

The reality is that over time the EU leverage will be deployed and will be used to enforce deals on issues like fisheries as they are not a significant part of our economy which will make those Referendum commitments by Brexiteers hollow as they will be abandoned and cheap stunts like Nigel Farage dropping fish in the Thames for a photo opportunity will be shown for what they were. In fact, Nigel Farage as UKIP MEP had only attended 1 of the 42 meetings of the EU Common Fisheries committee including votes on helping and supporting smaller fishing companies, despite making a big deal of fishing in the Referendum campaign and also after it. Perhaps this tells you more about the man than we realised?

The Government and the ruling class?

Although not often cited by Leavers as a reason for them leaving there was clearly an unhappiness with the government for various reasons including austerity of course and many sensed with David Cameron and George Osborne leading the remain campaign it was a big F@@k YOU to the government and the ruling class. It could also have been many thinking remain would win anyway so it didn't matter and shows how careful people have to be with their vote in all elections. According to British Social attitudes 65% of vote Leavers greatly distrusted Government and 62% distrusted parliament which would strengthen the idea above that it was not just the EU voters were complaining about. And there another reason reveals itself as to why referendums are not a good tool when addressing such a highly complex issue.

"It's not all about money" [IL]

This has been thrown at Remainers claiming they are only interested in money which is why they talk about the economy all the time and do not understand people's concerns outside monetary values etc. Obviously it is never just about money, but it is naïve if people do not think that money is very important because the more money a government has due to the success of its economy the more it can spend on the NHS, Social services, capital investments and other ways to improve UK society as a whole. But it needs a successful economy to achieve this and the single market and true free trade between all EU 28 countries has helped the UK achieve that.

With more money coming into the Government coffers due to a successful economy and tax receipts it can better address some of those concerns people had due to globalisation or the feeling of being left behind, the North-South divide, etc. If the UK crashes out of the EU and the expert forecasts from the Bank Of England and even the Government's "operation Yellowhammer" itself are correct then those people that had those concerns may be the ones that literally suffer most. With the risk of further increase in costs, rising inflation and job losses in manufacturing etc. the poorest in society will be disproportionately affected by such developments as, for example, they spend a higher proportion of their incomes on food, and basics etc.

But what this highlights are changes in attitude that some are so desperate for Brexit that they are willing to be poorer and don't care if their fellow compatriots are also poorer. But trying to get to the bottom of why this is can be difficult as they talk about a 'better society' which can mean many things to many people, but always felt like they were indicating fewer immigrants but believing it was not politically correct to say that. They had been sold a return to a Golden age that will never return now we live in a global economy where more interactions and compromises are needed, so are they again being set up for major disappointment when the Government has less money for social services, roads and the NHS, etc?

We must obviously blame the people that start the lies but then when do the people who believed the lie become those that are telling the lie when they start sharing lies on social media as they have ceased to be the person believing the lie but now the person telling and sharing the lie. So very quickly innocent, naïve people can be manipulated and become a part of the problem and escalate that problem and the Lemming effect can kick in.

Chapter 10
The Press & The Media

The British Media is largely right wing AND very powerful

This may be stating the obvious but many Brexiteers like to disclaim this claiming it is a biased left-wing media when their fanciful ideas about Brexit are dissected and disproved. But they never let facts get in the way of good propaganda. Although many people claim to not be influenced by the Press or any form of advertising as they want to be seen as independent free thinkers, especially in the case of Brexit for obvious reasons. But we should never underestimate the power of influence of propaganda and the Press.

Having now researched the press and their coverage of the EU the messages and reporting are very much negative and hugely inaccurate and sometimes plainly not true. When reading some items, they wrote it is difficult not to conclude that they are deliberate distortions which was for a specific political aim directed by the owners and Editors of many of these publications. When reviewing these false stories and dishonesty I was reminded of the reported quote by the former British Prime minister Stanley Baldwin in 1931 when he said, "The Press has power without Responsibility" (a phrase borrowed from Rudyard Kipling I believe).

It is impossible to know exactly how much the Press changes people's minds but that constant drip drip drip of negative stories must influence any normal person who, before the Internet had advanced, had limited avenues for consuming News. This is further exacerbated by the fact that the BBC and other TV outlets were greatly influenced by the Press and what stories they would lead on, especially as regards Europe. The other party who were greatly influenced by the Press was Number 10 and the Government which is obvious when one reads any political Biography or autobiography and this has resulted in many governments (perhaps Blair was an exception) continuously showing negativity towards the EU and regularly standing on the outside and not playing as big a developing role as they could from the centre. Even David Cameron started off as pretty EU friendly and even when negotiating the coalition agreement with Nick Clegg and the Liberal Democrats Mr. Clegg commented that "Europe was one of the easier points and not an issue" as they were both pro EU and saw the significant advantages of EU membership.

Unfortunately, like John Major before him he was pressured by and ultimately succumbed to the right-wing anti-EU side of his party, or the "Bastards" as Major labelled them. The constant pressure and small majority combined with the rise of UKIP and the megaphone voice of Nigel Farage led him to look more at self-preservation than national interest resulting in the Referendum and the Leave vote. This will be David Cameron's legacy no matter how much he tries to spin it as he achieved very little in government despite the positive picture or optimism he painted when first being elected to power, but he had no vision or strategy to achieve things and was ultimately too weak. The right wing of the Tory party would never go away and had a double role which was obviously competing for votes and influence within the party that feeds through to the leadership. But also, its 'pseudo partnership' with the right-wing press and the pressure they created also for the Conservative party leadership. Sometimes timing works against you and in a different time or situation may be David Cameron would have been a success, but as Harold Macmillan once said, "Events dear boy events". Although the decision on the referendum was his and his alone. The rest is history, but apart from gay marriage we struggle to see any great achievements of his premiership as he left a stuttering economy, the referendum as we have experienced was unworkable, and the governments whether it be Teresa May's or Boris Johnson's have been paralysed.

If we focus on the top selling Newspapers in the UK which are The Sun (1), the Daily Mail (2) they were and are unflinchingly anti-EU and report on its affairs with such hostility it is unhealthy but also add mockery and sheer contempt probably to hammer home their anti-EU message to their readers so there is no doubt what they expect them to believe. The Sun ran front pages such as "Up Yours Delors (Jacques Delors was the former EU commission president) with a two-fingered salute to the "French Fool"! But the Daily Mail is no better with one of its front pages claiming a "Blueprint for Tyranny" when referring to the EU constitution or when they claimed Germany was turning Europe into the "Fourth Reich"! The daily Express, although with a smaller readership, is not better having claimed such things as "Now EU wants to ban our kettles" or "EU brainwashes our children".

To show how bias the Press can be The Daily Mail ran a Front-Page story and a photo of migrants getting out of a Lorry apparently saying "we're from Europe let us in" when it transpired that police footage clearly showed the migrants saying they were actually from Kuwait and Iraq. Now how could they have got this wrong or did they deliberately make it up (i.e. lie)? But not to be outdone The Sun even tried to claim "The Queen backs Brexit" based on some 'anonymous' sources which was found by IPSO (Britain's watchdog) to be 'significantly misleading and not backed up by the text' which in layman's terms meant it was Bullshit!

Despite the cries of democracy from the press this was often crocodile tears when we saw the Daily Mail accusing high court judges of being the "enemies of the people" whipping up an already ugly mood in the country when all the judges were doing was interpreting the law which was and still is their job. This ugly side of the press did not help with the ever increasing and ever more repulsive attacks on the likes of Gina Miller and Deir Dos Santos, as they looked to have the law enacted on. Again, it appeared the poorer quality newspapers and media outlets wanted a "result" and had no interest in democracy or the rule of law. The law is the law whatever a biased newspaper editor may think. But this Daily Mail online article has not been withdrawn and can still be found online, further showing their disregard for the law. (54)

Now in each case each newspaper had to publish small corrections on the inside pages, but by then it was too late those and many other such false and unrelenting stories had become ingrained in the British Psyche, and where was the disincentive for the papers for publishing such stories again? Answer is there was none which is why it has continued unabated. The Freedom of the Press is clearly a hot potato as one witnessed in the phone hacking scandal where it took the hacking of the dead girl Milly Dowler's mobile phone to make something happen, but what stops such inaccuracies about the EU when it can cause such economic harm to the UK due to the referendum result?

Some Press stories about the EU verge on bizarre such as when they claimed "EU bureaucrats have banned children under 8 from blowing up balloons because they might hurt themselves" which turned out to be wrong on many levels where the journalist confused a "new directive" with a "draft text" and claiming that bureaucrats made laws which they do not. All that happened in reality was the commission recommend children under 8 be accompanied by an adult when blowing up balloons for obvious reasons (to stop them potentially choking). Now although in this case it was not a clear case of misinformation, it was lazy uninformed journalism that the newspaper either didn't check or was complicit in the ignorance.

But the above case highlights how a sensible idea is hijacked and spun in such a way that it is perceived by the readers as highly negative that the EU is apparently playing the 'Nanny State' big time just to continue a negative EU focus. Now obviously such dramatic headlines or claims were undiluted nonsense, but I ask myself how our press is allowed to write such drivel and influence its readership week after week, month after month and year after year. This constant drip drip drip of basic anti-EU sentiment obviously has an effect and has done, some damaging work over many years.

The referendum campaign will be remembered in history particularly for the amount of deception of the Leave campaigns and the lengths they were willing to go to defend or further exaggerate those falsehoods but you can now see how the Press contributed to those myths and assisted such fiction with their own lies and deceit over many years. Some may argue it was the journalists' ignorance of the workings of the EU which may be true and if so, DO NOT publish ignorant articles. But many stories including those cited above were not born out of ignorance but rather deceit and that should not be forgiven.

Some people over the years have tried to highlight this bias and inaccuracies but the tide of opinion and the power of the right-wing press that had built up was significant and to try to push back this tidal wave of EU abuse and slander was almost impossible. Going back to 2011 Alistair Campbell, the former UK government communications chief and close ally to Tony Blair sat before the Levison enquiry on the British Press. Campbell and Blair had during the Blair years had some very good press although one could argue the press were indeed backing the obvious winner when John Major's Premiership had run its course and had no chance of beating Blair at the time. But here he was trying to highlight the unacceptable anti-EU rhetoric. Campbell said "At various times, readers of UK papers may have read that 'Europe' or 'Brussels' or the 'EU Superstate' had banned or was intending to ban kilts, curries, mushy peas, paper rounds, Caerphilly cheese, charity shops, bulldogs, bent sausages and cucumbers, the British Army, lollipop ladies, British loaves, British made lavatories, the passport crest, lorry drivers who wear glasses, and many more." But how much press coverage or TV time do you think that got and how can it compare in effectiveness as front page after front page of Eurosceptic propaganda seeped into the British Psyche?

The thing with the press that Journalist James O'Brien highlighted was that 'if someone tells you in good faith, that an organisation or individual is dedicated to damaging your existence, in the very first instance there are only three possible responses: you ignore or dismiss the claim completely; you believe it immediately and come out swinging, or you examine the evidence and respond accordingly. Both sides are guilty of the same offence: picking a position and sticking to it without doing the heavy lifting needed to make it truly secure.' [41] But why do people not question things regularly anymore? Is it partly the social media effect or our trust of traditional media where we just accept what we are being fed? I personally (and it could be this shows how sad I am?) have read so many books, reports, and articles including those from very right wing or extreme Brexit organisations to try to understand their thinking, logic and fears, as well as where they received all their misinformation from which was astounding.

It was not just the anti-EU sentiment but also a horrendous callousness towards immigrants that reared its ugly head in 2015 when dead bodies were washed up on European beaches as rather than highlighting their extreme plight from war-torn countries the Sun (our largest selling Newspaper) wrote 'these migrants are cockroaches' which brought back memories of the Nazi and Rwandan genocidal language as propaganda. It is almost impossible to make direct links to press headlines and anti-immigrant sentiment to acts of violence that may have indeed been motivated by what they read. But is it really a coincidence that there was so much anti-immigrant rhetoric in the referendum campaign from many sources and the assassination of Joe Cox a pro-European and pro-refugee rights politician on 16th June 2016? This was the same day that Nigel Farage unveiled his anti-immigrant campaign poster entitled 'Breaking Point' which implied quite clearly that if we voted to Remain, we would be overrun by millions of Middle Eastern (NOT European) immigrants. This message was combined with other similar such messages including 1 million Turks would come to the UK, despite Turkey not even looking like becoming a member of the EU!

We can now see how specific not only the Press but the media in general has groomed the people over years to be anti-EU and then to give the impression if we vote Leave, we would, incorrectly, have fewer immigrants and foreigners, and many bought it.

But even if we think that Press bosses escape blame for their bias and lies we should act. A lot of people obviously say, "What can I do?" Well basically Boycott those papers you disagree with and if enough people do that, they may change their positions to more reasonable and honest. Answer by hitting them where it hurts in the pocket! Although, I agree it is difficult but not impossible, just see what the City of Liverpool did to the Sun, after their its fabrications and misinformation about the Hillsborough disaster! You could also write to and put pressure on your MP and make your feelings clear and if enough do this may be, he or she will bring it up in the House of commons, although they also fear the power of the press that could curtail or even kill their political ambitions.
In the 90s the Press treatment of the EU seemed to get nastier and more intense and we all remember the Sun's Headline 'Up Yours Delors' in November 1990, but if you read what was written below that headline the horrid and unnecessary nature of it that people were taking in was quite disgusting towards an ally and partner:

... Tell the Feelthy French to FROG OFF! They INSULT us, BURN our lambs, FLOOD our country with Dodgy food and plot to abolish our dear old Pound. Now it's your turn to kick THEM in the Gauls... Remember folks, it won't be long before the garlic-breathed bastilles will be here in droves once the Channel Tunnel is open. So, grab your megaphones... and let 'em hear the British Lion ROAR. [31]
The Sun by no means the only Press culprit but these Newspapers have dined out on fiction and half-truths including:

- "Now they've gone Bananas: Euro bosses ban "Too Bendy" ones and set up shop size of five and half inches'. (The Sun).
- 'EU judges want Sharia Law applied in British courts' (Daily Mail, April 2009).
- 'EU's plan to liquify corpses and pour them down the drain' (Daily Express July 2010).
- 'Children to be banned from blowing up balloons, under EU Safety rules' (Daily Telegraph, October 2011).

All incorrect and slightly ludicrous. But why? Brian Cathcart, the Founder of Hacked Off, the group that campaigns for the noble cause of media accountability put it like this 'when it comes to selling newspapers, xenophobia, racism, jingoism are very helpful. In a complicated world there is nothing simpler than identifying a faceless foreign baddie and blame everything on them.' So, in a nutshell it is about MONEY.

The advantages of size and volume was clear before and during the 2016 Referendum and despite The Guardian, Financial Times, The Times, and The Mirror supporting Remain those with the major circulations including The Sun, and Daily Mail etc. had the whip hand and by God they were going to use it. The University of Loughborough study found that 82% of the circulation was in favour of Brexit, which is a powerful machine to fight against. But as stated earlier it was not the power of the machine but the willingness to lie about almost anything to get people on its side. The Sun claimed in a huge Headline 'EXCLUSIVE: BOMBSHELL CLAIM OVER EUROPE VOTE. QUEEN BACKS BREXIT. EU going in the wrong direction she says.' This claim was based on anonymous sources which IPSO (Independent Press Standards Organisation) found to be 'significantly misleading'. But the damage was done. In fact, the Sun's Editor rejected the ruling and thirteen days later they led with a new headline about the Queen with 'WHAT QUEEN ASKED DINNER GUESTS: GIVE ME 3 REASONS TO STAY IN EUROPE. Sorry Ma'am, we can't think of ONE'. This shows 2 things 1. The lengths the Press will go to and 2. The tooth lessness of IPSO, which is concerning for our democracy.

The constant barrage of negative stories throughout the referendum campaigns must have an effect and that was clear when talking to normal people in everyday life. Even when you point out the nonsense in the story you would get replies such as "well what makes you right and not the newspapers?" and such questions are difficult to counter when the newspapers can effectively print what they want with little recourse. The following is just more examples of headlines and stories that were run during the Referendum campaign:

- 'We urge readers to BeLEAVE in Britain and vote to quit the EU on June 23' (The Sun).
- 'we must set ourselves free from dictatorial Brussels. Throughout our 43-year membership of the European Union it has proved increasingly greedy, bullying, and breathtakingly incompetent in a crisis.' (The Sun)
- 'Who will speak for England?' (Front page of The Daily Mail)
- 'As in 1939, we are at a crossroads in our island's history,' (The

Daily Mail) – always good for an irrelevant War anecdote!
- 'Criminal convictions for EU immigrants leap by 40% in 5 years: 700 found guilty every week in the UK.' (17 February 2016) – it should be noted here that it was in truth 'notifications' and not convictions, but the damage was done and why let facts get in the way of an anti-immigrant story!
- 'Report shows the NHS is nearly at breaking point as massive influx of EU Migrants forces Doctors to take on 1.5 million extra patients in just three years.' (Mail Online) – This statement was widely disputed.
- 'As politicians squabble over border controls, yet another lorry load of migrants arrives in the UK declaring ... WE'RE FROM EUROPE - LET US IN!' – This was proved to be totally untrue and the paper had to issue a correction as it was clear later from the video that the individuals were not from Europe at all but were from Iraq and Kuwait! Was this a mistake or was it deliberate to inflame anti-European fervour, I will let you decide.

But politicians are not immune from such dog whistle politics and it is not always the usual suspects such as Farage and Boris as we saw during the 2001 election campaign when William Hague raised fears of Britain becoming a 'Foreign Land' and although he did not go on to mention immigration many voters and anti-immigrant campaign groups felt they knew exactly what he meant!

The press constantly puts rebel conservative MPs on their front pages and uses language like saboteurs and traitors etc. which intimidates MPs in order to influence the democratic process, but of course few in the media call it that. MPs like John Redwood, Mark Francois, and Bill Cash are often and regularly featured or quoted on their anti-EU stance, but can you name one thing those individuals have achieved or are known for outside of being anti-EU and Brexit? No, they are MPs sitting in safe Tory seats throwing the proverbial stones at the EU in a fanatical manner without offering any solutions apart from 'Out at all costs'.

Since the referendum result and the perceived delay in getting an agreement with the EU the Press has increased the pressure on Teresa May and her team with words such as treason and Treachery being used. Treason was always a word used for spies or crimes against the state but now newspapers like the Sun have included headlines like "Treacherous Teresa" which is very concerning for the largest selling Newspaper in the UK. Such a partisan and not balanced media can fuel Far Right extremism or extreme individuals willing to carry out extreme acts. And really should not be as cavalier with its language.

The threat from far Right terrorism is, as we saw with the attack and murder of MP Jo Cox, growing alarmingly and while yes the violence tends to come from the fringes, the encouragement could come from the centre which is why such Media language and the rhetoric from the likes of Nigel Farage is very concerning and should not be underestimated as extreme 'sheep' are willing to carry out what they see or understand as the messages that they are receiving from various media sources or political individuals, who cannot control the outcomes of their extreme language.

It is not always extreme acts that the lies and pressure of the press can influence but also with the increase of the charges of treason etc. and trying to achieve the deselection of MPs that do not have the same philosophy or beliefs as the Editor or proprietor of a specific Newspaper, which certain Conservative MPs such as Dominic Grieve have had to contend with. This puts our democracy and our elected MPs in a very difficult position that they may bow to partisan Press pressure, and this cannot be right when a fair Press / Media is a cornerstone of our democracy and they are directly and indirectly negatively affecting it for personal gain.

The media often hides behind the myth that it just reflects and does not influence the public opinions, but this does not hold up to scrutiny and a convenient cop out for the stuff they write. Some articles written and leading headlines are totally unacceptable and inflammatory just to sell newspapers and that cannot be right in a modern society. Just think about Boris Johnson getting paid circa. £250,000 per year to write a regular column for the Telegraph, is he really going to reflect public opinions of the average man on the Street? When does he really have any contact with the average man in the street in any details or length of time to reflect their opinions? He is too busy quoting ancient Greek mythology or using Latin.

Even in a speech to party members at the Excel Centre in London in July 2019 he referred to bottles of PROsecco pronouncing it completely different from normal folk resulting in comments that this 'common man' of the people had never lowered himself to PROsecco but would have had no problem pronouncing Dom Perignon! This was the same speech where he produced the kipper claiming the EU were stopping kipper smokers sending fish through the post without ice when it was in reality the UK law aimed at reducing food poisoning! We will experience more farcical situations as this Brexit clown is now (at the time of writing) Prime Minister.

University researchers (Florian Foos or LSE and Daniel Bischof of Zurich University) concluded that due to the boycott of the Sun newspaper in Liverpool, due to the inaccuracies from the Newspaper about the Hillsborough tragedy in 1989, it led to reduced Euroscepticism. Liverpool voted 58.2% to Remain and their research showed that the mass media could influence public opinion, but the effects take place over years rather than a single political campaign. To see the full working paper please go:

http://www.florianfoos.net/resources/Foos_Bischof_Hillsborough_APSA.pdf

The Lies of the Press & political intent

You may feel the sub-title above is strong, and I have touched on it in previous pages. When one researches and analyses the history of the Press and its attitude to the EU over the last 20 or so years one realises that the amount of incorrect and inaccurate stories published could not in a sensible rational line of thought be accidental as the level of incompetence would be monumental. This leads one to the logical conclusion that it was deliberate and clearly had a political intent, possibly linked to the tax and financial positions of their owners?

There are so many fake news stories (as they are now refereed to since the election of President trump in the US) that the amount of research would be huge and I could not do it more justice than Tom Pride (https://tompride.wordpress.com) has done with his excellent analysis of such stories that had been published in our biggest selling and most influential newspapers and UK press over the last 20 years.

As he wrote:
Forget about Russian meddling or US companies pushing fake and 'dark' news on the Internet to influence the Brexit vote. Fake news to influence the UK public to vote for Brexit has mostly come from our very own so-called professional journalists right here in the UK.

Here's a list of fake news by the UK press over the last 20 years. Every single story here has been debunked as fake news. It's hard to pick just one but my personal favourites are "Euronotes cause impotence" by the Daily Mail and 'EU puts speed limit on children's roundabouts' from the always entertaining Daily

Express.[6] To see the huge list, some amusing and some bizarre, but all very dangerous when it comes to educating our public and society, please go to:

https://tompride.wordpress.com/2017/12/05/see-20-years-of-fake-news-about-eu-by-uk-press-vote-for-your-favourite-here/

Now reading these headlines and stories may bring a wry smile to your face but there is clearly a very important and worrying development as for democracy to work effectively voters need the information to do a proper job which requires a good flow of information and facts which should implore the UK Press to deliver that and this is clearly not the case. We would be naïve to expect completely dispassionate coverage of political issues and even the BBC which is meant to deliver this is accused of Bias, by both sides of the argument (which some would contend shows they are doing a good job). But we as a society should not expect or accept complete myths and misinformation to take people down a specific route, in this case, the dislike and distrust of the EU without fact or foundation.

We are told that reports should be balanced which I understand but it cannot be logical for any Media organisation to give the same amount of time to an argument that is based on misinformation and untruths than an argument that is based on facts and truth. How can that be correct otherwise our media is assisting lies and propaganda, albeit it may be unwillingly, as this is no different than a state-owned media agency? I appreciate the pressure organisations such as the BBC are under, especially in these times of 24-hour news and the restricted ability to fact check in live interviews, but Newspapers do not have such restrictions. Clearly people stay within their comfort zone and read media that meets their already preconceived opinions which creates a tunnel vision and especially on the internet we see this with so called "echo Chambers" with too many people all agreeing with each other rather than looking outside their peer group and considering alternative views. It has become clear that the advanced algorithms of programs like Facebook etc. know how to send more information to people based on their already defined interests which just exacerbates the issues highlighted above, and one we must address in our digital economy going forward.

We often heard from the press and Brexiteer politicians about the EU's plan for a so called "United States of Europe" but they never clarified where this came from or what it was exactly and it tended to link into this constant anti-EU scaremongering with no substance behind it, as there are no plans in the EU to create such a beast whatever it was that was created by the Press.

128

One of the problems for the BBC coverage was that it was in a difficult position and in some ways confused its traditional responsibility to be impartial with the requirement during an election campaign to be balanced. This requirement for balance seemed to restrict the BBC to scrutinise Vote Leave's claims and the many items of misinformation etc. that were fed consistently to the public. Probably with good intentions they mistook impartiality for balance and missed many opportunities to expose obvious untruths or plain fiction that the likes of Farage et al. espoused and this was unhealthy for a qualitative debate. This would by default give the public the impression that as they were not picked up on, the lies they must be true.

We should not underestimate the power of the BBC as a news and information organisation and due to this desperation to be balanced they did in fact affect the result in favour of Leave because they did not expose and highlight the distortions and misinformation from the Leave campaign day in day out which should surely have been their journalistic responsibility? Reporting things as news that were clearly not true such as claim that Millions of Turks were coming to the UK or the Breaking point poster using a Syrian refugee stock photo which had nothing to do with the UK's membership of the EU, but both looked like a warning about brown people coming to the UK which have a racist slant. So why was nobody being held to account on these untruths, as there should have been an arbiter of truth somewhere to rule on what was true and what was not, but this did not happen. Therefore, the lies and misinformation flourish.

It feels like Boris Johnson, whilst a journalist writing about the European union activities, appears to have created, albeit maybe inadvertently, a school of European reporting leading to a large part of the UK media peddling Euro myths, fuelling the type of Europhobia that no UK politician dared to counter. This could have been the beginning of the chaos we now face and the genesis of the Brexit vote.

One could argue that the news angle for the BBC was much more exciting by highlighting a movement to change the country potentially for ever and going against the current government and political class (as Nigel Farage would like to say) compared to a side campaigning for the Status quo which is a little bland. But that is not the job of the BBC who should be looking for truth and accuracy rather than just headlines and sound bites, as they should be better than that and have higher standards than that.

The Press and Tax avoidance

We see quite clearly the Press's position to the EU and its constant Eurosceptic headlines and articles including many lies and untruths, but could there be more to it and more from a selfish self-preservation point of view?

Many of the press barons and owners of many of our most popular newspapers are renowned Tax avoiders such as the Barclay brothers, Rupert Murdoch, and Lord Rothermere all held 'Non-Dom' status in the UK and perhaps they are concerned about the EU trying to tighten up on Tax avoidance? Especially the EU's Anti-Tax Avoidance Directive or 'ATAD', their latest and most forceful attack on Corporate Tax avoidance which became active as of February 2019, perhaps! Some of the act will tackle some of the most pervasive forms of tax avoidance, such as preventing companies from shifting profits to a third country to try to pay lower taxes. The act helps ensure companies pay tax in the EU before profits can be moved overseas, which surely is a logical and fair consequence? ATAD does much more but is not relevant and much too detailed for this book but is certainly food for thought as people have 'non-dom' status for a reason and it is not to pay more tax than they have to!

What did the media focus on during the Referendum Campaign?

The Daily Mail led on immigration on 18 of the final 23 days before the referendum vote, even though it had previously not advocated leaving the EU!

We have reported in a separate section of the book the amazing number of ridiculous anti-Eu articles and sentiment for decades but the focus in the run up to 23rd June 2016 was laser like and immigrants were the target. Such articles or headlines included:

- 'Top Police Chief: EU "free Movement" allows criminals to come to the UK and FLOURISH. THE European Union's open borders policy has allowed Islamist terrorists to roam the streets of the Continent at will'.

- Immigrants were accused of swamping NHS maternity services and taking primary school places (Daily Telegraph 6th May 2016)
- 'EU Migrants pocket MORE Tax credits cash and child benefit than British workers' (Express 24th March 24th, 2016)

- 'MIGRANTS SPARK HOUSING CRISIS: now EU tells the UK to build more homes and open borders send population soaring' (Daily Mail 19 May 2016)

Obviously if one looked closely at such headlines one can see how ridiculous they are when there is a high probability you would be treated by an immigrant within the NHS as without immigrants the NHS could not function, the tax credit claim is just a plain lie as how could it be true with so many more British workers and parents in the UK than EU immigrants? The lack of house building has been an issue for many years by consecutive governments, but the lack of social and truly affordable housing is the root cause of the problem NOT the immigrants that we need for many jobs in the UK. Alas many people will believe these accusations.

One worrying development throughout all this anti-immigrant sentiment from the Press, right-wing groups and individuals is there seeming to be an almost perceived hierarchy of how good or bad a particular race of immigrants are. The press seemed to focus particularly on Turks and Albanians (who are not even in the EU!) but also Poles and Romanians. The authors of the Kings College report on how the UK media covered the EU Referendum campaign noted the language used to describe migration was hysterical and drew on excessive language. Leave campaigners and partisan news outlets strongly protested against accusations that their focus on immigration was prejudiced or intolerant. Yet, based on most definitions, it is hard not to find their claims and coverage discriminatory. Out of 111 articles that expressed a view about Turks, for example, 98% (109) were negative. Out of 90 articles that expressed a view about Albanians, 100% were negative. Three metaphors were dominant in the coverage of migrants: migrants as water ('floodgates', 'waves'), as animals or insects ('flocking', 'swarming') or as an invading force. [12] has the Press created a hierarchy in the Psyche of the British subjects that certain nationalities are better than others e.g. Italian are better than French that are Better than Poles that are better than Romanians that are better than Turks that are better than Albanians, etc? If this is in fact the case it is overtly racist without even any justification. Would it be fair that all British men are thought paedophiles because of the stories about Jimmy Savile and Gary Glitter (real name Paul Francis Gadd)?

The threat of Turks coming to the UK was quickly seen as a red flag for voters so Leave.EU focused on that also to hammer home this point even though it was clearly misinformation and was never going to happen.

But was it immigration or also the growth and higher profile positioning of Islam that people did not like and ended up throwing all cultures and nations into one "Immigration Pot" even if many of those Muslims were 2nd and 3rd generation and were born in the UK, and therefore UK citizens? One only had to view Facebook on a particular day, and someone would post a video of similarly dressed Muslims coming out of the Mosque after prayers with the implications 'we are getting flooded by them' etc. This disregard as to whether or not they were immigrants is obviously aimed to be inflammatory but can seep into people's consciousness and then they believe whatever inflammatory language follow such videos. So, it was also a cultural discourse that the Referendum allowed people to exploit and allow racist tendencies to come to the fore.

You may question how influential the Press actually is, but successive surveys showed a strong correlation between voting patterns and what publications they read which indicates voters choose the publication that most meets their particular outlook. The danger with that is that it becomes an echo chamber and they are not exposed to, or do not want to be exposed to, alternative views or more thoughtful and accurate articles.

Below you can see a pictorial representation, created by Kings College London policy Institute, of the Media focus during the Referendum [22]. What is interesting is that the 2 largest areas by far are The Economy (The Remain focus) and Immigration (The Leave focus) and one worked but the other did not, but why? If one talks to average people and not people that work in banks, run companies, or economists etc. they do not understand in depth the running of the economy or the impacts of decisions made by the government, bankers etc. on their own personal lives. But why should they as they have never had that training, and the issues are often complex and interconnected to many other economic and political issues that are not visible when they are busy making ends meet and running their own lives? Immigration on the other hand is quite visible or audible in the form of brown faces and foreign languages or accents, which when they are told such people are taking their jobs or receiving benefits for nothing or are receiving hundreds of thousands of pounds in housing benefit creates dislike or hate bringing many prejudices to the surface, as highlighted after the Referendum result with the rise in hate crimes against minorities including examples such as cards left on cars near a school in Huntingdon saying 'No more Polish vermin'. On 5th July the Metropolitan police revealed that it recorded 599 race-hate incidents in the nine days after the referendum – a 50% increase over a typical period which was clearly not a coincidence and the vote brought out the worst in a lot of people, but would have heightened by the inflammatory rhetoric of the usual suspects.

Figure 5: EU Referendum articles referencing each policy issue (N = 14,779)

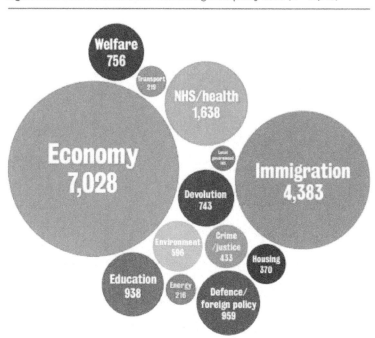

For a copy of the full report please go to:
https://kclpure.kcl.ac.uk/portal/files/109250771/UK_media_coverage_of_the_2016_EU_Referendum_campaign.pdf

Liz Fekete, the Director for race relations, told the Independent newspaper on 28th July 2016 'The referendum debate and result emboldened a lot of people. They thought they could say racist things in public. They lost their shame. (41)

Eryl Jones, from charity Show Racism the Red Card, said he believed

Brexit had been a 'major influence' on racism and the rise of hate crimes. "The feeling is that a lot of people believe they have the right to express their racist feelings or to show hatred." Home office statistics showed hate crimes in England and Wales rising from 2011 with a spike since 2016 blamed on Brexit. There may have not been any more hatred in the UK than in the past but based on the rhetoric and what happened at the referendum campaigns people felt emboldened to voice those thoughts and beliefs to do and say what they would not have done before. Some see a correlation with the rise in Anti-Semitism in the Labour party and Islamophobia in the Conservative party since 2016

When discussing this with Leavers I am often told they do not read Newspapers with the implication that as they do not buy or read newspapers they cannot be influenced by the Press, even if it was true (most won't even admit the bias, although they would struggle to justify that if in the previous breath they had just said they do not read newspapers!) But you do not have to even read newspapers to be influenced by our right-wing anti-EU press as many people walk past newspapers in shops, petrol stations, Doctors / Dentists waiting room, company canteens, the Chip shop, hairdressers, or see someone on the train reading a Newspaper, etc. The reason is you see the front page and many of the horrendous headlines such as "Migrants pay just £100 to invade Britain" (Daily Express 1st June 2016), or "Migrant Crisis in the Channel" (Express, 30 May 2016) demonstrate quite clearly how people can be influenced by such rhetoric being drip fed for decades as they expect (and so they should) that Newspapers are honest and professional rather than willing to write anything to sell newspapers and / or promote the political position of the owner of the publication.

Immigration - Prominence, volume and persistence [23]

Immigration specifically featured prominently on newspaper front pages. Over the 10 weeks of the campaign (70 days) across 15 national titles, there were 99 front-page leads focused on immigration. By contrast, for the 10 weeks leading up to the general election in 2015, across the same print titles, there were 14 front-page leads focused on immigration. In other words, there were just over seven times more front-page leads about immigration during the referendum campaign than during the 2015 general election campaign. Of these 99 front-page leads, 76% were in four titles: the Daily Express (21), Daily Mail (20), Daily Telegraph (21) and the Sun (13), each of which endorsed Leave. Immigration coverage was not only prominent but voluminous. Across The 20 news outlets over the course of the 10-

week campaign more than 5,500 articles referred to immigration in the context of the UK, and just under 80% (4,383) of those were related to the EU referendum. From the middle of the campaign onwards, coverage of immigration increased sharply week-on-week: by 44% in Week 6; 47% in Week 7; and then by another 51% over the final three weeks. As with the front pages, the volume of coverage was not consistent across publications. Three news outlets – the Express, the Daily Mail, and the Sun – accounted for just under a third (32%) of all articles published online on immigration in the 10-week period – 1,785 articles in total. Immigration coverage was also persistent. In no week during the 10-week campaign were there fewer than 250 articles referencing immigration. In each of the last four weeks of the campaign there were over 700 articles. The final week saw more than 1,000 articles published about immigration (this includes all immigration articles, not just those that also referred to the referendum). The Daily Mail, The Mail on Sunday, The Daily Express, The Sunday Express, The Guardian, The Observer, The Mirror, the Sunday Mirror, The Sun, The Sun on Sunday, The Times, The Sunday Times, The Telegraph, The Sunday Telegraph, The Financial Times. [23]

This power and impact cannot and should not be ignored and its influence on the final result.

Deliberate and horrendous Language

Certain news outlets (many highlighted in this book) used words normally used to describe epidemics, pestilence or any disastrous catastrophe including 'crisis', 'rampant', 'unsustainable', 'intolerable', 'influx' 'swarming', 'swamping', 'invading', and 'over-running', when referring to immigrants (yes the very same ones that could be saving your relative in an NHS hospital!). Some lead stories alone used the following words on their front pages: 'killers and rapists', 'plot', 'deception', 'chaos', 'soaring', invade', 'cover up', 'swindle', 'floodgates', 'terror', 'meltdown', and 'criminals' with the obvious aim of creating fear, concern and / or hate towards immigrants and by association minorities. We all know words are very important and these organisations are experts in language and the use of the English language so there is no excuse, and it is quite deliberate to get a reaction, regardless of how true the story is or not.

Reading back the above paragraph we should all be filled with a distinct sadness that a modern so-called free society has a press that can write such things or take such an extreme attitude towards often very distressed people to sell a few more newspapers and whip up a frenzy of hate. I have never really thought about it like that before but now it is quite obvious and actually quite disgusting and one that should make us all sick to be associated by our place of birth with such people. It is people who write these headlines and articles as well as the Editors that sign them off, not faceless organisations.

The deceitful use of images by the Press

We all know that a photo tells a thousand words, and many images used to illustrate articles about migrants etc. were similarly emotive, even though many of them were not news photos but stock pictures (from picture libraries like Getty and Alamy etc.). There are many examples such as generic images of overcrowded classrooms and doctors' waiting rooms used within articles about lack of primary school places and NHS problems for example but rarely confirming whether those in the photos were in fact immigrants, foreigners or British citizens that have lived in the country for years.

To illustrate, an article about jobless migrants coming to the UK the Daily Mail, used a photograph – from a picture agency – of four people around a park bench who appear to be homeless. The caption does not indicate who these four are, or whether they are migrants or jobless. [24]

But even worse and this is the extremes that some media houses will go to create fear and hate was The Express, when trying to support an article linking migrants to crime, used a photograph – from a photo library – making it appear as though a migrant had actually just shot someone, below which the caption read: 'Foreign criminals commit nearly 20 percent of crime in the UK'. Now surely this shows how reckless Newspapers can be with such language and the implications of the photo. What if someone took it upon themselves based on thinking that was a true reflection upon immigrants in our society and went out deciding to shoot / kill immigrants in retribution, as he / she expects our Press to report accurately and dispassionately, rather than raising tensions or potentially inciting violence. Who will ever know what Jo Cox's killer was thinking when he shouted Britain First or where he got his motivation from to take a life in that barbaric way?

All these things create the patchwork of fear, distress, hate and potentially violent actions with no positive benefits apart from the sale of Newspapers and clicks online. 'Blood for clicks' doesn't sound too appealing does it? Even in 2019

The Daily Mail's Richard Littlejohn wrote an article entitled **'What fun to hear the Remoaners squealing,'** where he wrote the following indicating that it is acceptable for our Prime Minister to lie to the Monarch 'Haven't stopped laughing since Boris bowled the Remoaners a short one which would have done Jofra Archer proud. Get that in the lower abdomen for a start, mate. Goodness knows how he's managed to keep a straight face, pretending that proroguing Parliament is all about preparing for the Queen's Speech. What hope do our citizens have when such despicable writing is mainstream, and no sense of morals or proportion is entertained?

Full article can be seen here:
https://www.dailymail.co.uk/debate/article-7409005/RICHARD-LITTLEJOHN-Melting-Pot-2019.html

Summary to Press

Although it cannot be exactly quantified as to how effective the constant attacks on, or disinformation about the EU had a direct impact on the result of the 2016 Referendum with 30 years of such hostile reporting, constant lies and disregard for truth or any standards or impartiality or even morality in places, logic says this must have had an effect and seeped into the British psyche. Such headlines and false stories would not easily be forgotten and that Drip Drip Drip feed into the British tabloid readers' memories and conversations down the pub or at home could have had the impact the Non-Dom Press barons and Editors had desired. Tony Blair was voted into Downing Street in 1997 and the Sun claimed, "It was the Sun what won it". Maybe the right-wing press did indeed win the EU referendum vote also?

Surely it is the Press' duty of impartiality is not to have one person saying it is night and one person saying it is day but rather pull the curtains back and see who is telling the truth? I suppose the basic concern is the litany of deceit and untruths of major newspapers almost exclusively bankrolled by multi-millionaires non-domiciled tax exiled individuals that avoid paying tax and major influence the news agendas as well as people's opinions and thoughts. It is not much to ask or expect as citizens that our press be free, balanced and TRUTHFUL? Sadly, it has been found wanting in these areas on many occasions.

Brexit and anti-EU feeling is as much a failure of honest fact based journalism and journalists, that should aid the checks and balances in our society of a free and truthful press, as it is politicians who receive all the vitriol whereas certain tabloid type journalists can hide behind an untrue or misleading headline and shabby research or simply a politically biased position that add no value but helps stir up hatred. During the referendum campaign and the years leading up to 2016 the press and many journalists and publications were found sadly lacking in the professionalism, truth and honesty departments.

Chapter 11
Brexit Options

In Out shake it all about

Clearly, the 2 extremes are the Remain (In) and leaving without a deal (out) and we then start from scratch with new trade deals and other related rules and laws. But as has been discussed (and actually voted on in the indicative votes in Parliament) there are also a number of many other options including Norway, Norway +, Canada +, Common Market 2.0, Confirmatory public vote, customs Union, revoke Article 50, plus others being added or tweaked as parliament showed its inability to get agreement on anything.

Two of the main options discussed as they are major deals with other countries, one geographically close to the EU in Norway and the other on almost the other side of the world in Canada, but what are these options that keep being discussed?

What is the Canada Option, and would it work for the UK post Brexit?

The EU trade agreement signed with Canada is called the Comprehensive Economic and Trade Agreement (CETA) and was signed in October 2016, it provisionally came into force in September 2018 with only the ratification from all the countries needed, although this could take several years.

In fact, exporters and importers have been working under its rules for a year, and many now believe the CETA model could be a template for the UK's trading relationship with the EU after Brexit.

In the agreement some 98% of all tariffs on goods traded between Canada and the EU have become duty free. Most tariffs were removed when the agreement came into force in 2018, and the rest will be removed within seven years. This means Canadian importers will not have to pay €590m (£529m) in taxes on the goods they receive from the EU, and European importers will see tariffs reduced to zero on some 9,000 Canadian products. Another aspect of the cooperation is the public project tendering process where public contracts at local, regional and federal levels to each other's contractors. For example, Canadian companies, could tender for building German or Italian builders bidding to construct a Toronto Police station.

It does also protect EU "geographical indications", meaning you can only make prosciutto di Parma ham in Italy and Camembert cheese in France, and Canada can't import something that calls itself Camembert from any other country inside or outside the EU. This is always an important part of an EU free trade deal as you can imagine. But the UK utilises such "G.Is" advantages to its advantages for such as the names / brands of Cornish pasties, Scotch beef, Melton Mowbray Pork Pie, Dorset blue cheese, Jersey royal potatoes, Whitstable Oysters, Rutland Bitter, Scotch Whiskey, Plymouth Gin, and Somerset cider Brandy to name but a few.

These are the kinds of changes CETA brought in:

- ■ EU tariffs on Canadian goods reduced to zero - frozen mackerel (previously 20%), oats (51.7%), maple syrup (8%), and auto parts (4.5%).
- ■ Canadian tariffs on EU goods reduced to zero - chocolate (previously 10%), textiles and clothing (16%), medical equipment (8%), and machinery (9.5%).
- ■ Tariff-free quotas (limits) on EU cheese exports to Canada: raised

from 18,500 tonnes to 31,972 tonnes.

■   Tariff-free quotas on Canadian sweet corn exports to the EU: raised from zero to 8,000 tonnes over five years.

Services? Although, not focused on services it offers more protection for intellectual property rights which in today's economies plays an ever-increasing importance but for example European artist can obtain royalties from a Toronto department store that plays music to attract new customers. The EU and Canada will co-operate on standards, so that a piece of equipment made in an EU country can go through all its safety and quality checks there without needing to have them repeated in Canada - and vice versa. CETA will also allow professional qualifications to be recognised both in Canada and the EU, making it easier, for example, for architects or accountants to work in both places.

It should be clear that CETA is <u>not a customs union or single market</u>, so the two parties are free to do trade deals with any other country. It does not remove border controls, but it encourages the use of advanced electronic checking to speed customs clearance. CETA does little for trade in financial services that is not covered by World Trade Organisation rules that both sides are already signed up to and Canadian financial companies will not get "Passporting", which would allow them to sell their products across the 28 nations of the EU. The same limitations apply for EU banks in Canada.

Tariffs will remain on poultry, meat and eggs. Several other Agri-products will be given quotas. For instance, the EU will allow Canadians to export increasing amounts of duty-free meat to the EU - up to 80,000 tonnes of pork, 50,000 tonnes of beef - as well as 100,000 tonnes of wheat. But the EU insists those products meet its quality standards - so that's no hormone-treated beef and tightly controlled GM cereals. [16] As we know agriculture is for the EU and other countries / regions critical and they can become very protective. The USA would be no different in any future trade negotiations.

Critics argue CETA will erode labour laws, not enforce environmental standards and allow multinational companies to dictate public policy. CETA does change the way trade disputes are settled, using a new type of tribunal, the Investment Court System (ICS). But not everyone is convinced. The French-speaking Walloon region of Belgium brought the whole process to a virtual halt by objecting to the way dispute settlement procedures were to be conducted. Even now Italy has threatened not to ratify it because it claims it does not sufficiently protect some of its "geographical indications". The threat could theoretically scupper the deal, but the European Commission has said as a last resort it may settle the matter in court. Meanwhile the EU (including Italy) and Canada have been trading under the terms of CETA for over a year, but as you can see it is not a smooth process which shows the UK how difficult such agreements can be. [16]

But is "Canada" or "Canada Plus" a suitable template or solution for the UK with the differences in the Canadian and UK economies? Firstly, you won't be surprised that there are many big differences between the EU-Canada and the EU-UK trading relationship. To begin with, there is a basic difference in the value of goods and services traded. Only 10% of Canada's external trade goes to the EU. Total trade between the two is worth about C$85bn (£50bn) but about 44% of UK external trade is with the EU. It is the UK's biggest trading partner. Total trade between the two is worth about £318bn.

In addition, the nature of the trade is very different. Canada's main trade with the EU is in precious stones and metals, machinery, mineral ores, mineral fuels and oils, aircraft, aircraft parts and pharmaceuticals. Agri-food trade between the two amounts to about £5bn. Canada's services exports amounted to £11bn and were largely in management, research and development (R&D,) financial and IT services. [16] In contrast, the UK exports £27 billion in financial services alone to the EU, and a total of £90 billion in all services. Agri-food trade between the UK and the EU amounts to about £30 billion.

The UK exports goods worth £236 billion to the EU across a wider range of industries than Canada. Motor vehicles and parts worth £18 billion are the largest single sector followed by chemicals and chemical products worth £15 billion. [16] Obviously many ask how effective the CETA agreement is, and it is early days, but most observers say it's good for business. Exports to the EU during the six months to July rose about 6% on the same period a year earlier, to Canadian $19.7 billion (£11.6billion), according to Statistics Canada. Jim Carr, Canada's Minister of International Trade Diversification said: "At the Port of Montreal alone, we have seen 20% more traffic in goods headed across the Atlantic.

"This enormous step in growth for Canada and the EU has been the reason why new shipping lanes have been added to accommodate container traffic." The European Commission is equally ebullient about the deal, pointing out the successes of small companies such as Belgium's Smet Chocolaterie which is

142

opening shops across Canada, or Italy's San Daniele ham producers who have increased sales to Canada by 35%. It estimates exports to Canada are up by over 7% year-on-year. [16]

The above makes crystal clear the importance of free trade and the potential for increased business and wealth, but we are withdrawing from the largest free trade block in the world as other countries, such as Canada, Japan and South Korea, try to cooperate with it. Doesn't make a good look does it? But, it may be by the end of this book we will see the light.

Is the "Norway" solution an option for the UK?

A number of people including Leavers in the Referendum campaign highlighted Norway as an option for the UK as a form of 'half-way house' (or 'soft' Brexit) although extreme Brexiteers would not consider Norway as they still perceived it was being dictated to by the EU and the UK with its 60 million people was more important that the 6 million of Norway and so we could get much more. But they forgot we already had a great deal!

The reason "Norway" has been suggested as an alternative to a no-deal Brexit was due to the significant opposition in the UK parliament to the draft agreement signed off by the EU and UK, the so called "Teresa May's Deal". Basically, using the Norway model, it is the closest we could get to the European Union without even being a member. It could also be used as a template to follow to keep trading relations as close as they are now. The other advantage it is a form of 'off the shelf' solution rather than starting from scratch, and so offer advantages to avoid a chaotic no-deal development where nobody really knows the impacts.

So, what is "Norway"? Norway is along with Lichtenstein and Iceland a member of the European Economic Area (EEA) and the European Free Trade Association (EFTA) which offers it full access to the EU single market, guaranteeing very limited restrictions to trade with the EU (Switzerland is also a member of EFTA, but it is not a member of the EEA and will be explained below.). In return, Norway makes substantial contributions to the EU budget although not as much as it would as a full member, and has to follow many EU rules and laws, but it has no say in how those rules are formed. So, Norway is effectively a rule taker and accepts this.

With regard to EU rules we should be very careful blaming the EU for certain rule changes as these are often set by other International bodies such as the WTO and the EU cuts and pastes them into its own rules for simplicity and ease of implementation and application. But tabloid newspapers often crucify the EU for such rules when they did not even originate from them. They either did not know (ignorance) or they did (misinformation!).

Norway like the UK has large fishing and agricultural industries and forms its own policy over these sectors by remaining outside the EU's Common Fisheries Policy or Common Agricultural Policy which would also appeal to many Brexiteers. Norway can also negotiate trade deals with other countries around the world, which would also appeal to pro-Brexit supporters, and it has agreed such agreements as a group with other EFTA countries. A Norway-type agreement would mean that the UK would not be ruled over by the European Court of Justice, another red-line issue for Brexiteers, which would make them happy.

The problem comes with certain Brexiteers and Mrs. May herself having set certain red lines and by signing up to EU single market rules, like Norway the UK would have to agree to the four freedoms - the freedom of movement of goods, services, capital and people, so it would cross another UK red line unless this could be changed. The British government's promise to retain control over its own borders and a say in who it lets into the country would be a major political issue to go back on and potentially unleash the unsavoury parts of British society that see immigration as the root cause of many ills in the country. Being a "rules taker" – following EU rules without having a say in drafting them – will not appeal to many Brexiteers because it does not give London control over its own economic rules, but also not really to Remainers who see that as a worse deal than we had previously as an EU member, although would accept that instead of a no-deal Brexit which is an anathema to them. The UK would still be held accountable by the EFTA court, so it would not be completely free of the EU and would open up many of the arguments we had previously.

But as the Irish border is a unique situation in Europe to make a Norway style deal work further steps would be needed because Norway is not in the customs union. To resolve the contentious issue of avoiding a hard border in Ireland, the UK would also have to agree a customs arrangement with the EU, another complication. This means the UK would have to have what is called a "Norway-plus" solution (i.e. a solution that does not exist!). This could limit its ability to negotiate its own trade deals and would with many Brexiteers in the British parliament be an absolute red line! This is showing again how complex all these issues are and that the electorate were sold a very simplified, and to be honest, a dishonest or ignorant version of an easy Brexit.

145

At the time of writing Boris Johnson's deal offers the solution of putting a front stop with a border in the Irish Sea, but he even disagreed with his own Brexit minister Steven Barclay and other cabinet ministers as to what systems and paperwork as well as checks will need to be carried out. It was not clear at all at the time. The Norway Sweden border is over 1000 miles long but there are only 8 crossings where it is legally allowed to cross with commercial goods. This is because both countries need to be able to check the goods entering their relevant countries.

The reason this has not been seriously considered by the UK government was because it did not tick Theresa May's boxes for the kind of Brexit she wants as she promised to take the UK out of both the single market and the customs union. Many commentators noted that because she had set so many firm red lines that could not be crossed her position for negotiation was limited and was the root cause of many of her problems as she had pandered to her right wing of the party for political reasons and was not focused enough on the country as a whole.

British MPs were considering the idea of a short-term Norway-type deal, including some form of temporary customs union with the EU, as a kind of holding arrangement until the UK and EU reach their own trade deal and to avoid a messy no-deal scenario if the current draft agreement is shot down by parliament. However, it is not clear whether the other EEA members or the EU would consider a temporary solution of this kind, or what could be negotiated before the UK's exit date. But this would again add cost to the UK and the EU a lot of money and time knowing that the real work would begin again, and this is obviously not a preferred solution even if it is a short-term plan.

Any deal would be a specific deal for the UK and would be a unique one so although the Norway and Canada deals could be used as templates there would still have to be a lot of changes and negotiations with potentially a lot of other different sticking points depending on each parties' priorities. We need to appreciate that once outside the EU we will struggle to have any influence no matter what form we take outside the EU (Norway, Canada+ etc.) in the setting of policies many of which will have a major impact on our national everyday life. EFTA countries have profited from their relationship with the EU whether by being in the single Market, as with Norway, Iceland, and Lichtenstein, or by mirroring it closely, as with Switzerland's large range of bilateral deals with the EU. All have a higher proportion of trade with the EU than the UK does.

The UK could be a member of the customs union without it restricting our ability to negotiate other trade deals with non-EU countries. Being in a customs union with the EU does not require the UK to sign up to the EU's common commercial policy, under which it negotiates trade deals with other countries. The common external tariff would though restrict the UK's room for manoeuvre, preventing us from offering tariff concessions, but it would not prevent trade deals being negotiated, particularly as regards services, the dominant part of the UK economy at 80% of trade.

Just the fact that Norway as a part of the EEA accepts European regulations but has no power of influence over it and pays a substantial contribution to the EU budget which our ardent Brexiteers are totally against and would mean the Norway solution would not be accepted by many Brexiteers. In fact, under a Norway type solution we could end up paying more than we could lose and the Rebates Margaret Thatcher negotiated for example as we would no longer be on the same deal. Since 1985 the UK has received a budget rebate equivalent to around 66% of its net contribution to the EU budget.

Could we be like Switzerland?

Firstly, we should be aware that Switzerland is a smaller less complex economy as our own and therefore managing such different economies are different to those of a large country like the UK. As in business running a smaller less complex organisation is simpler and so trying to get a one size fits all solution is not practical. The challenge with a Switzerland type deal is that as a member of the European Free trade Area (EFTA) it has signed many bi-lateral treaties with the EU, and we would have to negotiate and finalise hundreds of separate agreements with the EU for different goods and services. This would be an enormous task and we do not have enough of the experienced people to do this in any sensible time frame. Also, the EU did this with Switzerland as a unique case and now see the issues with this and may be very averse to doing this again, especially with a more complex economy the size of the UK.

Also Switzerland like Norway is highly integrated with the EU in terms of Trade relationships and they normally accept EU regulations in order to have access to the Single market and trade freely with other EU countries as they know the benefits of that, but our isolationist Brexiteers do not want this so this really rules out that as a possibility.

147

Although well intentioned to reduce the number of low skilled migrants in the country, Switzerland found the law of unintended consequences resulted in the isolation and regression of the country's research groups and academic institutions as well as being cut out of the EU research and innovation programme 'Horizon 2020'. The UK may also find that upon leaving numerous important bilateral arrangements with the EU may be undermined. Many of these negative 'knock-on effects' of the referendum are almost impossible to gauge beforehand but Switzerland found that after their referendum to change relationship with the EU issues followed down the line. The vice-president for research at the Swiss Federal Institute of Technology in Lausanne Andreas Mortensen said, "The whole thing created a lack of assurance – we saw a large decrease in the number of European projects led by our researchers." Also, according to the Swiss research institute EPFL, levels of collaboration with the EU dropped by a factor of 10. The UK is one of the largest recipients of research funding in the EU and to lose this could be catastrophic and we should not underestimate the impact of this in the medium to long term on the UK's R & D and science development industries. But it is not just the loss of funds but also the invaluable number of collaborative programmes and networks that could be lost, or excellent scientists etc. move to the EU to benefit from such advantages. Thousands of jobs are linked to these type of projects plus we should not forget the trickle-down effects their loss has to the wider UK economy!

We should also not forget that both Norway and Switzerland are at the time of writing a part of the Schengen agreement so no border controls which Brexiteers will not accept. But due to a referendum decision in Switzerland to impose immigration controls this does put the Switzerland relationship with the EU in doubt going forward and will play itself out over the next few months or years, especially as the EU has stopped quite a lot of cooperation with Switzerland due to such issues and complications in the relationship. So, as we can see all those leavers that highlighted Switzerland as a good option were ill informed or underestimated the complications of any alternative solution to the one we currently have.

You can never rule outWould a No-deal Brexit be so bad?

It is worth just clarifying that although it is called a "no-deal" as soon as the UK leaves the EU without a withdrawal agreement there will be a whole host of deals / agreements that will need agreeing between both parties. But the EU has stated that before they can take place three areas must be addressed and agreed which are 1. Citizens' rights, 2. Payment of dues (sometimes referred to as the divorce bill, but rather are costs that we had signed up to and agreed as a part of the 7-year budget round before we voted to leave, and 3. The Irish border.

The main factor would be the new costly friction with the UK's biggest trading partner in the EU which some commentators say could mean a drop-in trade of as much as 40%. This will also cut foreign investment, which is very high in the UK, one reason was due to us being a full member of the EU. Ending Free movement, although many Brexiteers feel this is a good thing, would curb valuable EU immigration of skills and labour we lack in the UK. Many Brexiteers do claim there will be great benefits that will offset such losses, but any expert analysis debunks this as pie in the sky. The Government's own analysis finds a benefit to GDP per person of only 0.1% from likely deregulation, but deregulation is not always a good thing as we saw with the banking crisis where more regulation and controls were required. Savings into the EU budget are relatively small for our economy as a whole and free trade deals with Australia, USA, and the BRIC countries (Brazil, Russia, India and China) would add just circa. 0.2% to GDP per head. But President Trump has said in the past that a trade deal may be impossible and although he changes his mind as the wind changes this may have been code for 'the UK will have to bend over backwards to meet the USA laws, regulations and requirements'? Remember "America First"? In fact we already have a trading surplus with the USA and although this may grow it would not be by much and could genuinely result in a trade deficit if we began to import huge amounts of Beef and chicken for example, as well as opening up our NHS to US drug companies in any negotiations that would be heavily pushed by the USA!

It always seemed a surprise after the referendum campaign and all the promises of easy deals with the EU and the rest of the world that suddenly we are even talking about a no-deal Brexit. What other country in the world has no trade deals with anyone in the world and feels that is a good position? The reason they have them is because they are advantageous to their country! Many Brexiteers including Boris Johnson, Jacob Rees-Mogg, Chris Grayling, David Davis, Liam Fox, Dominic Cummings, Owen Paterson, and Andrea Leadsom were all recorded in speeches highlighting a deal and NOT a no-deal Brexit, because they know how hurtful it could be to the UK. Suddenly in 2019 they have amnesia.

But it is more fundamental than that as many of the Brexiteers assume (never ASSUME, otherwise you make an ASS out of U and ME !) that we will slip out quietly with no deal and there will be a few months of 'Uncertainty' (as

Brexiteers like to term it, although that uncertainty could be peoples jobs and livelihoods negatively affected (not that that would affect the likes of Jacob Rees-Mogg or Nigel Farage that much) and then we will simply sign a new deal that would have to be negotiated from scratch as we are no longer leaving but rather would be negotiating as a new partner. In this time, they imply companies will simply adjust and get on with business as usual but in that time companies could cease trading and job losses ensure for very little benefit of advantage which is what is at the crux of this argument. The downsides are clear and palpable but the espoused advantages more of a wing and a prayer.

But the danger is that with only about 100 MPs on the periphery of this debate in terms of having a plan after Brexit there will not be a majority in Parliament for anything after a no-deal exit (unless the December 2019 election giving the Conservatives a working majority), so there would not be a majority for a Free Trade Deal with the USA or the new deal with the EU. This means we would be in a strange form of Limbo on some form of substandard WTO rules (which are only there as a safety net for trade, and something that nobody really wants) for quite some time whilst we then work out what we want to do on Tariffs, Quotas, regulations, Visa rules, Rules of origin, etc. That is when business confidence quickly collapses with no light at the end of the tunnel as to where this 'Twilight zone' period takes us. Basically, we enter a phase of stalemate. Brexiteers do not have a plan and have never had a plan so we cannot expect them to help us out of this as they just wanted out based on a dogmatic dislike of the EU but have nothing concrete or sensible to put in its place. Plus, many of them do not care as they are rich and comfortable surrounded by wealthy friends all of whom will not have a problem paying the rent or count the pennies before shopping. That will be left to the poorer in society who will be hit hardest, but why do these dogmatic Brexiteers not see that or if they do, then do they care?

We should not forget that there is only so much our government can do in a no-deal Brexit scenario as it is inherently bilateral requiring the EU to be collaborative, which will be interesting to see after all the complications and problems the UK had caused for them since 2016, and some may say years previous to that. We can throw open the port of Dover, but it will count for little if there are long checks at Calais. This is why the cry for independence is somewhat muffled now that reality is kicking in.

In March 2017 David Davis and the government's mantra was 'no deal is better than a bad deal' (which means nothing unless we know how bad the bad deal is and how bad no deal is so one can compare!), but then Mr. Davis admitted it was not underpinned by an economic impact assessment, in fact he actually told the Brexit select committee that there wouldn't be one until the following year! This is incompetence at work where Davis cannot hide it with his cheeky smile and hyperbole. He even claimed in May 2016 that "the first calling point of call for UK negotiator will not be Brussels, it will be Berlin, to strike a deal" which is a massive misunderstanding of how the EU works as it negotiates as one block. He was either talking bullshit again or was unaware of this fact, but whichever it was his incompetence is only outweighed by Chris 'failing' Grayling and his "Ferry Contract".

David Davis said we shouldn't fear the impact of leaving the Customs union and Single market as by autumn 2018 we will have negotiated a free trade area "ten times the size" of the EU, even though we are prohibited from signing free trade agreements whilst still a member of the customs union. Just another misleading statement by Mr. Davis, but that said as of August 2019 nothing that he spoke of and promised has been achieved, the emperor literally had no clothes.

The Bank of England predicts the economy shrinking by 8%, house prices potentially crashing and unemployment and inflation spiralling which does not paint a pretty picture. Police chiefs are even planning for civil unrest at the risk of a no-deal Brexit amassing the biggest ever peacetime reserve of officers in that expectation. How have we arrived at this? Make UK, an industry organisation representing 20,000 British manufacturers, has warned that a no-deal Brexit could threaten the already weakening sector, and other UK manufacturers have been stronger by saying a no-deal Brexit would be economic lunacy.

Responding to the UK Government genuinely looking towards no deal and planning to cut most tariffs to zero many business leaders and entrepreneurs were horrified. The Director of the Confederation of British Industry (CBI) Carolyn Fairburn described the prospect of no deal as a "sledgehammer for the economy" when on BBC Radio 4's Today programme. "This tells us everything that is wrong with a no-deal scenario. What we are hearing is the biggest change in terms of trade this country has faced since the mid-19th century being imposed on this country with no consultation with business, [and] no time to prepare." Also, Ian Wright, the head of the Food and Drink Federation said it was disgraceful that with just two weeks to go [before March 31st], restaurants, pubs, and catering businesses had to adapt to the new regime. "It is disgraceful that we are, only now, getting to see these. There must be proper consultation with business before a change of this magnitude is introduced," he said. [58]

One thing that is confused is regarding leaving with no deal, the transition period and negotiating new trade deals, and it should be made clear that the transition period is a part of the withdrawal agreement. So, leaving the EU with no deal means there is no transition period, so we would be able to still try to negotiate a free trade agreement following a no-deal Brexit, but we would be on the outside trying to get back in in some shape or form with limited negotiating power. This again shows the risk of a no-deal Brexit. Research from the UK Trade Policy Observatory in 2019 estimated that more than 745,000 could lose their job as a result of a no-deal Brexit, which is concerning and will mean many people are looking over their shoulder.

The Boris Johnson Government beginning July 2019 have been stating that they are making all these preparations for a no-deal exit (possibly as a bluff to the EU in the negotiations?) but with limited details implying that as we are making preparations everything will be fine. This is clearly not true as we can prepare to try to reduce the bad impacts of no deal, which some believe could be seismic for the UK and the EU, but it will not eradicate all the issues that will follow and make the UK poorer. As a friend of mine put it rather bluntly 'imagine I am going to punch you in the face and tell you to prepare for it which you do, and I then punch you, as promised, in the face. Did it hurt or did your preparations make it fine?' Not the best of analogies I concede but it does literally hit you in the face with it obvious reality.

Preparations and the readiness of business will not be uniform with larger businesses having the resources to better prepare and small to medium enterprises less so, with seasonal effects and factors such as warehouse availability, etc. The other aspect of what is hidden behind the narrative of 'preparations' is the huge cost to the UK, estimated at around £2 Billion + at the time of writing, whereas many voters were told leaving the EU would save us money which is definitely not the case currently and certainly does not look like the case moving forward after no deal. Even so-called simple things like the stockpiling of medicines incurs significant costs including renting massive warehouses of fridges to keep them at the required temperatures, all unnecessary if we had stayed in the European Union.

One thing that should not be forgotten when we talk about a no-deal scenario is that even if we leave in that way we will still have to go back for a deal and for obvious reasons it is a bilateral issue where we are reliant on the EU playing nicely with us when they will be at the 'bigger end of the stick' with the leverage which many British people do not comprehend or will not admit.

We have reached such a desperate place with Brexit as of August 2019 that the new PM Boris Johnson did not rule out the Proroguing of parliament, a word nobody outside the Westminster geeks had ever heard of or knew what it meant. Probably as it was most famously used by Charles I in 1628 believing he was ordained by God and was above all other 'normal' people. Basically, he thought he should be the dictator from God. Proroguing is basically the closing of parliament, the power of which rests with the queen and PM Johnson would simply have to go to the queen advise parliament should be prorogued and if she agrees then it is closed. In theory he could do it, but it would be such an extreme case it is very unlikely but shows where our democracy has sunk that our very own PM would not rule out such a move! Why would he do this? Well basically to stop MPs blocking a no-deal Brexit by for example holding a vote of no confidence in the prime minister as they would not be sitting.

I wrote the above paragraph in August 2019 but in September 2019 Boris Johnson did indeed prorogue Parliament for 5 weeks, but this was subsequently found to be unlawful based on the reasoning he had given to the Queen, i.e. he lied!

Before the G7 meeting in September 2019 Former senior diplomats / ex-ambassadors wrote to the new Prime Minister Boris Johnson urging him to rethink his no-deal direction as they know what negative impacts it could have on the UK. They were crystal clear when telling him: "An impending no-deal Brexit.... Would result in an unprecedented – and self-inflicted – diminution of Britain's international influence. We need a foreign policy based on long-term UK interests and a strong economy, and that requires close relationships with our European neighbours." "No deal represents the biggest unilateral abandonment of those interests in modern British History. It should not be allowed to happen. We hope the prime minister uses this G7 meeting to signal a different approach."

If the UK leaves without a deal, it will be back to the start in even more urgent need of a trade deal almost definitely having to meet the same terms as offered now but it is possible even having to make even greater concessions, and would be with no trade deals put pressure on trade, industry and the UK economy. This is why the threat to leave with the logic of getting a better deal had a very weak base. The threat of no deal to Brussels is greatly overestimated by the UK when any pain would be spread across 27 countries and they may be able to mitigate a lot of that by sourcing from / trading with / selling to other companies within the EU 27 that may have originally gone to UK companies. The UK companies will not have that option once we leave with no deal or even a bad deal with tariffs.

But if that did indeed happen it would be much harder to plan for no deal as without a sitting parliament we would not be able to pass laws to cushion the impact of no deal, for example allocating extra money or resources.

Luckily most MPs say it would be undemocratic and undermines MPs and our democracy with Amber Rudd calling the suggestion "outrageous" and some trying to put legislation in place to stop such an eventuality, but it's complex. But with some so desperate for Brexit and some being offered nice governmental jobs, you cannot rule it out, especially when the Boris Johnson Ego comes into play sense and logic goes out of the window.

If there was a no-deal Brexit and we had left on 1st November, there would probably have been chaos but on the other hand maybe not as the sky would not fall in, and on day 1 Brexiteers may have claimed everything is fine. But when we leave it will probably be more of a slow puncture to the British economy pushing the country into recession, destroying jobs that would otherwise have been there or created, as well as rising inflation and shrinking wages. The realistic expectations of no deal are so low anything that resembles anything other than a disaster will be declared by Brexiteers as a success despite no advantages and all the hate, uncertainty and Billions of pounds of spent when we were in a very good position before this chaos started in 2016.

We should all be clear that no deal or even Mr. Johnson's deal will not mean an end to negotiating with the EU but rather the beginning of a new, more complex set of negotiations, where the UK may lose any advantages it had as a full member of the EU. The reason for this is that any negotiations once we are out will need unanimous agreement from all member states and ratification by their parliaments almost certainly required for the kind of deal the UK will be seeking to secure. Those hoping for an end to the Brexit saga will be sadly disappointed as this is just the start of the post Brexit dramas to come. No-deal Brexit is not a solution it is just the start of a long and arduous journey.

Chapter 12
The Potential & Probable Cost of Brexit to the UK

Future Trade with the EU?

Regardless of a deal or no deal with the EU the UK still sells a lot of products to the EU and many Leavers seem to think we can just walk away without any substantial consequences and we can make our own rules and regulations. But the reality is that any UK products sold into the EU will still have to observe their standards just the same as it does when selling products into the USA etc. to meet the standard there. For the UK to have its own standards that do not conform to either the EU or USA (or maybe both) is fanciful due to the market size and economic power of both of those entities. It is going to be a tricky exercise to play on both sides of the street as we may get hit by a passing car! So again, this ideal of independence is a fallacy in an interconnected and interdependent world where we have to work with other countries and / or trading blocks to reach compromises or meet those required product standards.

One thing we have to accept is that if we do not want to be governed by supranational laws and courts, we cannot expect free access to THEIR market so we will have a worse deal than we currently have. This is not the EU being vindictive or difficult, this is just the logical extension of our decision to leave the club. We will have third country status, i.e. an outsider which is what many wanted, so get used to it and don't expect a lot of favours. This is just another one of those realities that Remainers told Leavers about that they either didn't believe or ignored. Perhaps because people like David Davis were telling voters that we would have a better deal or have an agreement signed sealed and delivered on the day of leaving? It was always nonsense, but some people believed it, or wanted to believe it. If one leaves the club you do not have the same benefits, this seems a simple fact to understand but some Brexiteer snake oil salesmen were still selling the unicorn dream, and many were still lapping it up despite the reality opening up around them.

Future of the EU Galileo project

Galileo is the EU's Global Satellite Navigation System and provides accurate positioning timing information which is the alternative to the USA-owned GPS navigation system, a critical strategic tool for the EU in the larger global world and to help their independence (I know we can all see the Irony of the UK argument of Independence!).

It states quite clearly in the EU rules that the UK will be excluded from more militarily sensitive parts of Galileo and the UK government has said it will not continue to see access to these for military purposes after Brexit. This is in some ways is logical as the EU will not want a third-party country involved in the development of the projects more secure elements.

But what will the UK do after Brexit in this regard? Well apparently we will develop our own which highlights some issues immediately which rail against the Brexiteer arguments such as 1. We have wasted all that money we have contributed to Galileo. 2. We were meant to be saving money with Brexit, but this is going to cost Billions of pounds in new developments 3. It will take years before it is up and running functionally and adding value to us as a country (i.e. lost time for no benefit!). And finally, 4. We have to rely on our own scientists and specialists and not benefit from the EU scientific knowledge base and experience when we know that we are short in such skill sets in the UK and may be pulled away from other important projects in the UK. Or we import those people, i.e. Immigrants, which again highlights the absurd position of Brexiteers to immigration when reality hits.

The above heightens the question again, 'where is the so-called Brexit Dividend' when it is costing us billions?

Universities and students

EU funding has helped our Universities become some of the most influential and sought after in the world. Between 2007 and 2013 the UK received 8.8 Billion from the EU for Research & Development and innovation but only paid in £5.4 Billion according to the Office for National Statistics (ONS). So, the EU support seeps throughout the UK economy and educational systems and the question is will this be replaced or how will Universities etc. have to change their systems and funding streams to maintain their status in the global world of university competition? In February 2017 UCAS recorded a drop of 7% in EU students applying to study in the UK which does not bode well and means a potential hole in the finances as fewer students means less money but also less potential talent once they graduate, and this starts to paint the picture of other long term risks associated with such decisions and Brexit.

People normally think of just students completing degrees etc. when they hear the word University, but Research is an important component of the link between universities and industry with many EU financed programs coming to fruition in the UK generating revenue, tax and jobs. This is put in doubt with the withdrawal from the EU and Lord Rees of the Royal Society has expressed his concerns, and the lack of a plan post Brexit is very concerning. Many successful companies have been spun off with great success from Universities which needed that initial funding or seed capital to make that leap to successful commercial entity on the global market.

We should not forget what a great income earner our university and education system is for the UK and if we make this more difficult for attendees from the EU and abroad it could lead to a reduced take up and influx of money into the UK economy. These students attending university, or a fee-paying school are registered as a services export for our balance of payments statistics which accounted for an estimated £19 Billion in 2016 (a 26% increase since 2010), so no small number. The UK has a target of £35 Billion in education exports by 2030 but Jo Johnson, the former minister for universities and science warned that we will not hit that target unless there is a significant shift in immigration policy, and he was not talking about fewer migrants coming here for their education. Education service exports is one of the bright spots in our economic performance, but an insular looking protective immigration policy could prove very detrimental and short sighted.

Linked to science in general future collaboration between the UK and the EU could be jeopardised if a no-deal Brexit happens. The potential problem has already been highlighted by the Russell group of Universities that saw a 9% decrease in EU postgraduate research students enrolling in its academic year 2019, which follows a 9% decline the previous year which has potential consequences on the UK's research capacity. The uncertainty of a no-deal Brexit and future funding streams and values could lead to further reductions from prospective students from the rest of the EU. This sector is not only an excellent money spinner for the country, but it also supports and estimated 944,000 jobs which is critical to the UK economy and that the UK universities flourish post Brexit.

Universities may thrive but it is yet another question mark and risk with no answers from Brexiteers as to what will happen in the next few years. But the risks are significant and again for what benefits?

Money Money Money - EU money around the corner from you!

The lack of knowledge or understanding of the EU includes not even knowing, or may be Brexiteers denying, how much money had been spent from EU funds on various facilities and projects here in the UK. If you've been to the NEC in Birmingham, used Liverpool John Lennon Airport or visited the natural history gallery at Manchester Museum, you've benefited from EU money, yes the EU part funded the projects. In many of our cities the EU funds have, for example, contributed £50m for Birmingham's International Convention Centre and Symphony Halland £25m for its Think Tank museum and City University.

There are also less well known or visible funding projects such as when the EU also gave £175m to help fund an emergency job-finding Taskforce for the 6,000 staff made redundant when MG Rover collapsed in 2005, and in 2018 gave £33m to help 16,000 young Birmingham residents into work. The funding goes all around the UK but does focus on poorer / distressed areas. In Wales, Swansea's National Waterfront Museum and university campus have received EU funding, as well as a multi-million-pound town centre regeneration programmes in south Wales valley towns including Aberdare, Pontypridd and Ebbw Vale benefiting from EU money. But how many of the local residents know this or will Brexiteers acknowledge rather than trying to imply the EU is a bottomless pit where we send our money for foreigners to squander or enrich themselves.

158

The above is just a small selection of EU funded projects but if you would like to know more and see what has been funded in your local area, please use good old Google (other search engines are available!).

It was clear we all knew very little about the EU and some knew nothing which is where the idea of referendum falls down as many of the votes placed were in ignorance and that is unfair to those people or the people who will suffer most from a Leave decision. Some call it democracy which it is but when based on such a weak foundation it cannot be GOOD democracy, that is just there for everyone to see.

Europe provides the UK with billions of pounds' worth of investment each year, both in the public and private sectors. Details of each year's EU spending in the UK can be found here: https://researchbriefings.parliament.uk/ResearchBriefing/Summary/CBP-7847.

But if you would like more details, you can go to the interactive map that highlights where a project was financed, or part financed by the EU and you will be amazed as to how many of them there are and there will be a number very close to where you live in the UK.

We are often accused of sending so much money to the EU that they waste, and we send so much more money than the other countries. But the UK's net budgetary contribution is a small net cost relative to the benefits. The UK's net contribution to the EU budget is around €7.3bn, or ONLY 0.4% of GDP. As a comparison that's around a quarter of what the UK spends on the Department for Business, Innovation & Skills, and less than an eighth of the UK's defence spend. The £116 per person net contribution is less than that from Sweden, Denmark, Finland, Germany and the Netherlands. So again, in the scheme of things and the benefits we receive it is an easy decision to be a member of the EU. The Think Tank Europe guesstimates that Norway's net contribution per capita is only 12% lower than the UK and Norway as an EEA member does not pay in full because it is not a full member – but it does have to pay contributions, although not being at the table to help set rules, regulations and laws that could be in their interest or not.

Another issue of Brexit and highlighted by the role of Multi-millionaires like Arron Banks and his huge political donation to the Leave campaign (the source of which is still being investigated) is the area of 'Grey Money' where it is not clear where it comes from, what its connections are, or where it is destined. Foreign money can be washed into our domestic market system and the transparency lost and whilst the EU introduces laws and regulations to try to clamp down and avoid this, the UK 'fiddles whilst Rome burns'. NO actions and an almost blatant disregard for the dangers of this Grey Money and the loss of tax revenues to pay for our roads and pay for street lighting, etc.

But we should not forget that it is not just about money as we are reliant on the importation of many products that we either do not make, or do not make enough of, or simply cannot manufacture / copy as they are subject to rules of origin or patented. This includes lifesaving drugs, radioactive isotopes, helium for MRI scans, chemicals, and even milk, yes milk! WTO disputes that lead from other members making objections to our proposed submitted schedule can lead to years of disputes and the UK being limited in its trading desires.

Every club has rules, get used to it!

Once we had voted to Leave the EU, it seemed like the Leave campaign were shocked and had no plan of what to do next or what they actually wanted, as they had never thought it through. Then the discussion proceeded to an act of cherry picking believing initially in some quarters that "they need us more than we need them" so the EU will give us almost whatever we want. This was obviously as a tactic (I cannot say strategy as there has never been one!) of "Cake and eat it". This obviously fell on deaf ears and reality kicked in as the EU was firm and clear in their position that we cannot cherry pick and that makes sense for anyone apart from the extreme Brexiteers. "Cakeism" was not working.

We must accept that the EU is a club such as a sports club, albeit a complicated one, that has rules and although they may be flexible on some of them to reach an agreement that works for the EU, they have certain red lines, i.e. fixed rules that cannot be changed. How can someone leave any club but then say I want the benefits of the club but few if any of the responsibilities or contribute to the running of the club?

Every club has its rules which we need to appreciate or we cannot be a full member but may be some compromise can be made if the EU so wishes with some kind of 'off peak' membership to carry on the sports club analogy which could be a Norway, Switzerland, of Canada + type solution. But all of those have their challenges as highlighted earlier in this book. The problem with that is that the extreme Brexiteers are at the time of writing so entrenched in their positions that there is almost no flexibility as they have so many demands with groups like the right-wing appearing to be holding the Government to ransom (as of 2018-19) and leveraging their position much more than the 50 odd MPs should do. But this is a fluid situation and logic would say they will move their red lines to back Boris and avoid losing Brexit completely. In recent weeks the tough man Mark Francois has resembled a humble pussycat rather than the strong British Bulldog he liked to portray as he has to hide under the table as he accepts compromises the ERG had never wanted.

Do Brexiteers honestly think that because we are leaving the club it will change its founding principles to simply suit the UK? This was some of the rhetoric we heard from Brexiteers in that if we simply leave without a deal, the EU will want us back so badly they will give us whatever we want, which was always nonsense. But Brexiteers twisted this into it was ill will and intransigence on behalf of the EU, when it is in reality just the norm, after all how many clubs of any shape or form do you know of when a member left the club it then changed all its rules based on what that one member wanted? It is folly, or was it disingenuous of some leading Brexiteers to suggest such folly knowing full well it was never going to happen?

The British media and Brexiteers appeared to not understand or deliberately ignore the fact that the EU cannot allow Brexit to result in the sort of benefits without the costs of leaving the club, or even threatening to do so, become a tempting option for others EU member states for obvious reasons. This really is basics that some people fail to grasp.

Our rules and only our rules!

When first hearing slogans like "Make our own decisions", "take back control" and "Independence" as Brexiteer leaders such as Chris Grayling and Boris Johnson had espoused during the referendum campaign and ever since, it always sounded of a desperate call for a time of imperialism when Britain did rule the waves, an imperialistic delusion that underpinned for many the Brexit cause. Many felt the humiliation of Suez in 1956 had shaken the British out of their dreams of empire, but Brexit exposed that some still harboured after such returns to the past.

Britain need to understand that it is now a medium sized economy surrounded by some huge 'sharks' such as China, USA, and India, and may be the EU once we leave, and therefore have to cooperate with other medium and smaller economies without this feeling of superiority based of past escapades.

But when one peels back the layers of the onion and actually considers such over simplified statements, you realise how either misplaced or disingenuous, they are. The reason for that is quite simple when you think about the UK complaining about having to agree to some rules or laws that the majority of the EU states wanted, even though when one really looks at how many Laws were passed without our agreement, they are very few and often minor. The simple logic is that there are at least 2 parties in any negotiation and therefore by default we WILL NOT be making all the decisions or setting all the rules as the other party will have their own ideas, aims and red lines in the negotiations. So how are we independent? How can we set our own rules or dictate the other party's red lines? It is pure fantasy, and these stated goals are just empty slogans and always were. The question is how do well-educated, intelligent people like Boris Johnson or Jacob Rees-Mogg ceaselessly continue with such rhetoric as it is obvious it is not accurate? One can only conclude that they do not fully understand how negotiations work, although I doubt it, OR they know full well what faces them in any future trade negotiations and therefore were deliberately being economical with the truth again.

The reality is that we have 'sub-contracted' certain laws in partnership with the other 27 EU partners as they are linked to the single market and makes things easier for us as a country. So, they effectively improve things, but other important issues as Crime, the NHS etc. we have total control over those, and this is why the line shouted by Brexiteers that we do not control our own laws is obviously untrue and out there to frighten people that do not know any better. Unfortunately, during the EU referendum campaign it worked.

As regards rules and the European Court of Justice (ECJ) the EU is not just about following common rules but also mechanisms for arbitration as well. From a practical point of view there would always have to be a body above the UK courts, otherwise who would decide on interpreting disagreements between the UK and the EU or another member state, or between the EU and the USA for example.

Now clearly economy with the truth or exaggeration of certain aspects of politics is well known and all too common, but the Referendum revealed what I feel is a much more dangerous trend. The ability to basically blatantly lie (and I cannot describe it as anything different as that is what it was) and to do it regularly and consistently had almost become the norm and this eats into the fabric of our democracy. Trump had made it a disgusting art form in the USA before he was president and subsequently when he was sworn in as the 45th President of the USA and ever since. Who would have ever thought it would be acceptable to just shout "Fake News" if he disagreed with something, without any facts or counter argument to challenge any accusation? It became worse when as incredible as it sounds "alternative facts" entered some people's vocabulary!

'Alternative facts' was a phrase used by U.S. Counsellor to President Trump Kellyanne Conway during a <u>Meet the Press</u> interview on January 22, 2017, in which she defended White House Press Secretary Sean Spicer's false statement about the attendance numbers of Donald Trump's inauguration as President of the United States. When pressed during the interview with Chuck Todd to explain why Spicer would "utter a provable falsehood", Conway stated that Spicer was giving 'alternative facts'. Todd responded, "Look, alternative facts are not facts. They're falsehoods."

Increased costs disproportionately affect the poor!

We should all be clear that Brexit is and will hit everyone in their pockets but will disproportionately hit the poor and less well off as they spend a greater proportion of their disposable income on such things as foodstuffs. The falling value of the pound since the Brexit vote in June 2016 has caused inflation to increase at a faster rate than other Eurozone countries which is hitting people in their pockets which can be seen below courtesy of research by the ONS, using Scotland as an example.

Food	June 2016	June 2018	Change
Bread, white sliced loaf 800g	£0.99	£1.05	£0.06
Sausages, per kg	£4.52	£4.97	£0.45
Ham, per 113g	£1.69	£1.79	£0.10
Milk, per pint	£0.43	£0.44	£0.01
Cheddar, per kg	£7.16	£7.30	£0.14
Butter, per 250g	£1.36	£1.79	£0.43
Apples, per kg	£1.98	£2.11	£0.13
Bananas, per kg	£0.85	£0.93	£0.08
Tomatoes, per kg	£2.01	£2.16	£0.15
Lettuce, iceberg, each	£0.51	£0.58	£0.07
Sugar, granulated, per kg	£0.61	£0.73	£0.12
Whiskey nip	£2.69	£2.87	£0.18
Wine, per 175ml glass	£3.60	£3.81	£0.21
Broccoli	£1.41	£1.7	£0.29
Salmon Fillet per kg	£15.07	£17.89	£2.81
Coffee, ground per 227g	£2.77	£3.03	£0.26

Source: ONS

Many Brexiteers choose to put their head in the sand or claim price increases are not true, just to protect their illusionary Brexit bubble having been promised all the riches and sunny uplands upon a Leave vote which have not transpired. Helen Dickinson, chief executive of the British Retail Consortium (BRC), said: 'The BRC has consistently made the case that a no-deal Brexit would see the prices of many everyday items rise. 'Our own research suggests that currency depreciation, additional documentation checks and requirements, tariffs on some goods, as well as delays at the border, would all contribute to higher prices and a reduced selection.' Research carried out by the GMB union suggested a family's shopping bill could increase by an average of £800 over a year!

Fuel is also another important factor to most families getting to work or driving their children to school but as we can see the increase in fuel pump pricing below they are significant and although fuel prices are influenced by many global forces Brexit and the subsequent devaluation of Sterling had a significant impact and it does not look like returning to pre-Brexit levels any time soon. Brexit is here to stay, and it IS affecting everyone in many negative ways.

Weekly Fuel Prices - Pump price in pence per litre

Date	Petrol (ULSP)	Diesel (ULSD)
30/05/2016	109.79	110.70
18/09/2017	118.85	120.59
05/08/2019	128.37	132.61

ULSP = Ultra low sulphur unleaded petrol
ULSD = Ultra low sulphur diesel

Source =   https://www.gov.uk/government/statistical-data-sets/oil-and-petroleum-products-weekly-statistics

Some of our older readers may remember Labour Prime Minister Harold Wilson in 1967, when the Pound devalued by 14.3%, claiming "The pound in your pocket was still worth a pound". This was obviously ridiculous as that same Pound bought less than it did before the devaluation as imported goods went up in price as they have since the referendum result. Inflation rose to 2.7% in May 2017 having been close to zero for the previous 18 months and could get worse after a no-deal Brexit.

We should be clear that the devaluation highlighted above was due to the judgement of the currency markets that the UK's growth potential was considerably less than it was before the referendum. This was exacerbated with a further devaluation when Prime minister Boris Johnson said we would leave the European Union on 31st October 2019 "Do or Die" i.e. deal or not deal. The markets reacted accordingly making that logical and sensible decision that a no-deal exit from the EU was very bad for the UK economy and Sterling devalued again accordingly.

Chapter 13
Social

Multiculturalism

Clearly, many Brits are concerned about this for many reasons some genuine concerns about the numbers but others simply from a racist view that they dislike or do not understand other races and cultures or cannot understand what they are saying etc. Although there are other more bizarre reasons for an anti-foreigner bias. We have covered racism in a separate part of this book so will focus here on the developments of our multicultural evolution in the UK and the impacts it may have had on the subject of Brexit.

London is the most multi-cultural city in the UK represented by circa. 160 countries, speaking around 200 languages and although it is far from perfect like any major city, we have a good ability to absorb new arrivals, but it will depend on tolerance, communication (helped by the Press and Media organisations) and obvious flexibility. Our history shows this is a national strength and not a weakness, but Brexit has allowed people to muddy the waters and blame immigration for many problems of which they are not the root cause. Clearly, immigrants must play their role by the basics of learning the English language to a good level and understand and appreciate the traditions of the UK as if they do not, they give ammunition to the right to demonstrate why certain immigrants are only interested in the UK money and NHS etc. As this book is about Brexit, it is not the place to go deep into extreme religions and cultures as it is a very complex subject and how certain cultures find it more difficult than others to assimilate and would distract from the focus of this book.

There are obviously some people that dislike and some in fact hate immigration full stop which is often voiced in many ways including statements like "we are losing our identity" or "it's not like it used to be around my way"[1A] etc. For these people it has nothing to do with the EU, but the referendum on the EU gave them the opportunity to highlight their dislike of the immigration developments over the years. The multiculturalism and growing number of non-Christian religions also played a part where the immigration became more visible in the way Muslims dressed and not just the colour of someone's skin. But it is not just this more extreme group as others have concerns about the number of immigrants and the pressure, they put on public services and our resources. More of that later.

"We are losing our identity!"

Identity is one of those concepts that we are all familiar with on the surface but would probably struggle to define, yet this Brexit identity crisis has consumed the whole question. But that aside and on the question of losing identity I always ask people "How would your identity be improved (that you fear you are losing or have lost) once we leave the EU?" The number of blank faces is amazing, as how do they legitimately answer such a ridiculous assumption?

But, this was seen and heard so much during the referendum campaign but also afterwards as the Leavers won the referendum it was almost as if Brexit had been a saviour for their valuable 'identity'. The problem was and is "What was their identity?" "What is British identity?" Who knows or understands what it is? Why were British Leave voters so frightened that it was being taken away? Was identity even the right word or was perceived 'superiority' what they felt they were losing as many people from various countries and cultures settle in the UK and are successful illustrations of superiority for just what it was, 'an illusion'.

It is almost as if there is a 'cultural drawbridge many British people want to raise to protect their culture even though they cannot tell us what that culture actually is. Many British people, like other nationalities, have strong opinions and

167

stereotypes many of which they know not where they come from, but they are strong, and they believe them no matter whether they can prove them of not. They have been fed these messages by friends, family and a powerful press which like an onion builds up layers of misinformation and fabrications that have to be peeled back. The only way to address this is to try to understand it and then educate with facts so that over time they may see the realities and not the urban myths they have followed for years.

Economic wastelands

Although it was clear that immigration played a major role in the Leave vote and those could use immigrants as a reason for their vote but when one scrapes the surface and ignores the extreme right wingers who just hate foreigners full stop, we saw that people had a genuine frustration and unhappiness with their life and circumstance. The referendum then gave them the opportunity to make a protest vote against the government or anyone that would listen even if the EU had been positive for the UK and immigrants were not the root cause of their personal problems including lack of money (greatly caused by austerity and growth in minimum (or zero) hour contracts etc.) and no perceived opportunities, leaving the future bleak in their eyes. The traditional Labour heartlands of the North, Midlands and some seaside towns felt they had been left behind, not listened to and the South had benefited from all this increased wealth. Generations of families who remember when Thatcher closed a lot of the industries where they earned their money but the government's replaced it with nothing, and now, they had the chance to kick Cameron (i.e. the establishment as they saw it) where it hurts whether or not they thought leave would win.

The above was clearly true even if these areas incorrectly blamed immigration as the root cause of their issues. But then we had anomalies of say Sunderland where Nissan was by far the largest employer in the area, but they voted to leave, despite one of the main reasons Nissan settled in the UK was due to it having tariff free access into the EU and a potential frictionless supply chain. Immigration in the North east of the country is one of the lowest of any region in the UK so surely immigration was not the issue? Once you start talking to people and trying to understand why there are a number of things that came up.

1.   People working at or associated with (e.g. family and local suppliers) no longer linked Nissan to the EU, but rather a local company, and never thought it would be an issue when we left the EU, as they did

168

not fully understand the interconnectedness of the EU supply chains or the importance of tariff free access or frictionless trade. This is understandable as who learns about such things or as had been clear over the years cared about the EU unless they saw the negative headlines in the British press? How many people or any of your friends do you remember talking about the EU before the referendum campaigns began? But then it became a behemoth of an issue that probably caught everyone by surprise and enveloped our whole society and revealed some very distasteful human traits.

2.   But the low immigration was still a threat to them, so they voted Leave? It is conceivable it is not actual immigration but rather the threat of growing immigration that scared them having seen so many negative headlines in the press and then millions of messages on social Media and Project Fear from the likes of Leave.EU or Vote Leave etc. throughout the referendum campaign. In some people, in all areas of the country, there may be an illogical fear or hate of foreigners that would be there whatever their circumstances and were always going to vote leave, which could have been inherited from, or influenced by, their parents as well as the stream of Eurosceptic scaremongering stories from the UK press for years.

Would people buy a house in the same way as they voted for Brexit?

What I mean by that is would they move to somewhere they have never seen and do not really know where it is, what the house looked like, what it will cost both short term (deposit) and long term (mortgage payments), what the area was like, and the amenities etc. This is also in the context of we as a country was very comfortable as the 5th largest economy in the world with the highest employment and lowest unemployment for decades, but then suddenly on one day it is all thrown up in the air!

Also the actual process as we know that Michael Gove basically dismissed 'experts' but would he buy his own house without using an expert Lawyer (who he would listen to and take advice), a surveyor (who he would listen to and take advice), or to a mortgage broker or bank (who he would listen to and take advice)? Of course, he would not, so why does he profess voters should do this or indeed he would literally ignore the expert advice of the Bank Of England and most economists, etc? If it isn't ignorance or a desperation to get the desired result that he will say anything to get that vote? So, if he would not do it, why would people do that?

One argument is that it is not their own money / house directly so they feel it is worth the risk as it will not impact them directly or have no clue about the implications or short medium and long-term effects on their lives, or their families and their society. They see it as almost an "arm's length decision".

But maybe it is because they see their lives as so bad with no future that any chance to improve it no matter how far-fetched or extreme it may seem they are going to go for it, and as they see it, vote for it. Why do people do the lottery when the odds of winning and improving their lives are almost 1 in 14 million? It makes no sense but maybe just maybe they could be the 1. It is the same sort of logic in that it may be a bloody long shot but if I do not go for it, I will never know. So, it is a shot to nothing, and you never know. The fact it is based on falsehoods and nonsense is irrelevant to them at that point.

Following on from this and looking at the house adage again if someone's renting a house that is so poor that they just cannot take it anymore as it is so cold, damp and the Landlord is a tyrant and they become so desperate maybe they would just go for a move of house blind just to get away. And we would all understand that. But realistically how many people are genuinely in that position as regards Brexit?

So why did so many people go for the Leave vote when they are clearly not stupid? Were the promises of a promised land just too inviting to resist and like the desperate person above just worth that "Lottery Punt" at a better life? The sadness is that it was never real and the Brexiteers didn't have a clue what they were selling or how to deliver it, whereas at least with the Lottery the rules are clear if you get 6 correct numbers you win the jackpot, but you may have to share it. They do not say once you have bought your ticket we are not sure of the rules and will work it out as we go along plus we do not know what the ticket (decision) will cost you for 10 years (or 50 years as Mr. Rees-Mogg stated!), but trust us we know what we are doing even though we have never done this before! Would you buy a ticket on this basis? I think not.

Leavers, Machos and football factories

It almost seems and feels snobby to write it, but this was my honest observation both from the TV, News, and on the two anti-Brexit marches myself but there appears to be some difference in the protesters for each side of the argument. When I looked at the People's vote march that I attended it was very peaceful quite middle class and a genuine concern of the direction of the country after the vote. Whereas often when I saw the Leave protesters it was much more aggressive, more obscenities were shouted, and it was very tribal, almost like a football factory feel with plenty of scowling faces and claims of 'traitors', 'garlic and sausage munchers' (French and German references I assume?), 'unpatriotic' 'snowflakes' as well as the accompanying profanities, that I personally witnessed before the police intervened to stop this group intimidating, or trying to intimidate, peaceful protesters with a different opinion.

This impression was further magnified when witnessing the aggressive intimidation of Anna Soubry, Femi Oluwole (having water thrown on him, abused and poked with a union Jack flag at a Brexit party rally) and Owen Jones harassment from a group of aggressive Leave voters. Now certain groups on the other side of the argument have also shown acts of unacceptable behaviour including towards Jacob Rees-Mogg and his family but in general the two sides appeared to show a different attitude towards protesting or getting their point of view across as well as their perception of being a 'patriot', but why is that I asked myself?

Knowing I was planning this book I spoke to a couple of the men on the pro-Brexit group, that were shouting some derogatory remarks to our group, why in fact they were pro-Brexit and against the march. I received the response "F**k off you gay C**t and take your rainbows with yer!" This was obviously a shock as I am not gay, and I couldn't see a rainbow in the close vicinity. One shouldn't laugh at such attitudes, but I did as I genuinely think he thought he was at London Pride and not a Pro-Brexit march. Shocking and hilarious at the same time.

Now there are many Leave voters that are not like that described above but why does the Leave argument attract such aggression from an almost stereotype aggressive, over patriotic (almost nationalistic) anti-foreigner football thug type carrying his St George's flag (not union Jack!) claiming they want 'their' country back? Do they genuinely understand the issues and what the implications are for Leave or do many of them join the group that seems to better fit what they look like or think, plus they feel this is the 'harder' group so they will march with them, rather like the kids at school kept close to the big bully so he didn't pick on them? A form of herd instinct may be? Did a lot of these men aspire to be one of the thug like individuals to feel tough themselves and give them a sense of power that they do not possess outside the group? This feeling of being feared when with their 'tribe' rather like the Quadrophenia film where he gets his buzz at the weekend before returning to his mundane life? I am not a psychologist so cannot even begin to answer my dilemma on this observation and it is just that 'an observation' which is fascinating. I am sure it is linked to the fact that with my own particular remain stance I was accused of being unpatriotic (often with a few war stories from non-combatants thrown in), which was bizarre and a total misunderstanding of the issues and reasoning for the remain position.

Were a lot of these men conveniently marching against the EU when it had nothing to do with the EU but rather a march of perceived British superiority – The British Bulldogs against the world so to speak? Only they would know, or would they?

Is it not better that countries work more closely together even if they pool a bit of sovereignty for the greater good to be a part of a much stronger trading and political unit where those countries work together and respect each other rather than fighting and bullying each other? Now I know that is not the language you will here on the football terraces too often but maybe we are talking about the future of the UK and we need to take a much higher ground than this base level macho attitude of The British Bulldog spirit, etc. The EU is based on democracy, the rule of law, non-discrimination, equality and human rights as well as the obvious support of its members which is a huge contrast to other parts of the world where the big boys bully the little guys – surely we all hate bullying and do not want to return to the world of dog eat dog?

Clearly the EU is not perfect and needs reforms as do most large multinational organisations but compare it to the dictatorships around the world such as Russia and China or the wars and conflicts in Syria, Ukraine, and Palestine etc. You only have to compare the Ukraine to Poland both originally a part of the Soviet Union, but Poland is peaceful and prospering whereas its neighbour Ukraine is poor and in constant fear of Putin and his nationalistic whims. Coincidence? I do not want to exaggerate this point and when we leave the EU there will not be a sudden third world war, but the EU can be a force for peace, and we should acknowledge that and embrace it. Let us not forget that in 2012 The Nobel Peace Prize was awarded to the European Union (EU) 'for over six decades contributed to the advancement of peace and reconciliation, democracy and human rights in Europe.'

Housing

Housing is a vast and complicated subject and could require a book of its own to go into detail, but we will touch on it here.

Clearly, consecutive governments have not built enough affordable housing or let's call it what it is 'social' housing that is subsidised by the government so low-wage workers, unemployed, and those with social difficulties that cannot work can live in reasonable comfort. 'Affordable housing' has become such an abused term by governments that it is literally useless especially when some ministers quote £350,000 as affordable showing they live in a completely different world. There are hundreds of cranes across London and big cities building thousands of apartments and houses, but the problem is someone on average wages cannot afford such a house or even raise the deposit to be in a position to purchase. We are suffering now and have been for over a decade now of Mrs. Thatcher thinking she was doing a good thing by selling off the council houses cheap but now we reap the law of unintended consequences!

So, what has housing got to do with Brexit? Well, the OBR (Office of Budget Responsibility) the Government's independent forecasting agency claimed house prices could fall by around 10% if we have a disorderly Brexit. These houses are people's savings and pensions in some cases and could leave them immediately with negative equity. Would they still have voted Leave if they knew this could be the case? One Brexiteer commented to me "great then house prices will be lower so younger people can buy them" not understanding that many won't move as the price is too low now for them or they will wait until price increases return, but also that it is accumulating the deposits is one of the major problems especially for first-time buyers.

With negative equity many people avoid moving so the housing market becomes stagnant and as the housing market is an important part of the UK economy generating billions in trade and taxes, this has a ripple effect. If this happens, this is really bad news for estate agents, surveyors, retailers of housing materials such as furniture, curtains and carpets as well as storage companies and

173

removal companies that may have to reduce their employee head count putting a further strain on the exchequer due to higher unemployment.

Shelter, the housing charity, said at the end of 2018 1.2 million homes are needed for younger families who cannot afford to buy and "face a lifetime in expensive and insecure private renting".

"In the years after the second world war, governments – Labour and Conservative – built about 120,000 social homes and council houses every year. In the last 20 years or so – we've built 20,000 social homes per year - and that is one of the biggest causes of the housing crisis." See the graphic below.

Fall in new social housing across England

Additional homes provided in the year ending March

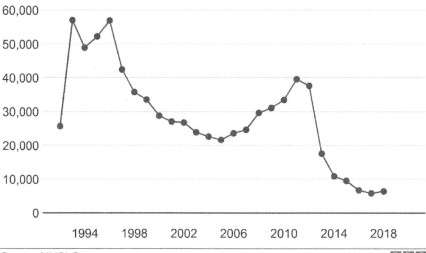

Source: MHCLG   BBC

Housing is a complex topic and one that we cannot go into great depth here in this book but the idea we must build more social homes seems obvious to a layman when we have a higher population, people living longer and more families splitting up etc. than in the past so two houses are then required. Clearly there is a significant cost involved with the estimation of building 3.1 million new social homes costing an average of 10.7 billion a year, according to analysis by research group Capital Economics on behalf of Shelter. But Shelter claims the government would save £60 Billion over 30 years if it can make renting cheaper. It said having more social housing would lower rents. [59]

Many Leavers like to blame immigrants who are helping our economy carrying our vital jobs and services, whereas it appears that the government inertia when it comes to building social housing is the root cause of this issue on housing. The Government has such briefing papers as "Tackling the under-supply of housing in England" by Wendy Wilson and Cassie Barton but there is so little action and implementation of any plans that gets any way near to the numbers that are clearly required. It is the execution that is lacking.

Chapter 14
Immigration

Just as a point of clarification there are many ways to interpret the term 'migrant', but nothing set in law. There is no consensus on a single definition of a 'migrant'. Migrants might be defined by foreign birth, by foreign citizenship, or by their movement into a new country to stay temporarily (sometimes for as little as a year) or to settle for the long-term. Some analyses of the impact of migration even include children who are UK-born or UK nationals, but whose parents are foreign-born or foreign-nationals, in the migrant population. None of these definitions are equivalent, and none fit precisely with 'migrant' defined as an individual who is subject to immigration controls. Moreover, in the UK 'immigrant' and 'migrant' (as well as 'foreigner') are commonly used interchangeably in public debate and even among research specialists, although dictionary definitions distinguish 'immigrants' – people who are or intend to be settled in their new country – from 'migrants' who are temporarily resident. Additionally, in some scholarly and everyday usage, people who move internally within national boundaries are called migrants.

Although there is no definition of 'migrant' or of 'immigrant' in law, there is a key distinction between 'Persons Subject to Immigration Control', who need permission to enter or to remain in the UK, and those 'Not Subject to Immigration Control' who do not. While the UK remains part of the EU, EU nationals are not subject to immigration control although they are often described as migrants.

So, we can see here some confusion with interchangeable descriptions, but let us get stuck into the big and diverse issue of immigration.

Shock horror - There are racists and racism!

It may seem surprising to address this issue head on in point one, but I felt it had to be addressed as the word RACIST was very evident in the referendum whether it be overtly or bubbling under the surface, with Leavers feeling they were being painted unfairly as racists when they did not feel they were. It is often the Elephant in the room so let's look at it closely. I often heard the words "I am not a racist but......" which leads one to ask what actually is a racist, and what better than the Oxford English Dictionary?

So, to get a base line this is the actual definition:

Noun

A person who shows or feels discrimination or prejudice against people of other races, or who believes that a particular race is superior to another.
'I had a fear of being called a racist'

Adjective

Showing or feeling discrimination or prejudice against people of other races or believing that a particular race is superior to another.
'we are investigating complaints about racist abuse at a newsagents'

Now you will see straight away that many of the people that are discriminating or prejudiced against immigrants in preference to British people are in fact according to the technical definition, racists e.g. the Brit saying "I want our jobs for our British people and NOT for those East Europeans or Spanish coming in etc." even though he does not necessarily know the British people he is referring to and probably never will! So immediately this becomes inflammatory as many British people look at Racists as a stereotype of a skinhead, with Doctor Martins aggressively abusing foreigners and telling them to go home flaunting BNP (or before that National Front) banners and flags! But the above definition tells you that we in fact have more racists in this country (and all other countries) based purely on this official definition. But clearly not all arguments are black and white, and many people are more protectionist and inward looking rather than being aggressive racist and this leads one to think 'Why do Brits prefer other Brits instead of foreigners even though they do not know the Brits they refer to and probably never will?

With this in mind I posed a question to a number of people who voted Leave or now supported Leave "Why would you, for example (and purely hypothetical), prefer a Mr. Smith from Sunderland who you are not related to, do not know and never ever will compared to Filip from Poland who has a job and is living close to you (other scenarios available of course)? But despite a number of them being strongly against the Free movement of people they could not justify their decision when it was put in such a format and they had to justify their prejudice, some even accepting they had prejudicial tendencies that they were unaware of or thought were acceptable.

When we boiled it down, it came down to comments like "well they were born here" or "they are British" etc. which as we now know ARE racist arguments but looking at it in a bit more depth this preference is based basically on a place of birth, or rather the luck of the place of birth. What they clearly did not appreciate was that this was privilege (yes privilege) voting for privilege i.e. someone in a country that was lucky enough to be born there preferring someone with the same luck compared to someone that does not necessarily have those same advantages and benefits. Privilege is relative of course but people often do not see themselves as privileged as they often focus on what they do not have rather than what they do.

There is a clear feeling by a number in our British society that they as British or us as a British race are superior to other countries and races, normally based on no evidence (of course) apart from dumb statements on Facebook or other social media channels as well as down the pub that 'we' won the war which in itself is obviously historically incorrect as if nobody else played a part, but like many Brexiteer arguments why should they let facts get in the way. One only has to see how many Facebook posts are followed by a number of St George flag Emojis. Note not Union Jack as many of those individuals feel the English are superior to the 'Jocks', 'Taffs' and 'Paddies' also. Perhaps this is revealing of the psyche of these types of nationalist / imperialist that craves Brexit at any cost.

This is also highlighted in the selfishness of many British people not wanting to give foreign aid as they add that to their anti-immigrant feeling. We only spend 0.7% of our Gross National Income, which accounted for £13 Billion in 2016, 1 billion of this is distributed via the EU aid budget. But for many Brits it is a case of charity begins at home and want to spend the money on so many things but would never stretch that far anyway. But when they argue for the money to help to get waiting lists down at their GP, it appears that it is a very relative world – privilege in the UK where a critical focus is getting an appointment with the GP within 2 days rather than a week for a non-emergency issue compared to starvation and no clean water in Africa or war and death in the middle east, etc. But as a famous person once said, "you pay your money you make your choices." What are your priorities? I have friends that see as a "charity begins at home" argument but I see it differently and maybe we just have different ideals, focus and priorities where for many saving a child from starvation in Africa is more important than Mrs. Jones needing her varicose veins looking within 5 days? We have great hospital and emergency services and if we have an emergency, we get seen and I have never heard of someone with a legitimate and diagnosed emergency being turned away from a hospital but cases of infants not having water and food are rife in Africa. That is my reality, what's yours?

There were some bizarre, albeit for some Brexiteers frightening, statistics calculated around the internet that 'More than a third of babies are born to foreign parents', which gave some the vision in the UK of being swamped by immigrants of the future and as Muslims on average have a higher number of children than non-Muslim families a higher proportion of Muslims in the UK. Clearly, some did not need to be asked twice to fan the flames of such xenophobic fears. But as with all such statements or statistics when one looks behind the headline (which unfortunately many do not, especially on Social Media such as Facebook) a completely different picture can be found. Firstly, in 2000 records show 21.2% of new-borns had at least one parent born abroad (not 2 but 1 so the other parent was British whereas the headline implies both parents were foreign!) so it was a British person having a child. Secondly, just because a parent was born outside the UK they may have been here for 30 years, would you still count them as foreign? This bodes the question when does an immigrant stop being an immigrant? Probably never in some people's eyes and in a racist's eyes a black person will always be an outsider as it is a race argument and not a place of birth argument in that case. But this place of birth throws up some anomalies that the people spreading such falsehoods had not considered in that this could also include Boris

179

Johnson (born in the USA) and Margaret Hodge MP (born in Alexandria, Egypt) and if he had another child also Nigel Farage whose wife is German and was born in Germany (I know, I know the irony is not lost on anyone!).

But it was not just anti-immigrant Internet trolls spreading such falsehoods but also The Sun on the 1st December 2016 quoted some birth figures incorrectly writing "The figures showed nine in ten London new-borns had at least one parent from overseas". That was wrong and not consistent with the rest of the Sun's article. The Sun subsequently amended its article to remove the inaccurate claim, but this shows how such inaccurate and inflammatory reporting from the British Press helps to fan the flames of anti-immigrant sentiment and the damage is done. What if someone read the first article but didn't see the amendment?

Just to show how the referendum and the run up to the referendum plus the aftermath increased the focus or concern about immigration, in 1995 the proportion of people who said that "immigration or race relations" was one of the top five issues facing the UK was around 2%. By August 2016 after the referendum it had increased to 34% according to Ipsos MORI. Obviously this does not tell us anything about what people think of immigration, just they think it is an issue. But if the public had been constantly told by many Media outlets or politicians and Brexiteers in the run up to the referendum that Immigrants were swarming to the UK (see Press section of this book), are criminals, 4 million Turks were coming to the UK in 2020, or they were claiming millions in benefits etc. is it any wonder that they would see immigration in a completely different way?

When does an Immigrant cease to be an immigrant?

It is now accepted that scientifically very few British people would be pure Anglo Saxons but rather would be a combination of many races and ethnicities which can now be simply identified with a DNA test. So, if we accept to a certain extent we are all immigrants, when does an immigrant no longer be an immigrant? Do we go back to the parents, the grandparents or even further back to decide who should be defined as an immigrant and potentially returning them home as many Brexiteers hint at? But what of even recent arrivals?

For example, a Romanian woman comes to the UK to do some jobs that cannot be filled by British people with her 3-year-old child who then goes to school and learns perfect English. 5 years later she is 8 and cannot remember life in Romania anymore and is fully integrated into British society with many close friends. So, would Brexiteers send her home when this is her home now? Would they send just her Mum home and split the family, what would they do? I have really struggled to get a clear answer on this from Brexiteers apart just saying "we have too many immigrants" (without justification or facts I must add). It literally shows that rather like Brexit these empty slogans reveal a lack of intellectual rigour or thinking through the arguments, or a plan to do something about the problem they perceive, and this is a real problem as it is pure emotion and a desperation for Brexit at all costs which hinders critical thinking.

Do people even remember or even know that famous and successful people that added great value to their countries such as Henry Ford, Walt Disney or Elon Musk were immigrants or children of immigrants? History shows us that immigrants are very creative and have a high success rate when it comes entrepreneurship, highlighted when one sees that they account for 13% of the US population but 27.5% of those that start their own businesses. This is also the case in the UK that many immigrants where possible look to start businesses and increase their independence. Perhaps this is because immigrants have experienced at least two cultures which allows them better scope to bring new and innovative ideas to the table in their new country they live in?

Another aspect that became clear talking to Brexiteers was that when the immigration issues was made more personal to them they retreated for example when I asked who or how many of their immigrant friends from table tennis should be sent home? Clearly, they avoided the answer for obvious reasons but surely I countered, "if we have too many they should also go home, or not?" This demonstrated how Brexiteers preferred to keep the immigration issue at arm's length and not get to directly involved, as they struggled to justify their original statements, and appeared to create a hierarchy of immigrants beginning with their friends or acquaintances at the top who were OK and work down.

Research by Christian Dustmann and Tommaso Frattini from University London found that immigrants are 47% less likely to receive state benefits or tax credits, immigrants arriving since the early 2000s have made net contributions to the UK's public finances, reduced the financial burden of such fixed expenditure such as defence by billions, and 35% of EEA immigrants (compared to 24% of UK citizens) had a Degree and strong educational background, so they add real value. Also, we have to consider that they tend to arrive in the UK after completing their education, so the UK has not had the cost burden of educating them which is estimated at around £5.8 Billion by the authors.

So, our EU immigrant workers are very productive, cost effective and this is often forgotten in the debate about the costs and benefits of immigration. [64]

Which immigrants that live in the country already would you remove, if any, and how would you decide who must go home?

"Most immigrants don't speak English.'

This was an accusation used when trying to justify the issues with immigrants and immigration on the UK and there are clearly areas where immigrants could make more of an effort to learn better English and integrate. But on the flip side why should British people not make greater efforts to understand other cultures and integrate with them? Surely in an ideal world both parties would try to create a better country.

This 'Immigrants don't speak English lie was spread and exacerbated by Nigel Farage when leader of the UKIP party knowing it was not true and was picked up a number of times including on his interview with James O'Brien on 16th May 2014 when it was quite rightly pointed out by Mr. O'Brien that it was in fact certain children listed English as their second language NOT that they could not speak English which was just Mr. Farage trying to extol this inflammatory language to create an anti-foreigner / anti-immigrant feeling to serve his own purpose. But even when exposed Mr. Farage really struggled to admit he was in fact wrong / spreading misinformation that can create hate very quickly. He also conveniently forgot that his wife speaks to his daughters in German at home!

We should be aware and British people should be aware that most communities wherever they are in the world tend to stick more with their own nationality, language and culture just like many Brits on the Costa Del Sol do not bother to learn Spanish, maintain their social groups and Bowls clubs to create a Little Britain in the Sun. So, to a certain extent everyone is to blame but in the UK some people use immigrant minority groups as scapegoats in this regard.

But how widespread is this non-English speaking issue in the UK? At the last census only 138,000 immigrants spoke no English which is less than 0.3% of population. But an interesting fact once I looked into this was that not all 138,000 were immigrants with only 118,000 being born outside the UK. The rest were born inside the UK and included, for example, people whose main language was a sign language! Yes, sign language is something many people would not consider when talking about people that do not speak English. So, we have to be very careful with statistics, how they are used, understanding them correctly, and being careful of disgraceful abuses.

The non-English speaking issue with immigrants is very much for those that come to the country after their 50th birthday and who struggle, like many older people, to learn a new language. But with the influx of younger Eastern European workers that may have actually had English at school it is not such an issue as they are looking for work and therefore need the English language to live. Therefore, this issue should be reducing considerably and should not be highlighted as a major issue with race relations and integration, when they are simply prejudiced and looking for scapegoats.

NHS gastric bands and Immigrants

Hospitals can be congested yes but not because of immigrants as many Brexiteers would have you believe but rather due to large and growing numbers of predominantly older people who have been treated but also there is a serious lack of beds / facilities for them to go to as they cannot go home yet, which is largely due to the lack of planning and spending on care services. This is a lack of joined up thinking and planning that has been present in our Health service for years and despite a good deal of different Health ministers tinkering around the edges it has not been efficiently addressed. So, we see here how Brexiteers focused on hospitals with a simplistic solution of fewer immigrants without really understanding what the real complex issues are and having workable solutions for those issues. Some almost want to blame Immigrants and look for ways of blaming them, even if without proof or justification.

I was even told by a friend on Facebook that he went into A & E in Liverpool and "it was full of foreigners"[KW] which is why he had to wait so long. Firstly, this rings alarm bells as only 14% of the population in 2017 were foreign born, so very unlikely the A & E just happened to be full of foreigners at that moment in time. But he believed it. When pressed, he could not prove it but it's conceivable he saw some Black and middle Eastern faces and assumed they had just immigrated into the UK even though they may have been in the UK for 20+ years? Perhaps he also thought The 2 people in the corner talking together in their native tongue had also just come over from Eastern Europe, even though they may have also lived here for 20+ years? It is those assumptions and inbuilt perceptions that cause significant problems as well as an intense longing for immigrants to be the problem which some truly believe they are, even if the reality and facts say something completely different. If you are looking hard enough for something you will find it, even if not based on the facts.

Another interesting statistic linked to the percentage of foreign-born immigrants in the UK was that 53% of our foreign-born population are women, which is contrary to Nigel Farage's contentions and Breaking Point poster that implied it was only men streaming into the country. But, we all know Nigel and his porkies.

When it comes to the NHS we always hear about Immigrants apparently being the root cause of most of the problems hospitals face but at the same time we know people that cannot or will not control for example their eating habits and receive free (well-funded by you, me and other taxpayers) Gastric Bands but nobody seems to bat an eyelid? Why is that? It is not clear why Brexiteers say nothing about such operations but would begrudge an immigrant child an important operation, unless it is pure prejudice and carrying the adage of "Charity begins and finishes at home". This attitude does not make us look great as a country or very charitable. We should not be proud of that or even allow such false rumours and stories to be widely shared without countering and proving these lies about immigrants and the NHS as incorrect.

What the previous hospital example exemplifies and appears often in many of the Brexiteer arguments is that many do not seem to know why they believe something, where the belief came from, how to explain it, and how to prove they are correct etc. which results in someone walking into A & E and convincing themselves that it is full of foreigners sponging off the system.

Leaving the EU is not the be all and end all for immigration as if it is a magic bullet that will stop the immigrants and cure all the country's ills. Leavers seem to forget that we control the non-EU immigration as they want but more immigrants enter the country that way than from the EU states. So, we cannot or will not control immigration as they want and get anywhere near the Government's own targets for 'tens of thousands' which must be 99,000 or lower each year. The problem with the Brexiteer logic and arguments are that are not based in reality and we need the immigration to help our economy function, but they will not accept that.

The other side of the coin to the abuse of the NHS by 'locals' and the fact immigrants are not a drain on the NHS as purported by many Brexiteers is that of the foreign Doctors and nurses (i.e., immigrants) that are an integral part of how our health service functions. Many Doctors have highlighted how since the referendum result they are feeling less welcome and the risk of losing many such skilled specialists with many years of experience could be an absolute disaster for our health service, including the fact that thousands have spent years training in our NHS. It was quite clear that after the referendum there was a rise in hate crime rose with the Home Office Statistical Bulleting highlighting 'In 2016-17 hate crime offences rose by 29% to 80,393' and although Brexiteers may conveniently say it is a coincidence from the timing and has nothing to do with Brexit but do you think Doctors and nurses are immune from such hate crime when dealing with very difficult and distressed individuals on the front line?

One factor that is often overlooked and underrated is that many social care workers leave the social care system to take up seasonal retail work as it is better paid. This creates a 'perfect storm' with existing problems exacerbated in the event of a no-deal Brexit with the exodus of EU workers. The Nuffield Trust estimated in its research that the UK could be short of up to 70,000 social care workers by 2025/26 if migration of such foreign workers is halted or made more difficult or less welcoming. The cost of care will therefore have to go up and it could be significant otherwise immigrants will not come from other such as poorer regions such as from Africa, or Philippines, India, Pakistan and others. Did Brexiteers really vote for this, or did they simply not understand the implications of putting a simple cross in a box having been lied to constantly?

When talking about the NHS people focus understandably on Doctors and nurses as they have the highest profiles but there are many other professions in the NHS that will have serious problems post Brexit. Midwifery is one of them with an ageing demographic with half of the nurses in the UK older than 45 and over half midwives over 50, and they can retire at 55! There are already thousands of vacancies in these professions unfilled, so where do Brexiteers, if they have even thought about it, going to come from? They will be the first ones to complain in their expectations of care in the NHS is not met, and the air will fill with hypocrisy!

The other often overlooked aspect of health and us leaving the EU with no deal is the possibility of many retired citizens living in the EU especially Spain and France who currently enjoy free access to local healthcare paid by their host member-state but in the case of a no-deal Brexit it would probably be either the UK taxpayer that would end up bearing the cost or the retirees return to the UK to become a further burden on the NHS and housing system.

One of the issues with the NHS being stretched for patients is that there are a lot of jobs still to be filled (96,000 the last time I looked) with the UK not having enough skills to fulfil a lot those requirements but also we have fewer beds per 1000 of the population with only 2 per 1000 whereas in Germany it is 8, and France is 6 per thousand. You can see the difference.

You should also be aware that the European Medicines agency has shut its UK office and moved it back to within the EU which makes the UK less attractive to global Pharma companies and the release of specific life-saving drugs could be delayed coming to the UK by up to 2 years as the UK decides what type of approval system it will have once outside the EU. The Pharma companies will want the released onto the biggest market possible which is the EU after the USA so the UK as in many areas will play second fiddle again! All Brexiteers should be ready to hold their hands up if lifesaving drugs are available in the Netherlands for example but not yet in the UK and people die as a result. Basically, how it works is the drugs / medicines gets approved for USA first as the biggest most profitable market, then the EU followed by other countries / regions such as Japan, China, and the Rest Of the World. The further down the ladder of approvals you are the later you get the approved drugs! So, it could be that British citizens needing new life saving drugs may have to wait up to 2 years after other regions which could mean they lose their battle before receiving the required drugs. That is a major disadvantage with no benefits to the UK citizens. I am sure you did not vote for this (or even knew about this, as I did not?) but that can be the result of your vote, but you were never told that.

Although the cry of Brexiteers is British jobs for the British but with circa. 24,000 vacancies (as of June 2017 after the referendum vote) for nurses with no Leave politician or political figure offering a solution as to how these requirements are to be filled. The number of applications to train as nurses have also fallen. We must also consider that with the falling number of applications plus nurses retiring, this is potentially an emergency in the offing. By 2020, just three years away, up to half of the current workforce will be eligible for retirement, a number of whom will be nurses. Ultimately, Brexit is looking like resulting in fewer NHS staff, including doctors and nurses, with growing work pressures due to reducing numbers and that does not bode well for our health or that of our NHS staff.

The Local Government Association said in 2019 that the government needed to reverse the £700 million reduction it had planned in public health funding since 2015 and plug a £3.6 Billion gap in funding for adult social care by 2025. This is how serious they see the shortfall and Brexit is not going to help .

In an article in the Lancet medical publication in February 2019 for "All forms of Brexit will negatively impact affect the UK national health service but a no-deal scenario would by far the worst with negative effects on the healthcare work force, NHS financing, availability of medicines and vaccines, the sharing of information and medical research."

Clearly, no one that voted Leave voted for a weaker NHS but there is a clear risk of that happening and with a drastic shortage we have compared to other European countries, rather than making these professionals unwelcome we should be doing all we can to encourage such healthcare workers to come here and support them and make them feel welcome. This shows another weakness in a referendum as many people would not have linked stopping immigrants coming to the UK but including the nurse that looks after their Mother and father in their old age or in hospital or the Doctors that help protect and save THEIR children. This is what we elect and pay MPs and other specialists for to have this joined up thinking and policy rather than exposing the public to such a complex issue with thousands of interrelated parts that can make or break the UK.

An example of this risk was seen in a letter highlighted in an Article in The Guardian online on the 9th April 2019 as follows:

'The day after the 2016 EU referendum, I happened to have an appointment with my GP, a Dutch citizen who had worked in the UK for over 30 years. I asked him his reaction to the result. "I've sadly realised that half my patients don't want me to be here," he said. He returned to Holland shortly afterwards. The people of Peterborough, a majority of whom voted to leave the EU, lost a very fine GP. **Author [this is very sad, and dangerous going forward]**

David Jost
Peterborough [39]

Don't forget our animals and pets!

Although not a major focus of interest during the EU referendum campaigns many of you have pets or a love of animals and it may surprise you to know that 50% of veterinary practitioners registered to practice in the UK are from overseas with the majority from the EU states so any reduction in immigration would damage the ability of this industry to support owners, pets and the food and animal safety industries according to Royal college of veterinary surgeons and British veterinary association. Basically, we do not produce enough vets and it takes years to train Vets so this time lag combined with the issue with immigration if the free movement is changed will create an issue.

But when we think of Vets we think of the doctor that deals with your pet dog or cat, but many vets are used in various other areas including farms, abattoirs etc. and it appears many British people do not wish to complete all that training to watch animals slaughtered! So, it is not just the more fluffy parts of the job but these less popular but just as critical areas that ensure animal welfare and maintaining food standards at source. An unforeseen circumstance is that it will become increasingly impossible to export animals and meat products if there isn't the veterinary oversight to supervise and ensure infection free products and animals!

So, you can see this is just one more area and there are hundreds where we as a country could be struggling to fulfil / control if many of the Brexiteers get their way with immigration as they do not understand the requirements of our economy or the implications of the demands they make. Unforeseen circumstances will make us rue the day we leave the EU with no deal and make the UK less welcoming to our foreign partners.

Areas of low immigration voted Leave, why?

This was an interesting development once the result was declared and one could analyse the results as many of the Leave areas were areas of low immigration so why the concern? Fear that London levels of immigration may come to their own area perhaps? Believe the scare stories of the Media or UKIP etc? simple dislike of foreigners? A desire to go back to the days of empire etc? what could it be or is it more complex than the above?

It was clear in the EU Referendum campaign that immigration, no matter how Leavers now try in a revisionist manner to deny it was that important, had replaced the economy as the single most important factor driving Vote Leave's focus, even though Bobby Duffy of Ipsos MORI said polling showed that 'the actual direct impact on people's local areas and lives is much less widespread than the general concern. That does not mean that the people's concerns aren't real (just the facts do not back up these concerns) – we can be legitimately worried about how immigration is changing the UK and putting pressure on other parts of society and services like the NHS. But it is still remarkable that the single most important factor driving the Leave vote actually has a direct negative impact on only one in five of the population, and the EU immigrants that tend to be younger, fit and working are not the strain on the NHS as Brexiteers dishonestly would have us believe.

A poll conducted on behalf of Lord Ashcroft shortly after votes had closed showed 33% stated their main reason for voting Leave was because "offered the best chance for the UK to regain control over immigration and its own borders". Yes, they were misled and yes they will be disappointed as the numbers will not dramatically change unless our country and economy changes, but they genuinely believed it. It is not them to blame, it is the liars that sold them this vision of the UK post 2019. On top of that the Ashcroft poll found 81% of Leave voters regarded multiculturalism and 80% regarded immigration as "forces for ill" compared to 19% and 20% of Remain voters, respectively. So, there it is, and we all knew this, even if it may not be politically correct to admit it.

The government did not help with these concerns or giving the perception of lacking control and Brendan Cox, husband of murdered MP Jo Cox, put it clearly when he said 'The UK government policy is a masterclass in how to get the crisis wrong: set an unrealistic target, miss it, report on it quarterly, and in doing so show a complete lack of control heightening concern and fanning the flames of resentment.' Critics would also highlight Cameron's insistence on boosting international aid while his government wrestled with the deficit and continued austerity, which fostered a growing feeling that the political class (greatly linked to the Remain campaign) were so remote from the people confirming for many their decision to vote Leave.

Big Leave areas like Midlands, Yorkshire and the North-West have a percentage of migrants living in each region between only 6-8%, so why the fear, or is it just a simple built-in anti-foreigner sentiment? Many market towns have seen rising crime, loss of well-paid quality jobs as well as the highly visible homelessness, which could be partly due to austerity since the global banking collapse, but many found immigration and foreigners as an easier simpler excuse for these ills whether that is justified or not.

It is clear that if British white individuals spent more time with ethnic minorities they would see that they are just normal individuals like themselves trying to do the best for their families, but this lack of contact allows the stereotypes to mushroom and the lack of understanding and assimilation to spread such concern, fear, and sometimes hate. What is also clear that in London these feelings are only there in a small minority of typically older white generations, whereas the children that grow up together in school despite coming from an immigrant family merge together in friendship and companionship seeing each other not as different races, creeds and nationalities but as friends. So, the problem seems to be the lack of contact, understanding, flexibility, and willingness to live and let live rather than being fearful and wanting them sent home or stop any more coming. This is not a uniquely British thing but the British 'island mentality' could play a role in this more isolationist attitude.

The irony of this issue of austerity and issues with our economy is that a no-deal Brexit would make it impossible, despite what the next conservative leader and Prime Minister promises, to spend a lot more on public services etc. unless they borrow heavily or raise taxes. As the economy is expected to shrink in those circumstances, where will the money come from and will those issues really be addressed by the vote to leave?

As highlighted in August 2019 net migration from the EU had fallen to a five-year low, based on the ONS (Office of National Statistics) figures, indicating that the market was successfully regulating the employment market that a rules and regulations-based points type system could never replicate. The aforementioned fall had fallen by more than two-thirds since 2015. There are many reasons for that including the change in the Sterling exchange rate and the improvement in certain economies such as Poland. The non-EU migration, i.e. the part we control, has remained broadly stable over the last 12 months following gradual increase since 2013.

Long-term net migration to the UK

Net migration by EU and non-EU migrants, '000s

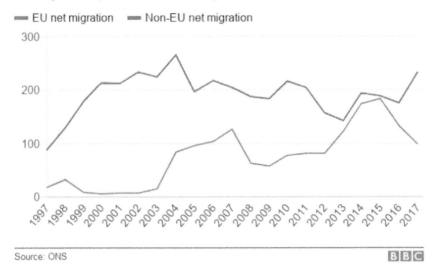

Source: ONS

B|B|C

There is genuinely quite a lot of variation in the share and spread of workers from EU countries once you look at different jobs, examples of which are highlighted below all showing jobs and skills (not even including Doctors, Nurses, Vets and social workers) we are struggling to fulfil with the local UK board citizens [55]:

- Basic construction - 34%
- Cleaning - 19%
- Food preparation - 14%
- Construction - 11%
- Basic hospitality - 11%
- Personal care - 6%
- Teaching - 5%

Has political correctness contributed towards the Racism we see?

Before the referendum there appeared a fear or reluctance to talk about immigration for the fear of being called racist even though many that have

191

concerns about immigration may not genuinely be racist. We are finding in society that the 'correct' or acceptable words used has become blurred creating confusion within society and resulting in people not using any word that could be construed or even twisted into being racial and therefore a potential step towards people not talking about immigration and their concerns.

When does one use the word coloured? Can one now use the word coloured? These are just simple issues that close down debate and then alienates people when we could be educating them about immigration into this country and how we could better integrate and work together.

This political correctness can lead to more moderate people not saying anything but the extreme right wingers and racists that maybe do not care about political correctness and so still espouse their anti-immigrant feelings either verbally or via social media which can give the impression that all those that are concerned about immigration are in fact racists. So, it skews the appearance of the immigration issue and those views towards it.

Some felt an example of this was when Amber Rudd appeared to call Diane Abbott a "coloured" woman which is no longer the acceptable language and Mrs. Rudd apologised as follows: "Mortified at my clumsy language and sorry to @HackneyAbbott," she tweeted. "My point stands: that no one should suffer abuse because of their race or gender."

I have listed Rudd's actual remarks below [56] and you can make your own mind up to the how bad Mrs. Rudd's slip was, especially in her position. But it highlights the issues the public face as to what language they are now allowed to use and how this changes over time. Mrs. Abbott is a black woman but what if she had been Chinese, Indian, North African or middle Eastern and she wanted to cover all those women as a group what adjective does she use? Would you as a reader know what word or words would be acceptable or your neighbour would they know?

The shame with this particular incident coming from the choice of language was that it was only Rudd's "coloured" comment and the storm that followed it which was reported, and the fact Mrs. Rudd was condemning online abuse of women and defending women and minorities like Diane Abbott. Even though politicians spend most of the time attacking their opposition, this was a missed opportunity to highlight the huge issue of horrendous abuse of women politicians online or as we saw with Anna Soubry outside the Houses Of

Parliament threatening behaviour in person.

Amber Rudd's actual remarks in full

Jeremy Vine - *"I've got a lot of tweets printed out - lucky me! - of things that have been sent to you. And the question is, given that all people in the public eye seem to get horrible tweets from strangers, whether it's worse if you're a woman?"*

Amber Rudd - *"It definitely is worse if you're a woman, and it's worst of all if you're a coloured woman. I know that Diane Abbott gets a huge amount of abuse, and I think that's something we need to continue to call out."*
"But there was a report done by Lord Bew into the amount of trolling there was, et cetera, and it definitely was the case that women get it more, black and black and minority ethnic women get it additionally. So, it is just a particularly nasty form of attack that focuses on gender and colour, and I think that we have to address it by calling it out, and we have to continually look at ways to stop it happening."

An interesting argument that was often put to me was when a Brexiteer found an immigrant that was against immigration so "they must be right then" and was used to say to me "see I told you so" and justify their position rather like the National Front groups that sometimes had a black member as "he is different and was alright, not like them" and basically like them enjoyed terrorising the Indian and Pakistani communities! But this is false as how is a migrant's opinion of future migrants more important than a non-immigrant and if anything could be perceived as hypocritical as they have enjoyed the same advantages that they now wish to prevent to others. But throughout history this has been the same as people have short memories and like the indigenous population feel threatened, often without reason of proof, to change and / or do not like the culture of those now coming into the country as it is not 'their' culture. This is a very complex area and cannot be covered in any detail but suffice to say that such an argument of the immigrant against immigration being a slam dunk reason for justifying immigration is bogus.

The whole immigration / racism discussion is a complex one as many people that are clearly racists have immigrant or foreign friends but as they know them and would find it difficult to discriminate against them as they may be, for example, a member of the same Tennis club they see them as different to those incoming or already immigrants they do not know. They somehow compartmentalise the two to enable them to justify their anti-immigrant / xenophobic position. And when pushed they avoid the discussion point or say it is only those coming in now that are important even though they have been

193

complaining about the number of immigrants for many years. There is a clear disconnect that does not make any logical sense, but it could be this is based around the fact that discrimination and racism are in reality illogical and dumb concepts supported by ignorance and an unwillingness to understand or get to know other cultures and views of the world. This is probably a whole section that a psychologist could investigate and expand on, but that is enough for this Brexit focused publication.

"We cannot stop EU immigrants coming in"

This was so often what we heard from many quarters at the EU referendum, but again this was based on falsehoods as Article 7 of the EU citizens' Rights Directive makes it perfectly possible for member states to deport citizens of other member states if they haven't found work after 3 Months or if they cannot demonstrate they have enough capital to sustain their lives here. So, once we know and can understand this the whole controlling of our borders argument, especially as we are not a part of Schengen, falls apart and was / is clearly bogus!

But why was this not made clear or exposed during the campaign to show the main argument of unlimited free movement we heard so often from Brexiteers could have been disproved and their immigration balloon popped there and then? The reason why Cameron and his team did not explain it as they would get accused of incompetence by never enacting it. But also, as anyone knows the facts of immigration and the horror stories invented about the sponging foreigners just coming for benefits was largely mythical and other such stories grossly exaggerated and out of touch Cameron probably thought people wouldn't believe the lies?

This is not a theoretical argument going on in Westminster as I have been told personally by people that Eastern Europeans come here to claim benefits and send the money home so they can build a house in say Bulgaria or Romania and then go home having fleeced our system. Yes I know it is bizarre but even once I ask them to do some simple arithmetic of how much someone receives in the UK on benefits and then subtract what they will need to pay for food, clothes and other necessities and inform us how much they will then actually have left by the end of the month. Once they have that 'disposable income' figure I ask them how many years it would take for them to buy a house in Romania or Bulgaria? Clearly, they have a look of embarrassment at first as reality kicks in and they feel embarrassed at the nonsense that they first espoused but then the defence

194

mechanism kicks in and they still claim I do not know what I am talking about and talking bullshit or I am not a patriot, etc. This desperation to demonise the foreigner runs deep in a lot of people and they have been fed with this 'crap' for so long that they struggle to look at things objectively or logically or admit their mistakes and they still continue with their fantasies. This is so frustrating, but pride will not let them move their entrenched position and these urban myths become fact in their heads and lead them to dramatic statements and thoughts and actions of hate.

The fact is the Freedom Of Movement directive allowed for the "old" countries (i.e. UK, Germany, France etc.) to restrict the rights of migrants from "New" countries for up to 7 years which varied from stopping migration completely or allow for selected categories of work on a work permit bases. But the UK chose not to use that power, not the EU!

The Freedom Of Movement directive is also clear when it comes to benefit fraud or welfare tourism for example that enabled the member state to adopt the necessary measures to refuse, terminate or withdraw any right the migrant had. The ECJ judgement (see below the so-called Dano case) on limitation of social benefits for EU citizens in another Member State made this clear. [56] Because the UK does not know or track accurately how many migrants are using the welfare system, it is unable to even try to exercise this power. Other EU states insist on migrants proving that they can support themselves and Belgium for example requires all migrants prove they have sufficient funds, health insurance and suitable housing.

So it is the lack of controls in the UK and not the abuse that is the root cause of the problem we face as we can legally request people to register so we can track all immigrants and ensure they are financially and medically self-supporting, prevent and / or prosecute benefit fraud and return home any migrants who are not economically active. So, we have those powers even whilst in the EU but choose not to implement them, and this applies to immigrants from outside the EU and is not an exclusively EU migrant problem.

The EU in its attempt to help David Cameron and the rise of the right wing of his party, UKIP and other Leave focused organisation gave further clarification and rights in February 2018: *'Whereas the free movement of workers under Article 45 TFEU entails the abolition of any discrimination based on nationality as regards employment, remuneration, and other conditions of work and employment, this right may be subject to limitations on grounds of public policy, public security or public health. In addition, if overriding reasons of public interest make it necessary, free movement of workers may be restricted by measure proportionate to the legitimate aim pursued'.*

Migrants already have limits to their access to Benefits based on EU LAW which is why the claims by many Brexiteers that a lot of immigrants were only here to take benefits is based on misinformation or stereotypes created by anti-immigrant individuals, groups and publications. Free movement has never been an unconditional right and an example case was shown in Germany in 2014 known as the Dano case [57]. A ruling in 2014 of the European Court of Justice confirmed the right of the German authorities to refuse unemployment benefits to a Romanian citizen who had no history of work in either country. But this was not a surprise as the ECJ was simply upholding the 2004 directive (known as the 'Citizens directive') that already limited migrants' access to benefits! Also, the Citizens directive states that those migrants that become an "unreasonable burden" (defined in the directive) on the welfare system of the host country can be denied benefits. Therefore, member states are allowed to expel those EU citizens who do not fulfil the conditions for legal residence.

As one that is always looking for facts I could not find much evidence of benefits tourism in the UK and nor could the European think tank CER (Centre for European Forum) or the European Commission, so it does not seem like there is this huge wave of eastern European immigrants flocking to the UK for benefits as some would have you think. We should learn the lesson of the Dano ruling and focus on the facts rather than blaming Brussels as there are clearly laws in place to prevent abuse of the benefits system. The UK could establish a compulsory register for EU citizens living in the UK like other EU member states to help ensure EU migrants fulfil the necessary conditions and could then be expelled if they do not. It is not a Brussels problem and leaving the EU will not address this issues many Brexiteers believe we have or at least play on the fears of others that immigration is out of control.

So why do Brexiteers call for us to fix something if it is not broken, unless they do not understand the factual situation but believe the empty slogans and headlines the Press or Farage etc. have fed them? Or is there another underlying reason that has nothing to do with 'controlling' immigration, but rather stopping it due to Xenophobia.

Still the basic maths says we have the highest employment and lowest unemployment for decades plus hundreds of thousands of vacancies to fill, so how can we have too many immigrants? If you want to cut them by say 1 Million who are you sending home? Doctors? Nurses? Social workers? Vets? Chemists?

Plus, why did David Cameron not make the above clearer to people as we are now probably leaving the EU based on lies, ignorance and the failures of our UK government? In this regard, he was inept.

I always like to ask those that say, indicate or post extreme comments the following Question: **Do you think you are a racist?**

Now as you can imagine nobody says "yes I am a racist" for obvious reasons. Have you ever heard someone say they are a racist? Even the BNP and such groups call themselves 'Patriots'. But this then leads one to a further consideration.

No, this is not a psychology book but poses the second question after the previous question *"why would people not offer people less fortunate (albeit of a different nation / race) the same opportunities as themselves when it is very unlikely it will affect them personally or those close to them?"*

I found many had racist tendencies without them even realising it but maybe they are sub-conscious feelings of discrimination that have always been there and are clearly stronger for those of 50+ in my experience. These feelings could have been built up over years when they have lived through the more overt racist years of the 70s etc. when the words such as wogs, jungle bunnies, Pakis, and niggers as well as other unacceptable language, were used frequently and openly in the era of the National Front. Have these people who do not think they are racists heard such terms and attitudes for so long that they and their friends and peer groups believe such discrimination is acceptable, but it was dormant and hidden from sight in this politically correct world? Only once the EU referendum campaign started and extreme right-wing groups on a social media etc. reared their ugly heads did these feelings come to the fore and in larger numbers they felt confident or comfortable to espouse such anti-immigrant / anti-foreigner sentiments especially when they got likes or shares on Facebook for such comments and thoughts that they had been told were unacceptable in the 21st Century.

This may need a much more in-depth analysis of the psyche of certain groups to get to the bottom of such a mentality, but it is definitely worth thinking

197

about especially if reading this you may think this is you! We should never be complacent with or underestimate the power of the emotive arguments of racists and right-wing groups. We only have to look back at Enoch Powell where he ignited the always present xenophobic elements in society and politics which has taken different forms at various times during our history. But Powell made unsubstantiated and bizarre claims in his 'Rivers of Blood' speech repeating stories that were allegedly going around his constituents about black children racially abusing white elderly women, and then claiming, 'the black man had the whip hand over the white man'.

Although one can claim Powell was ethically bankrupt and should not as a political leader peddle such myths, but a fair percentage of the public seemed to agree with him. This is dangerous stuff which is why some may see Farage as a harmless cheeky chappy troublemaker down the pub with a pint in his hand, he has a platform and he is using it. But if Farage is willing to stand in front of a poster of non-EU middle eastern immigrants implying they will all be coming to the UK if we do not leave the EU, just hours (yes hours!) before Jo Cox was so brutally assassinated by a racist right wing individual shouting 'Britain first', what other lengths would he go to and how would that play out in the wider public?

To put her death in context despite some MPs suffering some violence, Mrs. Cox was the first death in service since the Provisional IRA murdered conservative MP Ian Gow in 1990, and you may call it a coincidence that she was an outspoken campaigner against Brexit but this result of hate shows how important this act was and Jo Cox should never be forgotten when we are looking at such hate speech from UKIP and other nationalistic organisations and groups.

In typical Farage style he never apologised for the poser, so by default he thought it was acceptable, but he apologised for the 'timing' of the poster which is a bit of a cop out and showed a lack of empathy for the Cox family and friends, but for Farage it got the news cycle moving again and he made headlines and kept immigration in people's minds as that poster got more coverage than it would ever have done, on the back of the Jo Cox tragedy.

Even his comments after the death of Jo Cox told you a lot about the man when he said 'By Monday, the whole debate was on immigration again. Whatever miseries I had to withstand – and the Media was the most aggressive I've ever seen in my life, as if I'd actually done it (murdered Jo Cox) – but by the Monday morning, we realised the debate is back on migration.' So, it was all about Nigel, me me me, and seemed pleased we had quickly moved on from the Jo Cox assassination. Is this the real Nigel Farage a narcissistic animal with literally no empathy that knew if the referendum was lost he would fade into the background of political history having achieved very little despite 20+ years in politics?

Farage genuinely sounded like Enoch Powell when he stated in an interview 'It wasn't until we got past Grove Park (a South East London suburb) that I could actually hear English being audibly spoken in the carriage. Does that make me feel slightly awkward? Yes.... This country, in a short space of time, has frankly become unrecognisable.'

He has also stated on the record 'Any normal and fair-minded person would have a perfect right to be concerned if a Group of Romanian people suddenly moved in the next door.' When pushed on his choice of words in subsequent interviews he struggled to defend or explain them but was implying Romanians were undesirables and clearly less value than British people. Is that not discrimination? Imagine what he says behind closed doors! He was even criticised by the Sun stating 'This is racism, pure and simple. it IS racist to smear Romanians as being Romanian.' Now when the Sun is attacking you for racism, you have problems. Also, does that mean if I do not mind a Romanian person living next door to me I am not "normal" and "fair minded"?

Perhaps Farage is a bit more careful with his choice of language in public with the benefit of hindsight since Enoch Powell, but the message was very similar and many people would read into his sly comments as "they are taking over, and we need to do something about it!" This is totally unacceptable language and seems like an extension of Enoch Powell's philosophy, although one should highlight that with most of Farage's speeches, they always lack depth of argument and fact which appears with his moral inferiority he is carrying an intellectual inferiority complex as well. See how many of his interviews where he has to actually answer difficult questions, he goes off on tangents to avoid answering these and goes back to the diatribe he has learned parrot fashion down the pub.

Some are fanatics and genuinely believe the racist nonsense that they spout but some are charlatans and liars that use such fanatics and evoke people's darker side for their own gain and pleasure. Some may say they are worse. Which one is Farage? I will leave that up to your own discretion.

The advantage that Leavers had when it came to immigration is that it is easier to be passionate when you are against something and feel strongly in that belief and this became visible in the discussions or arguments we would all witness in the streets, pubs or on our television screens. Remainers in general calmly explained how at ease they were with immigration and the value they brought to the UK, whereas many Brexiteers saw them as a scourge on society and the cause of many of our economic ills and therefore were more forthright and "shouty" in the defence of their position and gave the impression they took the issue more seriously than the Remainers. It was interesting how the Remainers resembled quaint middle-class Waitrose shoppers and the Leavers more like football fans chanting for their beloved local team.

Clearly, I generalise but this difference became more visible as the lack of clarity and chaos in Parliament raised temperatures and both sides of the argument campaigned outside the Houses of Parliament. The disgraceful scenes of grown men campaigning in yellow vests and choosing to aggressively shout at and heckle female MP Anna Soubry including words such as "Traitor" and "Nazi" whilst pursuing her down the road just highlighted this difference in tactics or the way of protesting. Fortunately, one of the ringleaders James Goddard was arrested and released on bail in connection with the abuse of Mrs. Soubry. So, there is some justice in the world for such cowardly bully boys. Their families must be so proud!

One thing we should not forget, as many Brexiteers conveniently do, that the Freedom Of Movement works both ways and any limitations or changes in laws on the movement of people works against all the UK citizens wanting to live and work within the EU. This would also include Switzerland and not just the EU as in the event of a no-deal Brexit the current bilateral Swiss-EU agreement on the free movement of persons (AFMP) would cease to apply to our British nationals. So Brexiteers should not forget they are negatively impacting potentially millions of their fellow citizens that benefit from such freedoms, for the sake of an imaginary problem.

Australian points-based immigration system

If Leavers get their way and we are to dramatically reduce immigration, despite the positive impact they have on the UK and pay their taxes and therefore indirectly pay towards the state pensions of those that want them stopped or sent back, with an Australian points based system do we want the same issues faced by Australia who allow more immigrants per head than we in the UK have coming in on free movement any way. Australia has relatively high levels of migration not just compared to the UK but by international standards in general. In 2018 29% of the population of Australia were born abroad compared to around only 14% in the UK. Is that the system Brexiteers really want? Skilled migrants made up about 68% of the 2014-15 migration programme so 32% were 'non-skilled' which bursts the bubble of those that attempt to make out they only take skilled migrants.

Some aspects of the Australian immigration system are already quite similar to what happens in the UK, which is for non-EU citizens and admits more into the country than the number of EU citizens that come as a part of the free movement of labour from the EU! For example, employers can sponsor workers to fill specific vacancies in Australia (without passing a points test), much as they can in the UK, but they can change jobs once in the country, so the chosen system falls down.

It should not be forgotten that the Australian system is designed to increase immigration not to reduce it plus if the UK used such a system it would be a capping system (i.e. a set number of specific jobs) rather than companies working on a more qualitative system where they can get say the best Bricklayers rather than just a set number of bricklayers and then the drawbridge is pulled up for any more in that period. There is also no system in the Australian system to stop people changing jobs once they have been admitted to the country e.g. a Bricklayer friend of mine become a teacher, but what is Australia has enough teachers already? Surely he has now taken a teacher's job. Critics of their system point out that their system in no ways is an accurate indicator of their long-term contribution to the country as was the aim of the system. This is in contrast to the UK system where if the immigrant comes to the UK for a specific job they need permission to change that job. So, the UK system is stricter in that regard.

Their system also relies on the Government's perception of what's skills are valuable which can clash with employers opinions or even employers from different industries and market sectors who are actually the ones doing the recruiting. The other aspect of this is the dynamic nature of the requirements of economies with it being very difficult to keep up with changes and ensure the skills you are looking for are indeed the skills that will be needed in 12 months' time.

Separate to the immigration system above we have seen refugees in boats off the coast of the UK trying to enter the UK and once we leave the EU with no incentive for French police to stop them how will the UK Government handle that? Do we want offshore detention centres for asylum seekers / refugees and the reported human rights abuses that seem to accompany such centres or where are those awaiting Visas etc. going to go? At the moment the French police as a fellow EU partner stop them coming across the channel, what is their incentive once we leave the EU? As human rights lawyer Daniel Webb commented [The Australian] Government chose to build these camps on remote corners of remote islands in order to hide from view what they don't want the public to see – deliberate cruelty to innocent human beings. So, the Australian points system is not the perfect system some Brexiteers paint it to be as it is fraught with difficulty, is expensive to administer, and as we have seen in Australia has a human cost. Is this really where we want to be as a country addressing a problem that does not even exist. If you want to read more on this google, the writer (and former camp detainee) Behrouz Boochani who lifted the lid on these barbaric camps or Per Liljas who published an article entitled 'The human cost of Australia's offshore detention centres, where freedom does not equal opportunity.

Just for clarity this is the current UK Tier Points Based Visa System is a five-tier visa system consisting of the following:

- **Tier 1 Visa**: This visa category is for 'high-value migrants' from outside the EEA and covers entry of investors, and those very few people who come under the 'exceptional talent' visa.
- **Tier 2 Visa:** This category is for 'skilled workers' from outside the EEA with a job offer in the UK. It includes skilled workers who are transferred to the UK by an international company, skilled workers where there is a proven shortage in the UK, ministers of religion and sports people.
- **Tier 3 Visa**: This category was originally designed for low-skilled workers filling specific temporary labour shortages and **no longer exists.** The Government never allocated any visas under this scheme.
- **Tier 4 Visa**: This category is for students from outside the EEA who wish to study in the UK. Applicants must have a place at a registered UK educational establishment before they can apply.
- **Tier 5 Visa**: This category contains six sub-tiers of temporary worker including creative and sporting, charity, religious workers, and the youth mobility scheme which enables about 55,000 young people every year to work in the UK on working holidays.

Will those that voted Leave because of Immigration end up being more disappointed than anyone?

This was a question that I posed to many Leavers as those people's expectations were at one time so high and they were so jubilant once they had won the referendum with a Leave vote, as they expected immigration to be severely curtailed and they would hear less foreign languages or accents on their streets. But if we look at immigration into the UK in 2018 and 2019 it was higher from outside the EU which is the part that we CONTROL! So even with controls we still need and are welcoming non-EU immigrants in their hundreds of thousands from All Around the World. So even if we change the rules and immigrants need Visas or some kind of documentation they will still come because we have jobs that need fulfilling. Not long ago there was 97,000 vacancies in the NHS, and we do not have enough of the skills or willingness to do all those jobs, as well as many others in various companies around the UK big and small.

The fact that we have the lowest unemployment in the UK for decades indicates that immigrants are not taking all the jobs as scaremongers would have you believe as we clearly need them, otherwise unemployment would be very high. Also, if we were to leave the EU and stop Free Movement, we may have less EU immigrants, but they will be replaced by immigrants from Africa, India, Pakistan, East Asia, Vietnam, or West Indies etc. so we will have even more differing accents and cultures on our streets. Was that what those Leavers against immigration voted for? Certainly, a number I have spoken to or communicated with did not as they wanted things to return to better times (not sure that was exactly as before we joined the EU we were the sick man of Europe!) stating things like "It's not like it used to be round my way", or as Farage commented about not hearing an English voice on the train until he got passed Grove Park (a suburb of South London) before getting off at his leafy Kent dwelling. This real belief that immigration would go down dramatically because of Brexit is a dream sold to Leavers based on false information that they have been fed by the likes of Farage, Boris and Rees-Mogg, etc. The sad thing is that people still believe it will happen.

During the campaigns Michael Gove and Boris Johnson avoided attacking immigration for obvious reasons but neither actually promised to cut immigration, probably as they know we need the people and the skills and so in a rather disingenuous way they talked about control, points systems and taking back control of our borders etc. which just resembles the racist that knows he cannot be racist any more as it is not acceptable as it was in the 1950s-1970s and so resorts to saying "There are too many of them," "we are flooded", "we will sink soon etc. and then clarifies he has nothing against these people but we can't take any more etc." Reading between the lines has never been so important.

For example, if we could sign a free trade deal with India, they are not heavily interested in free trade with developed countries like ours but would rather build everything they can in India, and would rather demand a high level of Visas for Indians to come, live and work in the UK. So Brexiteers focused on Immigration may have less Polish immigrants but could have a lot more Indian immigrants – did they vote for that? Imagine if say 2 million immigrants just went home, and what the catastrophic implications of that would be including: 1. Who would do the jobs? 2. Companies would go bust because they either cannot get the skilled staff or have fewer people to buy their products and services as their domestic market had 2 million fewer consumers!

So sorry to disappoint those that voted Leave because of Immigration but reality is we have an ageing population we need to support, a negative birth rate, need the people to work in our companies and also to buy products and services to support other companies to help them survive and prosper, and pay taxes etc. and although you think you may have won you will in reality simply be potentially replacing one type of immigrant with another. So, it does bode the question, what have you won? We require immigration in this country to help drive our economy as we do not have enough of the skills or people to do specific jobs so whether this is controlled via Visas or not, they are already here many of whom will stay here, and more will come to fulfil our needs, and you have to adapt it.

The solution is to accept reality, embrace immigration, don't be afraid of it and just because they talk a different language or are a different colour or culture it does not negatively impact your life and if you engage with them it could be enlightening and enjoyable as you learn more about the rest of the world and its people. How good could that be? It's just a thought, but at the end of the day any immigration system comes down to supply and demand!

"We must control our borders (or "we have lost control of our borders")"

This was very much a core to the Leave campaign's strategy in combination with immigration of course with a simple message of the 'Threat of floods of immigrants from Turkey' etc. plus the take back control tag line which was originated by Dominic Cummings and pushed by the likes of Chris Grayling,

Michael Gove and Iain Duncan Smith as well as the other usual suspects. But we already had the control!

Yes, that is the irony of this 'argument' or claim as we had the laws to control this all the time and the very well-informed Michael Gove etc. must have known this, so were they conning the voters (again)? If Leave voters knew this, and it was in fact our own Government and not the EU that decided not to use the laws, they had at their disposal would they have voted differently?

In most other countries in the world they currently check your passport once you go through security whereas at our airports etc., we do not, and this goes back to 1998 when Tony Blair's government removed exit checks. It is true these exit checks were re-introduced in 2015 but they are nowhere near the usual airport enforced physical and visible checks carried out and the government does not release any statistics on these exit checks i.e. about immigrants leaving the country, so any records available are useless. Why do they not do that? That's simple as they know we have a lot of immigrants in this country, but we need them, yet they must play to their more right-wing voters and MPs and claim they are cracking down on immigration and genuinely aiming to get the annual levels of immigration down to the "tens of thousands". Basically, it is a clever game of 'smoke and mirrors', but allows the rumours to abound about immigrants arriving but not going home such as the often cited '100,000 international students overstay their visas as every year!'

The office for Statistics regulation even published a report stating we cannot rely on the immigration statistics for International students as they are based on inaccurate IPS (International Passenger Survey) numbers when, for example, surveys are not conducted after 10pm when many Internationals flights leave. This shows what a mess the immigration numbers are in the UK but are exacerbated by the fact that International students are treated as Immigrants whereas most other countries including US, Canada, and Australia classify International students as temporary residents when calculating their numbers. So, we are in fact targeting and scapegoating International students also in this war on immigration when we should be welcoming the money and expertise they bring. As mentioned elsewhere in this book immigration is based on many misplaced fears and misinformation when we have (at the time of writing) the lowest unemployment rate for decades at around 4.5% as well as the highest level of employment on record ever. If we did not have these high levels of employment how would we cover both the skilled and unskilled labour shortages? Yes, skilled also! There is this perception that immigrants take mostly the unskilled jobs of factory work, Labourers, and fruit pickers etc. but our NHS employs 26% of Doctors who are non-British and 39% of our Russell Group Universities academic staff are foreign, as well as many of our top executives and CEOs based in the UK.

Such anti-immigrant sentiments driven by a number of former home secretaries such as Teresa May and Amber Rudd are just as you can see economically illiterate but also, they could easily reintroduce exit checks very quickly, but they have not and show no inclination to do so perhaps cost is a factor. But that is OUR government and NOT the EU. Does the public understand that, or do they care?

The Times (Tommy Stubbington) reported on the issue of flower growers in the UK already (before Brexit!) having issues of employing pickers linked directly due to Brexit. Brexit uncertainty and the fall in the value of the pound have left growers struggling to recruit enough migrant workers for the harvest season, which runs from January to April. Lee Abbey of the National Farmers' federation said an increasing number of members said crops were going unharvested – a blow to the £45 million a year industry. "A large proportion of our crop has gone unpicked," said Jeremy Hosking, who grows 180 acres of daffodils on his farm near Truro, Cornwall. "The fields still look beautiful and yellow, but really it's not beautiful to us because it has cost us many tens of thousands of pounds." Hosking said that many of his workers, who typically come from Romania and Bulgaria, had chosen to work in other EU countries this year, where they feel more welcome. Locals did not want to work in the fields, he said. Without these people we haven't got a business. The costs through the year – land, rents, fertilisers – all go to getting the crop to a harvestable condition. If we can't harvest it all, that's the difference between a profit and a hulking big loss." [14]

There is a pilot scheme from the government to manage the number of such migrant workers coming into the country which is aimed at about 2500 but it currently only applies to edible crops such as apples and vegetables etc. and so would not help flower farmers for example which is just another area where the government does not understand the requirements of business and is more focused on keeping its pro Brexit wing of the party happy. It appears this scheme is not correctly directed but also the numbers are greatly underestimated and will not address the real needs of a number of farming sectors as well as not getting anywhere near the numbers required. When Leavers voted leave did many of them just see brown faces and East European accents as surely they did not realise they could be sending business like Mr. Hosking's above BUST?

The crazy thing is, and Michael Gove, Jacob Rees-Mogg and Nigel Farage all know that we could have indeed controlled our borders under EU law as under European Parliament and Council Directive 2004/38/EC (details can be found here: https://eur-lex.europa.eu/LexUriServ/LexUriServ.do?uri=OJ:L:2004:158:0077:0123:en:PDF)

This allows us to repatriate EU nationals after only 3 Months if they have not found a job or do not have the means to support themselves! So why is the government not implementing this directive? Simple, look at the unemployment AND the employment numbers and you will see we need such levels of immigration and they are paying taxes etc. to help run and fuel our economy. So to implement and enforce it would cost money and resource, to address a problem the government and civil service know does not exist. This is the reality not the scaremongering and anti-immigrant stories we hear from the likes of Farage that have made the anti-EU sentiment a life's work, despite 'working' for the European parliament (well when he turned up and not taking high paying speaking engagements in the USA!) and taking his salary, pension and expenses.

Even the Telegraph in its article entitled 20 reasons you should vote to leave the European Union on 2nd June 2016 Number 2 was "We could decide who comes into the UK" estimating that in 2015 257,000 EU nationals arrived in the UK but no estimation of how many went back or how many would be working in our NHS or carry out jobs where companies cannot find British people to do them! But also, not a word of mention about the above directive that could be used to do exactly what they were proposing. Lazy journalism or political expediency? I will leave that question for you to ponder.

You can now see we had the tools to control immigration easily if they did not have work or money so why did Cameron, Osbourne and his Remain campaign team not make the public very aware of this directive and controls we always had in our hands? Well, he couldn't really as on the one hand he is playing to the right with tough rhetoric on immigration but not using the tools he had at his fingertips for the reasons cited and no strong statistics to prove that many were in fact being repatriated so it would backfire on him and his governmental team, that was running the Remain campaign.

Many would have you believe the Australian points system is the best way to control our borders, but this is not as simple as it sounds as they have changed their system many times and still have an issue with immigration but also such a work permit based system for EU migrants would involve a lot of cost and paperwork and can be cumbersome. To be honest now that the UK is changing or has in fact changed already as regards its reduced welcoming environment for foreigners plus the 'hassle factor', why would they not now go to one of the other EU countries instead? Are we relying on their second language being English?

This artful deception (possibly the whole Brexit campaign) has been a 30 year game of smoke and mirrors where if the Leave voters knew and were given the truth about the EU and its rules as well as what we as a country could do they would quickly realise they had been conned and it had been the greatest sham carried out on the voters for as long as anyone can remember.

Race relations in the UK have actually been very good and the last race riot took place in Notting Hill in 1958 with other riots such as Brixton in 1981 and Broadwater Farm in 1985, or Tottenham in 2011 were more about certain groups of the black community being unfairly treated and targeted by the police. But these were definitely not anti-immigrant, and large cities have worked very well with the positive waves of immigration since the 1950s and it was interesting in the Referendum that the areas that had the most immigration such as London voted Remain and those that had seen every little immigration voted Leave. Some argued that it was all the immigrants that voted to stay of course but remember we are talking about membership of the EU so EU immigrants should be the focus and a lot of them were not British citizens so could not vote in the referendum anyway, just another fallacy that was spread on social Media with no foundation which was becoming a regular theme.

"Yes, but what about the other immigrants?" they say, to which the reply "you mean the black Windrush generations?" Or the Indian / Pakistani immigrants of the 60s / 70s many of whom that started business and employed people and have paid a lot of taxes. Once you get passed the blank faces, you realise that it was not just about the EU and EU immigration but immigration in general. Many people still cannot get it around their heads that these people that are of a different colour or speak with strong accents are still British subjects and have been for many years, so deep does this anti-foreigner feeling go. And for some this will never go. One can only hope with the younger generations see more integration as a good and normal thing and question why their parents try to demonise those that are just different.

As I highlighted to some friends and then on Facebook when one comment was about watering down the British blood and becoming a mongrel

208

race or words to that effect, I replied something to the effect of "what you mean our purified Roman, Viking, Germanic, Norman, Jute and Frisian bloodlines?" after all how far do these people think you have to go back to be deemed 'pure' British? Sometimes ignorance IS bliss, but it is also very dangerous in the wrong hands as some extreme groups like the EDL exhibit.

We must accept that the constant anti-immigrant and EU rhetoric from the British press makes it very easy for people to blame immigrants for unemployment, stagnant wages and poverty (some extremists would even say disease!) when such crises as the economic crash of 2017 hit the UK. Nothing to do with immigration but you can see that people have been set up with a scapegoat gift wrapped over many years.

It was not just the anti-Immigrant sentiment of the articles and using immigration as the scapegoat for most of the UK's ills it was also the number of articles that felt like a tsunami of such anti-immigrant articles and interviews etc. that swamped the UK for months, and before that years. A report completed by Kings college London in 2017 cited 4,383 online articles about immigration in the EU referendum but only 938 for Health or 433 on Crime / Justice [11]. It should also be noted this was for ONLY the 10 days leading up to the vote – 4383 articles about immigration in 10 days, and people try to make out the referendum was not about immigration, which is disingenuous at best.

"Are immigrants really the greatest threat to jobs in the UK?"

The jobs that many immigrants are filling are those where the UK does not have enough of the skills such as nurses, Vets, Doctors, and social workers as well as building trades etc. but also those unskilled jobs such as fruit picking, warehouse work, labouring etc. that not enough British people want to. So, although immigrants are an easy scapegoat, as they have been on many infamous occasions in history, with the lowest unemployment rate for decades and the most people in work for decades the accusation that we have too many immigrants does not add up, but for Brexiteers it was a real focus in the referendum campaign.

Adam Smith in his famous economics book 'Wealth Of Nations' first published in 1776 stated the following: *"The annual produce of the land and labour of any nation can be increased in its value by no other means, but by increasing either the number of its productive labourers, or the productive powers of those labourers, who had before been employed."*

This had been true for many years but technological advances and the rapid growth in Artificial Intelligence has changed the rules and highlighted the UK's poor productivity levels compared to many other economies.

The real elephant in the room is technological innovation and automation that will take many more jobs than any immigrants, but why are the public not talking about that? Is it because they are unaware of this as it slowly creeps into our consciousness with kiosks and machines replacing for example ticket office staff at the train station, Till workers at supermarkets or checking in staff at the airports etc.? Or is it that nobody like Nigel Farage with a megaphone is claiming immigration and free movement is taking your jobs and the jobs of your children allowing people to shout, scream and abuse something tangible like immigrants, rather than abusing a ticket machine at the train station? Why no screams against A.I. (Artificial Intelligence)?

The UK has some of the worst Productivity rates in the modern world due largely to lack of investment in facilities, skills and a short-termism attitude towards our industries and growth (unlike Germany that invests for the long term for example) and these structural weaknesses have been filled by immigration, but it is not the immigrants' fault. Any economic growth has failed to increase average prosperity creating a feeling of many being left behind who when they see a growth in immigration believed, mistakenly, that is the reason. It is not, but it is easy to blame immigrants as many have throughout history including Europe of the 1930s.

A.I. aside during the years of increased immigration from eastern Europe more jobs have in fact been created with record migration coinciding with falling unemployment, so there is no evidence that immigrants are taking jobs from the British. The so-called fourth industrial revolutions is already transforming the workplace and people's lives and new technology could bring amazing benefits, but it may create winner and losers through its disruption and governments need to be aware of that and have a suitable industrial policy in place.

Also, we have a rapidly ageing population (or people coming up to retirement age) and if we do not have a young source of working age individuals, we could very well be in real trouble come the next decade.

Have the lies about race ceased since the referendum?

Certainly, it became clear that after the Leave campaign vote had won the referendum that many people played down the immigration issue trying then to talk about Independence and sovereignty etc. and from personal experience I know many Leavers that never mentioned such subjects but often used alternative 'code' for immigration such as "It isn't like it used to be round my way" or "Too many bloody cars on the road these days" etc. Although usually not believable and appeared dishonest and somewhat cowardly it was more politically correct and avoided them potentially being referred to a racist or having prejudices, etc.

But Nigel Farage despite having won the referendum could not help himself often still using inflammatory language as well as lies. He told a US audience at Lock Haven University in Pennsylvania, that entire streets in Oldham are split along racial lines saying whites lived on one side of the road and blacks on the other, with no assimilation between the two. In the same speech he also called Teresa May "the most useless and dishonest prime minister I have seen in my lifetime" which was ironic based on his earlier lies. Obviously, this street does not exist apart from in his discriminatory imagination, because if it was he would march his army of Press that follow him around and show them.

I actually had someone send me an image with a sticker on a lamppost stating "you are now entering a Sharia Law zone" and people believed it and then they share it and send it to people like me as "Proof" we have sharia Law no-go areas in the country! Yes "proof" they think. So, if I put a sticker on my local lamppost stating "you are entering the Democratic Kingdom of Christopher Bartram VIII" would they believe it? Of course, not but when it comes to Sharia, they have read right-wing Newspapers and Facebook groups and so have a built-in prejudice and WANT to believe such posts and reports. The problem is and was people would jump from there to Eastern European immigrants and put them all in one 'bucket' and almost disable their critical faculties for some form of normal proof and the next thing is they are using Sharia Law as a reason to leave the EU! But the point here is when does ignorance and naivety become stupidity to then someone becoming part of the problem of lies by sharing and spreading such nonsense that some other people will believe?

There is an excellent article / report by Dan Kaszeta called "Debunking Maps of Alleged Islamic No Go Zones in London" (www.bellingcat.com) I would refer you to as it addresses very well the above nonsense spread by some Brexiteers to create further fear and division in our society.

So many people do bring up anecdotal arguments they genuinely believe in although it has not happened to them personally, and it always seems to be a "friend of mine" or "my brother's cousin's husband" etc. which gives them safety as they basically do not have to prove these things happened just that they had been told (even if they had in fact not been told) so they can then espouse it as the gospel truth and maybe embellish it also for effect. But whenever I tried to get to the actual exact negative personal experiences with immigrants, they were almost non-existent, or I would get thrown back "yes our local shop got robbed by 2 black kids!" as if that is proof of the immigration swamping we are told about. I then politely ask how they actually knew they were immigrants they look blank as they had obviously just put every immigrant, asylum seeker, refugee and black / brown person into their very own "unwanted" bucket. That is not proof, it is prejudice right there in the flesh!

The UK is a relatively low immigration region compared to Central Europe where a German meets a Dutch person and they live together one is an immigrant, the same when French, Belgium, Danish, Italian, Austrians meet and strike up a relationship, one becomes an immigrant and there is a lot of this in central Europe as people are people and not looked at so intensely and labelled as they seem to from certain quarters in the UK.

Regardless of the fact it is based on falsifications which do not seem to bother Mr. Farage in any way whatsoever, it is obviously attempting to be emotive and paint a horrendous picture to create some kind of uprising or revolution to benefit Mr. Farage and not many other people. Oswald Mosley used similar rhetoric in the 1930s. But it gives the impression that it is the immigrants or those of race that are not assimilating when we know that many Brits including those living on the Costa Del Sol do not assimilate or make any effort to learn the language apart from "2 cervezas por favor"! Some do note even do that due to numerous British pubs and Bowls clubs out there they create a 'Brits abroad' mentality and enclave. But does Mr. Farage clarify or delve into the issues or Solutions behind the issue? No of course not, he has an issue for everything but a Solution for nothing and just to stirs up hatred and will do almost anything to get to speak into a microphone or get himself on the TV again. It certainly seems like an Ego show as it lacks any substance, sensible logical thought or detailed plan, which he should have after having been in politics for 20 years.

It should be made clear that despite the fear and even hate of immigrants in many quarters experts believe that if immigration is significantly limited into the UK, it will have negative impacts on the UK economy estimated by the OBR (Office of Budget Responsibility) at around £6 Billion a year by say 2020-21 depending on any action taken. The IMF has argued that the hit could be worse still because of the impact on productivity growth. [51] Having spoken to many normal people that voted leave and remain few of them understood or appreciated the role of immigrants to our economy and had mainly read or seen the negative stories from the Media leading them to have a biased view of immigration in the UK.

One question as regards immigration is that after all the turmoil and hate will people still want to come to the UK, as opposed to looking for other more welcoming countries to settle? Recent immigration figures suggest a fall in numbers already which combined with a devalued pound and uncertainty about the future of migrants in the UK could mean it is unattractive to potential workers. Brexiteers may cheer and think 'job done' but who will do all those jobs we have vacancies for in the UK, especially where we lack the skills?

The question we should pose is "was it immigration itself that drove the leave victory or the <u>fear of</u> immigration? The paradox we witnessed was those that have experienced the highest levels of migration worry about it least which we can see with the highest levels of Remain voters being in the areas of the highest net migration.

The husband of murdered MP Jo Cox, Brendan Cox, highlighted that immigration was too important to leave it to the populist right and their obsession with numbers. He stated, "The UK government policy is a masterclass in how to get the crisis wrong; set an unrealistic target, miss it, report on it quarterly and in doing so show a complete lack of control heightening concern and fanning the flames of resentment."

Some believe the only sure way to cut immigration levels [when we need the migration and have many more vacancies to fill] is to crash the economy and maybe the Brexiteers are so clever and far-sighted and that is what they wanted to do all the same and we never realised?! Let us see if Project Fear becomes Project Reality or Project Fact.

As Philosopher Hasko Von Kriegstein made the argument, it is logically impossible for an immigrant to Britain to not integrate. The immigrant can adopt British Values and attitudes therefore the immigrant would be perfectly British. Or the immigrant can reject British values and attitudes but since moving to another country and then spurning that country's traditions, values, language and attitudes is a quintessentially British behaviour, the immigrant is again perfectly British! How true, albeit quite a sad indictment on our British and colonial past!

Chapter 15

An Age of Ignorance, Simplicity & 'Alternative Facts'?

No more experts please!

Michael Gove became well known, some may say infamous, for his comment 'people in this country have had enough of experts' which is concerning as it had echoes of the middle ages when religious leaders held more sway than experts and decided they were the experts in morality and life in general so decided to burn so-called witches, burned books they did not agree with, or carried out all sorts of wicked acts despite having no expertise in anything apart from a fictional religious book. Now I am not saying Michael Gove or Boris Johnson would partake in such atrocities but to disregard experts as they did not meet their own entrenched position was very unfortunate and sent the wrong message to voters (probably intended) but also wider society as a whole. Would they have been OK if the car they drove in had not been developed and manufactured by experts, or the aeroplanes they flew in? I fear not.

As David Cameron wrote in his memoir 'For the record' it was an appalling thing to say, where we were in an age when feelings were prioritised over facts....and Michael had become an ambassador for the post truth age.

This development of the dismissive attitude towards experts made them look like fact light journalists (which they both were / are) rather than serious fact-based politicians as they should be. Now you may call people naïve for thinking that as both these men were in a desperate battle to win a referendum and would say and do almost anything to get the result, they wanted but surely if our major politicians and cabinet ministers act in such a way, what hope is there for democracy in general? When we see such actions and disregard for facts and truth, it does resemble a posh boys' debating society where win or lose, they will be together having a bottle of Bollinger in their studies afterwards. How do these people no matter how intelligent (or should I say academic), think they are improving the lives of people on minimum wage or having to hold down 3 jobs to keep their head above water? The disconnect became frightening more so in this referendum than in any election before it.

But Nigel Farage has been just as bad making comments such as 'I think doctors have got it wrong on smoking.' On the surface you would think this is just plain dumb but Farage is far from dumb, rather he is a populist willing to say anything to get a small group cheering him or the press / media placing another microphone or camera in front of his face so he can spout more populist rants with little regard for truth, fact or accuracy. Farage has become a Media Hoare and with the growth of digital Media he has found another audience that may not have listened to the mainstream media of the BBC but are now members of various weird and wonderful Facebook groups which he can exploit.

The willingness to dismiss experts and believe people with no expertise in the subjects they speak of as it fits a certain perspective or view of the world should concern us all if critical decisions are to be made based on facts and not on emotion.

It always resembled the question of how would you buy your house?

■ First you would normally go to an estate agent who is an expert in their field. May be now you may go to a purely online company to promote your property but that is still and expert in online property promotion with an expert algorithm behind it produced by an expert programmer, etc! You would not allow David Davis to promote your house!

■ You would then have an expert surveyor survey the house for any issues. You would not allow Boris Johnson to survey your house!

■   Then you would employ an expert solicitor to cover all the legal paperwork and issues. You would not allow Nigel Farage to do your legal paperwork!

■   Once completed you would contract an expert removal company to move all your belongings from your current abode to your new house. You would not allow Jacob Rees-Mogg to move your goods in his pin stripe suit!

The point here, albeit laboured, is clear experts have their place and always will and we are in a dangerous place when we dismiss experts as they do not meet our own entrenched positions. But it bodes the question to many people - Would you have bought a house in the same way as you voted for Brexit?

Would Michael Gove with his dismissive attitude towards experts, allow a stranger to operate on him rather than an expert physician? Yes, it is an exaggerated example, but Michael Gove was telling voters to ignore experts and believe him and other voters that had their own alternative facts and truths! He was previously, and is again at the time of writing, a government minister and such an attitude towards experts is utterly unacceptable, but during the Brexit debate much was unacceptable, but was accepted by many.

Some voters clearly demonstrated the willingness to take a great uncalculated risk of a no-deal Brexit which they would never do in their own personal lives, that would directly affect them. Many saw no risk and much upside such as fewer foreigners on our shores etc., but would they be disappointed in the long run?

David Cameron made it clear of his position when he tweeted, after Vote Leave tried to silence Mark Carney and the Bank Of England from commenting on the risks of Brexit to the UK economy, 'It's deeply concerning that the Leave campaign is criticising the independent Bank Of England. We should listen to experts when they warn us of the dangers to our economy of leaving the European Union'.

I find this development against experts extremely concerning because as this anti-expert rhetoric from Michael Gove and Nigel Farage et al. has been picked up by the public which effectively 'dumbs down' and polarises discussion and certain unqualified individuals are more influential than those that really know what they are talking about. We have seen this with Nadine Dorries not understanding the Single Market or customs union but imploring people to vote to Leave it which is bizarre and is an example of blind dogma, i.e. I want out of something I do not understand! As I have said it is reminiscent of the middle ages where we were listening to religious zealots and were burning and drowning witches based on no facts or logic just a crazy belief in something non-experts had told them! Sound familiar? This may seem amusing and justified to some, but it is in fact very dangerous as we now have politicians like Nigel Farage espousing all sorts of thoughts and positions as if they are factual and true, when they are not, without any reference to the implications or downsides which can be inflammatory and lead to anger in the country. But due to his simplistic inflammatory language he listens to more than an actual expert on say immigration who explains things using facts and nuance etc. which may be very complex to understand and that cannot be right. I am not naïve to accept that people like Farage get a lot of coverage as he is good for a sound bite and will say whatever he likes, especially as he is accountable to nobody but since the EU Referendum campaigns it has gone too far, and experts are almost ignored.

Forecasting by experts is clearly not a science and can be wrong but we have to differentiate between short term forecasting when trying to predict short-term behaviour with millions of individuals interacting in a complex system, and long-term Brexit forecasting that has a far more reliable body of economic thought grounded in robust Methodologies. From this, two broad conclusion emerge. First, the longer-term forecasts are more likely to be accurate than their short-term brethren. Second, there is absolutely no logical reason to assume that, just because the latter have been proven inaccurate, the former will too. [48]

It is clearly impossible to be exact impacts of Brexit without even 3 years later knowing what the exact form Brexit will take and even leaving with no deal the impacts could be wide and revealing in the decade post Brexit. But with the above we should still take the Treasury's original long-term forecasts seriously. It estimated in 2018 that British GDP would be 3.4-4% lower in 2031 than it would have been had we remained in the EU with a type of 'Norway option'. The figures for a bilateral trade agreement ('Canada style' option) and reliance on WTO terms were 4.6-7.8% and 5.4-9.5%, respectively. [49] So, we can see the greater the risks the further away from the EU we move, which has logic to it even as a layman when we see how the single market and customs union gives the UK many advantages and benefits to its economy as well as its citizens.

218

More recent figures envisage trade with the EU falling by some 40%, in the event that the UK leaves the single market and customs union which would imply that the UK GDP would be smaller by 3% every year (or 2.4% net of savings from the cancellation of membership payments to the EU). In addition, foreign investment could decline by around 20%. By contrast the gains possible from signing trade deals with other states look tenuous, with a free trade deal with the USA would lead to an increase in the region of 0.3% of GDP. [50] Plus, the issues and complications that come with such a deal that are covered elsewhere in this book. GDP had been growing between 2.0 and 2.9% between 2013 and 2016 but then post EU referendum result it fell to 1.8% and then in 2018 it fell to 1.4% and had shrunk to 0.5% and 0.2% in Quarters 1 and 2 2019. Now clearly those reductions are not just because of Brexit but it has had a major affected as businesses have no clarity going forward and the risks of a no-deal Brexit and its impacts.

Despite the difficulties of such projections experts are saying that there is a strong possibility that Brexit will (and is beginning to already) severely and negatively impact the UK economy which would have many effects including impose significant constraints on the government as it will have less money for services, etc. The treasury estimated that the Canada option would generate receipts of £36 billion lower than in the case of EU membership by 2031, which is more than a third of the NHS budget and the equivalent of around 8p on the basic rate of income tax. This is money that could be spent on better supporting your family via the NHS or social services for your elderly parent. How much more in income tax would you be willing to pay for Brexit? Again, it has to be put in context – for what benefits?

It seems that the way Leavers discount experts is by saying they were wrong before about something such as the Euro etc. which means that they are basically saying we will only listen to experts who are perfect. This is obviously impossible as a lot of experts are being asked about the future and trying to forecast a few or many years ahead which is fraught with danger. This is why they discount most of the Economists that forecast a poorer country after Brexit despite the probability but then will gladly agree with the Economist Patrick Minford as one of the few Economists who thinks Brexit is a good thing as 'their expert'. But on the other hand they conveniently ignore that Mr. Minford claimed that Brexit would lead to running down the car industry "in the same way we ran down the coal and steel industries", In 2012, he told MPs on Westminster's Foreign Affairs committee that car manufacturers in the UK would have to be wound down if the UK left the EU. Patrick Minford and his "Economists for Free

Trade" organisation produced an unusual report which indicated it wanted to unilaterally abolish all our trade tariffs with the rest of the world after Brexit. That would decimate our farming and manufacturing industries, forced to suddenly compete with global giants, but Minford appeared relaxed about this. During the referendum he wrote that Brexit should "eliminate manufacturing" which must be very concerning for all those that voted Leave and are employed in a manufacturing company or capacity. Mr. Minford gets quoted more than his work justifies but that is because most economists are on the other side of the argument from him and disagree with his findings, so the Media do not have much choice but to use him for such quotes or debate.

With the above we can see the hypocrisy of the Leave position against experts but selectively choose their own experts that fit their already entrenched positions but conveniently ignore or hide some more concerning and extreme positions as highlighted above.

Give them simplicity

This was the logic of the Leave campaign which was focus on 2 key messages and did not get into too much detail as this was never thought through, which was highlighted by the fact that 3 years after the Referendum there was still no plan for Brexit from the Brexiteers or the ERG, etc. But we must admit that it was a very effective albeit simplistic message.

As we know simple is not always better as the negotiations with the EU and the complex issues that need to be addressed have shown but the slogans and arguments that won the Referendum were indeed very simple and were successful. Telling people, the 'Turks are coming', we will 'take back control' and 'fewer foreigners = more jobs for their British kids' etc. worked, but therein we find the problem as it was never ever going to be that simple.

Why was it, and still seems to be, that the Leave arguments and debating their points always seem to have scapegoats or people to blame? There never seemed to be a positive message or vision without it attacking or blaming various people or organisations. I looked back at the Leave arguments / focus and at various times and to varying degrees they accused / blamed or made responsible the following:

Teresa May, The European Council, Remainers, Remain MPs, The

Government, Michel Barnier, The European Parliament, Donald Tusk, immigrants, asylum seekers, Jean Claude Juncker, The BBC, Left wing Press, Specific British Civil Servants and the civil service in general, Jeremy Corbyn, Labour remain MPs, MPs that opposed Teresa May's Brexit deal, The EU as a whole, The Media in General, Economists, Experts (as highlighted by Michael Gove), the Bank Of England and Mark Carney etc. etc.

The blame game was everywhere especially as things were not going the Brexiteers way (largely due to the complexity of reality) and an example was the Twitter page of Lord Digby Jones, the Brexiteer businessman who spent a lot of time accusing Remainers of *"Undermining Britain from within" and "Doing Barnier's work for him....... we'll end up with a lousy deal and it will be Remainers who are to blame."* This is the same Digby Jones that said, "not a single job will be lost because of Brexit". Two years after that statement he waffled around the semantics of difference between "Brexit" and "uncertainty around Brexit" but everyone listening to him knew it was nonsense with thousands of jobs having been lost or repatriated to the EU with more clearly affected. The only question some were not clear about was how did this man ever become the CBI boss? What it exposed again is when a Brexiteer takes an entrenched position and reality smacks them straight in the face they double down thinking if they admit they were wrong with that aspect of their belief it may bring the rest of the Dogma come tumbling down like a house of cards.

As things became entrenched and reality was biting, Brexiteers had no choice but to accept it was much more difficult than they expected or had told people. It appeared there was in some circles almost a calculated campaign to almost move blame for any issues or lack of progress to Remainers. On the surface it was a clever tactic by claiming Remainers were "Talking Britain Down" just because they had a different view of the UK's future. Even Boris Johnson in the conservative leadership debates of July 2019 implied all we needed was a lot of positive thinking and positivity to make the country successful. Obviously no detail! This accusation of negativity was then pushed further onto Remainers not being patriots, or to the extreme level where MP Anna Soubry is being shouted at and being called Traitor by a group of bully boys outside the Houses of Parliament. This is an example of how politicians, celebrities and political figures like Nigel Farage need to be very careful with their language and playing the blame game as it can be very inflammatory and can lead to abuse and violence. These are accusations that Remainers must challenge as like other myths such as £350 million per week to the EU" or "5 million Turks coming to the UK" etc. if they are not and not nipped in the bud, they can take on a life of their own. We are seeing already that as Brexit is failing (in the eyes of Brexiteers of course) the knives (not literally) are out for Remainers as another suitable scapegoat for perceived failure. One can already see it that if Brexit fails, it will not be the Brexiteers fault or their lack of reality and understanding of the complexity of the world. It will be many people and organisations including the Remainers. In a worst-case scenario and say Leavers voted for a disaster scenario, say a disaster that will bring misery to themselves and their families, it won't be their fault but there will be a huge list (see above) or scapegoats and people to blame for the mess.

Remainers should be quite clear in their message to Leavers such as 'Don't blame me because YOU voted Leave.'

Brexit debate is not easy

How do we debate or argue with often intelligent individuals with legitimate concerns but who's arguments are based on incorrect information and nonsense in a reasonable and empathetic manner? John Major, always the pragmatist made it quite clear when talking about the EU and having to deal with his Eurosceptic backbenchers when he said there were basically only three options ' To leave is unthinkable; to stand aside and let ourselves be dragged along by others, which is untenable, or to be at the very heart of the community and help frame the decisions – which is our policy.'

But it has always been a battle with the anti-EU protagonists who seemed to not understand the concept of compromise and still don't or won't. During the Maastricht conference in December 1991 Major achieved several compromises which gave us one of the best deals of any member state including opt-out from the Social Chapter, the right of Parliament to decide whether the UK would enter the Single Currency, intergovernmental rather than supranational cooperation as the basis for deciding domestic defence and foreign policy, and retention of some control of security forces across Europe. This at the time went down very well within the Conservative party with only 7 of the expected 40-50 dissenters failing to vote for the deal. Even Boris Johnson commented at the time it is 'a copybook triumph for Mr. Major'. Funny how the smell of power can change people's positions!

Brexit debate has become so factious and entrenched that logic, facts and sensible observable reality is not even considered with the most bizarre ways of finding a way of claiming Brexit is still a good idea. There clearly are challenges in the UK as there are in all economies but to blame the EU and immigrants substantially for these perceived issues without any logic or facts is concerning as sensible debate becomes non-existent and people simply try to shout people down when attempting to address the real issues with real facts. Just look at the Brexiteer arguments cited in this book to see how ludicrous things can become when emotion overtakes brainpower.

Chapter 16
Digital & Social Media

Digital and Social Media were huge

Vote Leave and especially Dominic Cummings their enigmatic but effective campaign Director realised very quickly the power of Social Media. He claimed that Leave spent 98% of its money on Digital Media, especially Facebook utilising algorithms that allowed them to tweak messages towards individuals, and the specific concerns voters had. Remain on the other hand preferred campaign posters but even when they did utilise Social Media it was not very well targeted, thought through or effective.

Leave.EU claimed it reached 15 million voters in some weeks of the campaign, with one video viewed an amazing 9.3 million times of Facebook! Research shows, albeit not conclusively, that the Leave.EU social media campaigns and Nigel Farage's rallies achieved in getting out a larger proposition of blue-collar voters. Perhaps because it was well targeted but also because the messages were simple and clear, and they hammered home those messages even if they were not true. They were not talking about GDP and possible Quantitative Easing, etc.

What became clear in the referendum campaign, although whilst researching it was clear it had happened in the USA 2015 presidential election already, that the use of technology and social media data had gone to a whole new level of sophistication. Things such as big data mining, data analytics and micro-targeting had become an art form allowing campaigns to better identify their supporters and then mobilise them, even if that was for them to simply share an advert or article to start to spin that 'digital spiders web'.

The difference in the 2016 Referendum campaign was that Vote Leave appreciated this much more and implemented its strategy much more affectively. The Leave campaign even developed an interactive Smart phone App which was downloaded by tens of thousands of people which encouraged subscribers to sign up their friends and family and asking permission for Vote Leave to be able to access their smart phone contacts. This app provided further means of harvesting valuable data about potential Brexit supporters and disseminating key campaign messages...... In terms of political communication, both Leave and remain campaigns were fairly evenly matched – deploying similar digital approaches. The critical difference, however, was that the Leave campaign was much more successful at targeting than the Remain campaign. Although the result was close, that is the main reason why the Leave campaign was victorious. [20]

But rather like the tabloid press Leave.EU were pulling no punches in their headlines even if they were not factual and prayed on people's fears and were overtly inflammatory including the following:

■   'Are you concerned about the amount of crime being committed in the UK by foreign criminals?'..... Isn't it time to take control? (Facebook page)

■   Are you worried about the overcrowding of the UK and the burden on the NHS?' (Facebook page video)

■   'Islamic extremism is a real threat to our way of life. Act now before we see an Orlando-style atrocity here' (Tweet).

You can see how direct and inflammatory the messages are, written in a way that makes them sound as if they are based on facts, but also divert away from the EU arguments yet still fanning the flames of anti-foreigner and Islamophobic sentiment, which is just what they wanted to achieve. Even if you think it is disgusting, from a propaganda point of view it is clever and effective and was rarely effectively countered by the Remainers. Guess who won!

Right-wing social Media Groups on Facebook, etc.

There are also right-wing nationalist individuals and 'organisations on other Social Media platforms such as Twitter but it has been with Facebook due to its greater flexibility with images and especially videos, headlines and more words where these groups have been more effective, prevalent and have found many followers. Also, it allowed fanatics to rant at will whereas with Twitter they would have to think how they best got that across in only 160 characters. The general danger and lack of controls of Social Media in general and Facebook specifically is for another time, particularly when an Australian white supremacist terrorist ran amok at 2 mosques in New Zealand shooting anyone that moved whilst live streaming it on Facebook! 50+ people lost their lives, but these videos were then shared around the world! That cannot be right, but people now have the ultimate mask of anonymity and abuse it to its extreme.

But here I want to mention the number of these right wing, so called patriotic, Nationalist groups that can almost create and share posts containing whatever they want no matter how untruthful or inflammatory they are, which is concerning and allows such hatred to be circulated. This was clear during the referendum campaign and after the result as many anti-immigrant posts appeared regularly, or anti-EU posts comparing it to the Nazis or irrational links to the second World war, as well as many posts that were totally false. But people believed many of them. The nature of social media makes it worse than other forms of communication as posts are often shared many times without the individuals even reading the post but sharing ONLY on the basis of the dramatic headline! So, we can now see how quickly incorrect or deliberately false information can spread like a wildfire demonstrating that it does not only have to be the Press publishing false information, but The 2 together can achieve exponential results. This is where the negative 'viral' effects can begin. I have questioned many people about this on Facebook, but they don't care. It's like a dumb obsession to share an inflammatory or clearly untrue headline.

Controversially Leave.EU sought out overt racists to hit and energise with their messages (maybe this is what Farage and Banks meant with pushing the boundaries?). How do we know this? Tom Edwards of the Stronger In campaign

226

set up fake profiles for far-right extremists and found the Leave.EU adverts had been deliberately sent to members of the BNP and Britain First! When the story appeared, Leave.EU stopped it but it shows what directions campaigning and messaging were going and what sort of messages were being sent that would engage these extremists. Farage was happy as he said, 'I think we did very well on social media, the reach we were getting was absolutely huge'. Who they reached appeared secondary (or maybe not behind closed doors)? Banks confirmed 'even though we were not the designated campaign we had twice as much social reach as The 2 official campaigns combined. Our best did 8 million views.' If this is in fact true, this is a powerful campaign and felt like the Stronger In remain campaign was fighting against not one but two powerful foes and was struggling, certainly in the social media arena, to compete.

Andy Wigmore Leave.EUs spokesman, and Arron Banks confident knew what they wanted and where to go when he made clear 'Most of the people polled by big polling companies are up to speed with the news and current affairs. We are going after the type of people that watch Breakfast TV, Jeremy Kyle and a bit if Trisha. When you put anything out about economics, we would get three of four thousand likes on a tile. If you put out something emotive you would get something like four of five hundred thousand likes, and in some cases two of three million. So that's the kind of audience we knew early on that we needed to approach.' Call it cynical, call it 'dumbing down' by sending targeted simple inflammatory messages, but they knew their target market and they hit it hard. Emotion was more powerful than logic or even facts in this case and I saw this personally with my friends, contacts or social media connections where they would believe posts / articles online just from the headline and would not even read the article of body of the text as the title was enough for them to either convince them, change their mind or reinforce what they thought they knew in the first place. Watching this was very frustrating, but it hardened their opinions and stance and they were not going to change and whenever a factual logical argument was put to them, it would be something like 'there goes Chris with his fake news or Remainer Bullshit' but when challenged which bit was fake or Bullshit, they could not say and didn't feel they had to, tending to via off to some other unrelated tangent.

The rules were being bent also and Leave.EU knew how to do it in a desperate push in the last few days of the campaign to optimise its social media campaigns and results. 'In the final days of the campaign they donated £675,000 to a twenty-three-year-old fashion student who was running an online campaign called BeLeave (yes I know these number of obscure Leave groups were growing) and the timing of this donation meant that they did not have to be declared until after the result. Grimes spent this money with AggregateIQ (more of them and Cambridge Analytica shortly) but if the two campaigns had been working together this money would have to count against Vote Leave's £7 million spending limit – but the Electoral Commission would have to prove that Vote Leave told Grimes how to spend the money, and that was going to be almost impossible. So, we can see here that it is not just Arron Banks and Leave.EU who were pushing the boundaries of acceptability Vote Leave were now pushing the boundaries of acceptability in the desperation to win. Some may say this was breaking the rules some may say just 'bending' the rules, but it is very concerning that our democracy and such a critical decision to the UK's future was being potentially manipulated by some 'black arts'.

It must be said that the Remain arguments did need more explaining and the Leave arguments could be put in very simple short slogans and headlines and this fitted much better into a digital Media strategy where people flicking through Facebook were not looking for long explanations about economics but quick fragments of information, news or gossip and Vote Leave exposed this brilliantly. This combined with decades of EU scepticism in the Press meant the Stronger In campaign may well have been doomed from the start, although that does not mean that they made mistakes and could have done a lot of things better.

If we then combine the above with rich people like Arron Banks or even foreign powers financing Facebook adverts or targeted posts aimed at convincing voters to vote to Leave the EU, we have a dangerous and combustible concoction that directly attacks our democracy in the normal way it currently functions, and we should not underestimate these influences.

AggrecateIQ and Cambridge Analytica

These two companies were really unknown in the UK until it was put forward that they could have influenced the EU referendum result and made the difference for the Leave vote. I am not going to go into much detail on them in this book as it is very complex and detailed with nobody quite knowing what the facts are with an ongoing investigation at the time of writing by both the UK's Electoral commission and the UK information commissioner, Elizabeth Denham, for its role in the EU referendum.

Things livened up when a former employee of Cambridge Analytica called Christopher Wylie came before the British parliamentary committee in March 2018, and basically the Canadian based Aggregate IQ (AIQ) was accused of an alleged scheme to circumvent the Brexit spending limits in order to influence the outcome of the vote. The alleged connection between the two companies is disputed, but they either worked together or were actually a part of the same organisation but let us just concentrate on what we think they allegedly did.

Wylie claims the AIQ developed software that relied on algorithms Cambridge Analytica had developed using 50 million Facebook profiles harvested in 2014 and then used those algorithms for its clients' political campaigns to tailor the ads people saw. BUT we should make clear that it was not proven whether AIQ had direct access to Facebook data itself, but the waters are murky.

We know that the company helped Vote Leave and BeLeave target UK voters with advertising on Social Media, but did the two companies work together? Whistleblower Shahmir Sanni told CBC News that Vote Leave and BeLeave that the companies coordinated to spend more than legally allowed on advertising services from AIQ, although co-ordinating campaigns are supposed to share a single spending cap. Whether the company was in on the alleged scheme is not clear. Wylie in his testimony before parliament said he believes it is "reasonable" to conclude that financial "cheating" in the Brexit vote may have altered the outcome. But clearly this is not proof which is being searched for now.

The concern with these and such companies is that our data is being silently amassed, harvested and stored and whoever owns / has access to this data could own the future. It is clear that it is not just a story about social psychology and data analytics but rather it is so complex and sophisticated it resembles more of a military contractor using applying military style strategies on a civilian population. Plus this is on a global cross border scale for a simple IN or OUT domestic vote. Is this a sign of the future?

Has the UK become another "managed" democracy that can be influenced and paid for by Billionaires including foreign Billionaires? If it is indeed true, this goes much deeper than Leave or Remain at the EU referendum or even party politics and could be the future where it becomes less democratic rather than more due to the aforementioned influences at play.

'Echo Chambers' and Social Media

This phenomenon or development has existed for a while based on the logic of if individuals like a certain thing (e.g. Table Tennis) we will give / send / filter them more of what they like, which in the case of Table Tennis is fine although they may also want to see more Rugby for example as they are also a fan. But it is not dramatic if they do not see much Rugby in their news feeds as Table Tennis is their passion. The algorithms were designed for a purpose and were probably well intentioned for this requirement but as we began to understand the likes of Facebook and Twitter etc. it became very clear that when it came to The presidential Election in 2015 (and the Russian interventions via Social Media) and the Brexit campaign in 2016 for example, 2 things were happening.

■ People were very much in echo Chambers where they were basically only hearing one side, their side, of the political arguments which made them more entrenched and not exposed to the arguments and points of view from across the political divide which stifled debate and education. I found this and to counter this I joined, followed or Liked groups or individuals with whom I flatly disagreed just so I would get their feeds and information to give me a more balanced view of Brexit for example. Now I may look at some of them and decide they were bat shit crazy but at least I was seeing what others were receiving and potentially buying into so I can better understand it and counter the lies or misinformation where appropriate. The problem was I may like say Leave.Eu Facebook page but would get feeds from more obscure and extreme groups that could be run by some fruit cake sitting in his union Jack boxer shorts spreading lies, hate and misinformation to satisfy his own dark side and can do it in obscurity. But he feels his tribe are supporting him and are with him as he may get a few positive comments and 3 likes! You just do not know who these people are, or who is behind these extreme groups, or what their motives are and that should concern us all.

■ One lady, a robust Brexiteer, took offence on Facebook to me dissecting and correcting her reasons for voting leave (immigration basically) with facts but rather than take them on board and consider the points or even disagree she said that "if we were discussing this down the pub she would smash me in the face!"[AP] Polarisation in politics? Never!

But it revealed how powerful and negative at the same time a reality check can be where what Brexiteers were promised melts away before their eyes and their raw prejudices come to the fore.

Or

- People are deliberately targeted based on their interest and views meaning incorrect information or just plain fiction can be fed to them on a regular basis to further entrench their position and hate or even try to radicalise that position to make it more extreme than where they started. The Facebook platform can be used to do this very effectively as it uses visuals and dramatic headlines which are attention grabbing even before the person begins to read the propaganda. In actual fact it is worse as highlighted previously as I know of many people that simply share based on an image or headline, without even reading the content! You can see how dangerous that can be, as their friends and contacts they share it to may read the actual 'article' and it could contain the most racist extreme material and they become complicit in sharing such material. It may be ignorance, naivety, or laziness, but it is the same result, and where else in life could such a thing happen apart from Social media and to the same level and speed? We are now seeing that this collusion and impressionism cannot be underestimated or ignored, and with many groups it is an effective strategy.

My personal experience of Brexit on Social Media

The following thoughts observations and stories are true examples of what I have experienced, seen, read and taken part in which could be a microcosm of my world or may be just a lot of strange individuals (and I include myself in that) who take pleasure in debating the most important issue of our time as this is their only forum or platform for their opinions.

As a minority Remain voter within my peer Group social Media exchanges were always interesting with different leavers taking different approaches to their dislike of a minority position with some starting calmly and logically debating points but then would get excitable and inconsistent sometimes commenting simply with "Boring" and a sleepy Emoji as he no longer had any interest but would then re-join the debate in an excitable manner using words like 'disgusting' and 'nasty' etc.[SP] You then have those that want to debate but do not have enough knowledge of the subject and so just snipe from the sidelines concentrating more on comments that will get likes from his / her 'tribe' to gain a feeling of self-satisfaction sometimes simply stirring others up to a frustrated Brexit frenzy.[MG] They then hibernate for a while again feeling pout of their depth. Then there are the very direct and honest but totally committed to Brexit at all costs individuals posting anything that is slightly related to or could make Brexit appear positive plus a lot of St. George Emojis etc.[BH] I even experienced Ex-Pat Brits living abroad where Brexit will not affect them directly still with an amazing passion for Brexit but never really being able to confirm why but race was often bubbling below the surface as a justification of their position, but often with some bizarre unrelated arguments that lacked credibility. But they did not care.[PL] Still no matter the type of Brexiteer it was always good to try to understand their position, the logic and consider how they got there, but also then witnessing their growing frustration as Brexit did not develop in the way they were promised looked for people to blame for the lack of developments as they saw it. Rarely did they blame those that lied to them in the campaigns though, which we have covered elsewhere in this book.

The Nazis, the EU and Brexiteers?

When people become desperate to get what they want, in this case exiting from the EU, they go to desperate measure and one of the most bizarre that became even more prevalent was and still is comparing the EU to the Nazis for example. When looking at this one must ask the reason why. This could be a number of reasons or a combination of those. The obvious reason, and one a number of people peddle is the fact that we (yes believe it or not many Brits think we won two world wars on our own so exaggerated is their belief in British superiority) were successful in the second world war but had to put the UK in extreme debt to the Americans and the Germans which becomes the most powerful economy in Europe and have extreme influence over the policies and direction of the EU. You hear comments like 'The Germans are trying to take over or control Europe including the UK economically via the EU as they failed in two world wars and we died for freedom!" etc. Now on the surface one can understand that 'disappointment' that over time becomes an ingrained anti German prejudice that can be demonstrated by hating the EU, no matter how ridiculous it is in reality.

This falsified opinion of Great Britain won two world wars almost on their own when it was in reality supported and, in some areas, led by coalition forces including the USA, and the commonwealth countries BUT ALSO including brave fighters from Poland and Czechoslovakia as well as other EU countries who are still our allies. Plus of course the Russians fighting the Nazis on the Eastern Front, so the Germans had to fight on two fronts.

Alternatively, could this be genuine fear or jealousy of German expansion or just a simple tool to openly help discredit the EU to help ensure a clean no-deal Brexit?! and the obsession of Brits winning the war.

Perhaps I am over thinking this aspect of the campaign both during and before the vote because as a friend and fellow Remainer joked with me "forget it Chris, they have just watched too many war films and think they are Steve McQueen on their Motorcycle in The Great Escape!" Even though Hilts (Steve McQueen) was American... cue war film music!

But seriously these constant anti-German combined with anti-EU messages, opinions and press coverage became a powerful potent concoction when combined with other such emotive topics as immigration etc. and should not be forgotten when piecing together the Leave vote and what happened on the day or The 20 years running up to the 2016 referendum.

Chapter 17
Nostalgia, Imperialism, Sovereignty & the Illusion

of Independence

Nostalgia and Imperialism

From several comments, interviews and articles seen, mainly for older white males it must be said, there was a definite implication or longing for things to return to times of the past when apparently things were better. Only once you ask pointed questions or peel back the onion to those thoughts, opinions and comments do you find there is not much substance to it and it seems to come back to immigration although a smattering of comments about the second world war or when we ruled half the world (obviously omitting the fact the UK raped, pillaged and stole people's land to achieve a lot of that! The Vikings were rank amateurs compared to the Brits centuries later with the havoc they achieved!) and nostalgic references to the empire. Clearly, in history Britain has fought wars against France, Germany, the Netherlands and Spain and some cannot seem to forget that, and that the world has moved on in a spirit of cooperation and no wars. But, these were so long ago and those referring back to these events did not take part in them as they are too young and come across as the bravest keyboard warriors trying in some way link historical events as some justification of leaving the EU.

The British empire was basically dismantled in about 25 years after the second World war giving imperialists even more dislike of Germans or Japanese that lost the war but built modern developed economies whilst we lost our empire, lacked much economic strength or growth in the 40s and 50s leading us having to join the EU as it assisted our economic development, which we are now potentially walking away from. Obviously, the ghost of the empire exists in the form of the commonwealth, but we lack power over it and coming from a place where we 'controlled' a quarter of the world's land mass leaves the imperialists with great regret and sadness in their hearts of where they feel we could be in the world. Some may call this delusion.

Remember that when we speak of immigration and the empire in the same breath most of the early immigration was British people moving to the countries of the growing empire to improve themselves, which Brits obviously did not have a problem with but now this has reversed and the empire no longer exists and people want to better themselves and come to the UK there is a backlash against this. The hypocrisy is obviously clear, or perhaps just selfishness?

Here is an example of a comment I received on a Facebook post (unedited) that began with Leave.Eu (and shared) about the abuse Jess Phillips, but you can see how these items go off on perverse tangents as we end up with a one-sided warped view of British military history [RR]:

Well here is the view of this particular 'Baby Boomer' who has stepped up to the plate.
Apart from being aggressive to their neighbour's in the past, certain countries in the EU have been "Piss Poor" in the military support they have shown since WW2 despite the EU's laughable claim to have "Kept the Peace" for 70yrs or so.

Let's take the Falklands Conflict in 1982. It was only 37yrs ago!... we were in the "Common Market" let's see how our European Friends supported us then.

1. The UN resolution 502 called for the immediate withdrawal of all Argentine forces from the F.Is. - carried (Almost unanimously).. Spain and Poland abstained. Thank you Spanish and Polish friends.

2. When hostilities broke out, the French had an Exocet technical weapons team in Argentina which we hoped would either provide us with details of 'Radar Head Parameters' or at best, 'Be recalled' to France. Neither happened. (This undoubtedly cost the lives of British Serviceman) - Thank you French friends.

3. In anticipation of a lengthy conflict, we requested from Belgium a resupply of 7.26mm ammunition for the standard issue infantry rifle (The Belgium FN, or SLR in the British Army). Guess what ?.. they refused. Thank you Belgium Friends.

4. Germany had ship and submarine orders for the Argentine military which we asked to be cancelled (or at best delayed) .... Guess what?.. they refused. - Thank you German Friends.

We could go on.... perhaps the EU's underwhelming response to the war in the Former Yugoslavia (leave it to NATO seemed to be their contribution) .... they haven't clue. The sooner we are shut of them, the SAFER we will be.

Bottom line is, they are cowards and don't give a 'Fishes Tit' about those who actually get 'Stuck In' when the going gets tough.... as long as it's not them.

You can see how one can go quickly from Jess Phillips to the Falklands war "which is only 37 years ago"! But you can see from the above 'rant' it was for some never about economic cooperation in a modern globalised world, or the future stability and free movement for our children but rather highlighting perceived military misdemeanours of the EU in an attempt to reclaim a rock in the South Atlantic sea over 8,000 of miles away that have been claimed by the French, British, Spaniards and Argentines at various points over the last 500 years.   The hypocrisy in the piece above is that on the one hand there is uproar from such individuals of a possible European army (we have a veto against being a part of this by the way) and closer integration but on the other hand they want full compliance with the British requests. There are some Brits that think such an army in the right context may not be such a bad idea as it would reduce our reliance on the US military might which is where we find ourselves now.

It is clear that when imperialists and military fantasist's comment on these areas they deliberately forget to go back further in British history regarding slavery, and the raping and pillaging and stealing of people's lands, as that does not quite for the depiction they are trying to portray, resulting in a one sided (if even accurate?) 'rose-tinted glasses' view of the world, where watching a lot of war films may enhance this perception.

236

This makes clear another reason why the referendum was misplaced and fraught with danger when many people like RR with such imperialistic ideals never understood or wanted to be a part of closer European cooperation because in his head they are all "cowards" and not "British Bulldogs", and this is just one ideal that was floating around when people voted in 2016.

The root of the nationalistic attitudes is difficult to pinpoint but Professor Diane Purkiss believes it could be rooted in out dim and distant past of the Elizabethan period. She writes:

'The two ideas of nationhood espoused by Brexiteers and Remainers also continue a tradition, with Brexiteers reflecting the beliefs of the Elizabethan state in their insistence that patriotism involves separation from other powers and authorities. Their idea that England is an elect nation with a special destiny is also the direct outcome of the propaganda and legislation created by their Elizabethan forebears.

Remainers, on the other hand, have a more porous and an arguably humbler vision for the nation state as one among many such entities. That division arising from the first Elizabethan age has in many ways come to mark the divisions in English society still present more than four centuries later.' [52]

Sovereignty & Independence

Sovereignty = *"Supreme power or authority. The authority of a state to govern itself or another state".*
Oxford dictionary

Surely the UK never lost this but rather pooled it with other EU member states for the better good? The autonomy of the nation state has been eroded like many countries by globalisation yes, but the UK has still had its sovereignty.

We should appreciate that in today's global world, all nation states like the UK make various trade-offs and compromises in return for other benefits. Examples of this are membership of the WTO (World Trade Organisation) where the UK commits to various regulations and arbitration systems, but the UK deems that worthwhile. Or membership of NATO includes a clear obligation to come to the mutual defence of fellow members. This implies a loss of sovereignty over deploying UK forces, but again the UK deems this as an acceptable compromise. Likewise, membership of the EU requires some compromises on sovereignty for the better good and despite the Brexiteer misrepresentations the UK was in control of a lot more than they would have you believe. These included control of our borders, limiting EU immigration (even though the British government chose not to enforce the laws available to them). The global world now requires compromises and common-rule books to make international trade work and the EU is one of the most efficient trading blocks in the world. Retaining benefits of the EU single market or any other global trade arrangement will mean concessions on such common rules and that impacts this notion of sovereignty in practical terms.

Brexit could lead to less sovereignty / autonomy and not more for a number of reasons such as a weaker economy leads to a loss of sovereignty including the weak currency leading to international investors picking off UK national assets as they are cheaper due to the devaluation of Sterling since the EU referendum. Linked to corporate influence we have the risks of US companies, as a part of TTIP (Transatlantic Trade and Investment Partnership) agreements, could sue Governments for loss of profits, or pressuring for the privatisation of most parts of the NHS which all could erode the UK's sovereignty as such International trade agreements are inherently designed that way, and it is obvious without common rule books the administrative and time burden of trading will be much greater and expensive.

Often the focus is on the sovereignty of the country, but personal sovereignty can also be affected such as losing their freedom of movement and that of their children throughout the EU without restriction, plus the privileges and rights when travelling in the EU member states such as Healthcare (e.g. EHIC cards).

When one looks at the probable developments closely and analyses such changes it appears that Brexit will cause the UK to give up more control and sovereignty than it will ever take back.

Thatcher is often portrayed as this extreme anti-EU figure, but she signed agreements with the EU as, unlike say Enoch Powell, she did not see Sovereignty as an absolute and some diminution of sovereignty was a price worth paying for the economic benefits to the UK that she believed would arise from the creation of the single market, and so it proved once she signed the Single European Act in

1986. When John Major was Prime Minister and the Maastricht treaty debates took place Thatcher's disdain came to the fore, but that was more her incapability to give up power gracefully and work positively in the background. Her venting was not so much against the EU but rather her bitterness as to how she was ousted by her own party and desire for revenge. Major in contrast has taken part in debates but always been respectful and shows no signs of bitterness at the loss of power. No matter what you thought of them as Prime Ministers Major has held his head high whilst Thatcher did unfortunately diminish her reputation after leaving office.

Thatcher and her government were instrumental in creating the EU's single market and expanding the EU to encompass many of the old Warsaw Pact countries, and if we were not leaving, there was no reason why we could not have helped shape the EU's digital, financial and defence policies as well as help fight climate change more effectively.

David Cameron on the Andrew Marr show highlighted his opinion of sovereignty and leaving the EU and the fact it would reduce the UK's ability to do things. 'You have an illusion of sovereignty, but you don't have the power, you don't have control, you can't get things done'. Cameron hit the nail on the head in that it is the Leavers illusion of sovereignty and independence as if other countries we have to work with or negotiate trade deals with do not have the same sovereignty and independence and will leverage that against us. The logic of being a member of the EU as well as a number of the other benefits is that pooling of sovereignty and working together as a cooperative, giving the member states more sovereignty and power to make things happen and get things done, but this just did not break through against the more emotive Leave arguments and the misinformation of course.

One could almost understand (reluctantly) the arguments for economic harm if there was some true sovereignty being achieved. But there are no true realistic arguments for more sovereignty from the Brexit side, even "take back control" is a colossal lie as every trade deal we sign around the world is a compromise with sovereignty and will chip away at our sovereignty – that is what trade deals with compromises means. Membership of NATO is a compromise of sovereignty, Good Friday Agreement, and even the Paris Accord impact our sovereignty as we must live and cooperate with other nations. This dream of sovereignty is an illusion, and it always was, even when the lead Brexiteers sounded so convincing. We already have good trade deals with 50 other countries in some shape or form as a member of the EU which could take a decade to replicate and finalise, but the search for this so-called sovereignty has taken on religious levels of belief that do not bear out in reality.

In summary, absolute sovereignty is a fantasy (with may be the exception of the isolated North Korea, although it could be argued without China it could not survive) and we must make compromises with other countries to our mutual advantage. Sovereignty is always bartered for commerce and very rarely reversed.

Other countries have sovereignty too you know!

Yes as strange as it sounds many Brexiteers and Leavers spoke of sovereignty as if we were the only country that wanted it or could have it, and they may be in for a big shock when it comes to trade deals, international regulations, working with the WTO and other third countries like ourselves, and realise we cannot standalone in the world, we are not completely independent and we have to work with countries where compromises (i.e. give and take) are required. The EU 27 believe that pooling their sovereignty enhances that sovereignty as they are able to have more influence and power in trade negotiations or the setting of industrial standards that they would not have as a single country. I am not saying the argument to take back control of borders, money and laws is not a valid one, but what Brexiteers need to understand is that there is a price to pay for all of those in some shape or form and sovereignty for sovereignty's sake may not be what they had expected or had been sold.

Yes there were very positive documents produced by such organisations as the ERG (albeit never a fully formed and costed detailed plan, that is realistic!) that were a form of "Have your cake and eat it" type wish list that was never going to fly, but under pressure they had to get something out into the public domain to attempt to demonstrate their credibility whilst they seemed to resemble more of a party within a party of the official Conservative party as their obsession with EU knew no bounds. They would not admit that trade-offs will be important and significant and would dare not show these even after winning the referendum for fear of themselves introducing reality into the arena and being exposed for the misinformation they and many of their Brexiteer colleagues had espoused.

It is not clear why Brexiteers (apart from their uniquely 'rose-tinted glasses' view of the world) cannot appreciate that once we enter into free trade agreements, we give up a certain amount of independence to regulate certain sectors of our economy as we would like because there will be compromises with any other major economy as to what THEY want (as a part of THEIR sovereignty / independence) whether that be to tariffs / quotas / regulations, etc. They either ignore or do not appreciate that all trade deals restrict or pool sovereignty to some degree and sometimes significantly so we can get what we want in other areas. This is what the single market does – we pool sovereignty for the better good. It is clear that when listening to some Brexiteers they clearly live in the distant past (or maybe wish those times to return?) when Great Britain was sailing around the world raping and pillaging and taking people's land with limited negotiations or intrusion on our sovereignty. Don't say it too loud as it may come as a surprise to them that these times are not returning any time soon.

This is indeed one of the reasons Jeremy Corbyn (leader of the opposition) and John McDonnell (shadow chancellor) are anti-EU as this constricting of sovereignty would limit their visions of 'Socialism in one country' and their various extreme economic ideas which would work against the EU's control your national budget and fiscally responsibility agenda.

The reality is that you can have as much sovereignty as you want or as you perceive but there is a web of international standards, rules and regulations that we will have to meet as an independent country going forward which by default reduces that so call sovereignty or independence as countries in the world are not going to meet the standards of the UK if different from the USA or the EU for example as it would make no sense. This is literally reality. Sovereignty or not the customer will decide what standard they will purchase, and it will be an international standard.

Taking back control has costs!

To move from our trading, political and legal base of the EU will not be a simple case of change and carry on and improve as many Brexiteers would have us believe. It may sound very privileged to have this perceived total control and notional freedom, but we WILL be affected by the Norms and rules and regulations set by the EU when we are not in the room (as we are now) which will limit our freedom of manoeuvre in many areas. We should not underestimate the huge cost of compliance and / or deviation from a set rules that our companies will incur when previously our delegates and representatives were in the room to help mould those rules and regulations to our liking. This is a massive change and if we feel we can ignore them or make our own rules to suit the UK alone, we are

241

kidding ourselves that our market will be largely domestic one where we know companies will struggle to grow and expand. This applies not just to the EU, but we will come across the same issues with the likes of the USA, China, Brazil and India etc. once the details of such agreements get negotiated. The world is not simple, it is not independent and complete sovereignty is a myth as we will find out to our detriment.

Could Leaving the EU make us less Free?

We currently have the right to travel, work, do business, retire and live / marry etc. in the EU which many millions of Brits have done over the last 40 years and if we leave, we will obviously lose those freedoms, or they will at least become much more difficult and therefore worse. Just consider the European Health Insurance card that has benefited many Brits and Europeans to access medical treatment wherever they are in the EU.

■ This has been of special importance to people with chronic conditions, such as the UK's almost 30,000 dialysis patients. This is something they could probably not afford once we leave the EU as the insurance would be so expensive, so when people talk of freedom what about these poor people who have a difficult life as it is?

■ We forget we could not use our mobile phone minutes and data abroad without horrendous roaming charges, which the EU changed.

■ Even relatively small things like taking your pets abroad with you on holiday without lengthy quarantine processes we once knew are a thing of the past with EU pet passports now common place.

■ Recognition of professional qualifications are now mutually recognised meaning nurses, vets, solicitors, engineers and many other professions can apply their trade across the whole of the EU. Once outside the EU this may change, or regulations / laws change, and we are no longer compliant.

■ Do not underestimate the free movement of capital allowing the easy movement of money across the EU, which with stricter money laundering laws may make this much more difficult moving forward.

As we can now see that this Braveheart cry of "Freedom" from Brexiteers is a perverse type of freedom where many of their countrymen will be less free and have many more laws, rules, and red tape imparted upon them. Now it may not affect the Brexiteer that has no pet, never goes abroad on holiday, or sends money abroad to relatives, does not use a mobile phone etc. and so it will never affect him, but it will negatively affect many, and as usual the question is 'for what tangible benefit' rather than some abstract feeling of being 'free'?

Chapter 18
Economics

Money NOT economics

Why do I say Money NOT economics? Well basically because the average man or woman in the street does not feel economics affects them as how many have studied or even had economics lessons at school or have to deal with "economics"? Yes, I appreciate economics is a lot wider subject than money but when talking about Brexit and how well-off people will or will not be it is all about money (and of course the emotive / emotional aspects such as immigration etc.). We have to talk to a certain extent about economics here, but we should bear in mind most people care about money and have never heard of John Maynard Keynes, Adam Smith or price elasticity etc., even though these could indirectly affect and filter into their lives, if it hasn't already.

We heard frequently that it was not about economics and that it was about people's feelings and opinions which on reflection was probably true but what to do when the feelings and opinions are based on false information and not facts?

Many people used the referendum as a protest against whatever they thought had put them in the position they were in and they were not happy with it. It is clear to us that the economic benefits to the UK have been skewed towards

London and the South East and like a snowball effect that has grown a pace. Despite a few bright spots based in big cities such as Manchester, Birmingham, Glasgow and Edinburgh many across the UK felt that they have been left behind and saw the EU and immigration etc. as someone or something they could blame and that combined with kicking the Tory government seemed an excellent opportunity they could not refuse. To them it made sense. But there is no evidence their relative disadvantage is because of those factors and in fact could have been worse if we had not been a member of the EU and the UK remained the sick man of Europe rather than the 5th largest economy in the world. Actually, post-Brexit the UK dropped to 6th behind France! The worry is that these so called 'left behinds' could be the ones that pay the highest price if our economy shrinks as forecasted with a hard Brexit. The North-East and North Yorkshire are also set to lose £668 million of EU funding after 2020, do they think that will be replaced by a conservative government that does not have a great record of investment into these poorer Northern regions?

Even though you may think the South of England is reliant on its trade with the EU, It is not well known but the poorer regions in the UK are more reliant on Exports to the EU as this is very much where more of our produce and products are made. That is the irony of some leave areas voting to leave the EU but may be that power of the immigration argument was so powerful that nothing else counted.

The single market and its value

During the campaign it became clear that many people did not know about, care about or understand the single market or the customs union etc. as it never, they felt, touched their lives and only really heard these terms when politicians or political figured bandied these terms around when trying to convince voters of the pros and cons of their positions. But if we leave the single market and have no free trade deal, they will start to feel the pinch of us no longer being a part of the European Single market.

For clarity I should just explain what the Single Market is, and although that may sound strange after a long referendum campaign and subsequent discussions, it was clear that people still did not know exactly what the single market is or the customs union for that fact. This includes Brexiteers from the ERG as was exposed when it was leaked (see below) that Nadine Dorries did not understand the Customs Union, having campaigned to leave it! Even Kemi

Badenoch who she was asking for advice wasn't even sure. Yes, I know you couldn't make it up, and the blind leading the blind comes to mind!

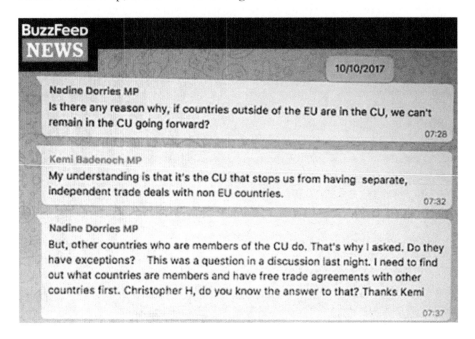

BuzzFeed NEWS

10/10/2017

Nadine Dorries MP
Is there any reason why, if countries outside of the EU are in the CU, we can't remain in the CU going forward?
07:28

Kemi Badenoch MP
My understanding is that it's the CU that stops us from having separate, independent trade deals with non EU countries.
07:32

Nadine Dorries MP
But, other countries who are members of the CU do. That's why I asked. Do they have exceptions? This was a question in a discussion last night. I need to find out what countries are members and have free trade agreements with other countries first. Christopher H, do you know the answer to that? Thanks Kemi
07:37

This lack of understanding by MPs as well as the general Public was highlighted by campaign Director of Vote Leave, Dominic Cummings, frustration with the likes of Boris Johnson getting dragged into various potential options and alternatives to the single market as he was quite clear nobody understands the Single Market so don't go there and stick to the simple messages he and his team has laid out, i.e., 'immigration' and 'take back control'.

The Single Market

The Single Market for EU member states have effectively created one territory without any internal borders or other regulatory obstacles to the free movement of goods and services. A functioning Single Market stimulates competition and trade, improves efficiency, raises quality, and helps cut prices. The European Single Market is one of the EU's major achievements. It has helped fuel economic growth and made the everyday life of European businesses and consumers much easier in many ways.

The European Union Customs Union (EUCU)

This is a customs union which consists of all the member states of the European Union (EU), Monaco, and some dependencies of the United Kingdom, which are not part of the EU. Some detached territories of EU members do not participate in the customs union, usually as a result of their geographic separation. In addition to the EU Customs Union, the EU is in other customs unions with Andorra, San Marino, and Turkey, (with the exceptions of certain goods) through separate bilateral agreements.

The customs union is a principal component of the European Union, since its establishment in 1958 as the European Economic Community. There are no tariffs or non-tariff barriers to trade between members of the customs union and – unlike a free trade area – members of the customs union impose a common external tariff on all goods entering the union.

The European Commission negotiates for and on behalf of the Union as a whole in international trade deals (such as those with Canada, Japan and many others), rather than each member state negotiating individually. It also represents the Union in the World Trade Organization and any trade disputes mediated through it.

This means that for example:

■ no customs duties are paid on goods moving between EU Member States
■ all apply a common customs tariff for goods imported from outside the EU
■ goods that have been legally imported can circulate throughout the EU with no further customs checks

The European Free Trade Association (EFTA) was formed in 1960 and the UK was one of the founding members as it recognised what a good idea it was and how it could benefit the UK and other member states. But if we leave without a deal and do not have access to the single market where almost half of our trade is going it could be a very expensive decision indeed. Some economists estimate the loss could equal £75 Billion, which is about what the UK spent on defence and transport in 2016 / 17! [17] True we will not be paying the £9 billion towards the EU budget each year but the losses far outweigh the benefit to the UK.

The argument about savings from leaving the EU is often misrepresented and misunderstood as Brexiteers claim that we will save £9 billion a year from leaving the EU which is technically true and looks like a good deal but then stop there, as this is only half of the argument of course. Economists are saying we will lose potentially £75 Billion so that does not seem such a good deal does it? It's almost like if one changes their £1,000 car for a car costing them only £500 they can say they have saved £500 (Brexiteer argument) but if the engine goes pop as it was so cheap and costs them £700 and it costs them £100 more to run each month within 12 months it has cost them an additional £1900 or £1400 in real terms. So not such a good deal now is it, but it would sound it if I gave you only half of the information? There are a number of instances when Brexiteers like Jacob Rees-Mogg are very careful (some may deceitful) and clever with their language to not give the whole picture or all the information.

But there are other knock-on effects of losing access to the single market which would include unemployment where economists estimate the unemployment rate could increase to 6.6% due to a recession influenced by such developments which could be a loss of up to 500,000 jobs which would mean loss of tax income for the government and higher benefit payments, making the country poorer with little obvious benefit. We may be able to counter that slightly by generating more low paid zero-hour contracts and companies using Apprenticeships as cheap labour, but this could become a race to the bottom and is this really where we want to go? After all, one of the calls from the Brexiteers was immigrants squeezing wages of the indigenous population, but they may well have been successful in achieving what they were apparently trying to avoid.

Clearly, the above are potential issues and nothing is guaranteed, but even if it was only 50,000 jobs it would bode the question "for what benefits, where is the Brexit dividend promised?"

The big risk if we are no longer in the Single European Market is the potential reduction in foreign internal investment into the UK, and we have already seen this with companies like Honda, Nissan, Panasonic, various banks, Dyson and other companies either moving their operations, stopping production, redirecting other investments, no longer investing in projects in the UK they had planned to do, and focusing on other countries and regions outside the UK now. Many Brexiteers claim it has nothing to do with Brexit, but I suppose they would wouldn't they but there have been a lot of "coincidences" in the 3+ years since we voted to Leave. But Logic says that companies will vote with their feet and if we are a less inviting place to invest as we are standing alone outside the EU single market then it's going to happen isn't it. Nissan came to Sunderland for a number of reasons, but one was to access the single market and avail itself of a frictionless supply chain system. This cannot exist if we are outside the EU. Yes, Honda's senior Japanese management will say that their decision to take production back to Japan from Swindon has nothing to do with Brexit, but one has to understand the Japanese business culture and politics of the situation. This includes the fact they are very courteous and do not want to offend anyone, especially those Leave voters that they want to buy their cars. Imagine they had said it was because of Brexit they are leaving, and hundreds of people are losing their jobs and the public reacted by boycotting Honda cars and products, would that have then been a wise business announcement? Of course not. We should not be naïve when it comes to these job losses of plant closures.

But the Honda example showed how we cannot as an island stand alone in the world of trade and economics because with Japan having signed a free trade deal with the EU, they affectively had access to the EU market, albeit from further away. The EU HAS a signed and functioning trade deal with Japan, but we have nothing, and nothing is on the horizons. Yes, people like Liam Fox told people it would be easy, and he would have all these trade deals ready to go once we leave but reality is, he is nowhere near. Even if he says he is 95% of the way there that is because the 5% remaining are the difficult aspects where countries enter into intransigence and final agreements take years. Was he so naïve or was he another Brexiteer trying to con the public?

When it comes to internal investment half of the UK's Foreign Direct Investment (FDI) stock which amounts to around a staggering £1 trillion come from the rest of the EU and if after Brexit higher tariffs and trade costs will probably cause the investments into the UK to drop. Estimates vary but some official analysis indicates that leaving the EU could reduce inward investment by 20% + as they could face additional costs, friction of trade, uncertainty and loss of opportunity they could find within the single EU market. This is just logical and Brexiteers can stick their head in the sand as much as they like it is a reality. Never underestimate uncertainty in the business environment especially when decisions have to be made 5-10 Years hence. Many companies including Vodafone, EasyJet, Jaguar Land Rover, Virgin Group, John Lewis, Visa, Siemens, HSBC, Barclays and Tesco's as well as many banks have seen or fear the negative effects of Brexit and have had to or are planning to make decisions that could result in less investment, moving jobs, cutting jobs or a range of other measures in light of the negative effects or dangers of Brexit.

Even with Small and Medium Size business (SMEs) they are not immune with insolvencies predicted to rise in 2020 onward compared to previous years as they are also hit directly or indirectly with the results of Brexit. A small exporter to the EU working on low margins may not be able to pass on increased costs to his customers and may not make enough business to stay solvent. Or maybe his EU customers are now looking harder to find a supplier within the EU and the Single European Market? Or he is hit by import duties or a devaluation of the pound making imported goods more expensive coming into the UK so his costs rise but he cannot raise his prices as a French competitor is within the Single market and doesn't suffer from the aforementioned disadvantages. Upon confirmation of the referendum result and leave winning, the Pound Sterling fell by 12% (the Bank Of England has warned about this but it was again referred to as 'Project Fear'), and if we left without a Deal, this would happen again and all the repercussions that go with that.

Even the 12% reduction should have seen our exports soar as they got cheaper after the Referendum but they didn't greatly as trade and economics is much more complex than that but if we suffer a further devaluation when we actually leave this could cause the UK a real issue if the confidence of the International financial institutions in our economy and our future is low, plus the potential huge increase in the cost of imported goods including food could help increase inflation. People feel this will not affect them, but it will affect everyone, although the poor will be hit even more than the rich as they spend a higher percentage of their disposable income on such products and necessities. The public debate of such issues and threats need to be based on the realities and not the fantasies we hear from prominent Brexiteers.

The Confederation of British Industry (CBI) conveyed a special committee in 2018 of their most senior policy-making committee and made it quite clear "we must not go backwards" following Brexit. It was clear to them that a no-deal Brexit is unacceptable as companies are clear it would negatively be affecting supply chains that could result in shortages including critical services. No deal some forecast could lead to our Gross Domestic Product (GDP) being 2% lower by 2020 (Oxford Economics) and up to 5-8% lower in the long run (IMF) which would obviously have serious consequences for jobs and living standards in the UK. But the risk or uncertainty about no deal is already causing companies problems both immediately and for planning purposes.

Marnie Millard, CEO of Nichols and CBI North West Regional Chair, said "No deal is not an option for firms in the North West. Many of our businesses are already investing heavily in contingency plans. This is money that could otherwise be spent on investment, innovation or colleague pay. Leaving in March without a transition deal would severely impact complex supply chains and worsen inequalities that already exist." This is often underestimated how much time and money companies spend on preparing for various scenarios and the uncertainty. This is a cost for business with no obvious benefits.

Clearly, the exact impact will be in part considerably influenced by what kind of deal we can negotiate with the EU or in the extreme case a no-deal Brexit but there is no doubt the ripples will be significant, and the tentacles of International trade will entwine itself all over the UK trade policy going forward. The world has quite clearly moved towards trading blocks and after Brexit we will be one of the few countries without any signed and functioning trade deals. Yes, we can then negotiate trade deals that are in theory much more to our liking than ones negotiated by us and the EU in partnership which has to take into account the opinions and needs of 27 other countries. BUT (and this is a big but!) trading Blocks or big countries will know how desperate we are to get trade deals signed as we have nothing so that they will not make it easy and trading with major powers like the USA, China and India as a much smaller entity is fraught with danger and not as easy as many Brexiteers like David Davis would have you believe? How often has he been wrong?

We should be in no doubt that that there will be a substantial hit on the balance of trade and public finances as companies relocate or do not invest in the UK where they may have done in the past when as we were a full member of the EU as we have now simply made supplying products and services across EU borders much more difficult and costly. You do not have to be a rocket scientist to work out what implications that will have. You go to the gym and make a weight heavier and therefore more difficult to lift, then you will do fewer lifts.

The EU and services

Although a lot of the talk is about trade in products this only accounts for circa. 20% of our trade with the other 80% being in services which are much more complicated when it comes to international trade and which we will cover in more detail under the WTO section of this book, but the importance of this should not be underestimated.

It seems the government's own Department for Exiting the EU doesn't (or at least didn't) understand the single market and services as it tweeted (subsequently deleted) on 27th march 2019 claiming that "[staying in] the single market and customs union...... would not cover services," which was totally incorrect as the single market is based on the 4 freedoms of goods, people, capital AND SERVICES. This means that services can establish themselves in any single market country and operate freely across all other member states of the single market, WITHOUT BARRIERS. This is not the case in other countries which is why for example some architects or advertising businesses have to set themselves up in a foreign territory e.g. The USA to be able to work freely and effectively, which obviously adds cost to that business.

It seemed and still does that politicians find goods trade and tariffs more understandable than services trade, even though this is 80% of our trade. It is indeed more complex and not a simple case of a product = a tariff and they rarely grasp how incredibly tough it is to deliver freer cross-border trade in services which, by definition gets you deep into domestic sovereignty questions in a way which makes removing tariff barriers look easy.

To put it into context UK export of services into the EU in 2016 was £90 Billion a year which is as much as we export to our next eight export markets put together. It is significant and although the EU cross liberalisation of service trade is not perfect by far (but still simpler and more efficient than trade between many US states or the Canadian provinces) politicians should understand how difficult it is for anyone negotiating such services with the USA, Japan, Brazil, India or China for example. This is why there are in reality relatively few far-reaching market opening service deals benefiting major cross services traders. In fact, to avoid this these companies have to invest huge amounts of money and resources to be based in those countries to be able to compete on a level playing field. But the reality for services of a no-deal Brexit is that they will be sacrificed in favour of many people's priority or the end of the freedom of movement, when the UK has a trade surplus in services with the EU compared to a significant trade deficit in manufactured products further highlights the issue.

The UK government's determination to curtail the free movement of EU citizens to the UK will mean in turn our exporters of services will lose free access to the EU's single market, and we will be treated like any other third country and although it will vary by sector, most if not all will take a hit. We will find that opening up new markets for services is historically difficult and in general do little more than what the WTO base line trading agreement defines, i.e. we may not have any of the advantages that we have now as a member of the EU. The "Global Britain" chant sounds great from Brexiteers, but reality could be an uncomfortable bedfellow.

For services you obviously need the people and the UK has been loathed to offer to many places in the UK to non-EU citizens but any trade deal with say India will mean the UK will have to issue a lot more business visas for Indians, and I am not sure that is what many Brexiteers voted for, but then they couldn't know that as the likes of Rees-Mogg et al. never told them.

We should understand that the Free movement of services and free movement of people are not the same and one does not exist for the other. But for the European Union they are indivisible because they create a market for the workforce as well as a market for the service providers, and on a political level it is also a positive and tangible result for many Europeans to be a part of the EU and the advantages that brings.

Clearly, the free movement of people and services cannot easily be separated, practically or politically and if we leave the single market and cannot accept the free movement of EU nationals, then it follows that the free movement of services must end. Most free trade agreements do not extend to services, and those that do only offer minimal coverage unlike the EU single market which is the most advanced in the world. So, it is likely we will suffer and in any EU-UK free trade agreement post no-deal Brexit which will have to be quite broad and in fact more radical than anything signed before. But again, it bodes the question for all this pain, hate and added cost what will be achieved for our citizens?

Lessons of Japan?

Many of the Brexiteers genuinely feel this isolationist position where we leave the best club on the planet and go it on our own starting from scratch with no trade deals so that we can 'control' many things (that we apparently cannot influence at the moment) such as stopping or reducing immigration, it should remind us of Japan. Japan has nearly stopped immigration completely with now less than 1% of the population foreign born but the problem is their economy is stagnant, and they have a decreasing population (as like the UK they have a negative birth rate without immigration) and still believe in their great past and an almost dogmatic belief in their own uniqueness (some may say code for superiority) which has resulted in a closed narrow minded inward looking society. Does this not remind you of some Brexiteer rhetoric where we can do everything on our own, do not need anyone else and do not need any more immigration? It is not easy to work or live in Japan beginning with securing a Visa and even the basics of finding somewhere to live, as it is legal and common place for landlords to discriminate against foreigners! Is this really the country and society we want to replicate dreaming of the halcyon days of the past when we ruled the waves and raped and pillaged our way around the world or Japan was once the preeminent industrial power around the globe but now this isolationist prejudiced society and economy has floundered with no good, young, dynamic immigrants there to help kick start their country's fortunes.

The success of UK financial services

With UK exports now made up of 80% services, it is not all about goods and although bankers do not have a great reputation (may be still better than political figures?) their successful role in the UK economic success cannot be denied. But at the same time the role the EU has played in that should also not be forgotten. Over the last decade our financial transactions have been more focused on the Eurozone area and financial services and insurance make up the largest proportion of the UK's services trade, accounting for £22.7 billion (26%) of services exports to the EU.

In 1997, other EU member states accounted for 30% of the accumulated stock of foreign direct investment (FDI) in the UK; by 2012, this proportion had risen to 50%. In 2013, no fewer than two thirds of EU financial services were handled by the City, while EU banks held £1.4 trillion of assets in London, about 17% of the country's total bank assets, far exceeding those from the US. In 2019, even before the UK has left the EU or come to some agreement a number of banking institutions have moved assets to other EU states such as Ireland, and the question will be how far will that continue over time to weaken our banking appeal to foreign investors?

The Financial Markets are important

Most people do not see that the markets have any impact on their everyday lives or how their vote for Leave had any impact on this as 'that is all about London and the City'. But clearly this is not the case and the trickle-down effect of decisions made in the markets or the Bank Of England do impact everyday lives.

The Leave result resulted in the markets going crazy as share values fell dramatically especially for those major corporations the markets felt would be most impacted by Brexit and fears of a recession sometime soon or if Brexit is extended (as it has been twice already) once we leave the European Union. To highlight how quickly these fears can develop the FTSE 100 dived by 530 points, or 8.4% within the first hours of trading and investors sold Sterling as it plunged against the Dollar by 12%. The Bank Of England saw the problem and to calm markets and mark Carney made £250 billion available to the banks to ensure their liquidity, that was how serious he saw the risks. His actions seem to calm many investors but that was not before more than a £100 billion had been wiped off shares to the detriment of those companies, including large pension companies that manage millions of peoples pensions. These developments were what Gove and Boris Johnson dismissed as project fear that had now become project reality, but it was only the start as we have not left yet and the loss of jobs or cancelling of future investments etc. has only just started.

It should be remembered that previous recessions produced economic shocks equating to circa. £2500 loss for each household in the UK, as well as increasing unemployment by one million. Clearly, some were affected more than others depending on their particular circumstances but some older Brexiteers [MW & 1A] I communicated with claimed they never even noticed the previous recessions which I found astounding as they were either very comfortable and ignored the plight of others in society losing their jobs and their houses etc. or it was just another way Brexiteers pull up the draw bridge and ignore anything past or present that may negatively impact their weak arguments and desperation for Brexit. I had to question the honesty of people apparently not noticing a recession and all the difficulties and misery that come with such a time in economic cycles when it is on the news, in the newspapers etc. and one can normally not avoid. Maybe it is more of a feeling of I was alright so the fact others less fortunate than themselves were suffering was of less importance?

The issue when speaking to normal people that have no contact with the markets, take no interest in shares or the Bank Of England etc. is that they see or make no link between these developments and their lives. But what is clear that these developments do or will have an impact on their lives as loss of share values negatively affect pension companies and therefore peoples pensions, the devaluation of Sterling will mean more inflation and more expensive goods in the shops over time, and the more debt the Bank Of England / Government takes on the less money there is available for public services including repairing peoples roads, street lights, etc.

Some may say correctly that with a lower Pound our exports should rise but this is not always the case as it depends on a number of other factors including price elasticity of those products but there is another important factor here. Being a part of the Single market and union but not part of the Euro gives us the best of both worlds as we could technically devalue if we wanted to, but that would be a decision for the Bank Of England as a strategic fiscal move but the recent devaluations since the EU referendum were and are outside our control and are basically the financial markets saying we will be worse off outside the EU single market and especially with no deal.

This is project reality, not empty scaremongering and people need to understand that.

Did the Bank Of England bail out the UK economy?

So Mr. Carney and his team took the following actions to support the economy and to help smooth out the market sentiments regarding the result of the EU referendum.

■   A Cut in official interest rates to 0.25%, which is the first since March 2009!

■   Up to an additional £100 Billion of new funding to banks to help them pass on the base rate cut. Under the new term "Term Funding Scheme" (TFS) the bank will create new money to provide loans to banks at interest rates close to the base rate of 0.25%. The charge would apparently charge a penalty rate if banks do not lend and get the money out into the industry, so it starts working for the economy!

■ A further £10 Billion in electronic cash to buy corporate bonds from firms "making a material contribution to the UK economy".

■ Will pump an additional £60 Billion in electronic cash into the economy to buy government bonds which was an extension of the previous Quantitative Easing (QE) programme bringing it to a whopping £435 Billion!

Clearly, the usual suspects accuse Carney of over-reacting and sticking their head in the proverbial sand, but the Credit ratings agency Fitch said the bank's package was a "proactive policy response" to the EU referendum. "But it is only likely to cushion, rather than fully offset, the shock to UK growth that June's Brexit vote will cause," it said. And this has proved to be true since 2016.

As Fitch noted this is not the magic bullet as we have issues in the economy such as poor productivity, under-investment, inadequate physical and human capital, and this cannot be rectified by cheap money or Quantitative Easing (QE). More is needed but the BoE can only do so much and the government i.e. the Treasury needs to do it's best to support the economy, but if in 2019 Sajid Javid and Boris Johnson do not think there is a problem how can we trust them to make the right decisions?

But it does bode the question again, was it all worth it? What have Brexiteers won to warrant such chaos and emergency actions on behalf of the BoE and the Treasury?

The Brexiteers Economist even told us the problems of Brexit!

Patrick Minford is really the poster boy economist expert (even though a number of them including Michael Gove did not want experts involved, but struggle to find many economists that think Brexit is a good idea) of the Brexiteers who selectively use statements from Mr. Minford as he is one of the highest profile economists in favour of Brexit. Some may say the only high-profile economist in favour. But if we delve into his comments / projections / forecasts in papers, interviews or conversations with select committees even Brexiteers should be concerned.

In 2012, Mr. Minford told MPs on Westminster's foreign affairs committee that car manufacturers in the UK would have to be wound down if the UK left the EU. Brexit would lead to running down the car industry "in the same way we ran down the coal and steel industries", as stated above.

The transcript which is in the public domain lists Mr. Minford saying 'it is perfectly true that if you remove protection of the sort that has been given particularly to the car industry and other manufacturing industries inside the protective wall, you will have a change in the situation facing that industry, and you are going to have to run it down". He does go into more details, but you get his point. I do not remember Jacob Rees-Mogg, one of Minford's supporters, highlighting that in the referendum campaign or warning workers at Honda, Ford, Nissan etc? A bit disingenuous I hear you say.

One of those that will be affected is Toyota's plant in Deeside, Wales and Plaid Cymru's MP for Carmarthen East and Dinefwr, Jonathan Edwards said he was alarmed but not surprised by the 2012 comments. He said "The reality is if we do leave the single market and the customs union there will be a huge hit for manufacturing. The same people who took away our coal mines and our steel plants are now going to be pursuing the same ideological economic philosophy in the post-Brexit era...."

Chapter 19
Trade

Trade is not a simple Profit and Loss account

International trade including imports and Exports are often misunderstood as a sort of Profit and Loss account whereby imports (costs) are bad and exports (revenue) are good, but this is fundamental misunderstanding otherwise it would be a zero-sum game with one country's exports cancelling out the other countries imports. The world benefits from international trade as it allows a country to focus on the items it is relatively good and efficient at producing and then importing those where it is not, for example, it does not have the natural resources such as Gold, Oil, or the climate for growing grapes, etc. But it is not an absolute advantage but rather what the country does in relative terms to its trading partners giving them a **'comparative' advantage** which has been vindicated by the improvements in real incomes due to globalisation over the last 40 years.

The topic of **Tariffs**, so much in the news due to Brexit, have also suffered from a misunderstanding with the idea that if you put Tariffs on your imports, it generates great money for the Government and helps protect the country from foreign imports. But the Government can raise revenue from various other sources and Tariffs are more about the efficient allocation of resources and maximising income and welfare which can include foreign countries selling their produce into another country. For example, the UK imports oil as we do not have enough which then allows cars to drive or plastics manufacturers to make their plastic products. Another example is automobiles where we do not manufacture enough cars to fulfil the demand in the UK.

The reason for highlighting the two above points is that I so often heard from Brexiteers, admittedly without a sound knowledge of economics and only repeating what they had heard from somebody else, that we should stop importing and make everything ourselves like in the 'good old days' or 'pull up the proverbial drawbridge' and slap Tariffs on all imports to help protect our British manufacturers. Clearly, this is nonsense, but I felt it should be touched upon before we cover aspects related to trade and Brexit.

It will all be so easy, quick and painless!

What became clear after the referendum result was the letters WTO were used a lot more. I say AFTER because during the referendum campaign it was almost never mentioned partly, because Leave did not expect to win so focused on their core fear tactics of 1. Immigration and 2. Turkey joining the EU and millions of Turks coming to the UK, which is obviously linked to immigration also, combined with the fallacy of taking back actual control. The control argument is a fallacy in that to trade with another country we must negotiate with them to arrive at a deal like we do as a part of the EU currently. It was clear that many Brexiteers seemed to think we would just offer a country a trade deal and they would accept everything we stipulated which is obviously nonsense and probably goes back to our imperialistic history of raping and pillaging and of empire where we did exactly that, before many of these countries secured independence like India, etc.

So from a position of not expecting to win the referendum the Leavers were suddenly put in a position of having to add some meat on the bones and explain exactly how this Leaving the EU would work in a clean and orderly manner, although there were still many that seemed not to not understand or even care about that, they just wanted out. They were now being asked about trade deals, where are they, who will they be with and initially the silence was deafening, or the glib answers of with 'everyone', or just 'wait and see'!

We have to accept that access into the EU will worsen whatever the post-Brexit deal we eventually strike as it has to be as we now have a frictionless free trade agreement. If Brexiteers claim it won't then they are greatly misinformed, disingenuous or even simply lying. Trade flows and money generated via trade with the EU will diminish and will hit us immediately after exit (there are some signs we have actually been hit already due to the lack of confidence or clarity of the future).

As reality set in after the referendum suddenly we were faced with complexities and interconnected regulations and laws etc. the Leavers failed to mentioned this could be a problem and people like Liam Fox the International Trade secretary no less who stated Coming to a free trade agreement with the EU should be 'one of the easiest in human history' because our rules and laws are already the same [3], were found to be completely wrong on many issues including the deal with the EU. But this meets with the thread that run though the Leave campaign and subsequent months that everything would either be simple and easy, or if not, they revert back to the basic excuse of 'it is somebody else's fault (the EU, the Remainers etc.) and not their lack of understanding, grasp of reality, cavalier language or downright lies to win a vote.

But we shouldn't think that it is poor old Liam Fox as the sole lone wolf who did not understand these issues and was the only one exaggerating or misunderstanding what was going on in the world and how it worked. David Davis, the smooth-talking Brexit minister, made numerous claims such as "Within minutes of a vote for Brexit the CEO's of Mercedes, BMW, VW and Audi will be knocking down Chancellor Merkel's door demanding that there be no barriers to German access to the British market."

Or

"That means immediately seeking Free Trade Agreements with the biggest prospective markets as fast as possible. There is no reason why many of these cannot be achieved within two years."

Or

In July 2016 he indicated Britain will outperform the EU in 12 months when shortly after being appointed Brexit secretary he claimed "Be under no doubt: we can do deals with our trading partners, and we can do them quickly,"

261

The negotiation phase of most of these deals, would most likely be concluded "within between 12 and 24 months" and would comprise a free trade area "massively larger than the EU", most likely including Hong Kong, Canada, Australia, India, Japan, the UAE, Indonesia – "and many others". Now I am not sure what his idea of "quickly" is but at the time of writing (August 2019) we had only secured the Faroe Islands. Incidentally the Faroe Islands is a part of the Danish realm and follow EU rules and regulations!

I could go on, but you get the picture and we could fill this book with examples from lead Brexiteers including Boris Johnson. Jacob Rees-Mogg and Nigel Farage etc. where the rhetoric sounded amazing in what was once again to be our green and pleasant land, but then entered the reality zone and it was somebody else's fault or it will happen you just have to be patient. So, patient that Rees-Mogg in one interview indicated that it may take 50 years to see the benefits of leaving the EU, when obviously (well presumably he and I will be dead). Yes 50 years! I don't know about a crystal ball, rather Mr. Rees-Mogg thinking he is Nostradamus!

So, we have this discord between some Leavers saying we will see the benefits of leaving the EU immediately but others saying it could take 50+ years which does indicate some of them or all of them do not have a clue and are winging it as they go along. But do they all think we will be more prosperous? Not necessarily according to Nigel Farage who stated he never promised that Brexit "would be a huge success", he said on LBC radio. "I never said it would be a beneficial thing to leave and everyone would be better off," said Farage – who has repeatedly said we would be better off – "just that we would be self-governing." So, Farage is coming clean and admitting that we could be worse off as many economists, industrialist and other experts have confirmed just so we can have this illusion of self-government, even though the Parliamentary white paper after the referendum confirmed our government is sovereign and always has been.

A prime example of the Brexiteer ignorance of trade as previously mentioned was the case of Nadine Dorries a member of Rees-Mogg's right wing ERG group and advocate for a no-deal exit from the EU admitting in their WhatsApp group she had been stumped in a conversation with a politics teacher and didn't know enough about the trading relationships of the customs union's members to argue the point. After her colleagues replied on WhatsApp with arguments for leaving the customs union, Dorries said: "You have just convinced me what my gut always knew – it is so complicated and convoluted, we must get the hell out." So, her logic was I do not understand it so must get out. And she is an MP!

Dorries didn't respond to requests for comment after this (obviously), but a couple of days after tweeted a picture of the Times newspaper and a message to Philip Hammond urging him to "stop trying to confuse" the issue surrounding the customs union! [4] I mean you couldn't make this stuff up. We only ask for a little intelligence from our MPs, it's not much to ask surely?

Now it is clear that many of the leave arguments were built on sand with lies, misinformation, untruths, fabrications, double counting, exaggerations and blind faith the basis but absolutely no joined up thinking of a plan or strategy and now condemned by Farage implying we may be worse off. But for many that is a good deal which is concerning.

But the lies, misunderstanding and misinformation was not just about immigration, foreigners, sovereignty etc. it was also about trade as that was going to be super easy also with us apparently quietly slipping onto WTO rules, and everything will be fine and smooth, and nobody would know the difference. How so wrong they were!

With the confusion and uncertainty of Brexit there has been a steep decline in business spending such as investment in new machinery and premises which is crucial for any manufacturing business in order to keep developing and staying ahead of the competition. This saw in 2018 according to the national manufacturing barometer only 37% of SMEs (Small and Medium-size Enterprises) increasing spending in this area compared to the previous year. We have also seen the mixed messages from government leading to stockpiling of products in case of delays, tariffs and border checks etc. which creates its own issue. For example, what if the company cannot finance this or the suppliers' stocks are already running low and they cannot replenish in time? It may be a popular and perceived as an easy way of heading off Brexit, but it could be high risk for many companies if it ties up their cash reserves that they need for cash flow / running costs and to pay their employees! It is fraught with danger as it is not the normal way these businesses do business and the problems are seen by many businesses as self-inflicted and unnecessarily diverting much needed resources, which will not allow them to grasp other opportunities that may arise. Cash is the lifeblood of any business and our businesses could end up being anaemic due to Brexit with a huge hidden opportunity cost!

In theory when talking about immigration and trade / business the influx of immigrants should give business the access to a pool or skilled and unskilled individuals as well as a new pool of customers which should increase profits (and tax revenue) which should lead to further investment by companies and the government creating new jobs and then the native population benefit from such job creation.

As the UK is looking to leave the EU with no deal it faces less free trade than we currently enjoy which flies in the face of Teresa May's argument for the UK becoming "the strongest and most forceful advocate" for free trade in the world. This is similar to her position on being open for global talent whilst at the same time she (and now Boris Johnson and Priti Patel) are looking to tighten border controls, which does not make it easier to attract the right talent as well as making them welcome when they arrive. Brexit has created so much confusion and chaos with no tangible benefits.

This logic of being a more powerful voice within the EU whilst being outside is obviously nonsense and any EU changes in trading standards etc. without our input will still affect the UK whether or not we like it.

Percentage of World Trade and the EU

I was talking to a leaver friend of mine and he told me the following 'fact'. I say 'fact' because I don't know if it's true:

He said that when we joined the EEC, their trade accounted for around 35% of world trade. Today EU trade accounts for around just 15% of world trade. I am not sure if that is correct, but it is definitely falling, although what is important is what products a country sells and how competitive they are on the world trade and also how profitable those products are to those companies and countries. Since the 70s the Far east low cost manufacturing has risen sharply especially in China, so the world trading landscape is completely different. But that does not mean we can sell billions of pounds of goods to these countries to replace the largest market that is the EU which is next door.

There is no doubt, and he admits it that the EU is still a major trading bloc, but he went on to say that while the EU is but a shrinking trading bloc, in world trade terms, the rest of the world is a faster growing area and accounts for a much larger percentage of world trade. That is why the U.K. should leave because outside the EU is where the opportunities lie.

Obviously, I disagreed with him, but it did make me think, does he have a point particularly if his percentage trade numbers are correct?

Percentage growth is a tricky one, and it is quite possible there is a far higher percentage growth outside of the EU. If some country's economy grows by, let's be crazy, say 50%, even with that growth it may only be a tiny minuscule fraction of the economy of one of the EU member states. 50% of 100 is considerably less than 1% of 50 billion... but in percentage terms it sounds better.

But to highlight this issue let's use an actual factual example with Ethiopia (8.5% growth in 2018) the fastest growing economy in Africa 2018. Situated in eastern Africa, Ethiopia has a whopping 107-million population with 30% made up of young people. It was no secret that Ethiopia's economy is booming, and its economic growth had been hovering around 8-11% for over 10 Years now. As for the average rate, it's 5.85% from 1981 to 2017, with 13.9% being the highest economic growth that this country has seen, with-11.10% being the lowest rate recorded. But to put this growth into context the GDP of the country is currently around $84 Billion which is less than Sri Lanka, Ecuador or Slovakia, so even the fastest growing economy in Africa has limited potential for the UK. But it is actually worse than that if you ask yourself what we would in reality sell Ethiopia to make a significant change to our economy when a lot of their industry and country is still very underdeveloped. Around 45% of Ethiopia's GDP is from agriculture but are we really saying Ethiopian farmers will need our excellent financial services or brand-new motor vehicles we manufacture in the UK, etc? There may be some products we can sell them, but it is limited and will make no significant benefit to our economic development post EU membership. Again, it is just another example of a naïve risk for limited, if any, gain [i.e. leaving the EU with no deal]!

It really is nonsense. Emerging markets, as in countries that can only afford to buy from you if you lend them the money in the first place, then they can't improve their education services, infrastructure or healthcare because they carry too much debt. The Chinese are big players in all these developing markets because their goods are a lot cheaper than we can produce them. The whole of Africa has the same GDP as France. Being in the EU has never held the UK back, in fact being in the EU has kept the UK up there with the bigger boys. The UK has for many years performed above its real potential mainly through foreign investment, as foreign investment into the UK because the UK is (or was!) a gateway into the world's biggest market I.e. the EU. Anyone who thinks the UK can be an economic powerhouse as a standalone nation is sadly deluded, it's why the UK government won't cut the cord and walk away, it's why the UK economy hasn't already tanked, all the smart money is on the UK not leaving, or at least staying as close as possible to the EU whilst still being able to tell the Brexiteers we have in fact left.

Another aspect linked to the EU and trade moving forward is that there will be a number of new technological innovations and developments such as electric cars etc. and all the regulations and standards will be set by the EU so our companies, even if we are outside the EU, will have to meet those new regulations if we want to supply into the EU and we will have no input on those rules and regulations. No seat at the table means you are a rule take not a rule maker and depending on how these technologies and products develop over time we could get left behind or the regulations introduced work against our manufacturers leaving them, in a much weaker position compared to EU manufacturers.

We should also not forget that trade is often linked to geography so, for example, the UK does more trade with Ireland than it does with all the BRIC countries combined despite their size due largely to the close proximity and this is something, Brexit or not, that will remain and the UK will have to deal with it.

Trade Deals are NOT that easy

This is a well-known fact but Brexiteers such as Liam Fox and David Davis et al. preferred to sell to the public that they would be easy and effectively countries would be queueing up to sign OUR trade deals. But this is disingenuous and plainly wrong. They may queue up, but they will have a list of demands knowing we are on our own and desperate to sign deals as quickly as possible due to the political importance to the EU and the outside world. Such deals are rarely just about trade and include such things as environmental regulations and human rights to name just 2. Liam Fox learned this the hard way when he said that a group of unnamed countries would prefer not to sign a deal that includes basic (human) rights. Welcome to the real-world Mr. Fox, but did you not realise this would be an issue before you started negotiation? Is this naivety, or just previous misinformation or ignorance again? Brexiteer politicians often had an 'off pat' answer but rarely a solution for the impending problems.

We had as of July 2018 116 Trade deals as a member partner of the EU which were either in place, partly in place, being negotiated, pending or being updated. Plus, we have free trade deals with the 50 poorest countries in the world (known as the "everything but arms initiative" [57]) to try to help those countries develop. So where are all these other countries that we are going to do the trade deals with that we cannot already? It is something that is often trumpeted by Brexiteers but with no details or ideas of how long this will take (some take years to finalise!) or the actual benefits we can offer or will obtain as 60 million people compared to the EU's 500 million?

The reality is that once we are on our own striking deals with unsavoury governments and regimes will be a fact of life as it was for the EU. The big difference is that the EU had the clout to make these governments accept a lot of their terms as they had a market of the aforementioned 500 million people and not the 60 million, and this makes a big difference as to what you can expect to be able to drive through. This can include human rights expectations, meeting the Paris climate accord or ensuring governments set their own laws for the good of the whole country and not that they are heavily influenced by large multinational corporations that do not want any negative developments that could affect their profits. This can happen in many countries where say the oil and gas industry wields major disproportionate influence in the country where it is based.

An example of the above is the deal the EU and Singapore signed in February 2019 whereby the EU had Singapore commit to reduced CO_2 emissions, a focus on Human Rights and a watered-down Investor-State Dispute Settlement (ISDS). Would Singapore have agreed to this with less on offer from the UK?

So often we heard that the USA was the big prize and a trade deal was workable as Donald Trump said it would be. It is difficult to say whether Liam Fox and his team are naïve or desperate but to be excited by Donald Trump's hyperbole when he has made it quite clear it is America First every time is more than naïve it is dumb. Obama was realistic when he said the UK would go to the back of the queue, especially in light of the US negotiating with the EU on a much bigger grander scale. And the EU will begin negotiations again with the US and we will be back on the side lines, and we need to get used to that as that type of deal will be a long drawn-out process (unless we just cede to all their demands of course) and the EU is in it for the long-term working towards securing the deal when Mr. Trump is no longer in office!

But even if that was not the case a trade deal with the USA is very difficult as they normally stipulate it cannot be just for products but for agriculture also which brings us into the realms of chlorinated washed chicken, GM cereals grown with the help of glyphosate pesticide, hormone injected beef and the US insists on the ISDS system IN FULL! Is that what we want? Is that where we have got to going from being a partner in the largest trading block in the world with the highest standards to a country reducing our food standards with its begging bowl at the table of a compulsive liar. Perhaps he was going to grab Mrs. May by the proverbial, or perhaps it's Mr. Johnson's lucky day!

Yes, of course, we could get a deal with the USA if we are to drop our pants and our principles, but we would pass from one economic union to another and be a rule taker as effectively the USA's 51st state.

One of the perverse arguments of great success Brexiteers put forward it that we can (and must) easily leave the EU Free Trade Agreement and area to trade on WTO rules like we trade with many countries around the world, and it is fine as many other countries trade in this way. But in the next breath claim once we are out we will negotiate and conclude as many free trade agreements as we can as WTO trade is (Presumably) rubbish? In reality it is like us going from the Premier Division to Division 3. This really is talking out of both sides of their mouths or they just simply do not really understand what they are saying or trying to confuse the public. How can moving past WTO rules to free trade agreements be a major step forward whilst moving away from our membership of the largest free trade agreement in the world not be a step backwards?

We need to be careful of all these so-called trade deals with pluses behind their name such as Norway +, Canada + (Super Canada was mentioned at one stage) etc. which could be compared to going large at McDonalds and if not necessarily being good for us. The + simply highlights the deficiencies in these deals and means the politicians suggesting such deals do not have to explain in any details what the + would mean, plus the likelihood of the other parties actually agreeing to our requests. But they are nonsense anyway as for example none of them ever got close to addressing and finding a solution to the Irish backstop.

There were some extreme fantasies with one being referred to as "no deal +" which was basically if we just walk away with nothing and refuse to sign the withdrawal agreement the EU would see we were serious and the EU would then come running to us with a series of mini deals basically giving us all the befits we have now with none of the down sides of compromises. Plus, we wouldn't have to pay a penny. Yes, I know it is pure Unicorn fantasy, but this is what happens when politicians and Brexiteers get desperate in the face of reality and the fact they have got away with so many fabrications up to now a few more will not make any difference. It is feeble mindedness and / or dishonesty of the highest order.

Will the UK always be a rule taker in the big world?

The reality is that the single market has been very good at increasing trade as it has worked very hard at liberalising the rules across all the member states and shared standards is a prerequisite for a successful trading block. With this in mind the Brexiteers need a good dose of reality because in the global economy rule making is the privilege of the powerful which is why the EU as the largest trading block in the world has been so successful in this. When it comes to negotiating any free trade agreements with the likes of the USA, China, and India (or even the EU if we leave without a deal) etc. the UK will be made very aware of this, as it is simple economics and economies of scale as well as the fact we may not have any trade deals at that time and will be therefore languishing on WTO rules. So Brexiteers may have us accepting rules, not from the EU but from other major economies which bodes the question to Leavers "what have we won?" This was quite clear at the 'winners' press conference when Boris Johnson and Michael Gove stood in front of the cameras not really knowing what to do or say as they had never thought about it in depth and that Press conference was so downbeat it was awkward. Conservative MP and Leader of the Scottish conservatives Ruth Davidson may be put it best when she said 'I have seen more cheerful wakes than that press conference. It really did look like a couple of teenage arsonists that had been caught red-handed burning the house down.' And three years after that neither seemed to have a plan of how to deliver an effective Brexit apart from saying "we are off with no deal", which would be disastrous.

Obviously, we will still trade with the EU but the costs of trade for both sides will increase but will hit us harder when 44% of our trade is with the EU and their pain is spread across 27 nations and not one. This has been referred to by some commentators as a Lose Lose scenario with no winners.

Yes, we can manufacture a more powerful power-hungry vacuum cleaner as Dyson had planned, but the problem is nobody in the EU will buy it. So will Dyson, despite having moved its Headquarters to Singapore, produce a vacuum cleaner, as they had planned previously before running into the European Court of Justice, for just the UK market? Very doubtful when one considers the economies of scale argument in global trade, but perhaps they will prove us wrong?

Financial services 'may' be an exception and The Bank Of England seemed to think that the UK may have enough clout as an international rule maker

269

in this arena, but only time will tell. Obviously other financial hubs such as Paris, Frankfurt, Dublin and Amsterdam are trying to lure companies and individuals away to weaken London's position as that predominant financial centre. And if they all chip away at a part of that London centric financial centre, in 10 Years' time it could look completely different.

It is clear that reality is now sinking in and the dishonesty of some Brexiteers as to how easy Brexit would be and countries would be queueing up to sign trade deals with the UK are now becoming quite evident either through ignorance or intent. The world of trade is INTERdependent NOT independent as we will be reliant on, for example, the port authorities in Calais to help ensure our trade flows being as frictionless as possible or US rules on Agriculture or the number of annual Visas required by India, but the list is endless. So, despite the rhetoric of the Brexiteers we will be in some shape or form a rule taker and not just rule maker as the Leave campaign and Nigel Farage etc. had us all believe.

We must remember that no other developed country has left such a trade block before, let alone in a disorderly fashion, but also one that has developed into a lot more than a trade bloc, with all the complexities that go with that. We can expect disruption on a significant scale and of a length that no other country has experienced in recent years, but the worrying thing is that many commentators and press houses are so complacent as if it could never happen to a modern economy like ours and we are Great Britain, etc. Britannia may have ruled the waves it its distant past, but it has a considerable shock coming to it, especially with no deal.

Frictionless Trade and Lorries at Dover

Surely anyone talking about trade and frictionless trade with the EU especially someone working in Government as the Brexit secretary should know of the importance of the Calais Dover trade link? Well it appeared to have escaped arch Brexiteer and one-time conservative leadership challenger Dominic Raab who came under fire for saying he "hadn't quite understood" how reliant UK trade in goods is on the Dover-Calais crossing!

The Brexit Secretary's remarks came at a technology conference as he discussed the "bespoke arrangement" the UK sought with the EU after it leaves the bloc. At the time Shadow Brexit minister Jenny Chapman suggested Mr Raab "doesn't even understand the very basics of Brexit". Conservative pro-Remain MP Nicky Morgan simply tweeted: "Gulp." Which may be said it all. Someone also tweeted "has Raab just recognised we are an island?"

Now although this is an isolated and slightly doltish statement it may show that 2 years after the referendum what people were actually voting for in detail is not understood. Even if it was, the implications of that wish were not, even by Government ministers. It looks like dogma for dogma's sake.

But to put it into context according to the Port of Dover official Road traffic statistics in 2018 2,497,804 Road haulage vehicles passed through Dover, which is a huge amount by any calculations. The Port of Dover says EU lorries as a part of the Customs Union are processed in 2 minutes, whereas it takes around 20 minutes to clear non-EU lorries. This means that if we leave the EU with no deal every foreign Lorry coming into the UK could take up to 20 minutes to process which add time and cost and limits any realistic frictionless trade and Just In Time (JIT) delivery requirements.

Many Brexiteer MPs and political figures were claiming this would not be a problem (some even citing some technological solutions that do not even exist – more Unicorns!) but what does the Port of Dover - the experts – say? It says that it has no additional space to carry out an increased number of checks, adding that in order to avoid long queues at the port after Brexit, checks will have to be concluded away from the port.

The government has said it would continue to recognise medicines that have already been approved by the EU after no deal so they can still be supplied in the UK. But there are concerns about the risks of short-term disruptions to the supply if there are delays at the border. The government did say it has plans to stockpile six weeks' worth of medicines (on top of normal stocks) in the event of no deal. So effectively we are potentially preparing almost for war like conditions and the risk of slower or no supplies of critical products and was highlighted in the Government's own research 'project Yellowhammer'.

The Government's plan was to use the Manston disused airfield to ease lorry congestion if there is UK border disruption in the event of a no-deal Brexit. Charlie Elphicke Conservative MP for Dover criticised the idea as nearly 100 lorries descended on Manston Airport near Ramsgate in Kent on a Monday morning in January 2019 to test out using the runway as an HGV holding bay to prevent traffic jams on roads to Channel ports. But a 100 lorries, one of which was a dust cart (refuse collection truck) tells us nothing when the Port could be expecting around 7,000 per day. It resembled a Dad's Army exercise with Chris Grayling playing Pike and making our Brexit plan lamentable and laughable. But it isn't even well thought through as normally lorries drive to Dover down the soon to be widened M20 motorway passed Folkestone into Dover, which is relatively simple. To go to Manston, they have either got to go to Dover and then away from the port to come back again adding circa. 45 minutes each way to their journey or cut across land bypassing Canterbury on the much smaller A28 road which is not designed to take that number of huge articulated lorries. Either way a logistics nightmare, and for what benefit?

Mr. Elphicke agrees but his proposal as he tweeted on January 7, 2019 was "Routing lorries via Manston is not the answer. Far better to extend the tried and tested traffic management system on the A20 at Dover to Kent's motorways. That way lorries can be effectively managed, got most speedily to the ports and all our motorways can be kept open". So, he basically wants a constant Operations stack with miles and miles of lorries parked along the side of the M20 Motorway with all the dangers that brings! Operation stack was meant to be an emergency last resort operation not an everyday inconvenience due to a boneheaded idea that had not ever been thought through. We can flower it up but basically it is a lorry park where lorries should not be parked. This combined with stockpiling of medicines and foodstuffs is derisible for an advanced economy like our own.

Now these are experts highlighting the real risks from the heart of this industry but we still have Brexiteer MPs in interviews saying it will not be a problem and it is all exaggerated without a scintilla of a plan of how to avoid such issues and risks which must be seen as cavalier at best or possibly incompetent or even contemptuous. Will it take a death or absolute catastrophe for those nay Sayers to see this seriousness of the issues or are they blinded by the dogma of Brexit?

But many won't care as they won't see the lorries or suffer the inconveniences and additional accidents this could cause and why? Because "it's not on their doorstep." It is rather like everybody wants a better phone reception, but nobody wants the mobile phone pylon to be next to their house. Perhaps for Brexit there is a parallel there where lots of people voted for it as they thought we will have fewer immigrants, but they did not think it would negatively affect their lives as they do not link a smaller poorer economy with paying for the roads and street lights to be repaired etc. Was it a vote for "Doesn't matter as I will be alright"?

The Institute of Government noted that "To scale [existing customs clearance] organisations up to the point where they have the capacity to manage 100% of trade would require more systems, staff and infrastructure." So basically, adding huge cost for little benefit and with unemployment at only circa. 4% (almost full employment) where are the extra workers going to come from?

We should be clear on something and that is that there WILL NOT be frictionless trade if we are outside the EU I am afraid, no matter what far-fetched conclusions some Brexiteers come to. Frictionless trade will come with Free movement of people, you take both or you get neither.

'Forgotten' or 'hidden' industries

Creative industries – do not think it is just cars and aircraft wings and other heavy industries that you see in the news that may suffer and therefore our economy will suffer with the demise or reduction of these industries. The creative industries are one such example which includes IT, Music, film and television which are worth circa. £88 Billion but may be more important to people to understand that this is circa. 3 million jobs in the UK. The exports of the creative industries in 2014 (when the latest set of figures was available) was 19.8 Billion, up 10 percent on the year before. Over half of these exports, 57.3% were sent to Europe, generating £11.4 billion in revenue. [9]

These industries are dynamic growth industries with big futures unlike some of our more traditional manufacturing sectors with our Games development sector being the largest in Europe with circa. £2 billion in revenue and growing. To make trade or the ease of employing talent from around the world more difficult with additional immigration rules and regulations could reduce the expertise coming to the UK, and other EU states will become more appealing to those individuals and cities such as Berlin, Amsterdam, and Paris who are enticing such talent to go to and reside there with their own versions of 'Tech City' that was previously created in London. Their gain is our loss, and for what? Do not think that such changes will not affect you as all these negative effects of Brexit will

273

trickle down and lead to potentially a reduced size economy, less taxes and therefore less money for public services or simple things like street lighting, road repairs etc. that all have to be paid for somehow.

Independent Trade Policy

The Brexiteer arguments for an independent trade deal as if it would all be so quick and easy, albeit very positive, is at best naïve and possibly deliberately misleading as those people stating such things must have appreciated even if they did not fully understand the true complexity of world trade today. Today's advanced economies are extremely interconnected spanning many countries with some components and sub-assemblies passing over multiple borders and countries. Now I know Brexiteers standing up and shouting "Independence Day" and independent trade for the UK can stir a feeling of our imperialistic past and Cries of 'God for Harry, England, and Saint George!' but this misses one irrefutable fact. And that is the fact that it is not actually in any shape or form independent as the other negotiating party has a massive say in that deal and getting the best deal for their respective country also and flexing their own sovereign muscles! So how can it be independent? This regular nonsense or ignorance was regularly spouted with no consideration for the complexities and realities of the International world of trade.

Brexiteers constantly talk about major trade deals and by which they are normally talking about the USA, but also China and India, yet without the combined power of negotiation and market size we lose bargaining power with any of those countries and a lot of them do not want free trade deals unless we are willing to give them a lot. India has shown little interest in free trade deals with developed countries like our own as they do not see the benefits when they are the fastest growing economy in the world anyway and would be more interested in a huge quota of visas to the UK as a part of any free trade deal. Was that what Brexiteers voted for? China is very protectionist and with its huge market size it would want a heavy price paid for free access to its prosperous, rich middle classes. The USA would insist on such free imports of chlorinated chicken and hormone infused cheap beef which could send many of our farmers out of business very quickly. The size and low cost of these USA farming conglomerates should not be underestimated, and this was one of the reasons the trade deal with the EU faltered as the EU wanted to keep food standards and standards of animal welfare high which the USA disagreed with or could not be guaranteed. In essence it would be a lowering of food standards which can quickly become a rapid race to the bottom. Is that what we want? Would we realistically have any choice as the significantly junior partner potentially with limited or no other trade deals? We export more to the USA than we import from them, so could this lead to a huge trade deficit from the current surplus if a deal was concluded? The EU could counter such USA demands but 'little Britain' may be so desperate for a significant trade deal that we will accept almost any requests to achieve that. Let's face it Brexit has created some crazy scenarios and you cannot rule anything out. remember Chris Grayling the Transport minister in 2018 handed out a contract worth £13.8 million to a new ferry company that had no ships! You couldn't normally make this stuff up, but Brexit has made people do futile things and make rash decisions due to the pressure, lack of planning and no clue where we were /are going. But the 'Ferry farce' got worse as the whole process was botched and Eurotunnel received an out of court settlement of £33 Million having done nothing as Chris Grayling's department did not follow the correct procedure as negotiations and tendering was carried out in Private. This is at a time when Brexiteer Chris Grayling was telling us how much money Brexit was going to save us!

The UK chamber of shipping spoke of long potential delays at ports for pharmaceuticals and 40% of our food. The Financial Times reported a large Japanese pharmaceutical company in the UK would be shifting 60 of its medicines to Germany (i.e. an EU state). Another example of a negative development is Surrey Satellite Technology is moving its security-sensitive contracts elsewhere within the EU. Although many Brexiteers will say "so what?" These are just 2 examples of the negative 'drip drip drip' effect of the UK losing its position, influence, and strength whilst some still believing that this idea of having an 'independent' trade policy is great, but it is just an illusion of the real-world scenario.

So, despite the cries of freedom and independence a no-deal Brexit will mean there will be certain international rules and regulation we will have to follow including rules determined by the WTO, the European Convention on Human rights (ECHR), and certain international obligations on fisheries for example. This is why Bob Sanguinetti, Chief Executive of the UK Chamber of Shipping said: "Those hoping for a no-deal Brexit have a duty to explain in technical detail why this risk is worth taking." Clearly that has been sadly lacking due partly to intransigence on behalf of Brexiteers and the Government as well as the total lack of a plan or clear strategy still!

British waters and fishing

Firstly, on fishing regardless of the EU the UK is signed up to the UN Law of the Sea Convention, which requires countries to cooperate to conserve and manage marine resources, including fisheries. It's impossible to say exactly what would happen to UK fisheries once we leave the EU without knowing what sort of deal will be negotiated. But the House of Commons Library does say that "many of the underlying issues that affect fisheries management would remain unchanged".

Once we leave the EU, we will become an independent coastal state and able to negotiate access to our waters in return for access to other markets and territorial waters. Even the government's white paper [16] on sustainable fisheries acknowledges that there are other international obligations on fisheries the UK will still need to abide by. Basically, this means we cannot just plunder everything in our fishing waters because it makes no sense and fish move so it becomes a global issue of security of food stocks.

Fisheries has always been overblown in its economic importance by the Brexiteers to hype up the British patriotism and was easy to put a few flags on a few boats and sail up the Thames and throw symbolic fish into the water for dramatic effect and then argue with Bob Geldof via a megaphone. But this simplified argument of we will take back our waters and then everything will be OK is so misplaced it must be by many Brexiteers a simple act of misdirection. If the UK leaves without a deal, it will affect the UK in 2 ways, and these are not simple and can be very complicated and we cover that more in the section of the WTO. This plays or could play a major role if no free trade agreement is agreed between the UK and the EU.

1.   Where we can fish (not a WTO issues); and

2.   And what it can sell to the EU and elsewhere (very much a WTO issue)

If you want more information specifically on the EU, UK and the Fisheries issue please go to this link which gives you more detail than will be covered here:

https://researchbriefings.parliament.uk/ResearchBriefing/Summary/CBP-8396

The above is what will take place in negotiations in the transition period which again highlights that this illusion of independence is a Brexiteer dream as we have to work with other countries to get a compromise solution.

Actually, the MEPs have legislative power in this policy area and are proposing amendments to a European Commission reform plan for the CFP which shows they are looking at reforms and cooperation between the different bodies, but there will be more negotiations with the 27 fisheries ministers going forward before the changes become EU law. The reason for this development was that they realised that the current system was not meeting the European market's needs. Fish imported from non-EU countries now accounts for two-thirds of the fish sold in the EU. The UK government is enthusiastic with UK fisheries Minister Richard Benyon saying more work must be done to encourage consumers to buy a wider range of fish. A message echoed by Sainsbury's which said "it is imperative that supermarkets such as Sainsbury's help create the consumer demand for lesser known species by promoting them to our customers.

Here we can see a positive look at issues and finding solutions and compare that to Nigel Farage's attitude to the fishermen he claimed to be supporting in that during the three years that Nigel Farage was a member of the European Parliament Fisheries Committee, he attended only 1 out of 42 meetings. Greenpeace research released shows that during the three major votes to fix the flaws of the Common Fisheries Policy (CFP), Nigel Farage was in the building but failed to vote in favour of improving the legislation.

In 2013, Nigel Farage was again present but chose not to vote on the part of the reform of the CFP that introduces an obligation on governments to give more fishing quota to sustainable fishermen who contribute the most to the local, coastal economies. This would see the government giving more fishing quota to local, low impact fishing fleets, such as the fishermen featured in UKIP's poster.[27] This does just show the hypocrisy of Mr. Farage who appears either not to understand the issues or not care about them or the people affected by these issues but claims to support the common man and the fisherman. Perhaps he prefers to be in front of the camera pushing his newly formed personality cult called the Brexit Party than actually doing some hard graft in the committees to achieve change? But how many people question this?

Remember that if we ban other countries from fishing in our waters, then other countries will do the same and although we have plenty of cod in the North Sea a lot of our white fish comes from seas around Norway and Iceland so the costs of those would rise or we would have limited access. We export most of our shellfish such as Crab and Langoustines so with import duties into the EU many of our exporters of such shellfish could find they are no longer competitive and could go bust. This is a more balanced picture of fishing and not the one-sided Brexiteer view that the evil EU and their fishermen are all against us and stealing our birth right, etc. In Thatcher's time these quotas were actually commodified, and the "owners" of the quotas sold them to the highest bidders, including foreign "investors" from Holland, Spain and elsewhere and in that way the ports were depleted of boats as they were not needed and now we are reaping the downside of those decisions made decades ago, but as usual it is easier to blame the foreigner fishermen rather than look at the root causes of issues.

Will the planes be halted and grounded?

Post Brexit airlines operating inside the EU (between member countries like France and Germany for example, without going through the UK) will have to comply with EU majority ownership rules. These rules say that the majority of shareholders in an airline have to be based in the EU - UK shareholders will no longer count towards that threshold after 29 March 2019. In order to operate flights within the EU, air carriers with UK shareholders will have to change their ownership structure to ensure they meet that threshold. For example, EasyJet has established a new branch, EasyJet Europe, in Austria in order to maintain full access to the EU market. The owner of British Airways, IAG, was reportedly in talks with European governments to ensure it meets EU and UK ownership requirements after Brexit. Ryanair has the same issue of lack EU shareholders, but CEO Michael O'Leary has confirmed they will have this organised by the time we leave the EU.

EU agreements also govern flights between the EU (including the UK) and a number of other countries, like the USA. These also need to be renegotiated. The UK has been discussing these with relevant governments to ensure flights can continue and so far has signed agreements with the USA, Canada and eight other countries.

It is quite clear that due to the pan-European / global nature of flights and aviation that agreements, even if short term, will be agreed and flights will not be halted or grounded. But it just demonstrates another area of this Brexit story where there is a lot of time, work, and additional costs (again!) with no discernible advantages and benefits to anyone.

Chapter 20
Brexit and Foreign Direct Investment into the UK

How could Brexit affect Foreign Direct Investment into the UK?

To know exactly how much Brexit will affect the UK in the years to come is impossible to say but certain economists, investment banks and other experts will and do make forecasts and estimations but the one thing that is clear is that it will have a negative effect. You do not have to be a rocket scientist to realise if you make it more difficult to do business with the largest trading block in the world, as we have left it and are outside looking in there will be less investment and therefore less jobs and tax revenues and even less highly skilled engineers, technicians et al. in the UK. When Brexiteers tell us this is rubbish I am firstly amazed they think things won't or can't get worse because of Brexit but when I then push them to better understand their position many clearly have no idea or they spout genuinely pie in the sky ideas of, for example, we can trade more with the Commonwealth and Africa you realise the knowledge is lacking and you have to ask why did they genuinely vote Leave? But even regarding the Commonwealth we do not have to choose between say the commonwealth and Europe but rather we can be at the heart of the commonwealth and utilise our historical position whilst still benefiting from our free trading status and close proximity to continental Europe to benefit the UK. I also asked what and how much we would sell to the Commonwealth to justify leaving the EU, but little coherent replies.

As regards what is happening at the time of writing we see experiences even before we have even left, with Japanese car makers building models elsewhere, European research bodies moving staff back into the EU, or International Banks shifting staff to Frankfurt as well as household names such as Panasonic cutting jobs. What should not be forgotten is the fact that companies such as Nissan, Honda et al. get the headlines but other smaller companies and SMEs that are not household names will lose jobs too, either because they are a part of the supply chain to companies such as Nissan or buy and sell from the EU and will also be significantly hit and that will mean less jobs and less tax receipts for the exchequer. This is not project fear this is Brexit reality although many Brexiteers will find many other reasons as to why these companies were cutting jobs or moving elsewhere and some may have some basis BUT it is quite a coincidence of timing and we haven't even left with many companies still hoping we will remain in or the Brexit will be so soft it will not dramatically affect their business moving forward. Some companies are affected by Brexit even though they do not deal with them directly as their customers or suppliers do, and so they are indirectly affected, and their businesses could suffer for that reason.

There has been FDI despite the referendum result but with the plunge in the Pound after the referendum Leave result it meant foreign companies could buy British assets at a much cheaper price after the 23rd June than they could do the day before, one only hopes it is not the cynical asset strippers or those making off with our hard earned Intellectual Property. But there are some concerns as the UK was the top destination for cross-border mergers and acquisitions involving American tech firms in 2014-17, but in 2018 had dropped to eight place. Now there may well be more complex reasons for this drop but we would be naïve not to consider that Brexit played a role especially in those companies that were originally investing in the UK to also have easy access to the EU for their products or services, when now nobody has any clue of what the rules, regulations and laws will be for the UK as a third party country trading with and inside the EU. Could these companies now take the risk that it would be OK rather than investing in say Amsterdam knowing that they would definitely have direct access to the largest trading market in the world?

In October 2018 the UK Trade Policy Observatory at Sussex University modelled a counter factual Britain that had voted Remain, and found that the Leave vote had reduced inward investment by a fifth.[29] You may argue with the amount or the degree but it appears irrefutable that there must be a drop in FDI unless something significant changes.

But Brexit affects domestic firms, too. In January 2019 Barclays bank received legal approval to move Euros 900 billion ($213 billion) of assets to Dublin, fearing no deal. The London School of economics recently found the Brexit vote had caused a 12% rise in investment by British firms in the rest of the EU. That capital might otherwise have been used at home. FDI remains strong, but it could be even stronger if it wasn't for Brexit. And Britain has not even left yet.[29] So we can see it could be worse but it could also be a lot better and the theme running through this book is that it is clear it will cost us money, that is not really in doubt, its just a question of how much, but what are the tangible advantages we will see and experience upon leaving taking into account these costs and losses?

It has been argued by some Brexiteers that despite the UK voting to leave job creation is at an all-time high, so things are fine. Obviously this is false as firstly, job creation takes time and for jobs to be lost in times of poorer economic growth etc. But also, just because overall 1000 jobs are created but 400 lost due to a no-deal Brexit this is still 400 lost jobs for our UK citizens and should not be seen as just 1000 jobs which is great because it is not as good as it could have been if we had remained in the EU. This is just one example and there are a lot more, with more to follow of lost opportunities and the opportunity cost could be significant!

Should you want some more information on job losses in the UK since the EU referendum this is at the time of writing a good resource. https://smallbusinessprices.co.uk/brexit-index/.

The EU has helped open global markets to UK firms on strong terms

The EU is a springboard for trade with the rest of the world through its global clout: it accounted for 23% of the global economy in 2012 in dollar terms. Through 37 trade deals negotiated by the EU, including the Single Market itself, British firms now have full access to a $24 trillion market. The recent deals with Canada and Japan and the US could double this to $47 trillion - the UK would struggle to achieve the same quality of trade deals independently. The average man on the street is not aware of this and has no interest in this when they are concentrating on putting food on the table BUT this filters through to the wealth of the country due to huge taxes paid by major multinationals which allows the exchequer to better deliver public services such as the NHS or even basics such as street lighting. The stronger the UK businesses the stronger the economy and therefore the wealth of the country and the EU membership has facilitated this very well.

By exiting the EU with no deal the UK will be so far behind the curve when it comes to trade deals when we lack the required economies of scale and do not have the time to wait around in long drawn our tedious trade negotiations (which is what they are) when our business and our economy needs free low cost trade to prosper. The latest significant trade deal is between the EU (yes the EU!) and the key emerging markets in Latin America building bigger economic opportunities for its citizens, while our Brexiteer ministers boast of a potential archaic no-deal Brexit success as if they have achieved something. The political agreement was reached with Argentina, Brazil, Paraguay, and Uruguay to enable free trade between their South American trading bloc, Mercosur, and the EU. It is estimated that the free trade area of circa. 780 million people will save EU exporters £3.6 billion a year in tariffs. But this has been worked on and negotiated for over 20 years, which puts into context the nonsense that is coming out of Whitehall and Westminster since Boris Johnson became Prime Minister.

Certainly in trade terms with a soccer analogy, it looks like we were in the premier division for Manchester City looking very comfortable only to decide to slip down into the non-league team to try and get back up again, all because we made an atrocious decision, that the people may never get a chance to confirm was what they wanted.

Jobs

It is sometimes underestimated or not known how millions of jobs are linked to the UK's membership of the EU and they are at risk. Many industries / sectors such as manufacturing, and nursing could experience a slump in skilled labour as the UK simply does not have enough of the skills that we need. It really should not be underestimated that the EU helps us maintain millions of jobs, and therefore generate wealth and therefore pay more taxes!

Sometimes there seems a disconnect between the public, who have other day to day priorities, and the understanding that successful businesses lead and drive successful economies around the world – otherwise where does the money come from? The CBI estimates that the net benefit of EU membership is worth 4-5% of GDP to the UK, or £62-£78billion per year which is huge.

A report by the Centre for Economics and Business Research, released in October 2015, suggested 3.1 million British jobs were linked to the UK's exports to the EU, but there are also a variety of other jobs such as research etc. which would increase that number. Clearly, if we Leave the EU, especially on a no-deal scenario, those jobs will become vulnerable despite some restructuring and adjustments that will be made.

Free movement of labour has brought benefits to the UK economy

Inextricably linked to Brexit and jobs and immigration is the Free movement of labour. Despite the disappointing vitriol and negative press from certain Newspapers, individuals such as Nigel Farage, and media outlets in the run up to the 2016 Referendum the free movement of Labour has been critical for the growth and development of the UK economy over many years. Free movement helps UK business plug skills gaps. 63% of CBI members say that the ability to recruit and transfer staff from across the EU has been positive for business, including 48% of SMEs. Overall only 1% of members said the impact had been negative – and only 2% of SMEs said it had been negative.

So, businesses are making it quite clear that this is an advantage to them and adding real value to the economy, but this was jumped on by the Leave contingency as immigration was 1. Taking jobs off the British and 2. Suppressing wages. But let's look at those two accusations.

a. With unemployment at its lowest levels for many years this does not stand up to scrutiny as many immigrants do jobs that the British workers / residents don't traditionally want to do, and I have asked many UK residents (non-immigrants) of how many of their kids "want to wipe patients bums in a hospital?" "dig up and pick cabbages in the cold and rain for 12 hours per day?" etc. and the answers were always negative although often followed up with a lacklustre caveat of 'well they would if they had to ...' etc. But from

284

an employers' point of view this is not good enough and they need commitment to maximise the input / output. Clearly, it can be highlighted that there are British workers who actually do those jobs BUT there are nowhere near enough and never will be. But rather than be thankful for our EU immigrants doing these jobs and looking after our parents and grandparents in hospital or helping supply food to our supermarkets a part of our society turned on them and used them as scapegoats for all their own ills and problems, and that was very disappointing that these were my compatriots attacking people that were helping our economy and our society.

b.   As regards the suppressing of wages research has shown that for most of the jobs and trades there is no evidence that this is true. So, despite some plumbers, builders etc. saying that is true and may be offering anecdotal stories there is no actual evidence and it is probably more a case of they have may be suffered due to the recession after the financial crash and austerity, but it was not due to immigration. Sometimes in this regard people are hypocritical as they complain about what a plumber costs them or even how difficult it is to find a good reliable one. But where immigrants can help them with that issue many don't want foreigners although will still use them if it is in their own interest (hypocrisy?). We cannot have our cake and eat it.

It was clear during the campaigns that many people were not buying this, did not understand it and did not want to learn and just thought the end to free movement would solve what they saw as many of the country's ills. A position many cannot be blamed for as this was a message used many times in history, but the charlatans sending the messaging and being disingenuous to the general public should be blamed as they were the liars and the messengers that are now proving to have been wrong or were simply being false. Even since the referendum and the observable reality of many of the promises they made not being realised they still hold the public in the dark with highly convoluted and technical language to again confuse and bamboozle people to try and hide the truth of what is actually happening. And some of them are very good at it.

According to the Food and Drink Federation (FDF) the industry's skills gap could also be exacerbated by Brexit. Currently more than a quarter of the industry's workforce is made up of EU citizens, which are critical for this manufacturing sector.

An interesting point was when I asked Brexiteers if when voting for 'British people' as they liked to say whether they ever considered the free movement and rights of the 2 million British citizens living abroad in the other EU member states to which almost to a man was the reply was silence, a blank look or "I hadn't even thought about them". Many were so focused on Eastern Europeans coming to the UK to work that they did not even consider the rights of those fellow citizens. It seems all UK citizens are equal just some are more equal than others!

Do not underestimate the Long-term effect of investment!

At the time of writing job creation and levels of employment were doing very well, although pointing this out too many Leavers that this had been achieved whilst a member of the EU tended to fall on deaf ears for obvious reasons. But we need to be careful that we do not become complacent as these jobs have been created from investment from 2-3 years ago but up to April 2019 there had been 4 quarters of declining business investment which is storing up problems for the future as there is an obvious lag as there always is between the time investment is allocated and when the companies and economy benefit from this.

This reduced investment is partly due to the global slowdown but also Brexit and the lack of visibility or confidence in what the future holds, which if this was then combined with a no-deal Brexit could create real ripples through the business economy and result in a serious lack of investment and more focus on belt tightening as the economy would then be forecasted to shrink.

The Financial Times reported on 1st April 2019 that Goldman Sachs says Brexit costs the UK 600 million per week in their study. This number is revealed as Goldman said Brexit has cost Britain about 2.4% of Gross Domestic Product (GDP) and estimated that the UK economy had underperformed other advanced economies since mid-2016 as a result.

The UK went from the fastest growing economy in the G7 in 2016 to the joint slowest with Italy in the first quarter of 2017, and the slowest rate of growth of the other 27 countries of the EU Clearly, it is not as simple as saying this was because of the vote to Leave but we would be naïve not to think it was a major impacting factor for various reasons.

It is not just the long-term effects but also those already present, but the average person will not notice for a long time and even when they do with, for example, higher taxes they may not link the two.

Now many of my Leaver friends quite rightly point out like forecasts they are just estimates and not a science, which is amusing when some of the items they have read or heard and take on board as gospel because it came from Boris Johnson's lips (some of you will get the Irony there). But even if it is not 2.4% and only say 1% it is a loss and an unnecessary loss with no tangible benefits apart from some Brexiteers still believing we will be more independent, more sovereign and have less immigrants. It just highlights the difference between what was promised and the sunny uplands of old England and the actual real interdependent, interrelated world that is very complex and where true cooperation is needed. Cooperation and not isolation are the name of the game in the 21st Century.

Investment into non-financial assets, including machinery and factories etc., had reduced since the EU referendum vote result and as of August 2019 falling in five of the last six quarters which is now about 1.5% lower than in 2018. Many surveys have demonstrated many businesses have been deterred from investing in the UK due to Brexit and the uncertainty including barriers to trade etc. The results of the Government's own research project Yellowhammer added to this concern and justified many companies' decisions not to invest into the UK.

Cost versus Investment

This is often a misunderstood concept especially by everyday people that do not run businesses, may not invest money for higher gains and focus on making ends meet and balancing their household income and expenditure. But it is one of the important advantages of our EU membership.

An example is when people complain about the amount of money the EU "COSTS" us as if it goes into a bottomless pit, but it does not, and we can use Poland as an example. In 2004 Poland did under £4 Billion in trade with the UK now over £14 billion per year so we have benefited greatly from that and that is just one country, whilst our net contributions to the EU £8 billion per year. So, the simple maths show that it is a good investment. As these Eastern European economies develop they buy more of our advanced goods, their economy improves, as well their wages increase which in turn takes pressure off the UK immigration (if people feel it is an issue) as a lot go home or stay home as the wages have risen. So, although a longer game it creates a win win and is not a zero-sum game as some Brexiteers would have you believe! As of 2019 we have seen this with more Polish going home for exactly that reason, plus also the more unfriendly the UK is perceived towards foreigners since the referendum in 2016.

Future of Jobs and pensions

Clearly modernisation and automation of working processes etc. will play an ever more increasing role in our economy and job creation programmes but statistics show that we will still need a large immigrant workforce to cover these jobs where we have a serious lack of skills or specific jobs that Brits traditionally do not want to do or WILL NOT do. Now many of these jobs that immigrants fulfil cannot be replaced by such technology and automation. At the time of writing We have a shortage of many skills including HGV drivers (not enough qualified Brits), the huge and growing hospitality and tourism industry which is very labour intensive, a huge shortage of trained carers for the elderly, NHS workers where there is currently 45,000 vacancies, as well as the lack of teachers in those subjects that are more popular in a modern society which is dependent on specific high education and skill levels needed.

The UK has done very well as regards employment in recent years as a full member of the EU but there are some signs on in Q3 2019 that with Brexit looming and a global slowdown the UK jobs market may have lost some steam, but the vote to leave the European Union possibly on a no-deal Brexit has exacerbated any issues there were in the system, and were unnecessary.

Linked closely to the future of jobs and the number of workers in the British economy are UK pensions and how they are paid for as it accounts for 40% and rising of welfare spending in the UK. Two major sources are:

1. The success i.e. profits of corporations large and small which if our economy shrinks will cause a real issue; and

2. The taxes from workers and the more workers earning more money the better. These sources are critical as people live longer and therefore must be paid for and draw pensions for sometimes 30 years plus. This is an economic ticking time bomb that could be alleviated by more younger workers paying their taxes into the exchequer but obviously the success and profitability of UK companies also. This should not be underestimated but say, for example, 1 million immigrant workers were ejected or went home, imagine the huge drop in tax income from those workers and the money they no longer spend in our economy on food, petrol, household goods etc. Have Brexiteers ever thought about that?

One aspect rarely covered is the fact people's pensions may be affected if they do not have final salary guaranteed pensions. The reason for this is that pensions are reliant heavily on the performance of the stock market and if the UK crashes out with a no-deal Brexit which way will the markets go? The obvious casualties will be those that are UK focused and make most of their profits in the UK as opposed to the giants like BP, but it could be detrimental to people's pensions, and I wonder how many of them would have voted Leave and risked the performance and ultimate pay-outs from their own pensions. Some may say this risk is limited but again I ask, 'why risk such things and for what real tangible benefits?' Another potential risk people did not consider or know about when they voted I fear.

Only time will tell but Brexit and especially a no-deal Brexit could be a job killing machine that nobody realistically expected as only now are the true ramifications of such a mover becoming clear.

Chapter 21
World Trade Organisation - WTO

The reason for including this section which reared its ugly head in 2018 was that it was hardly ever mentioned or covered in the referendum due largely to the Leavers so positively pronouncing how easy it would be to get a great deal with the European Union which has proved much more difficult than they promised. But from Farage advocating what great solutions Norway or Switzerland would be great for the UK he has now gone to the extremes claiming a no-deal WTO Brexit is the best option for the UK, which probably says more about his dogmatic desperation to the leave the EU than his well thought out balanced reasoning for the best solution for his country. The Brexiteers would, beginning in 2018 sing the praises and advantages of a WTO solution in broad brush strokes but avoiding the details due to the complex nature explained in the following pages. In reality it gives the UK less control than the country had within the EU, which is the bizarre irony of the Brexiteer position they have taken in 2019.

What simply is the WTO?

I was not going to write much on the WTO as it was not really a significant part of the Referendum campaign or even after the result in 2016 as we were told by Brexiteers that Norway+, Canada+, Switzerland or a negotiated deal with the EU would be easy. Unfortunately, as reality kicked in the Leavers realised, this was not the case and so had no choice but to claim that leaving with no deal on WTO terms would be perfectly acceptable even though no other country in the world works on purely WTO terms, because it is naturally a last resort back-up plan and not an intelligent strategy to improve any country's economic position.

The WTO came to prominence NOT during the Referendum campaign when we were told by many of the main Brexiteers that we would get a great deal, an easy deal, or we could be like Norway, or Switzerland etc. only for them to meet the harsh face of reality and suddenly a no-deal WTO type exit deal would be the best option, albeit it did sound desperate and not at all well thought through. So, what is it? Well, the easiest way to begin is to go to the horse's mouth where on the WTO website it states:

'The World Trade Organization (WTO) is the only global international organisation dealing with the rules of trade between nations. At its heart are the WTO agreements, negotiated and signed by the bulk of the world's trading nations and ratified in their parliaments. The goal is to help producers of goods and services, exporters, and importers conduct their business.' It is in essence an international organisation aiming to reduce all barriers to trade and literally tries to achieve this by acting as a forum for countries to constantly re-negotiate to remove blocks they have on trade, and these renegotiations are called 'Rounds'.

Barriers to trade include the so much talked about Tariffs (taxes) on products or services being imported into a country, as well as added tariffs that a foreign product or service may pay within a country. Unlike other economic organisations like the IMF (International Monetary Fund) each country has only one vote though decisions are generally made by consensus. The exception you won't be surprised is the EU which has a block vote of 28, soon to be 27 of course (well unless somehow Brexit is cancelled or voted down). The WTO does not have a set of minimum tariffs or rules which each country must comply, instead it has two main elements which are critical.

One point of clarity is that there is in fact a difference between 'WTO rules' and 'WTO terms'. 'WTO rules' govern all the trading relations between the UK and the EU, including the single market, customs union, and any other form of free trade agreement or even a 'no deal'. Agreements can go beyond WTO rules in some areas, but not in others. The rules remain the foundation for any arrangement. 'WTO Terms' means particular conditions that countries have agreed in the WTO, such as their individual 'commitments' (pledges) on tariffs, agricultural subsidies or opening up of services markets. Its meaning is therefore much narrower than WTO rules.

Firstly, it requires each country sets out a list of its tariff rates for each product and service. Each tariff set for a product and service is subject to negotiation with each other member of the WTO, which we will return to. Whether another member seeks to negotiate these Tariffs will depend on whether they have a vested interest in those products. For large trading states like the USA, China, or Brazil these lists, or 'schedules' can be extremely long and therefore can take a long time (sometimes years!) to work through. The UK as a part of the EU has a single 'schedule' for ALL its members and it is quite extensive.

Secondly, it requires states to apply their own individual schedules, and non-Tariff rules on packaging or licensing etc. in a non-discriminatory way, which basically means they cannot use one tariff for one country and another tariff for another country for the same product or service.

The non-discrimination aspect breaks down into two basic rules and forms the so called 'Most-Favoured Nation' and 'national treatment rules'. Firstly, Most-Favoured nation means you must give your best treatment to all foreign products coming into a country to all WTO members, e.g. if a country cut the tariff on imports of Sheep from 12.8% to 5% for exports from one country, we would have to charge 5% to every other country as well.

Taking sheep as an example there are the import quotas (e.g. from New Zealand and Australia) but any sheep imports outside those quotas are subject to Ad Valorem (in proportion to the estimated value of the goods or transaction concerned) tariff of 12.8%, PLUS a fixed amount ranging from Euros 902 to Euros 3118 per tonne, depending on the cut. In many cases this is equivalent of an Ad Valorem tariff of 50% +. This obviously seriously impacts on the ability of imported sheep to compete with EU meat as the prices are uncompetitive, which is the aim of the EU system. The result any sheep imported is within quota, but we will now once we leave the EU have the same problem that our meat will be uncompetitive. What quota we will be granted by the WTO and its members is at this stage unknown and again shows our lack of independence when we leave the EU.

The 'National Treatment' rule means that you must give your best internal conditions to foreign products or services e.g. if you do not require domestic products to have a warning as to say sugar content in food you cannot require it on foreign products. So, you can see that it is a way of trying to achieve a level and fair playing field. These requirements are set out in detail in the WTO's core treaties which are:

- General Agreement on Tariffs and Trade (GATT)

- General Agreement on Trade in Services (GATS)

- Trade-related Intellectual Property (TRIPs)

BUT there is one exception, and that is if you are in a customs union like the EU and then you can treat products and services from your customs union better than you treat other WTO members, which is why countries are always trying to get mutually beneficial free trade deals / customs unions such as the EU, NAFTA etc. and why the UK if it leaves the EU with no deal would be almost the only country NOT to have any free trade Agreements (FTAs).

So, seems fairly straight forward and all good so far for the Brexiteers, as that is the noble aims but how do they get there and who makes the decisions, can countries make up their own rules, etc? This is not a trade and economics book so we will not go into huge technical details but as Brexit has thrown up critical questions about trade and the WTO we will investigate this form of trade and what the implications are for the UK, the EU and our other potential 'Free Trade' trading partners as the WTO is not as simple as implied by Brexiteers and is not just an organisation for tariffs.

What became clear when listening to the lead Brexiteers and Leave politicians and then listening to the trade experts was that like us the voters they did not seem to understand how the WTO worked and were quickly turning to Wikipedia to try to avail themselves of some information to try to sound at least partially convincing. Also when they had a decent grasp of this like Jacob Rees-Mogg he would avoid highlighting the complexities and issues with trading on WTO for obvious reasons so describes it in idealistic tones as he doesn't really care as his sole focus in life is leaving the EU and has been for many years and possesses that lassaiz faire attitude of "It will be alright in the night". He would clearly be as happy as a pig in the proverbial once we leave the EU so he can celebrate with a glass of his favourite tipple with his chums in his £5 million mansion in Westminster to celebrate and then worry about it after, whilst the poorer in society suffer the most.

The WTO is not some panacea to easy trade because the US right wing (who does not like following any International Trade rules) for example hates the WTO dispute settlement regime and sees it as the UK right wing sees the European Court of Justice which is basically a supranational affront to sovereignty when all they are trying to do is create and introduce common laws, regulations and rules to create a common playing field to the benefit of as many as possible. Sound familiar?

The question is obviously what happens when there are disputes or countries not keeping to the agreed 'rules'. The WTO addresses this with a Dispute Settlement Body (DSB) where countries can take their cases against other countries they think are violating WTO rules. The DSB is a busy body showing you that it does not work as smoothly and easily as Brexiteers would have you believe. The EU and the USA as well as China, India and Brazil are the most common participants in disputes which indicates the larger stronger bodies are either accused of violations or claim violations so maybe it is not as egalitarian as we would like and if we are outside the EU, we will not have the same influence. At the time of writing President Trump and the USA have begun a trade war with China which the WTO is struggling to control.

If a country is found in violation of WTO rules it is required to change its laws to comply with them, but if countries choose not to do so the winning country can take retaliatory action in the form of trade sanctions such as introducing higher tariffs.

The accusation against the WTO is that is lacks teeth and is only a forum for negotiation but even that can take years with the latest round called DOHA achieving little success despite starting in 2001! The willingness of its members to negotiate with each other will dictate how successful or not the WTO will be now and in the future, and we see with the USA and China this is often NOT the case.

What would it mean for us to crash out of the EU on WTO rules?

There are advantages in theory of trading on WTO rules such as Free Trade Deals with non-EU countries, we would not be beholden to the European Court of Justice (ECJ) and have more independence or sovereignty over trade deals, although as we will discover not totally which makes a mockery of the independent claim.

The government's default legal position at the time of writing is that we will leave the EU without a deal. With this in mind both the UK and the EU have submitted their plans for trade to the WTO on which they wish to trade with the rest of the world. But they are different reflecting the UK's and EU's own specific positions and priorities.

UK wants to replicate the rules they already have as a member of the EU with some minor technical changes which seems very optimistic as the original deal with the EU was based on a group of 500 million people but now we want the same for a smaller group of 60 million. Once this is submitted the other members of the WTO i.e. all those countries around the world had 90 days to submit their objections. Yes, you heard right 'they can raise objections to our plan', so this bodes the questions where did our sovereignty go to make such independent decisions? And this is where reality begins to creep into the Leave plans and distortions as they were never realistic as sold to the public. So, we cannot see that 164 countries plus the EU block, so 164 in total can and will have input on our WTO trade plans in the rest of the world. Were you ever told that at the referendum campaign? In fact, the WTO was very rarely mentioned as we were told by David Davis and Liam Fox etc. that we would have all these deals secured on the day we left.

This system of 'objecting' has already started as the USA, Brazil and New Zealand do not agree that the UK can simply replicate the current agreement shared with the EU that share an import quota system for the importation of sensitive products such as Beef, sugar, and lamb, etc. They will put forward an alternative proposed arrangement based on historical trading volumes which will then be considered by the WTO and some form of agreement will be reached. So, in reality independence in the sense it was sold to the public does not exist and whilst the UK is trying to reach a trade deal with the EU it will also be negotiating directly and indirectly in the sense of the WTO with 164 other countries all of whom have their own interests at heart. Was that the independence Leavers were sold?

Although at the time of writing it has not been confirmed but New Zealand would almost definitely not accept the UK proposal for splitting quotas on Lamb and other products, but for the UK and EU farmers it is in fact much worse. The Tariff quotas mean that, with no deal between the UK and EU, trade between them in some agricultural products would dry up completely. In others, it would be severely reduced. Some may say that it's only New Zealand and its only

Lamb etc. but this is missing the point as this is just one example of the problems we could face on WTO terms and there are many other areas that do not make the news that could put UK businesses in jeopardy.

So, in a nutshell 164 countries CAN affect our trade plans, schedules and legality of what we want to achieve. But how long does this take? Roberto Azevêdo, director general of the World Trade Organisation highlighted in an interview that some agreements can take decades, but this will depend on what the UK's proposals are towards import tariffs, etc.

One fallacy we need to squash is that upon leaving the EU and moving on to WTO rules we would be outside the jurisdiction of the European Court of Human Rights (ECHR) which is not correct as this has nothing to do with the EU. So, outside the jurisdiction of the ECJ yes but ECHR no. I do not understand why people are against the ECHR unless it is ignorance thinking it is a part of the EU (so anything +EU is bad for them) as despite not being perfect (which organisation is?) it holds national governments to account, and with regards human rights, surely that is a good thing?

But we should not forget that hardly any countries trade on WTO rules as they have so many further protocols that avoid such terms, and there is a reason for that which is basically that the WTO rules based trade is a last resort, almost a safety net and not something to be celebrated when we go off the cliff.

David Davis is renowned for his hyperbole and broken promises as a government minister elsewhere in this book which includes his understanding of the WTO but the former head of the WTO Pascal Lamy through his proverbial hands up in exasperation at the erroneous statements being made by Mr. Davis about the WTO. Mr. Lamy is a polite and well-mannered man but basically he was saying that Mr. Davis was, in everyday parlance, talking bullshit! Mr. Davis is not alone in Mr. Lamy's horror at Brexiteers understanding of the WTO which has been skewed many times to fit their narrative. For example, Iain Duncan Smith the desperate and lifelong anti-EU advocate when referring to article 24 of WTO to solve the UK-EU border issues in Ireland (i.e. countries in discussion to form a customs union can ask other WTO members to consider their trade schedules "as if" they were already the same, pending final ratification. This is nonsense and none of this applies to either the withdrawal agreement or a no-deal Brexit. More fantasy, more lies and more unicorns, years after the vote, all because Mr Duncan et al. did not have a shred of a plan when the vote was won. That is shameful when it is most probably the poor will pay the highest price of a no-deal Brexit.

"UK can simply scrap all tariffs with the EU and the rest of the world."

This is an option that was put forward by some rather poorly informed Brexiteers as although strictly true the UK would then have to do this for all other WTO countries otherwise we would be violating WTO non-discrimination rules particularly the most favoured nation* principle. This would mean there would be no Tariffs, inspections nor paperwork on any imports, and there would be little control over the safety of products from anywhere, and that obviously would not be an acceptable situation to the 6th largest economy in the world. Also, there would be no protections for any of our manufacturers and farmers etc. which could put them out of business so would not be a very clever strategy to help ensure we have a regular reliant supply of home-grown products of a high standard. Is this really what we want or where we have got to as a nation since the Referendum vote?

*This means that countries cannot discriminate between their trading partners. If country x grants country Y a benefit (e.g. a simplified licensing process), that same favour must be granted to all other WTO members.

"No problem as the average EU import Duty is only 3.2%!"

This again was an argument put forward by Brexiteers which on the surface seems OK until you look into this in a bit more detail. The first problem of this argument is for UK companies that export a lot to the EU and work on low single digit gross profit margins which some industries have to as it is so competitive. If they incur an additional 3.2%+ Tariff cost this could send them into liquidation as they may now be competing with a competitor in France, Germany etc. that does not have those additional costs (or paperwork and potential delays at the border).

But also, those businesses that do not work on low margins may be totally shafted if we went down that route as the highest tariff rates are in fact way above 25%, which includes 1 in 10 agricultural products, which are the equivalent of 189% for some dairy products and 116% for some animal products. For processed foods they are even more complex as they can change if a recipe is changed by say adding or reducing sugar content. This demonstrates that the trade in food and agricultural products will be hit hardest for both importers AND exporters.

Theoretically we could import more food from outside the EU but due to a small percentage of our imported food coming from non-EU countries and the distances involved in importing from those countries we would have to significantly change / lower our food standards, inspection regimes, and import policies for these countries to meet anywhere near our requirements plus shipping costs etc. would be higher. The impact on the carbon footprint if we suddenly wanted more from the other side of the world would be significant. Not exactly a step forward, and from a practical point of view this will not happen any time soon.

Although we talk about Tariffs, the UK's National Farmers Union seems more concerned about the lack of agreement on regulations and standards in the event of no deal and when it comes down to it, we may find that these become more important than Tariff barriers. This just highlights again the lack of understanding by Brexiteers about the intricacies and implications of the WTO world.

"We can become like the Singapore of Europe with Zero Tariffs"

Many are concerned about this should a conservative government go in this direction due to the deregulation and the fact that Singapore, like Hong Kong are de facto 'Cities' really and completely different from the UK.

As highlighted previously slashing import Duties would negatively affect some most protected industries including strategic industries such as agriculture and food and drink. But the reason for protecting agriculture and similar industries is to protect local production and keep farmers in business to continue a long-term supply of food and foodstuffs. Singapore and Hong Kong do not have a significant farming industry and therefore it works to their benefit of their Islands as they rely on such imports.

If the UK unilaterally scrapped import duties, it would also weaken the UK's negotiating position for any free trade agreements if it had already scrapped duties, although agreements also include services, regulations and standards so it is not just Tariff rates that would play a role. Singapore literally used these in its negotiations with the EU as they had no high import Tariffs to use as bargaining chips.

298

You can never rule out such a development, but this is very unlikely and is usually referred to by uninformed Brexiteers especially with the high percentage of immigrants in Singapore. The non-resident population increased at an unprecedented pace in the first decade of the 21st century, according to the 2010 Singapore census. During this period, it accounted for 25.7 percent of the total population, up from 18.7 percent in the previous decade. How many Leave voters and Brexiteers would want those percentages in the UK?

WTO and Services

As 80% of our economy comes from services how would moving to WTO terms impact our economy or how does the WTO deal with Services as this is not as simple as products, Tariff codes and percentages? Just for clarification when I first started looking into services I had to look up some examples which are extensive and cannot all be listed but include maintenance agreements, lawyer to financial services, tourism, installations, architecture, design, and catering, etc. So, the list is vast.

Compared to Products the management of Services is much less stringent partly because it is a much more of a recent historical growth phenomenon compared to products that began in 1947 and are changing at a pace including a lot of the online and digital Media services with the WTO often, understandably so, behind the curve playing catch up.

The trade in services is regulated by the agreement known as GATS (General Agreement on Trade in Services) which is a part of the WTO agreements.

As it is not as visible or as simple as a physical product crossing borders the WTO covers services in 4 ways as follows:

1.   Mode 1 ('cross-border supply'): as with trade in goods, in this mode the service itself crosses the border. This is the case, for example, with an architect working in a UK office sending building plans to a client abroad.

2.   Mode 2 ('consumption abroad'): here the consumer travels to the country of the service supplier and consumes the service there. Think of a Japanese tourist taking a train in the UK.

299

3.   Mode 3 ('commercial presence'): this refers to a service supplier setting up a presence in another country to provide its services. For instance, a UK bank might establish a branch in France, or an Italian restaurant chain might open a restaurant in the UK.

4.   Mode 4 ('presence of natural persons'): this is where a person crosses a border to supply a service, which includes foreign construction workers and even British footballers playing in Madrid, for example

The above was taken from the document "What would 'trading on WTO terms' mean for the UK? From 'The UK in a Changing Europe'. [32]

I did not want to go into huge detail on services for this book despite its importance as some books cover these aspects in much more detail but here the question was "can the UK comfortably fall back on the General Agreement on Trade in Services as some Brexiteers wish to take us down this route as an easy trade deal has eluded us? If we do not agree an FTA with the EU in 2020 we will be in this position anyway. It is certainly a step backwards compared to the EU's much more integrated system for services with greater clarity and cooperation including equal treatment and mutual recognition of qualifications, etc.

That will be enough here on WTO and services but suffice to say that it is complex not easy and not clear how our service companies will fare under WTO rules when it comes to services. One final example to finish on is that we could lose access to intra-EU air traffic rights (or at least have disadvantages compared to full EU members that will result when we leave the EU and this cannot be compensated for by the WTO law which does not contain any obligation to grant market access. What will happen or what will we have to concede to get this access is unknown and again we ask the question – 'For what great benefit?'

"WTO rules will solve the Irish hard border"

If this book had been written before the referendum campaign we would not even be mentioning the Irish Border as it was hardly covered, and as it was so 'English centric' the whole debate and nobody really considered it, or it seemed to care. But as it is a frictionless and seamless border it does play an important role, especially in light of the Irish history of political violence and the Good Friday agreement.

In this agreement both the Irish and UK governments agreed on two very important principles, which must be adhered to whatever after the UK's withdrawal from the European Union, and if WTO rules were to work, they would have to meet both these requirements, and this is where the complexities begin:

1.   A had border must be avoided; and

2.   The operation of the 1998 Agreement must be protected

The problem with WTO and the EU is that they require a hard border i.e. some kind of physical infrastructure and the means to track deliveries and shipments such as when a truck has left its destination and arrived at its destination, and therefore no chance of changing the cargo. To do this, it would include data surveillance, data submission, monitoring of the shipment and full registration, supported by targeted spot inspections. We are told by many Brexiteers that they have been told that the technology is available to do this, but such a solution is nowhere else in the world being used and implemented – why not you may ask yourself if it is so developed? This may be another illusive unicorn. As mentioned previously in this book the Norway Sweden border is over 1000 miles long but there are only 8 crossings where it is legally allowed to cross with commercial goods. This is because both countries need to be able to check the goods entering their relevant countries. If it could be achieved without border checks, they would have implemented it.

There is no confirmation or proof that these technologies can be effectively utilised so WTO rules would introduce a very unwanted level of friction in a very political place where such border controls represent a step backwards in politics as well as economics and would not be an advantage in any shape of form. So again, we ask ourselves, is this really a distinct advantage for the UK and what real tangible advantages are there for the UK taking yet another negative step backwards.

Nothing so far highlighted by Brexiteers removes the need for risk based inspections at the border, new import and export declarations, and associated red tape that is required when being a 'third country' importing into the EU, and this applies to any EU border and not just the Irish border, no matter how many pie in the sky so called 'solutions' Brexiteers pluck out of the air with no specific examples of where this is happening already. This is the reality Brexiteers now face and again is proving the emperor literally has no clothes.

Boris Johnson's deal pushes the customs border into the Irish Sea (i.e. the proposed backstop is replaced by a 'Frontstop' but even Brexit secretary and Mr. Johnson could not agree the checks, paperwork or systems that would be in place to make that function! Dad's army is rearing its ugly head again.

"Agriculture and fisheries will be much better off under WTO terms."

These two areas played an important part in the EU Referendum being kicked around like political footballs, but these are two areas that are both very vulnerable to Tariffs and Tariff quotas as well as regulations on food safety, etc. Also, fisheries for example is a very small part of the UK economy but received a disproportionate amount of coverage, probably for its emotive memories of when Britannia ruled the waves.

Let us look at Agriculture and the WTO as it is a mixed bag with potential winners and losers, well when I say winners they are not winners as for them not much would change but it's the Losers that concern me, as they will ask quite legitimately "what are the real tangible benefits of Brexit when many of our businesses could go bust and leave the supply of some of our foodstuffs etc. at risk?" Producers who are able to supply the protected domestic market would probably benefit but costs of things such as animal feed could rise, and cross-border supply chains would be disrupted, and this would be highlighted across the Irish border.

But WTO rules and the UK's commitments are unlikely to have an impact on agricultural subsidies as both the UK and EU are phasing out agricultural export subsidies under a deal agreed with all WTO members in 2015. But because some of the EU 28 still have objections and the WTO has not yet been able to certify it as a legally correct document for the EU28 and the scrapping of those export subsidies. This again highlights the issues of the WTO and should, in normal circumstances, be real warning signs for Brexiteers that the WTO is not the simple answer to all their problems but when blinded by Brexit they either do not understand how the WTO works or are deliberately fooling the public about this, knowing most people will not look into the details as they are getting on with their lives. Despite Brexiteers talking about independence it is so clear it is an INTERdependent world we live in in a similar way that we work closely with the EU in an interdependent manner.

There are many further complexities of agriculture and the WTO including 'Geographical indications', 'legislation' 'intellectual property', and 'seven year transition for farming', but the British 'no deal' paper on geographical indications warns UK producers that they may have to re-apply for protection in the EU if the EU requires the names to be re-registered, but if there was an agreed Withdrawal agreement with the EU then these same companies would not have to re-register if this was included. So, as you can see 3 years later it is still as clear as mud and makes it almost impossible for companies to prepare effectively. But still Brexiteers claim the WTO is a great option for the UK.

Even the free market and pro-Brexit economist Roger Bootle in his book "Making a success of Brexit and reforming the EU" on page 233 (4th update) states 'Admittedly for the UK's agricultural producers after abolition of Tariffs there would need to be considerable adjustment, which would be painful for some. But the end result could be positive for the UK as a whole – And even for quite a few producers themselves.' My concern with this position is that the 'considerable adjustment' and 'pain' he speaks of could mean many businesses go bust not to return, plus the 'end result' has no indication of timescales attached to it and is prefaced by the word 'could'. A very risky idea / strategy from an economist / Author who would not feel that 'pain' and 'considerable adjustment'. Reality for those involved in agricultural businesses or suppliers to those businesses could find reality is an uncomfortable bedfellow.

Further on in the same book on page 256 the author, in the section "weighing up costs and benefits" [of Brexit}, states 'I suspect that in 20- or 30-years' time, the British people will wonder why they ever doubted the wisdom of leaving the EU'. Again using "I suspect" is worrying and I cannot help that some people (not necessary the author) look at this as some kind of laboratory experiment and let us see how it looks in 30 years' time by when many people may have suffered, had more limited job and travel opportunities, suffered years of uncertainty as regards citizenship and hate crimes as well as Xenophobia with no obvious end goal or realisable improvements to our country and our society. The textbook very rarely gives a template that fits nicely and snuggly into real lives of those at the sharp end of such proposed changes.

303

Fisheries is different especially because of geography and the interaction with other fishing countries from the EU and EEA. But there are 2 main areas where fishing will be affected:

1.   Where one can fish (this is a major issue but not in reality related to the WTO); and

2.   What it can sell to the EU, which is a WTO issue.

As many Brexiteers want a no-deal exit now (and if we cannot agree a FTA with the EU that will be the default position) let us focus on that eventuality for fishing as this means that there is no cooperation between the UK and the EU which could mean both parties preventing the other entering their waters, but if it got to that stage it would make the option of cooperation very difficult and all parties much less willing to cooperate on trade. The Leave attitude and philosophy was a very simplified 'only British boats can fish in our waters and we can keep all out fish and sell it anywhere we want' scenario but without highlighting, for obvious reasons, the issues our fishermen and industry will face in reality.

This will include in a no-deal scenario that we would face tariffs and tariff quotas, as well as complicated licensing and clearance procedures under the EU's food safety and animal health regulations. British products would no longer automatically be recognised as meeting EU standards which creates complexities and confusion for many of our fishing companies that do not know what the future holds and could mean companies go bust if they cannot sell their produce in the same frictionless and tariff free manner as they had enjoyed in recent years. Some examples of Tariffs on fish are as follows:

■   Fresh cod of the species = 12%

■   Sardines of the species = 23%

■   Prawns of the genus Penaeus for processing = 12%

■   Squid, prepared or preserved = 20%

These extra costs as well as delays at the borders could be fatal for many of our UK businesses fishing and selling these products.

One only has to look at some of the prohibitive Tariffs for these business sectors to know, if an agreement with the EU is not reached for these areas of UK business people will lose their jobs and businesses will go bust. How can these companies export to the EU, one of their biggest markets with Tariffs of up to almost 40% or even their customers accept such a price increase in a world where profit margins are being squeezed, anyway? If politicians do not understand this or cannot do anything about it, then they do not deserve to be in their jobs.

- Preparations of meat or fish = 39.9%

- Dairy Produce = 39.4%

- Meat = 37.8%

- Cereals = 23.9%

- Preparations of vegetables and other parts of plants = 17.7%

- Preparations of cereals = 12.7%

Some political figures have indicated may be some companies have to reduce their profit expectations, which is easy for them sitting comfortably in Westminster in comfortable Non- Executive positions, but many of these companies do not even make those sort of gross profit margins! Apart from vehicles it is the food and agricultural sectors whose exports would suffer the most from the introduction of tariffs with meat, dairy and other agricultural products being hit the hardest. The future could be bleak for many of these companies, but the interesting thing was a number of them voted Leave. Hopefully this book describes and explains why they went down that path.

In the UK's proposed WTO schedules they proposed reducing some import tariffs to zero a number of which will not hit UK producers for Oranges (currently 16% into the EU) but others such as Carpet manufacturers (currently 8%), Battery manufacturers (4.7%), Spoon manufacturers (8.5%), and Jams, jellies, and marmalades (24%) could mean UK producers potentially going out of business and also laying off workers as the profits are no longer there to support them. So, this move is risky and there will be a number of losers in such a WTO exit, even if we can trade on WTO rules from day one after we leave?. We should also not forget that the WTO's "most favoured nation" rules mean the UK cannot lower its tariffs just for the EU or any specific country but rather any changes will be for every WTO member in an attempt to achieve a 'level playing field'. So, we have to follow such rules and regulations again, so no independence to be found here. Is this really what Brexiteers voted for?

Summary of WTO and Brexit

As stated this book is not the place for an all-inclusive detailed exploration of the WTO as it is so vast and complex but hopefully the aforementioned issues and considerations give a snapshot of the WTO and its implications to the UK after a no-deal Brexit. WTO terms basically give a 'bottom line' for world trade but clearly is not perfect and has inadequacies, is very political and relies on negotiation and interdependent working and cooperation, which is similar to the cooperation we have with the EU which kills the Brexiteer arguments that we will be totally Independent and can do whatever we want and everyone else will agree.

Several legal experts have highlighted how simply moving to WTO rules are not as easy as Brexiteers would have you believe in the usual over simplified manner and this focuses around 2 reasons:

1.   The huge amount of domestic legislation that will need to be passed before being able to actually trade under the WTO rules. There are nine statutes and 600 statutory instruments that would need to be adopted. That is a significant undertaking for the government. And

2.   Our schedule of products and services needs to be agreed by all the other 163 WTO states, and several states having already raised objections to the submitted schedule, so far including 20 over goods and 3 over services. The UK has no 'default terms' to crash out on leading to great complications and potential years of back-and-forth negotiations and the UK will be, to a certain extent, in 'Limbo' as it waits for these negotiations to play out. Where is the independence Brexiteers craved and said we would have post Brexit?

If one looks at it logically and calmly analyses the situation, falling back onto WTO terms is 'suboptimal' (that's the political language) in terms of trade, economics, politics, security, and some form certainty for business planning etc. despite how Brexiteers try to spin it. We see all these complexities, issues, challenges and problems with a no-deal Brexit and ask ourselves what the real tangible benefits are considering the issues faced and the things we are going to lose. This WTO development being loaded by Brexiteers really is not a good option and many issues will surface if we end up going this route.

Chapter 22
Future Trade Deals & The Big Wide World

Problem with a trade deal with India

One of the most common non-tariff barriers is the prohibition or restrictions on imports maintained through import licensing requirements. Though India has eliminated its import licensing requirements for most consumer goods, certain products face licensing related trade barriers. For example, the Indian government requires a special import license for motorcycles and vehicles that is very restrictive. Import licenses for motorcycles are provided to only foreign nationals permanently residing in India, working in India for foreign firms that hold greater than 30% equity or to foreign nations working at embassies and foreign missions. Strict Indian standards, testing, labelling, certifications, service and other barriers makes the Indian market a very difficult one to crack. Some domestic importers can import vehicles without a license provided the imports are counterbalanced by exports attributable to the same importer.

India maintains a "negative list" of imported products subject to various forms of non-tariff regulation. The negative list is currently divided into three categories: banned or prohibited items (e.g., tallow, fat, and oils of animal origin); restricted items that require an import license (e.g., livestock products and certain chemicals); and "canalized" items (e.g., some pharmaceuticals) importable only by government trading monopolies and subject to cabinet approval regarding import timing and quantity. India, however, often fails to observe transparency requirements, such as publication of timing and quantity restrictions in its Official Gazette or notification to WTO committees.

We can see here that with such restrictions and protective laws a trade deal would be difficult, and they would push such a hard bargain with the UK as they have a huge market and are growing significantly. Although we do not like to admit it we would be the junior partner to our former colony!

Another big issue with India will be the requirement for student visas that is a problem for Indian students currently wanting to come to the UK as the demand is high and growing, and this is not what a lot of Leave voters voted for i.e. less Polish but more Indian immigration

A free Trade Agreement with the USA?

This almost seems the panacea that Brexiteers are hanging their hat on but this will not be easy and the UK will have to make significant compromises as the USA will know we are desperate for a significant trade deal and they are the huge market and we are the little brother in that relationship, whatever we would like to think. Brexiteers like to say we saved Europe from the Nazis in the second world war (ERG Brexiteer Mark Francois is quite partial to an out of context war related observation) but the Americans will tell us very quickly THEY saved us all from the Nazis with some justification, although the Russians may dispute that making the Nazis fight on two fronts, plus other millions of soldiers around the world, that Brexiteers conveniently forget.

Some examples of the issues we will face are that the USA would require the UK to agree the USA approach to food safety and animal and plant health i.e. we would have to lower our standards, but then if UK companies wanted then to export to the EU this would cause issues as these standards would be too low, so the costs would rise for our food industry as they wrestled with maintaining two different standards. The other big issues would be the US requirement that there should be more private health competition in UK health services, which could signify a movement to a more privatised NHS if our government agreed such a deal. With the current USA-China trade war there would almost definitely be a clause stating we would not be able to negotiate an agreement with China, as is included in the latest revision of the agreement between the US and Mexico and Canada. So, we would be accepting more rules from a bigger 'partner' which was exactly one of the reasons the Brexiteers hate the EU apparently, but this is where reality meets Brexiteer rhetoric.

There is this illusion that outside the EU the United Kingdom would have more power and clout than inside it with a solid block of 28 countries being a part of the largest free trade group in the world. But the Obama administration made it clear to the UK as far back as 2012 when the US ambassador in London, Louis Susman warned Nick Clegg that if you guys left, 'you may soon not count in Europe anymore.' [37] Yes there is a new administration and policies / opinions can change but it only seems logical that the USA would prefer to finalise a trade deal with the EU than the UK due to its size and impact and although that is difficult due to both sides being very stringent on their requirements it must be the focus. Obviously if the UK would roll over and have its belly tickled and accept most of the US requirements no matter how detrimental to the UK, then clearly a deal could be done quickly, even if it is not in our interest.

The comments of President Trump when visiting the UK in June 2019 were contradictory at best (no surprise there) when one day saying the NHS would not be on the table in a negotiation but then claiming 'everything' is on the table this poses a big question as to what direction a trade negotiation would even go between the UK and USA and potential further pressure to increase drug prices paid by the NHS or more privatisation of the NHS in the future. For Brexiteers to believe we would be negotiating on a level playing field when the USA is a country of 330 million people with some important trade deals in place and we have 60 million, with possibly no trade deals, are obviously being disingenuous at best.

President Obama was clear commenting when in the UK saying "...may be some time down the line there will be a US-UK trade agreement, but it's not going to happen any time soon as our focus is in negotiating with a big block, the European Union, to get a trade agreement done. The UK is going to be in the back of the queue." Again, no matter how Brexiteers would like to believe the contrary this makes sense to the USA when so much work to try to finalise a deal that has been negotiated for some years. They would not want to waste that time. We should also remember that the UK does not have enough experienced Trade negotiators (and we would need a big team of these for such a major agreement) as we have not had to do this for the last 40 years. One thing that should be said that despite Obama's comments being correct and honest they may have worked against the Remain campaign as it was twisted by the Leavers to be someone meddling in domestic issues and therefore he should 'mind his own business' and they felt it helped them with anyone sitting on the fence as it spiked their patriotic blood resulting in a Leave vote.

The US healthcare industry sees a huge opportunity with the British NHS as it is the largest purchaser of medications and drugs in the world but at the moment keeps the pricing down due to its purchasing power which the large Pharmaceutical corporations and the lobby groups in the USA do not like. Now they see an opportunity if we are desperate for a trade deal to cash in and break this monopoly and price fixing as they see it by removing the barriers to entry. The lobby groups also criticise the NHS drug approval system, the National Institute for Healthcare Excellence, often referred to as NICE.

Problem with a trade deal with the USA

Although president Trump and his team say to Boris Johnson he wants the greatest (of course) trade deal with the UK we know Trump will do only what is in the USAs interest and we know from experience that if he is at the big end of the stick then he is going to go into bully boy mode and then we will be exposed, as he knows we are desperate, and what are our option, China? India?

The USA has already indicated it wants to use negotiations to open up market access to the UK for American Agri products (including meat) by loosening standards on what kind of food we can import into the UK, which according to the NFU (National Farmers Union) could harm UK producers. Some of their concerns involve practices banned in the UK and the EU including feeding poultry litter to Beef cattle, administering banned additives to Bacon, use of hormone-treated beef as well as chlorinated washed chicken. The differences in animal welfare and expectations are also major concerns.

The UK's food regulations are considerably different and much more stringent than the standards in the USA which means the UK cannot currently import certain foods from the USA as they don't meet our standards. For example, GM foods are sold without labelling in the USA or use pesticides banned in the EU and therefore the UK. Standards would probably have to reduce in the UK to secure a trade deal with the US as the US would be opposed to raising their standards when they find them totally acceptable and they would be the senior partner in any such agreement / trade deal by far (including the powerful US Pharma lobby).

There will be pressure to remove bans on certain food products as the US negotiators always have to get something for their powerful agricultural lobby. This is standard for US agreements. But this is not just scaremongering this is real as the US made clear itself when laying out its negotiating objectives with the UK when it stated, "remove expeditiously unwarranted barriers that block the export of US food and agricultural products." This was not what voters heard in the campaigns and were led to believe. But there are basic dynamics at play here with the US economy being seven times the size of the UK, we are not going to be able to cherry pick in such a negotiation. But even if we achieved a half decent FTA with the USA, it would not make a significant impact to the 40%+ of trade we had just walked away from with the EU if no agreement is reached, and could create more problems that it solves especially when it comes to food standards / quality and animal welfare for example. Also, we have a trade surplus with the US already.

The USA has already indicated that they would like the NHS to pay more for its medicines as part of a trade deal as they do not like it's purchasing power and want its Pharma corporations to make more profits as they do in the USA and elsewhere in the world. But this is British taxpayers money so we should be cautious of the pressure put upon our National Health Service by the US administration in trade deal talks as this could become a very strategic and political bargaining chip no matter what our government and negotiators say. Put simply the US trade representatives will try to increase their market access and revenues for US Pharmaceutical companies as this is the jewel in the UK's crown and with the fact we will have no trade deals of note when we leave the EU the pressure will build. We should not underestimate the power of the US Pharmaceutical lobby in trade negotiations.

Is that what we want? Environmental regulations, consumer protections, safeguards of the NHS etc. all reduced across the board, so we are effectively selling off our prized sovereignty we took back from the EU to the USA who will probably be the highest bidder.

Another important factor in USA trade will be the pressure and influence silicon Valley has on US trade policy due to its size and global reach. They are not happy about the EU's strict rules on use of personal data (to protect its citizens) and again the USA will put pressure on the UK to reduce these standards as they see it as restrictive to THEIR companies. The threat of EU fines is real, will US firms really take any threats from their junior partner as serious? The chipping away of our rules, standards and ultimately sovereignty would be compromised.

If we leave the EU with no deal and enter into negotiations with the USA about a Free Trade Agreement (FTA) I fear we will find to our cost Britain's new place in the global pecking order with the US as an economic giant and its demands on the UK proving very tough indeed.

The simple question is whether it is in the UK's interest to cosy up to the USA and Donald Trump at the expense of other relationships and some Brexiteers will say yes but this is often poorly thought through if at all and not understanding the implications of such a choice due to the blindness and dogma of Brexit at all costs!

Problem of a trade deal with China

It sounds great when politicians say we can have a trade deal with the largest manufacturer in the world but that is oversimplified and omits the issues and challenges that it will bring with it. For example, straight away a trade deal with China invariably means larger trade deficits, and sometimes huge deficits. Currently it is very much already in China's favour with the UK having a £23 billion trade deficit with the country. If we signed a trade deal with China, this would not be looked upon favourably by the USA and we may find we get dragged into the trade war that began in 2019 being used as a small pawn amongst two giants vying for global dominance.

Another issue when trading with China is the issue often known as 'debt-trap diplomacy' which begins with a country becoming dependent on trade with China and then China moves on to strategic targets within that country. This is not a theoretical issue as one only has to look at Sri Lanka when it had to hand over its largest port Hambantota to China when it could not pay off its debts to Chinese countries. This is not an isolated instance as in Burma China also took a 70% controlling stake in a strategic port. Critics may claim we are much bigger and more powerful than those aforementioned countries which may be true, but the long-term creep of China influence should not be underestimated, as can be highlighted with their interest in the British strategic nuclear energy infrastructure.

313

China wants to become a global leader in nuclear power and the UK could be very strategic if it is to achieve that ambition. It is possible that in the UK up to six new nuclear power stations could be built over the next 20 years and China has already made inroads into our strategic energy sector. If China buys a stake of up to 49% in the UK's existing plants (via the state-owned corporation General Nuclear Power Group – CGN) as has been discussed this is a significant expansion and is for some a concerning development. The CEO of chinadialogue.net Isabel Hilton, said the UK opening up vital infrastructure to China was without parallel in the Western world. "No other OECD country has done this. This is strategic infrastructure, and China is a partner but not an ally in the security sense." Is this a sign of things to come post Brexit where we feel exposed as no longer a part of the strongest trading block in the world and have to enter into deal and agreements that are not necessarily in our long term interest and foreign counties (but not allies!) take control of significant chunks of our strategic infrastructure?

Some argue we are leaving the EU to regain our sovereignty from the EU (even though it is argued elsewhere in this book that we never lost it) but doing business with China, or USA for that matter, results in a certain amount of loss of sovereignty which many Brexiteers appear to not appreciate. The decisions our government makes in the next few years will be critical for our nation as we try to balance the ambitions of China and the USA both of which will try to get us to conform to their own interests. We may decide to sit in the Middle of the Road but as the adage goes 'you may get run over by both parties!' It is quite clear how strategic this is going to be for the UK and with our government's expertise and handling of Brexit that does not bode well and once in the spiders web there may be no escaping, and the EU with hindsight may have seemed like heaven compared to the hell we may enter into.

It is ironic that probably our best chance of securing a good rules based trade agreement is as a part of the economically and politically strong EU that can call a lot of the shots and negotiate on parity with the likes of the USA and China including avoiding the dumping of products below its market value. We should never forget that as an open economy the UK is always seriously influenced by what is happening in the wider world economy including any trade wars and the politics that goes with that.

Non-Tariff barriers are also an issue and a form or protectionism used effectively by China as it is by other countries including India with such uncommon standards it makes it very difficult for International companies to fulfil these requirements. It could be labelling or classification requirements and necessity of certain tests to be undertaken. The country enforces strict sanitary rules, requiring significant administrative requirements consisting of vast amounts of documents and health certificates all in Chinese.

The big issue here will probably be the Chinese role in our energy infrastructure where Beijing will request significantly more access to the market which has strategic implications for the UK going forward. Did Leavers vote for less control from Brussels only to have Chinese companies heavily influence our energy plants when controlled by the Chinese government? This has started already even before they put pressure and demands forward for more input into the British energy infra-structures including Hinkley Point C nuclear power plant, a new project at Sizewell, and Bradwell in Essex

The other growing issue in China that may spill over into any negotiations with the UK regarding a trade deal is the huge number of Chinese graduates that they do not know what to do with as their economy growth slows resulting in fewer opportunities. China produced a record 8.3 million graduates in the summer of 2019! If we are to negotiate a free trade deal with China, like India, Business and student visas could become a pivotal request from China resulting in a glut of Chinese people looking for jobs to help improve their English and practical commercial experience. Again, was this what Brexiteers voted for – less Poles and Romanians but more Chinese and Indians? I think not.

What about Chemicals?

With a number of the countries we would look to strike deals with, chemicals could be an issue due to the important and potentially dangerous nature of them. If there was no deal, companies registered with REACH would no longer be able to sell into the EEA market without transferring their registrations to an EEA-based organisation. Companies would therefore need to take action to preserve their EEA market access, with a lot of paperwork, red tape and costs involved with no added benefits to them. The UK 'downstream users' currently importing chemicals from an EEA country would face new registration requirements. Under the UK's replacement for REACH, importers would have a duty to register chemicals. Similarly, UK downstream users of authorisations could no longer rely on authorisation decisions addressed to companies in the remaining EEA countries. So a lot of uncertainty, potential delays and unnecessary costs and some companies will look to set up offices within the EEA to better manage the whole process which means fewer jobs in the UK.

Also, the spectre of a USA trade deal would impact chemicals and how we deal with them as the USA have different standards, often lower than those of the EU and the UK. For example, REACH has the guiding principle that where there has been no evidence to prove the chemical has been shown to be safe it cannot be used. But in the USA if there is no evidence to prove harm the chemical is allowed until there is proof it is harmful which is obviously a lower standard. USA from the position of strength will put pressure on the UK to accept its rules and not vice versa. The issue facing the UK is if it wants to sell those very same chemicals into the EEA the EU will not accept untested chemicals that have not gone through the strict testing criteria, which the UK uses now. This is just an example of the issues faced by any UK negotiating team that does not have the strength in numbers it had when an EU member and as a part of a huge negotiating team. Again, Brexiteers never mentioned or even hinted at these issues, which they either didn't know, didn't consider important or just kept it to themselves as it wouldn't necessarily help their cause.

When it comes to chemicals, we should not forget water companies that need a regular and reliable supply of critical chemicals. They hold significant stocks and carry out extensive monitoring of their chemical supply chains (including transport and deliveries) and sharing agreements in place. But a supply chain failure could be costly, and some Remainers would say unnecessary now due to the limited benefits, if any, of Brexit.

Other EU countries will exploit our Myopic Leave decision

Many of the EU countries especially The Netherlands and France see Brexit as a huge opportunity for their countries, despite the difficulties it will cause them also, to take over large parts of UK business especially in financial services and high-tech industries. It is also possible that protectionist policies may be put in place going forward to exacerbate that development and makes it more difficult for UK companies to compete once the UK is outside the EU and a 'third country'.

The UK will be foraging for trade deals at one of the worst possible times as it will be in a position of weakness with no significant deals and only those with smaller countries desperate to gain access to the UK that have no leverage. This combined with the rise in trade protectionism around the world leading stock markets into a tailspin resulting in the worst of times when negotiating trade deals from a weak position and potentially walking away from the strongest free trade area in the world, especially when we have a good deal.

Chapter 23
Politics

Clearly, politics as well as economics or patriotism / nationalism etc. would play a major role both in the UK and the EU but also outside Europe as the UK looks for future trading partners and support for this momentous decision. Both the two main parties namely the Conservative and the Labour parties were riven with internal disagreements about Brexit and a host of other issues, so there was no conformity in either party, which seeped into Parliament. Some of these bitter divisions still remain and the divisive impact of the referendum and Brexit generated a number of unintended and unanticipated consequences. This was clear when Boris Johnson stripped 21 conservative MPs of the whip for voting against the Government and this included Winston Churchill's Grandson, Nicholas Soames and former Cabinet Minister, MP since 1970 and Father of the House Ken Clarke. This in light of the fact he voted against his own government on a number of occasions seemed hypocritical and desperate. The Conservative party had now ceased to be a broad church, and the so-called One Nation conservatism all but dead, maybe to return one day post Prime Minister Johnson.

Article 50 and the timing

Just to be sure we all know what Article 50 is as it has been spoken about so much but very rarely explained.

"Article 50 is the only legal mechanism for a member state of the European Union (EU) to leave. A short paragraph in the Lisbon Treaty agreed by all EU member states in 2009, it sets out the steps a country needs to go through to withdraw from its treaty obligations."

With hindsight most would agree that the enacting of Article 50 or more accurately when it was enacted was a mistake from the simple fact that we did not have a plan or a strategy (or putting it harshly a clue!) as to what the negotiations would hold (and some may argue Brexiteers and the government still didn't in 2019!). Perhaps the government buckled under the pressure from Brexiteers to do it as quickly as possible or thought it's no problem as we have 2 years to do this? But how wrong they were as those 2 years flew past and after we still had no acceptable solution that had a majority in parliament. A prime example of the problems that can ensue is when one tries to keep everybody happy, even if it was with the best of intentions, including adding unnecessary red lines at the beginning of the negotiation and boxing ourselves into a corner with limited flexibility without U-Turns. Courage in the face of adversity is an underrated attribute and was needed by Mrs May but instead she got boxed in by the ERG and her Brexiteers. The disappointing aspect of Article 50 is that those that are now condemning Teresa May's deal were the same ones putting on that pressure and cheered the loudest when she made that fateful error of invoking Article 50. Be careful what you wish for may be comes to mind or more accurately they had not the 'back of a fag packet idea of a plan'!

It could be argued it made no difference from a timing point of view apart from it may have delayed the process. There has not been and will not be a political consensus about a United Kingdom outside the EU, which combined with the adversarial nature of British politics would make a deal across the political divide very difficult indeed.

Had any thought gone into the transitional arrangements we would need when leaving, as it did not appear so? Did Mrs. May and her team also believe it would be "the easiest trade deals in human history" that would be signed sealed and delivered by the exit day or were they just rabbits in the headlights? What did happen was that within 2 years we were begging for extension after extension as it was quite clear we were never going to be ready to leave on 29th March 2019 or

319

indeed 31st November 2019. But even if we did with Teresa May's 'deal' it was a worse deal than we had as a full member of the EU, and Prime Minister Johnson's is even worse.

David Davis is quoted as saying the Government should 'take a little time before triggering Article 50" because "the negotiating strategy has to be properly designed, and there is some serious consultation to be done first." So, what was he doing as this simply did not happen and there was no strategy or plan (remember Mr. Davis looking ridiculous turning up to a meeting with Michel Barnier with nothing but a pen but the other side was fully prepared with quite a few lever arch files packed with papers!) but rather a list of unicorn dominated demands.

The bottom line is that we have a long-drawn-out process of negotiations and planning because we were tied at the hip for 45 years, there was the total absence of a serious plan of the process or the end destination. It became clear that the "no deal was better than a bad deal" mantra was nonsense, plus we were not in these negotiations on our own so the other side would be doing what is best for their club, the one WE wanted to leave.

Lies, damn lies and statistics

Yes, most politicians are thought to be economical with the truth, but the referendum campaign went to a whole new level where everything seemed to be fair game, especially as the combatants seemed untouchable due to the differences between a referendum and a general election which is covered in more depth later in the book.

It was not clear when Boris Johnson wrote the following (after the referendum result) he believed in unicorns or was just being dishonest?

'I cannot stress too much that the UK is a part of Europe, and always will be ...EU citizens living in this country will have their rights fully protected, and the same goes for British citizens living in the EU. British people will still be able to go and work in the EU; to live; to study; to buy homes and to settle down. As the German equivalent of the CBI – the BDI – has very sensibly reminded us, there will continue to be free trade, and access to the single market.
(The Telegraph June 26, 2016)

But this is typical Mr Johnson, as it is for Farage, in that they say and write things do not care about the accuracy or consequences and will fudge through it afterwards. Boris never had and would never have the authority to claim such things or make them happen. It was rather like something he hashed together on the back of a 'fag packet' which he turned into an article! But being paid £200,000 + per year by the Telegraph can act as a bit of a motivator I suppose. But we have to put this in context as the journalist who is flimsy with the facts and truth and has been dismissed twice for lying is our prime minister. This is no joke.

One statistic that was so often put forward as a reason why we should leave the EU was that the rest of the world was growing more quickly than the EU which was very selective and although in certain areas of the world true it was a very simplistic argument. But did appeal to the Brexiteer vote as they were looking for any crumb of hope to justify a decision that as time went on after the referendum was looking very weak. There are a number of reasons why this argument is weak as it just takes a number in isolation and does not take it in the context of the UK's product / service offering or abilities to exploit or deliver to those areas of great growth. So, let us just look at a couple of the reasons this argument does not offer us the land of milk and honey Brexiteers would have you believe.

Brexiteer "illusions"

1.   Growth rates sound great but if that growth is from a very low base then it is minuscule in the scale of things. For example, Africa is cited as offering the UK great growth opportunities but the GDP of the whole of Africa, and this includes wealthy countries such as Nigeria (oil) and South Africa (gold, diamonds and other raw materials) is only about the same as the GDP of France. Yes, correct of just one EU country not 27! It may be worth reading that again as you pick your jaw up off the floor. Another fact in 2019 linked to France is that since Brexit (another coincidence some may say) it has now overtaken the UK as the 5th largest economy in the world.

2.   The Commonwealth is also cited but has the same issue if scale, plus many of the commonwealth countries are smaller so opportunities are smaller, and we must ask ourselves what we are going to sell them that will give us this great International growth? There are 53 countries in the

commonwealth but 31 of them have fewer than 3 million people) Many of the goods we sell internationally are targeted at highly developed economies, which is why the EU is such a good trading partner for us, and we are obviously hugely successful in financial services but will a farmer in Trinidad & Tobago have a huge need for some of the complex financial instruments the City of London offers? Of course, not and despite there being some opportunities in these countries and regions they are overplayed by the various Leave groups, and we could still continue to trade with such countries on WTO rules (which apparently is great!) whilst still a member of the EU. Commonwealth countries such as Tanzania, Ghana, and Cameroon etc. have GDPs less than Manchester in England. This is not the massive market Brexiteers would have you believe and what products will they buy from the UK?

3.   As a member of the EU we can still partake in and benefit from any great growth in these other areas of the world and do not have to leave the EU to do this and put at risk a fair proportion of our trade with our largest and closest trading partner which is around 44% of our exports.

4.   The power of the EU Trading block has exhibited its power to strike good deals for the EU as a whole, and although we may get slightly better deals in specific areas on the whole, it is the big powerful trading blocks of the EU and the USA for example that get a lot of what THEY want and the UK on its own does not have that clout and never will. It's all about power and influence, pure and simple.

5.   The Brexiteers assumed countries would be queueing up to quickly sign trade deals with us but as of March 2019 that was not the case and Liam Fox the minister in charge of completing such trade deals had completed very few but tried to sell a trade deal with the Faroe Islands as a success, which demonstrates how rhetoric had met reality and we had fallen from the heights of the Brexiteer hyperbole to the depths of frustration and desperation.

6.   Complex trade deals with major or at least significant trading partners can take years and years which puts us way behind the curve, and a prime example is the fact the EU has now a fully working free trade deal with Japan and we are years away from such a deal, and Japan has made it clear it cannot simply be rolled over to the UK! It may be coincidence (I

will leave that for you to decide) but Japanese companies such as Honda and Nissan decided to either take some production back to Japan or no longer to invest in certain models or developments in the UK going forward. Some argue that it has nothing to do with Brexit and cite the management of those companies stating it has nothing to do with Brexit. But this is naïve and misunderstands the Japanese business etiquette of not wanting to offend or get involved in domestic squabbles, plus the obvious fact that they still want Brexiteers to buy their automobiles. It may not be just Brexit, but a number of the coincidences possibly linked to Brexit have been growing and continues to.

7.   Some of the high growth countries such as India would drive a very hard bargain as they are traditionally protectionist and do not look enthusiastically for free trade deals with developed counties as president Narendra Modi has made it clear he wants as much produced in India as possible and not to import such products that could be produced domestically. India will probably become the third largest powerhouse behind the USA and China, advancing all the time. But what they would like is a huge quota of work and education Visas for its educated citizens to work and train in countries like the UK and then return to utilise those skills at home. Did Leavers vote for a huge influx of Indian immigrants, even if they are temporary, as once they had gone home the next wave would come? For the UK this can obviously be a benefit bringing certain skills but many Brexiteers feel we have too many immigrants already, so the message to them is 'be careful what you wish for when we leave the EU'.

We can see the politics and economics of this high growth outside the EU has its flaws and is not as easy, simple or in some instances true that it will easily add lots of value quickly once we leave the EU and sacrifice some of the current business, we have with our largest trading partner.

The campaign of misinformation was so strong that many people still believed we would still join the Euro, which was never on the cards and would never be agreed by any UK government, especially in light of the issues the Euro has had and created a form of straitjacket for some of the countries such as Greece that could not devalue. Although, it must be said that a lot of the problems Greece caused for itself with such things as its poor systems for and record of collecting taxes. History now shows that Greece should never have been admitted into the Eurozone as the economy was not strong enough and too effectively manage such diverse economies as Germany at one extreme and Greece at the other was always going to be a challenge, and the global financial crash exposed those weaknesses.

Some of the political justification of Brexit were statements from a number of Brexiteers such as "The world will not end", or "we will get by", "We will be OK" or indeed "We will work it out" but this is such a mediocre attitude towards our future and an obvious way of deflecting arguments that we were going to make the UK poorer, or to explain in any details what their plan was for the future. Could you imagine an Olympic athlete preparing for the biggest race of his life by saying "it will be OK," or "we will work it out"? No, he would be laser focused with a carefully calculated plan with timescales working towards a specific date, originally for the 29th March 2019, and now 1st November 2019, to achieve the best result possible. But Brexiteers choose this mediocre route where the promises they made cannot be even close to being delivered and politician speak takes over with the poorer in our society probably bearing the brunt of the economic backlash.

The almost 3 years after the referendum has shown us how dangerous a group of ideological individuals with money behind them but no plan (although a few good orators!), and a weak Prime Minister can lead to absolute chaos, which makes the UK look so incompetent to the International community. The same one we want to take us seriously when it comes to complex trade deals! I was approached by an American Doctor at Heathrow Terminal 3 on the 28th March when he asked "I have to ask you guys what is going on with Brexit, first you're out, then you are not and now I cannot work out whether you are in or out, what's going on? What's the plan?" Try explaining our impotent parliament, Brexit delusion, plus all the deceit combined with the backstop and the conversation spirals from the sublime to the ridiculous. We did then move on to Trump but that's another story.

But the hope or belief that "In the long run it will be OK" is often based on very little apart from blind faith and reminds one of rebellious or religious zealots that will not change their belief despite the lack of facts or science to back up their position. They JUST BELIEVE, and you cannot argue with that as it is not based on any logic or reason. As Brexiteers hope and pray for the sunny uplands and the land of milk and honey on the horizon, the religious fundamentalists believe Jesus Christ will return again in their lifetime or they will go to a better world than this one. In the middle ages or before I understand they believed but now with the development of science and logic, I would have expected or hoped that people would think reasonably about such important critical issues. But the world shows us it is not so, and human beings will believe in many crazy things such as the world being flat, aliens on earth or numerous conspiracy theories and they will not be separated from those beliefs no matter how impossible science and observable reality show the beliefs to be. Brexit may not be so extreme but with many it carries some of the same traits.

Leave.EU and Vote Leave were very economical with the truth and kept the message very simple to get the result they wanted. One example from Vote Leave was a graphic showing how the EU had started as 9 countries and now it's 28, but then progressed to add that Bulgaria, Croatia and Romania had joined since 2007. Why did they list those countries as a supplementary bullet point? Well obviously trying to tap into the anti-immigrant feeling towards those specific countries (is there a national hierarchy of how good or bad British people think immigrants are i.e. are Romanians and Bulgarians at the bottom of the pack? If yes, why? But this particular graphic went a step further from whipping up anti-Eastern European fervour by telling readers the EU will continue to grow with the next countries set to join being: Albania (2.8 Million), Macedonia (2.1 million), Montenegro (0.6 million), Serbia (7.2 million), and last but not least the cherry on the cake Turkey with 76 Million! They knew this was just project Fear and had no grounds or that Turkey had next to no chance of becoming an EU member for many differing reasons including Greece's history and loathing or as human rights record etc. But they could get away with such lies without suffering any comebacks and people believed it. But even if they didn't, it is best to err on the side of caution and vote leave as "you never know!" Yes, you do, but they chose not to.

How many British people would recognise Irish people from Dublin living in London as immigrants? So why the difference between them and Polish or Bulgarians? A built-in discrimination or they have not yet got used to living with or near Polish and Bulgarians whereas they have with so many Irish having settled in the UK for decades? But the government would still have to reassure Irish citizens that their rights to live and work in the UK will not change post Brexit, but many are not sure and are faced with this uncertainty for themselves and their families.

Regarding Turkey, Vote Leave also published a provocative poster with the words 'Turkey (population 76 million) is joining the EU' when we all know that is not the case and is not even on the horizon. But Penny Mordaunt ramped up the Fear factor of Turks coming to the UK as a Security issue as 'crime is far higher in Turkey than in the UK' and 'gun ownership in Turkey was widespread'. She also claimed the UK will not be able to stop Turkish criminals entering the UK ignoring the fact that we are not in Schengen and due to closer workings between us the EU and Interpol there is a better chance that we can recognise and locate such undesirables. But it was clearly Project Fear with no substance and literally full of inaccuracies.

But also in a May 2016 BBC Television interview, also Mordaunt denied that the UK had a veto on Turkey joining the EU, despite Article 49 of the EU constitution requiring a unanimous vote of all 28 members of the General Council to allowing accession of a candidate state, thus creating a power of veto by a dissenting member nation! Was this ignorance or misinformation to benefit the leave campaign? The worrying thing is this badly informed or duplicitous individual became International Development Secretary in 2017! A political appointment to keep the right wing of the Conservative party happy or scraping the bottom of the barrel? But even with such incorrect information Number 10s response was muted and weak rather than calling it out for what it was, which was becoming a regular occurrence, a position for which they would pay a heavy price. It may be in this case yes Cameron did not want to negatively affect relations with the Turkish Government, but Dominic Cummings and the other side had no such concerns and were going for the jugular whenever they could. In Cummings 'Campaign Grid' Turkey was there every week, yes EVERY week!

But it wasn't just Vote Leave as The Telegraph in its article from 22nd June 2016 '20 reasons for you to leave the European Union' had at number 9 'We wouldn't have to worry about Turkey' further perpetuating this myth that Turkey will join the EU. It is obviously Project Fear, and it worked.
But give it a few years and the Brexiteer promises and mis-selling of the EU will come back to haunt us. Not 'them' as many are rich and connected so will not feel the same stress that manufacturing workers in the North of England will). They are realising this already in 2019 with Job losses and lack of business investment which will get worse upon us leaving, but they choose to continue the misinformation and spinning of the still ever bright future without any facts, indications or a plan. At some stage they will have to let those communities down that they had lied to and the fact there is no Brexit Dividend. But they will blame someone else as for every Brexiteer issue there is a scapegoat which goes with the territory of deceit and fabrications.

Even after the result it was difficult to tell whether MPs were still misleading people or whether they were just delusional as the example of Daniel Hannan Conservative Member of the European Parliament who said 'every

326

internal poll we did reflected the published polls where the biggest issue was sovereignty or democracy', whereas we all know that immigration and the fact many people thought and still think we have too many people coming into the country. Perhaps he is being disingenuous or maybe his pollsters were being told by people that it was "sovereignty" as it was more politically correct than saying immigration with the chances of being called a racist, even though they can often not name one limitation on their sovereignty or one EU-wide law that is negative to their life! The Leave campaign may have cleverly, or perhaps it was an unintended consequence, given Leave voters that were anti-immigrant or anti-foreigner another 'acceptable' reason for voting Leave and literally getting what they wanted – fewer immigrants! Daniel Hannan also stated before the referendum "absolutely nobody is talking about threatening our place in the single market". Well obviously it is Daniel.

Nigel Farage when, after the referendum result, realising he could no longer sell the great benefits of Brexit as they had been exposed he said on LBC radio "he never promised that it would be a huge success", just that "we would be self-governing. That's the point. I never said it would be a beneficial thing to leave and everyone would be better off". He did say those things as we all know but it clearly highlights that for the elites such as Farage and Banks etc. they will be fine whether or not Brexit is a success, and it will be the poorer in our society that will pay the price, and Farage etc. will blame someone else. Farage though will be in demand for highly paid political speeches and radio / TV performances, but Mrs. Jones will be counting the pennies for the food and rent as inflation and unemployment potentially rise and she struggles to feed the kids. Well done Nigel.

We should appreciate that it is sometimes easier to believe a statement is true if it is easier to process, or if it has been stated multiple times regardless of its actual accuracy. This so called "Truth illusory effect" Dominic Cummings understood very well which is why he hammered home "Millions of Turks coming to the UK" and "Taking back control" to create an easy-to-understand mantra that people could share. It worked very well.

The fascinating aspect of lies and the impact of the lies is that often people suffer from the so-called 'Third-person effect' which is basically 'a belief that mass communicated media messages have a greater effect on others than on themselves'. I have communicated with and come across many Brexiteers / Leavers that genuinely believe that they were not influenced by the propaganda and lies of the Leave campaign or some even claiming they read nothing about the EU and the referendum issues before the vote and they made "their own minds up". But when challenged as to where they really got their information to make an informed decision, they could not confirm, obviously because the initial claim was nonsense or would have to admit that they had in fact heard and listened to many of the media messages we were all surrounded by before and during the EU referendum campaign.

Remember £350 million and the Big Red Bus?

Now regardless of your position Leave or Remain the Bus was a marketing and propaganda master stroke even if it was, like many Vote Leave arguments, based on inaccuracies and / or untruths. But it was simple and punchy like any of the best marketing messages in history. Now looking at it from a truth and honesty point of view (some may say that is naïve, and they would be right in the context of the referendum campaign) it was really unacceptable in a modern democracy.

The £350 million per week quoted that we allegedly sent to the EU was our contribution to the EU budget according to Vote leave. But due to rebates negotiated previously £4 billion NEVER left the UK, so the number was incorrect by about £185 million per week! The actual annual numbers from the Office of national Statistics are £19 Billion was the gross figure, which in reality is £11 billion considering regional funds, and farming subsidies etc. that the EU commission pays back into the UK. Still what is a little £8 billion per year difference between 'friends'!
But it did the job and being honest even if they had quoted the net figure I believe it would have had the same effect as for any normal person it was a lot of money and they could not relate as to how it contributed to their life. But according to the Vote Leave it could ALL go to the NHS, which was never ever going to happen.

This number was Vote Leave's, and the likes of Boris Johnson etc. but even when he was cornered in an Interview on Channel 4 news by Fatima Manji to accept that this figure quoted was misleading and indeed incorrect due to the rebates we receive he struggled even with such basic honesty sticking to the Vote Leave line, despite it being clear and highlighted to him that the Institute for Fiscal studies and the UK Statistics Authority stating quite categorically this number was incorrect. Despite the bumbling language and the look of a rabbit in the headlights during the Manji interview he still managed to carry on with the pretence, which is a skill in itself. But that's Boris, the new PM who can lie for fun

John Major went onto the Andrew Marr show on 7th June 2016 and dismissed Johnson as a 'court Jester guilty of 'deceit' on the £350 million a week claim and was running a campaign 'verging on Squalid' on immigration.

But this was not the extent to all the lies with numerous being highlighted during the campaign. We have highlighted the official Leave campaign publishing an image of a map aimed to strike fear into British residents that stated the next countries set to join the EU including Syria, Iraq, Turkey, and Albania, which was obviously completely untrue, but how would the casual viewer know that? They would expect that an official campaign would not be allowed to write such lies without some kind of truth behind them and therein lies the problem of such a referendum.

Nigel Farage even said when interviewed the day after the result that he could not guarantee the £350 million windfall saying, "he would never have made that claim", although he did not correct it at the time! Even David Davis and Iain Duncan Smith who campaigned in front of the bus claimed they never made such a claim. This is political semantics and deception of the highest order that makes politicians such a disliked group as it is obvious deception to get a result, which it did. But are any of them held responsible? No, and that is why it will continue and is sadly a part of our political discourse now. We should say that there are some very good honest constituency MPs that do their best for all their constituencies that get tarred with the same brush unfortunately.

Alistair Campbell, who would use all sorts of tactics to win an election was also shocked stating "the 350 million was a veritable lie". I can't remember campaigns where you mount the campaign based on a lie, and then when it is exposed, you just keep going, as Johnson and co. did.' Unfortunately for Mr. Campbell and the Remain camps was that it did cut through and many people believed it, even though Michael Gove was also promising the Farmers all this money to replace their subsidies they would be losing. But offering subsidies to say Sheep farmers who have thousands of sheep they can no longer sell into the EU due to large import duties is worthless and not addressing the root cause of the problem and merely papering over the cracks. To highlight the potential issue with sheep farmers and exporting sheep is the fact that 38% of our sheep and lamb production goes to the EU now. But with high tariffs it could kill many companies and a large selection of the industry.

Some Eurosceptic Brexiteers like Matthew Ellery (Research Executive at Eurosceptic campaign group Get Britain Out) claims it was not a lie but rather Remainers cannot tell the difference between 'net' and 'gross', forgetting conveniently to say that neither of these words was on the bus, and the fact that we get that money back means you cannot spend the money twice. But I appreciate his desperation to try to 'polish a turd' of an argument. He actually made a poor attempt at highlighting some so-called 'lies' in a vain attempt to justify the Leave lies, but reading though it on the Huffington post from 27th September 2016 (https://www.huffingtonpost.co.uk/matthew-ellery/leave-lies-remainers-need_b_12191462.html).

He was struggling claiming lies when they were points highlighted as possibilities, forecasts or concerns etc. which can obviously not be lies as they have not happened yet and even if incorrect would be just that incorrect and not lies, such as Turkey is joining the EU etc. But his understanding and use of the English language is very good so he knew exactly what he was doing, and it just resembled an extension of the language and misinformation the Leave campaigns employed in the EU referendum.

One point and an important one highlighted by Mr. Ellery showed that not as many jobs had been lost as feared by Remainers even though we haven't even left yet and stated 'in July the claimant count fell by 8,600 to 763,600, despite an expected rise of 9,500. Another 'Lie'. But this ignores the fact that claimants can go down as low-level jobs could have been created on zero hour contracts at some well-known warehouse companies but skilled jobs have been cut by Honda, Ford, Panasonic etc. due partly due to Brexit as those companies need to be within the free trade area of the EU and the single market. Also, a number of these companies have announced withdrawal of future investment which will cause job losses or no additional jobs as they again need to be within the Single market area. He even throws in the European army argument when it will not affect us as we have a veto, but we wouldn't like the truth to get in the way of a bit of propaganda would we.

The irony was lost on Mr. Ellery in that he was being misleading about so called lies that were not lies, or maybe it wasn't and just didn't care?

Would the leave campaign still have won without the lies on the red bus? Well obviously one can never be sure, but Dominic Cummings seemed sure when he wrote in his 19,800-word Spectator essay on 6th January 2017:

330

'Pundits and MPs kept saying 'why isn't Leave arguing about the economy and living standards'. They did not realise that for millions of people, £350m / NHS was about the economy and living standards – that's why it was so effective. It was clearly the most effective argument not only with the crucial swing fifth but with almost every demographic. Even with UKIP voters it was level-pegging with immigration. Would we have won without immigration? No. Would we have won without £350m/NHS? All our research and the close result strongly suggests No. Would we have won by spending our time talking about trade and the Single Market? No way.' [61]

Well Mr. Cummings seems quite clear and has the NHS seen a penny of the promised money or been promised all this money by the incumbent Government? Of course not. Welcome to the referendum result!

A plethora of lies (claims and reality)

1.   The red Bus and £350 million per week extra for the NHS.

a.   OK we are not genuinely getting that, and it was made up!

2.   David Davis said it [EU Trade deal] would be the easiest deal to complete.

a.   OK so in reality the statement was fabricated also!

3.   We will be better off outside the EU.

a.   OK literally most informed commentary and experts say we will be poorer as a country including the Government's own research due to higher costs of trade etc. Which leads to less company profits which will lead to less tax receipts for our government to spend on public services etc.

4.   Immigration would be dramatically cut.

a.   It looks like that will not happen as the government is not guaranteeing that anymore and stats show we really need these workers and figures show they contribute positively to our economy. It is simple supply and demand.

5.   Five million more migrants could enter Britain by 2030 if Turkey and four other applicant countries join the EU.

a.   OK we see now that it was all made up as a part of project fear by Dominic Cummings, Farage et al., but it was convincing at the time, especially that poster of the Syrian refugees allegedly in Europe already and all coming to the UK. Yes, it was racist, but effective.

6.   The UK loses out because other members favour a highly regulated and protectionist economy

a.   OK That claim that the UK is constantly being overruled by other EU countries is false. Research by UK in a changing Europe shows that the UK has been in a minority on 57 legislative acts at the European Council since 1999, when the decisions were made public. Since then it has been in the majority on 2,474 acts and abstained on 70 occasions.

7.   No short-term economic disruption "After we Vote Leave, there won't be a sudden change that disrupts the economy.

a.   OK now all the major Brexiteers are saying there will be disruption and not sure for how long, with Mr. Rees-Mogg saying it could be 50 years before we reap the benefits of Brexit! Do you not feel misled? Costs have already risen due to the devaluation of the Sterling and jobs lost or moved because of Brexit, and we haven't even left yet.

8.   We'll get brand new trade deals all over the world, we would immediately be able to start negotiating new trade deals... which could enter into force immediately after the UK leaves the EU – Chris Grayling.

a.   OK that has proved to be totally false and will Leave us with no significant trade deals which makes us poorer and vulnerable on WTO terms. All countries in the world are looking to be a part of Strong trading blocks to enable them to be more competitive. It feels like we have been lied to and will now go backwards.

9. There'll be no damage to trade with the EU, "There is a European free trade zone from Iceland to the Russian border and we will be part of it... Britain will have access to the Single Market after we vote leave... The idea that our trade will suffer because we stop imposing terrible rules such as the Clinical Trial Directive is silly.

a. OK this has proved to be totally inaccurate and total nonsense. We are desperately searching for a deal with the EU. We could still crash out of crashing out with no deal at the end of 2020 despite Boris' deal as it will be the Free Trade Agreement that is critical and the deciding factor.

10. With a new system in place by 2020, "By the next general election, we will create a genuine Australian-style points-based immigration system.

a. This system is designed to increase immigration, so immigration may remain the same or even go up as we need the workers. Although now we have more information since the referendum that is a good thing as we know we need the immigrant workers to fill the jobs which many did not realise.

11. There will be no change to the border between Northern Ireland and the Republic.

a. This is clearly a huge ongoing issue and not as simple as was described either through their ignorance or deliberate deceit, but it is clear this WILL change even if the customs border ends up in the Irish Sea which Mrs Ma's government rejected as it split the union.

Deselection of MPs just for their opinion of Brexit? Really?

As a constituency MP Ministers of parliament are expected to represent their constituency as a whole in parliament covering many local, regional and national issue including voting in public but also potentially representing Mrs. Jones who comes to his / her surgery as her rubbish bins have been stolen and not replaced by the local authority. This is one of the advantages of our system. But clearly in the case of Mr. Dominic Grieve Conservative and pro Remain MP for Beaconsfield, Buckinghamshire facing deselection by his local Conservative party is just plain bizarre, and Mr. Grieve is not the only MP facing such actions. Mr. Grieve's local association were not happy with our independent sovereign parliament and their MP doing what they are paid to do but resorted to abusing Mr. Grieve by heckling him loudly calling him "Liar", "traitor" and "disgusting" as well as shouting "how f*****g dare you?"

The above has many implications that both the Conservative party need to consider but also our politics in general that such a polite professional man can be abused in such a manner and a few hundred people can make the decision for thousands of constituents. But Beaconsfield could be seen as a microcosm of the Conservative party that has torn itself apart for decades over the issue of Europe. The conservative membership is known to be consisting largely of the older generations and not very representative of the UK as a whole and this may have worked against Mr Grieve and his principled stance but also shows the obsession it has with Brexit specifically. The strange situation of this development was that the motion for deselection was tabled by Mr. Jon Conway who believe it or not, stood AGAINST Mr Grieve as a UKIP candidate in 2017! Yes Mr. Conway is now a member of the local Conservative party and can simply leave UKIP behind and try to deselect Mr. Grieve. This system clearly has obvious flaws that need to be addressed but seems to reflect the issues the Labour party faces with Momentum as many now feel this left-wing infiltration means the Labour party will never return to the days when it had real success with Tony Blair as Prime Minister.

The Conservative party could be suffering from the same phenomenon as the Labour Party but from the right as UKIP and even more right-wing people join and slowly infiltrate the Conservative party to move it more to an extreme right-wing stance. Call this exaggeration but Ed Miliband and his Labour party underestimated the power of the Left-Wing Lobby (many of whom had joined from more extreme Left-Wing organisation like the Socialist Workers Party (SWP) to now influence party policy or intimidate local organisations and more centrist

MPs. See the parallels with Mr. Grieve?

This and many other issues are going on in local party-political offices and this phenomenon of 'entryism' could be the scourge of both main parties taking them both in undesirable directions and to the extremes. How bad this development will be only time will tell?

In a poll carried out by YouGov poll in 2019 established a strong presence of English (not even British!) nationalism running through the party that a number of them would countenance the breaking up of the UK for the sake of Brexit. Yes, this is how desperate it has become, and these very same people chose our new Prime Minister! In this poll some horrifying and confusing replies were returned including a clear non-interest in Scotland or Northern Ireland, such as:

- 63% of the party were willing to accept significant damage to the UK economy!

- 59% were even willing to see the Conservative Party itself destroyed in order to achieve Brexit!

Now that is surely an unhealthy obsession or is it a case of they still do not understand or have ever understood what is at play and the implications for the whole country as that is what it indicates to me, as nobody without mental illnesses could wish such things upon itself?

It appears the Conservative party members no longer see it as a contest between the Conservative party and the Labour party but rather a battle between their party and the 'Brexit parties' and feel they have more in common with those that share their view of Brexit such as the Brexit party than members of their own party! This is a major shift.

The Guardian's political commentator put it best when he observed the "bottomless appetite for anti-Brussels grievance" that really does motivate the party's grass roots as it does UKIP and the Brexit party.

Where the bloody hell was Corbyn?

If we go back to 2015 Ed Miliband and the Labour Party made a clear case for membership of the EU as well as the position of power and influence it gave the UK, although many in the party wanted a much more positive pro-EU stance. But it was tactical as Labour did not want to alienate the anti-EU voters and was playing a tactical game in its search for power and Jeremy Corbyn during and since the Referendum has continued this 'tightrope game' of trying to keep both sides of the argument happy. Why did Miliband not go for an 'IN-OUT' referendum, even though polls showed it could be to his electoral advantage? Well he commented it was 'an unnecessary gamble for the UK'. Sensible reply.

So the Labour Party was pro EU, albeit cautiously, but Corbyn's history is of someone very ambivalent to the EU and this proved a real issue for the Remain campaign, as Corbyn would not commit to one side or the other and although he was eventually with the Remain side he was not very positive about the EU or very high profile during the referendum. The question is whether Corbyn did it for tactical political reasons and effectively sat on the fence or he still dislikes the EU and doesn't believe in it, but was not willing to back the Leave campaign as he did not think they would win or to get into bed with the likes of UKIP, Farage, Rees-Mogg and Boris? It may have been a combination of the two but Corbyn was meant to be a leader in waiting and all the referendum made him appear was indecisive or insincere.

It almost seemed like his deep hatred of Cameron and Tories would not allow himself to be associated with them even for the country's good. It could be he saw the demise of Nick Clegg when he did just that and worked with the Tories in coalition, went back on a couple of his pledges including free tuition fees, and paid the price with the Liberal Democrats getting routed at the next general election and Nick Clegg losing his seat.

This lack of statesmanship or leadership (albeit honest!) was when Jeremy appeared on the Andrew Marr show and was asked by Marr how he felt about the EU on a scale of one to ten, one being weak and 10 being very strong. He thought for a moment and then replied shrugging his shoulders 'seven or seven and a half' No more was needed to say but the leaders of the remain campaign must have sunk in their chairs as soon as the words left his lips. Episodes like this do show the difference between the statesman and the protester, which is Jeremy's background and may stop him ever entering Number 10.

But it was not just Cameron and his team that despaired, his very own party members found him extremely frustrating. The 'Labour In for Britain' campaign led by Harriet Harman and the popular Alan Johnson could not get him engaged with Johnson claiming the Labour Leadership 'undermined (Labour In's) efforts'. It was quite clear Johnson felt like Andy Burnham, Yvette Cooper or Liz Kendall the campaign would have got more money, support and been much more successful with Corbyn and the shadow cabinet behind it. The strange thing is it would not have been difficult for Corbyn to highlight the benefits of the EU to his voters including workers' rights that had helped soften the blow of globalisation, the poorer Labour regions of the UK that had benefited from regional funding, environmental protections, fair-trade, and other social protections. It could be that Jeremy Corbyn and John McDonnell were more focused on winning total control of the labour party, and the future of the country could wait. At the time of writing this section almost 3 years since the referendum result they are still fighting this battle with a number of resignations including Chuka Amuna*, Luciana Berger and Chris Leslie who set up The Independent Group and thought to become a political party, plus the ongoing battle with antisemitic and racist fringes within the party that Corbyn has again been indecisive in condemning for some reason.

*Chuka Amuna moved on to the Liberal Democrats in June 2019 and Luciana Berger also moved to the Lib Dems as The Independent Group all but disintegrated with Anna Soubry trying desperately to hold it together.

Just weeks before the referendum vote most Labour voters had no idea what the Labour Party's position was. It was such a weak position that lacked any communication and was probably Corbyn's 'Charge of the Light Brigade' where like the generals afterwards claiming it was a success and was the right thing to do. The sad thing is that those that Corbyn claims to be in politics for, the disadvantaged citizens of the UK and the least well off and lowly paid, will probably pay the biggest price for Brexit and surely that must be seen as a dereliction of his duty?

There is no doubt that had he come out positively for Remaining in the EU and took his vast number of supporters with him that the Remain vote would have won comfortably but his lack of passion or campaigning to Remain was taken by the Labour heartlands as a signal to kick Cameron and the perceived establishment even if as happened we damage the UK's prospects. Perhaps they never thought we would leave, so it was a low risk but tactically appealing strategy?

If so, it backfired, and many could pay the price. His lack of engagement or clarity meant Farage and his team could campaign almost unhindered in those Labour heartlands they had to win over, and they could not believe how easy Labour were making it for them. That lack of Labour Remain presence was great for the Leave teams and as they heard no contradictory messages from Labour, who were they going to believe?

There were many well-known Labour MPs and politicians including Gordon Brown, Ed Miliband and Harriet Harman that helped Alan Johnson and Labour In for Britain but Jeremy is the 'cult Leader' or pied piper who could have rallied his troops and Momentum to be clear that Britain was better as a member of the EU but he did not and this sold the Remain campaign short. Even 3 years later and going into a general election nobody really knows the Jeremy Corbyn and the Labour Party's position which seems to have deliberately been vague almost hoping the Conservative party will tear itself apart, the Brexit party takes Tory votes and he walks into number 10 without having to do very much at all. But this is a dereliction of duty and if this was the case and a conscious strategy, then this has helped the growth of Nigel Farage and the Brexit party. But the Brexit Party then announced it will not stand against Conservative MPs which changed the whole dynamic. Mr. Corbyn should be held to account for that as he has chosen party interest over the interest of the UK. Labour seems to have now moved towards a second referendum but in such convoluted evasive language people are not at all clear what they meant and are still not in December 2019!

The above combined with Corbyn's unwillingness to achieve good news coverage by delivering positive stories about EU membership or the concerns should we leave especially with no deal resulted in Corbyn being impotent during the campaign and adding very little value which could have effectively handed victory to the Leave campaign, especially when we see how many voted Leave in the traditional Labour heartlands in the North of England.

Corbyn's refusal to make a clear case for Remain many trace back to his obvious Eurosceptic past where he felt the EU was a bureaucratic device to service the interests of uber-capitalism (Shipman 2016).

The morning after the result the Labour campaign team were looking for Jeremy, but he was nowhere to be found and then they were informed he was still in bed and they didn't know how to get him up. Brian Duggan who worked with Alan Johnson from the Labour In for Britain campaign had had a strained relationship throughout the campaign with the Labour Leadership team and was a mild mannered man but when it got to this stage he had had enough and commented out of frustration 'Are you seriously telling me the markets are crashing, the pound is falling, we've just left the European Union, the Prime Minister is about to resign, and the leader of the opposition is in bed?' You can see his anger when this man should be portraying himself as the Prime Minister in waiting but will be at some obscure rally somewhere protesting against something else. This highlighted to many that he is not suitable to be Prime Minister as he does not have the understanding or recognition of seeing the wood for the trees and remains, and probably always will be, a protester at heart.

The continuing saga of Corbyn and his bewildering position on the EU and Brexit has a direct impact on today's politics as the absence of a credible opposition makes Boris Johnson a more powerful Prime Minister than he should be as the official opposition Labour party is not holding the Government to account. Despite all of Johnson's issues as PM including losing the first seven votes in the House and found guilty of acting unlawfully when advising the Queen but is still favourite to win the next general election because Corbyn is just not popular with the wider public.

Did Angela Merkel help the Leave vote?

Although a great believer in the EU and the cooperation of member states, especially with her history of having lived in the former East Germany and the isolationist attitudes she lived under, her decision to let 1 million Syrian refugees into Germany very quickly even if well intentioned, created real social issues for Germany and the Brexiteers obviously jumped on this, albeit with the usual economy of the truth. She made this decision with the right humanitarian intentions and social conscience but as it was badly planned and thought through it did not work efficiently, although it did save many Syrian refugees from a war-torn country and potential death which should not be forgotten. Basically, it was too many too soon without any planning for housing, integration or what would happen with these people in the medium and long term, resulting in some chaos. Many sport centres and large halls were meant to be temporarily allocated for immigrants and asylum seekers, but they were still camped there years later, and this reflected very badly on Angela Merkel who is normally very calculated and a very safe pair of hands.

This decision made by Merkel in Germany allowed the Brexiteers and the Leave campaign to exaggerate the issue with immigration in Europe implying it was uncontrolled rather than it was a conscious decision by the German government, albeit misplaced, to allow in that number of Syrian War refugees in one wave for humanitarian reasons. But, regardless of the real reason the Brexiteers rightly so for their campaign jumped on this and tried to convince people if they are in Germany they can simply walk across borders into the UK which was not the case and a total fabrication. Then, not surprisingly we have Nigel Farage in front of his racist poster implying those in the photo are all EU residents walking to the UK. Nonsense yes, lies Yes, deliberate yes, but effective and that was the clear aim of Farage, and the Arron Bank's funded campaign.

So indirectly Angela Merkel did help the Leave campaign build their case, albeit with misinformation, but they used clever focused tactics to get enough people to vote for their ideals (I cannot say vision as they never painted a vision, but rather focused on people's fears and prejudices) and get the results they wanted, by any means necessary.

Teresa May's 'Deal'

As we know (although some still try to contest this!) there were many reasons that 17.4m people voted to leave the EU and they were complex and, in part, contradictory such as we want a better NHS BUT we want fewer immigrants, and it is beyond any doubt that a desire to control immigration was the most important reason confirmed by hundreds of reports and videos filmed by most of the mainstream news networks in the run up to the Referendum, although once Leave won suddenly people were quiet about immigration (well apart from the rise in the reported hate crime) and suddenly 'sovereignty' and 'control' were the buzzwords being espoused, and obviously more politically correct.

As a Remainer I dislike many aspects of Teresa May's deal, but she tried to keep everybody happy probably in line with the 52-48% result of the Referendum but in reality pleasing nobody. Why as a Remainer do I think it is a bad deal? Simply because it is worse than the deal, we already have with the EU in almost every respect. We currently possess the benefits of the EU whilst opting out of the Euro, we are outside Schengen and have our own passport checks, plus we receive a very nice rebate which other countries do not receive, and this ignores all the many downsides coming our way when we leave.

But when looking at the issue of immigration and many other concerns by Leavers her deal; met many of their concerns including no longer sending large sums of money to Brussels, stopping free movement of people, the ECJ no longer taking precedent in some areas of law etc. but they were not satisfied.

Times Columnist Daniel Finkelstein said of the European Research Group (ERG) in February 2019 'when Teresa May returned from the negotiations, the deal done, all they had to do was vote for it and Brexit would have been secure. Now it isn't... You betrayed You. You can't count and you can't compromise, and you can't take yes for an answer.' Now this goes to the root of the problem with the extremist ERG position and attitude where they could not compromise and were looking for any small issue to try and crash out with a no-deal Brexit to almost prove a point that they had won and never had to compromise on anything, as they had implied all the time. But then reality bit them firmly in the posterior and the group started to split from the extremist head bangers and those that could smell the coffee and felt a more sensible approach would be wise to at least guarantee Brexit. The ERG had been playing poker without fully understanding the rules and kept playing for 4 aces when with a full house or royal flush they could get most of what they wanted, and we would all have to move on.

The future will require honest leadership which is far more honest than we have had so far in setting out the fundamental and realistic choices we really have and the difficult trade off we have between sovereignty and national control whilst keeping frictionless market access for our goods and services in our biggest trading market.

With May's deal having failed to get parliament approval and failed in 4 votes it is now dead. Now with Boris Johnson's deal that aims to avoid a no deal, which is a similar deal in a different guise, with some minor changes, he is now claiming enthusiastically it is a great deal. Some may call this 'polishing a turd' with others more generously 'putting lipstick on a pig'.

How could Brexit have ever been delivered effectively?

How could it have ever been effectively or efficiently delivered when the people pushing it didn't know what they were arguing for (in any details whatsoever) or have a clue how to deliver it or where it was even going once the vote was won? It was a clear gamble, probably not realistically thinking they could win, with the chances of a successful delivery even after a Leave result very fine indeed. I am sure many Leave voters and Brexiteers could (and maybe still can?) imagine a world where Brexit IS delivered quickly and effectively. But that is clearly an imaginary world as has become all so clear with the events of the last 3 years, but some still believe it and all they need to do is get all their Unicorns in a row!

Let's say for argument's sake they achieve some form of acceptable Brexit; it has still cost us so much time and money still with little benefit so as business and economists say the opportunity cost has been huge and expensive. This is because our MPs have NOT been spending time on Health, Welfare reform, NHS reforms / improvements, employment, schools, homelessness, food banks, dangerous cladding on high rise blocks of flats etc. but rather messing around with indicative votes, many of which were obvious they never had a majority (rather like Teresa May bringing back her deal times and wasting more parliamentary time). It is unintended consequences, but Brexit has caused many many issues and effectively paralysed parliamentary procedures to the extent that is has become all encompassing. And again, I ask the question "for what tangible benefits?" By any calculation of a cost Benefit analysis for this process it does not seem very clever or indeed warranted. Just shows you how a seemingly innocuous decision by David Cameron and his cowardly folly to protect his own job and keep the right wing of his party aligned can lead to such costs, chaos and confusion. But that will, I am afraid, be his legacy.

The current parliamentary arithmetic means that Teresa May and now Boris Johnson will find it difficult to get anything through parliament as Labour will not support them, the Lib Dems are at the other end of the spectrum now confirming they would revoke Article 50 if they win a majority at the next election, the DUP for example will do quite simply what is in their own narrow interest, and the ERG would dance around naked in the House of Commons to get a no-deal Brexit, that is unless enough MPs fear losing their seats at the next general election and vote for an easy option so their constituents do not reject them.

At the end of the day there was no plan, lots of false optimism, and false expectation we would get an "easy free trade agreement with the EU", "they need us more than we need them", "it won't cost us a penny" etc. All we are left with is Prime Minister Boris Johnson telling us less negativity and more positivity will get us through like some born again Mr Motivator? How dense and short sighted is that when he is just 'winging' it on the fly'. It is in fact Boris deceit, pure and simple, but he is the master.

Are we really 'Lions' and are we really led by 'Donkeys'?

It is so easy to witness on social media or even in our right-wing press so many references to the wars Britain had taken part in (normally the second World War) referring to how brave and successful we were and still are as a people. What all those people posting or highlighting such items forget is that it was over 70 years ago, we would not have won that war (WW2) without the help or the Americans, the Commonwealth soldiers and many other countries including many now EU states. So it is a great perversion of history, but it is portrayed by mainly middle aged and slightly older people that have never had to shoot a gun in anger or experience the horrors of war and one of the reasons they have not is because of the longest duration of peace in Europe of which the EU and the EEC before it have helped.

As Churchill commented "better Jaw than War War"! So it is great for these men (and is tends to be men) sitting in front of their keyboards in their Union Jack (or St. George Cross) underpants being so brave and extolling our virtues as a race, but they have never ever had to witness such horrors so are in no way qualified to state such nonsense or claim such propaganda as "we beat the Germans twice, so we will beat them again!" as if it is the third world war. The 'underpants brigade' may see or perceive it as that but this is plainly incorrect and being honest bizarre. So, are we as 'Brits' 'Lions' as a race? May be but we do not know and certainly no more than any other race unless you feel we are superior to other races of course? But when one sees such comments on social media, it appears the union Jack underpants brigade would love a war to prove how great we still are (as if that was the only way to demonstrate that!) especially as they will be sitting at home like Mr. Mainwaring and Pike saying "they don't like it up 'em" (if you have just said or thought to yourself "it was corporal Jones who in reality said that on screen" then you are missing the point of this serious book!).

As regards Donkeys looking at our political establishment and what happened during the referendum campaign as well as the aftermath, it is difficult not to conclude that we have many donkeys or at least a lot of politicians out of their depth showing incompetence and no sense of strategy or conviction. For this reason, it has helped the rise of the likes of Nigel Farage that has shown no intellectual rigour apart from being a good orator, having Multi-Millionaire backers and a few empty slogans.

We only have to look at David Cameron not having achieved much of note as Prime Minister including never getting anywhere near his immigration targets who then calls a Referendum loses it and resigns. Teresa May takes over and achieves very little and showed such poor communication skills and resigns (yes you could say it was the poison chalice, but she took the chalice and ran with it). Nigel Farage despite lots of bluster resigns two weeks after the referendum to avoid being held responsible for the implementation of the referendum result that he did not expect to win and had no clue how to implement it. Chris Grayling, the former transport secretary had a disastrous privatisation of the probation service but then was the minister that authorised awarding a key Ferry contract to a company WITH NO FERRIES, but ALSO tried to justify it afterwards! Yes, I know but it's true, although it could be the prime example of what a cluster fuck Brexit had become. The end result of this phase of Brexit is Boris Johnson, a serial liar and philanderer in the top job.

We cannot cover all the 'Donkeys' but let's finish with the aforementioned Boris Johnson, our new Prime Minister, who became a real disappointment as Foreign Secretary, where he seemed to idle around achieving nothing until he had to agree to a workable Brexit model, and then he cut and run. The repeated gaffes and inappropriate remarks alienated the UK's allies and opponents alike including the jokes about dead bodies in Libya and the recitation of inappropriate verses by Rudyard Kipling in Myanmar, plus his inaccurate suggestion that the detained British Iranian national Nazanin Zaghari Ratcliffe had been in Iran training journalists, which her family and supporters said had damaged their campaign to secure her release. The above does not include his newspaper articles including references to Muslim women looking like "letterboxes" or referring to homosexuals as "Tank Topped Bum boys" The image of Boris and Michael Gove after the Referendum result that they won, and had been promoting intensely for months, not having a clue what to do next was telling. It was like rabbits in the headlights and this was 2 of the most experienced politicians in our Parliament at the time. That image is imprinted on many peoples' minds. We address other issues with Boris Johnson elsewhere in this book including his exposed deceptions which makes it even more astounding that he has become our latest PM. May be just that very fact shows that we must be led by Donkeys and it answers the question. But as an eternal optimist I hope there is / are young bright conviction politicians coming through or who will emerge that will take us past this time of hate, discrimination and inflammatory language from career politicians like Nigel Farage to get press and social media headlines or clicks. I hope they govern for all the people and will do all they can to help and protect the less fortunate and poor in our society to raise everyone up to a better standard of living. Wishful thinking maybe but we must all be hopeful and not drown in cynicism.

This isn't really what this booked is focused on but Simon Kuper wrote a brilliant article in the Financial Times and had an interesting explanation for this incompetence of leadership writing how leaders like George HW Bush or Clement Attlee had their formative experiences in fighting WWII, while Bill Clinton and John Major for example experienced poverty and through these experiences knew that government really mattered. "But both countries have now fallen into the hands of well-off baby boomers, born between 1946 and 1964 – the luckiest members of the luckiest generation in history. These people had no formative experiences, only TV shows. They never expected anything awful or unknown to happen. They went into politics mostly for kicks."

Now although some may say it is a bit of an exaggeration, there is no doubt that politics appears a rich and privileged playground with so many Etonians having important jobs in Government and common Etonian rivalries between Cameron and Boris Johnson seeming more important than raising the living standards of our poor to help avoid the disenfranchisement of certain parts of our society. We only have to look at our last 2 Prime Ministers before Johnson in David Cameron and Teresa May and strip away the speeches and rhetoric and ask ourselves what was their conviction? What did they really stand for or more importantly achieve? And looking at that the cupboard appears bare and history will not treat them well. A startling example of the position of PM being the playground of the privileged, is that 20 of our PMs were schooled at Eton Mr. Johnson being the latest.

A pluralist democracy has checks and balances in part to guard against incompetence by a government or ministers. That is why Trump and the Brexiteers so often attack elements of a pluralist democracy. The ultimate check on incompetence should be democracy itself and incompetent politicians thrown out. But when a large part of the media encourages rather than expose acts of incompetence, and the non-partisan media treat knowledge as just another opinion, that safeguard against persistent incompetence and deceit is put in danger. [30]

Is the European Research Group (ERG) a most unpatriotic group?

You may find this a strange title to this section as their claim to be the ultimate patriots, but when I look at what this group of unusual individuals resembling a gang of ideological misfits including the minister for the nineteenth century Jacob Rees-Mogg, Mark Francois resembling a character out of dad's army with some bizarre opinions, and Nadine Dorries who didn't have a clue about the single market and had to ask her ERG colleagues even though she had been campaigning to withdraw from it as it was so bad! Where else but in such a small narrow-minded group of ideologues would such characters be seen together? The reason I use this title is that what they have been promoting with their no-deal WTO leave at all costs position makes our country and society weaker and poorer, and what true Patriot would do that?

You may disagree with that description but the plummeting pound, job losses, raising costs, and movement towards recession prove that this direction of travel is detrimental to the UK and we need Billions to bail out business and the economy from the Bank Of England and the Government. Yes, this is for something they told us would be quick, easy and so good for the UK!

They went for years not really producing anything with any detail as to what they were proposing or anything that resembled a plan or direction of travel and these are the supposed Gurus and experts of a no-deal Brexit. Eventually on the 5th of June, almost 3 years since the vote the so-called tough man Deputy Chairman of the ERG Steve Baker MP put pen to paper to put the ERG position and future 'plan' although it lacked detail or clarification as you will see below. Mr. Baker called it "A clean and managed Brexit", the title leaving a lot to be desired as I will highlight below. Note it is by the deputy Chairman and not the more high-profile Chairman Jacob Rees-Mogg who has cleverly kept his fingers off this document should it come back and bite him in the posterior. He always uses "common Sense" does our Jacob. Surely a document from Mr. Rees-Mogg would have more gravitas and achieve more column inches that a man who is hardly known outside Parliament and his own constituency? Unless he thought it was nonsense of course.

I have copied sections from the document to avoid any typos or mistakes with my comment or commentary after each actual section prefixed by a letter. For clarity Mr. Baker highlighted some important facts in the introduction as follows below, but let us quickly address the title of the document which is a misnomer before we begin as a Brexit is as we are seeing and never will be "Clean" or " Managed" unless the EU help us mange it, so where is the independence in that and we haven't even got to Page 2? So nice title for Brexiteers but in reality nonsense and another fantasy, but I am sure sense will follow.

The following is from and his copyright is fully acknowledged, of Mr. Steve Baker MP, in the document from 5ᵗʰ June 2019 called "A clean and Managed Brexit" You can google the document to get the original full copy as it makes interesting reading.

> *a.* **This document draws heavily on previously published work listed in the references, and especially the alternative written ministerial statement – A Better Deal and a Better Future – published in the aftermath of the first defeat of the agreement on 15 January.**

> *b.* **This work could not have been prepared without the contributions of colleagues. I am particularly grateful to Sir William Cash MP, Iain Duncan-Smith MP, Mark Francois MP, Sir Bernard Jenkin MP, Lord Lilley, Craig Mackinlay MP, Owen Paterson MP, Jacob Rees-Mogg MP, Theresa Villiers MP, Barney Reynolds, and Shanker Singham for helpful comments. Errors and omissions remain my own.**

Author: – So some prominent names have contributed, and one would assume agree with the content of the document otherwise they would not have allowed their names to go forward. Not surprising Nadine Dorries is not mentioned, but she is probably still trying to understand it!

1. including tax cuts, to mitigate any potential negative effects of leaving the EU on WTO terms, to compensate businesses and sectors for exceptional costs of adaptation, and on measures to increase business investment, training and research and development, and economic growth (Page 6)

Author: So, we do not pay what is internationally recognised as our commitment to the EU budget AS AGREED, which will be frowned upon in the financial markets, but this also shows how low we have dropped that we try to default on part of our commitments! What message does that say about the UK as a future partner?

If no deal is better than a bad deal how can there be negative effects to mitigate?!
But that aside it is basically admitting there will be significant issues, albeit using weaselly words to help, support, and compensate our businesses and economy, presumably as they know if will be an absolute mess?

As of November, they have eventually succumbed accepting we must pay the divorce bill, plus the UK's credit rating has been downgraded, partly because of the Brexit chaos caused and still ongoing.

2. Citizens' rights - The UK should, under our own domestic law, unilaterally guarantee the rights of EU citizens currently in the UK to continue to live and work in the UK broadly as they do today. EU citizens will enjoy national treatment and indefinite leave to remain, without additional rights in excess of UK citizens.

Author: So, the individuals that were telling us that immigration was out of control and had been for years and we should never let in so many people are now telling us they can all stay, and we will start a fresh from sometime in the future? So, either we have too many immigrants or we do not, which is it gentlemen? This is clearly a point when they stop all the scaremongering and anti-immigrant rhetoric and meet reality and have to try to use some careful wording to try not to look racist or out of touch with what is genuinely going on in the country and those people they did not want, are doing the important jobs we do not have the people or the skills to do!

3. The Government should accelerate work to mitigate the consequences of exiting without the Withdrawal Agreement in place, including taking unilateral and reciprocal measures, and reaching stand-alone agreements in our mutual interests where that proves possible.

Author: So, they admit there will be issues with a no deal scenario even though they have been pushing it with the usual enthusiastic rhetoric of "they need us more than we need them" etc. This is also disingenuous as it knows that such agreements can take years and avoid deliberately putting timescales on anything, why? Because we are reliant on other countries and regions to agree to our requests! So where again is this so-called Independence they told us we would have?

4. The UK should propose to the EU that we continue our free trade under a temporary FTA in goods with zero tariffs, no quantitative restrictions and full cumulation under rules of origin to provide for at least a two-year General Agreement on Tariffs and Trade (GATT) XXIV compliant standstill arrangement, pending the negotiation of a comprehensive advanced FTA.

Author: So basically, we are leaving the club, we have been very rude and obnoxious about the EU yet still expect to trade on the same rules with the same club which the ERG told us was so bad? This is what Boris Johnson called having your cake and eat it which is ridiculous and such 'cakeism' resembles a kid asking for something at Christmas that he knows he has no chance of getting and should not really even be asking Mummy and Daddy for it as it is too high a price to pay for such an irreverent child!
In fact, this 'standstill' period does not actually cover this scenario as it is for countries that have agreed an FTA and are then preparing to implement it. There is no agreement on a Free Trade Agreement (FTA) currently and could take years, so the point is mute.

5. The UK should continue to uphold high standards, including in relation to food safety and animal welfare.

Author: If their priority is a USA trade deal then this is just pie in the sky again. We are going to tell the Americans you cannot have any extra access to the NHS and its potentially huge pharmaceutical market, plus you must Mr. Trump supply food meeting our food standards which are already higher than yours and does not include hormone infused beef, or chlorinated chicken etc? Fantasy land, and they know that!

6. Tariffs and quotas In default of such an agreement, the UK should take such measures on agri-food tariffs and quotas as are necessary to avoid inflation in the UK, including on agri-food products. This will include a) unilateral applied tariff reductions on a WTO Most Favoured Nation (MFN) basis or b) applying erga omnes (That is, quotas open to all) Tariff Rate Quotas (TRQs) for agricultural products and c) opening FTA agreements with agricultural exporters such as Canada, Australia and New Zealand (TRQ or otherwise) in contemplation of fuller agreements in due course.

Author: So basically their vote and decision to leave the EU has already created and will create more inflation (yes their decision) but it could be the Farmers and other businesses and industries that could pay the price when they cannot sell their product to the EU as they have done up to now due to extremely high Tariffs plus be exposed to huge US and Australian farms that could blow them out of the water on price and kill their business. So, we can see a trend here where the poor or business pay the price for rich ideologs like Jacob Reece-Mogg whose greatest problem linked to this may be is the price of Dom Perignon going through the roof or will his nanny demanding more money as the cost of living has risen!

7. Services The UK will seek to implement two-way arrangements for mutual recognition on services, including enhanced equivalence for financial services, which continue services trade for the benefit of both parties5. The drafting for services can be relatively simple, and could be implemented in final form, effective from exit day.

Author: So, where is the independence they told us we would have when we leave the wicked EU? We do not have it as any agreement or cooperation means interdependence NOT independence, those days have gone, but some imperialists still believe in and dream of such times.

8. Independence will bring new opportunities for our economy.

Author: We have already conceded it is an interdependent world and independence in the sense they use it does not exist and they are simply making empty promises here but obviously with no details, timescales or an idea of how that will actually happen or why! We leave somewhere that gives us great opportunities already to somewhere that may offer some benefits, but we cannot tell you where or how! It's like someone offers to cut your leg off saying we have some great prosthetics over here that 'may' make you faster, just believe us!

9. Many EU regulations impede growth

Author: Again, no specific details, but maybe they mean the **EU working time Directive** that stops employers abusing the working hours of their staff to help protect their physical and mental health? It is possible they are thinking 100-hour weeks are acceptable or once out of the EU we can send kids back up Mr. Reece-Mogg's chimney? But seriously we can see where the ERG wants us to go and become a very lowly regulated economy so all their mates can profit?

10. The Government should seek to replicate the EU's agreements with third countries

Author: So again, we are not independent we are asking pretty please for other independent countries that have their own Sovereignty (not just us!) when it comes to negotiations. But in this case many countries including Japan and Turkey, have said they will not roll them over for obvious reasons i.e. the original deals were done with a market of 450 million people not 60! They know we will be cut a drift from any trade deals so will be most accommodating to their demands if we want to trade with them. Also, they will have some loyalty to and an eye on the EU who will not take too kindly to the UK getting the same deal as them with all the power they wield. Welcome to the real-world ERG as these are the realities we will have to deal with whilst becoming poorer as a country at the same time. Well done guys great job.

But there is an obvious flaw in this argument as we were told so often by Brexiteers and the ERG that the United Kingdom could do so much better on its own. So why would we simply want to roll over International Trade agreements that were negotiated by the EU to our benefit, if we can do SO much better on our own? The rhetoric and the reality do not add up!

11. The Government should conclude bilateral agreements with other states concurrently while negotiating a UK-EU Free Trade Plus agreement. Those should include FTAs with the US, India, China, and other partners

Author: Such agreements can take years plus we do not have the manpower to do all these trade deals as we lack the numbers and the experts as all the recent trade deals of the last 40 years have been negotiated by the team in Brussels (perhaps with some Brits on the team) but now we are on our own. But to even start this we will need foreign negotiation experts i.e. more immigrants, which the ERG has failed to mention.

12. Simultaneous discussions will include partners for more difficult FTAs in the longer term.

Author: I thought countries would be beating their way to our door to do quick trade deals? Oh no the ERG has changed its tune now it has won the vote and a seed of honesty has entered the conversation as again reality hits home. So why are the difficult FTAs? Obviously they do not say but just get their warning in and to confirm what they were saying before was nonsense and a lot of these agreements will take years, whilst our citizens suffer! Do you remember these ERG Brexit experts telling us that during the referendum campaigns? No, me neither. Funny that!

13. While wishing to advance all these agreements, priority will be placed on a UK-US FTA.

Author: see above regarding USA priority and the issue with NHS access and lower food standards but also Lower food standards, lower chemical standards, lower consumer rights, lower animal welfare, and no recognition of rules of origin.

14. The Government should use the UK's WTO membership to reinforce the other pillars of our strategy and to promote wealth creation for the UK economy and the world.

<u>Author:</u> So we are leaving the EU as we felt we did not have enough influence, and they were not working in our interest when we were 1 of 28 countries but now we will be 1 of 164 with 1 vote but we are going to make such an influence and change? And this is why President Trump (who hates the WTO) is undermining the WTO and stifling its development as I write. This is just word spaghetti from the ERG hoping people do not do their homework or understand the WTO. Basically, we are leaving the Premier League and going into the 3rd tier and as a Charlton Athletic fan I know what that is like!

We should also take into consideration that influence within the EU could have been higher still, but we chose to constantly work against the aims and desires of the EU so were seen not to be rowing in the same direction. How can you ask for more influence but then constantly remain a lone wolf within the club? We had much more influence than the smaller countries, but we chose not to use it in a positive cooperative manner, often to keep the extremes of our political parties or right-wing media happy and onside.

15. The Government should promote active UK membership of recognised WTO groups as soon as possible, and seek to establish new ones, showing the UK is a committed liberaliser of trade, committed to open domestic settings, for instance:

      The UK should seek to join the Cairns Group of agricultural exporters;

      The UK should launch the 'Manchester Group of Services Exporters', named for the city's role in the historic free trade movement, to support advancement of the Trade in Services Agreement (TiSA);

      The UK should join the e-commerce plurilateral initiative and take a leadership role in services liberalisation.

Author: So, we are leaving the most powerful free trading block in the world with all its advantages and the ERG's idea is to join more free trade groups that most people have never heard of or understand. This literally looks like Mr. Baker wanted to get to double figures with 10 pages so needed a bit of padding to get there, as it is nonsense and is scrambling around on the ground looking for pennies as I did ads a kid at the amusement arcades rather than looking to be in the elite club. It rings desperate and a bit pathetic that this is where we have arrived, and the ERG seems happy for us to be in this position.

16. The Government should accelerate the development of the UK economy so that we will continue to generate high levels of skilled employment, in which people, families and businesses are able to succeed based on the merits of their ideas and their hard work. An economic system based on fair and open competition and social responsibility will maximise participation in wealth creation and lead to more money in people's pockets and more money for essential public services.

Author: This is just a generic statement to finish with when these people have been a part of the same Government that have not developed the UK economy with high levels of skilled employment, so what have they been doing apart from meeting up to talk about Brexit rather than helping develop policy in this and other important areas. They have helped paralyse our economy for almost 4 years due to their obsession with this one subject. The irony is that many companies that do generate high skilled employment such as Honda, Nissan, The European Medicines agency or some of the financial institutions etc. have left, are leaving or have stated that they will not be investing in the UK either at all or not as much as was planned. This is like the ERG saying I am going to cut your legs off so you can become an Olympian in the Para Olympics! Either these people are really dense, unprepared, not realistic, or don't care about the implications of their actions and a no-deal Brexit may be all of the above? And let us not forget that these are the same people who hoisted Austerity on our citizens since 2008 and now this. They must be so proud.

The previous sections were from and credited to with his copyright is fully acknowledged, of Mr. Steve Baker MP, in the document from 5th June 2019 called "A clean and Managed Brexit". You can google the document to get the original full copy as it makes interesting reading.

<u>Summary from Author:</u> A fanciful wish list lacking detail and timescales (for obvious reasons) that has taken 3 years to concoct to try and justify the rantings of years that now had to be backed up in writing and Mr. Baker was the one that stepped up whereas Mr. Rees-Mogg took the back seat to avoid any collateral damage that may arise from this fiction J K Rowling would be proud of. They are crossing fingers and toes hoping this is not such a disaster as it could become as they clearly have no plan or strategy apart from the aforementioned fantastical ideas. If this is their 'Bible' for Brexit and they get their way we are really in trouble.

Leaves one with the question were they unpatriotic, ignorant of duplicitous or may be all of the above?

Chapter 24
The Confusion between referendums & general

elections

A referendum and general elections ARE different

In the run up to the referendum vote most people seemed to treat it like any other election albeit with a lot more emotion and implied importance as for many it was not blue versus red or Right versus Left but rather the Brits against Johnny foreigner and the evil empire of the EU and the immigration it brought with it. Having once won the referendum Leavers regularly compared it to a general election win with the same first past the post system and the claim that democracy had won. But there was one major difference which made the vote more critical than any general election and that was the fact that in a general election you can vote again in the UK in a maximum of 5 years, NOT so with the EU referendum. Although even if we exited you could not rule out the possibility of joining again sometime in the future, but this would be very unlikely, and the deal would not be as good as now. Out literally would mean Out and an unknown future with the risks of job losses, high costs and lack of future inward investment highly likely.

Although not all political parties when they win a general election keep completely to their manifesto, as circumstances do change, but at least we have some document in black and white that we can attempt to hold them to account with. But with the referendum it is quite clear that such accountability is almost non-existent as the organisations that fight these campaigns then just disappear into the background and anyone having produced such ugly racist posters or lying social media posts are not held to account. Can we hold Dominic Cummings, Nigel Farage, Boris Johnson or Jacob Rees-Mogg to account for any inaccuracies or misinformation they may have communicated in the campaign? Even the accusations of foreign money having been used to win or at least influence the result can only be investigated, which may take years, so would be too late even if found to be true but even then what actions could be taken against whom. The damage would have been done. So, in reality people and groups could promise whatever they wanted to the electorate to get the result they wanted without any risk of discourse or being held to account, and that is not a great position to be in if we want a true and accurate democracy. We saw how the Leave campaign effectively promised 350 million a week to the NHS but as soon as they had won Nigel Farage when interviewed on breakfast TV claimed he cannot promise that and would never have promised that, almost disavowing himself of that promise as he was not a part of that wing of the Leave campaign. But he never came out and distanced himself from that claim during the campaign. OK yes, I agree that is Nigel Farage so what more can you expect. But it wasn't just the promises for the NHS, there were also promised subsidies for farmers and higher education support which is clearly just a case of segmenting the market (as marketers would say) and promising each segment whatever they want so they get the result they want and then disappear knowing they do not have to deliver on anything. This is a major difference to a general election and the Leave campaigns recognised this and used it accordingly.

Even Dominic Cummings admitted the £350 million was a 'controversial claim' but having noticed how effectively it was picked up by the press and played well to the households around the country he continued with it. Dr Martin Moore of Kings College London found that The Express repeated the £350 million no fewer than 24 times during the campaign, even though it had been proven to be false! Was this lazy journalism, a disregard for truth and honesty or just a continuation of the British Press Eurosceptic and anti-immigrant sentiment, and implying in this case the NHS would get all the money we are sending to those foreigner types? Again, we see what people can get away with during a referendum that they probably could not during a general election campaign, although the Conservatives were having a good attempt on the 2019 general election campaign with the number of lies, contortions of the truth and pure deceit racked up by the day.

Yes Remain was also accused of Project Fear or scaremongering but their seemed to be a difference in that the Remain arguments tended to be based on research or information from other organisations such as the IMF or Bank of England etc. and were more focused on future risks such as huge loss of jobs (for logical reasons that could be explained such as lack of access to the single market and customs Union etc.) or we would become poorer (due to less internal investment, smaller economy and increased costs). But they were mainly speculative warnings about the future of the UK based on observable reality and basic economics such as the success we had achieved whilst a member of the EU. They were not misrepresenting the true situation regarding millions of Turks coming to the UK very soon, or posters of Middle Eastern immigrants and asylum seekers implying they were queueing up to come to the UK as the leave campaigns did. Surely the two are clearly different both in their implications but also in their aims and honesty.

The immigration issue was central to the Leave campaign and the difference between a referendum and general election allowed the Leave groups to be more visceral and direct as they would not get help to account, than they ever could like an incoming government in a general election. There is no doubt that whipping up the anti-immigrant fervour allowed Arron Banks and the Leave campaign to move more people to Leave that may not have ever voted in the first place, but now saw a reason to go to the polling booth, and could have made the difference between a Leave instead of a Remain result. We should be concerned for our democracy that people like Arron Banks with lots of money can heavily influence our politics without the same accountability as MPs have and seem somewhat carefree with his position on the rules of our elections. This became clear when he commented rather flippantly to the question about a fair contest "I don't give a monkey's... we pushed the boundaries right to the edge... no one cares!" Well may be The National Crime Agency will care as they investigate allegations of multiple offences by Arron Banks and his unofficial leave campaign in the Brexit referendum?

The reality is that EU immigrants contribute substantially to many sectors including building trades, warehouse workers, hospitality and healthcare as well as hundreds of other digital Media and high-tech sectors and if they leave the

359

UK, there will obviously be a huge gap between the demand for skilled workers and the supply we now see. The figures show that in 2016 2.1 million EU immigrants were working in the UK, so only about 1.2% of the population so why are British people and workers getting so excited and angry about this when it is those same people that wipe their arses at the hospital, or serve them their coffee at the coffee shop, etc. It makes no sense or logic and is very much an emotional and irrational reaction, probably fed by the right-wing press and social media.

Immediately after the referendum result came in, we realise that the Leave campaigners did not have any idea of what would happen in specifics to make Brexit a success. But as it was effectively the government that had to make this dream a reality, many of whom were Remainers, it dawned on them very quickly that they had no idea how to take this forward, and this is where the chaos began. The sudden drop in Sterling proved the markets thought that the result was a bad one for the UK but also that they had no confidence in the government to make a success of this withdrawal, and so it turned out.

One of the biggest issues with the referendum that has become very clear since the result is that those that have helped created the chaos, the likes of Farage, Rees-Mogg et al. do not have to sort out the mess but rather can snipe and serve critique from the side lines. Plus, the person that opened Pandora's box, David Cameron, has taken himself out of the firing line and Teresa May was expected to sort out the mess others have created to help ensure the country does not end up being a lot poorer than was ever necessary. Having said that, she should have known what was in store for her, although she probably envisaged it being a lot easier. Obviously that undertaking now falls to Boris Johnson and his new government.

One clear difference between the EU referendum and a general election, despite at GE the Conservatives do seem to carry more support from the Newspapers (Tony Blair with his more centre Left positioning is may be the exception), was that Leave very much had the Newspapers cornered and had done for years consistently printing anti-EU headlines and articles, which had a huge influence and effect on the outcome of the vote, even if a lot was fabrication.

Finally, we should not forget that all those on the Leave side of the campaign was in a position to deliver on the pledges they made! Another clear problem with calling such a simple IN OUT referendum.

Chapter 25
The March of The Right, The Angry & The

Disaffected

The rise of national populism

As someone coming from what I see as a liberal centrist politics the rise of national populism in the UK and across Europe is concerning. Concerning from a historical point of view knowing where such parties or politics can take their countries, Europe and the world into dark times and we should not underestimate this threat again. But from a more personal perspective it always seems like it want to be isolationist, discriminates and aims to divide people playing off one part of society against another and that is a negative development and a very risky game to play, which can be seen in the UK with Nigel Farage and his inflammatory rhetoric and dislike of say Romanians.

They offer the politics of protest and scapegoats promising to give a voice to those who feel that they have been neglected and ignored holding in contempt the so-called elites, but without offering any detailed solutions as to how their lives would be improved. Excitable rhetoric and excellent speakers such as Nigel Farage are important as there is rarely much substance in their proposals so the accusations of 'Traitors' 'Treachery' 'the elite' etc. must have traction. The irony of such calls and accusations are that they are often made by people like Nigel Farage who is a lifelong politician, a political elite, and a publicly educated former city trader who then tries to say he is a man of the people. But, there is nothing further from the truth. But when people are desperate, and you keep the message simple it can be very powerful to a specific part of society that are looking for something to believe in and feel left behind in the face of globalisation.

The issue of immigration appears at the core of the current national populism as in fact it has many times in the past, including Adolph Hitler and Mussolini to name but two, as it is an easy visible target and we should not underestimate people's concerns and certain people's ability to tap into that concern and mobilise their disenfranchisement with detrimental effect. People, especially older people, are genuinely worried about the speed of change and the increase in immigration as our economy needs further immigration of people and skills as well as the rapid ethnic change which is slightly different if not linked. But we must avoid this leading to heightened Xenophobia and racism stirred up but certain right-wing party leaders and politicians with detrimental effects.

Immigration does bring people out to vote that do not normally vote as shown at the EU referendum where 2 million more people voted than had voted in the 2015 general election, many of whom did not understand the EU as they couldn't as it had not been explained to them or any of us accurately and our image of the EU has been formed through the warped Eurosceptic press which has unfortunately consistently lied and published incorrect stories and misinformation. But even if people are not that political they may be looking for a club to join where they feel at home and powerful as they go out on rallies with like-minded people waving flags and shouting anti-government chants etc. to give them a real buzz and high which can lead to extreme and eventually dangerous views and actions.

Many voters are absolutely correct when they see the UK's political system has become so much less representative of their views and hopes because in fact they have. The proportions of degree holders, those that have never had a job outside Westminster and affluent politicians who sit in the houses of Parliament and the Lords has grown greatly while the proportions of politicians with working-class backgrounds have diminished and do not look to return. But one way of reengaging the working class could be to somehow once again get more people from those backgrounds into Parliament.

Some of those voting for populist parties are undoubtedly racist though many are not, and it has become more difficult to tell one from the other in these times of politically correct language that those who are on the verge of being a racist curb their tongue and are much more careful with their language in public. But, that does not mean those beliefs and sentiments, however illogical and unfounded, still exist and only education, patience and the raising of living standards for those who feel society has left them behind could change that. Only then will they look less to scapegoats and more to the opportunities life and the future hold. The EU is very concerned about the rise of populists in EU countries and petrified that the likes of Le Penn in France or the AfD in Germany get into power, and understandably so as last time that happened millions of lives were lost! Brexit has shown a very polarised and toxic environment in the UK, but could this spread throughout the EU with disastrous effects?

Is Brexit and the burning desire to leave the EU the Brexiteers 'Religion' where they believe so deeply like many believe in their holy books, which are not based on fact but rather stories passed down initially verbally through generations including people walking on water? Belief is powerful even in such holy books like The Book of Mormon being clearly a fake. Many are not looking for or do not want to believe observable reality and facts as they identify too strongly with the Leave movement and will continue to believe with this 'tribe' no matter what is put in front of them. I have never actually heard a Leaver say "Brexit moved in mysterious ways" but I could imagine it as it simply bats away any examination of the facts or their position.

There is almost too much pride in Leavers to admit they may be wrong or are even will consider the alternative arguments now the shortfalls in the arguments they were given are clear. It's almost a fear of admitting mistakes to highlight weaknesses, maybe they already know exist? There is even reluctance to agree on certain points that are clearly true and factual for fear of sacrificing their whole Brexit position / ideal based on those shortcomings. It is almost a paranoia that their idealistic bubble will be burst and all the ills of the world flood out, and the dream is over. That scares the life out of them, and so much so that they would prefer to wallow in ignorance and live a lie to keep the 'Brexit fire' burning.

Don't underestimate the populist right!

It may in some ways be amusing and entertaining to watch or hear people like Nigel Farage on TV remonstrating or standing up in front of the European Parliament unloading his prepared one-line gags and insulting many of our European partner MEPs. But we should not underestimate these type of unprofessional antics as they can stir up people's fear and hate which can mushroom and grow very quickly. We know how in the 1930s Europe how Hitler and Mussolini to name but 2 whipped up extreme nationalism and we all know where that ended for Europe and the rest of the world with millions of lives lost!

It appears now many people do not believe that could ever happen again and so are very complacent almost like after the First World War many people felt we had learned our lesson and it would not happen again, and that is the problem that we fail to learn from history. The fact is that there are a number of extreme political parties and movements in Europe who are making waves with the EU countries and cannot be underestimated. These developments are also in countries such as Netherlands (Geert Wilders), Sweden with the Swedish democrats, and in Germany via the Alternative for Germany (AFD) who achieved 13% of the vote in the last German general election. So, if it can happen in these countries then it can happen anywhere and of that we need to be very vigilant.

Clearly, such developments as social Media, racism, inequality and austerity after the financial crisis have heightened people's frustrations and more extreme views and search for reasons, albeit they often result in scapegoats. But this is a reality and especially Social media and the speed of sharing and distribution of misinformation or pure fabrications is frightening, and that has to be addressed.

What often happens with the far right is they start something and then break away let the lunatics do their worst and then they come back into the fold not as extreme as the previous group and so by comparison makes them look acceptable. This is exactly what has happened with Nigel Farage and his Brexit party who come with a nice slick message while UKIP, his previous project have gone even further right attracting the extremists like former Britain First leader Tommy Robinson and Carl Benjamin the individual who tweeted that he "wouldn't even rape Jess Phillips, the Labour MP. He had refused to apologise for the remark made in 2016, arguing that "any subject can be the subject of a joke." Now I am not sure what comedians he has been watching, but to stand then as a UKIP MEP again is bizarre. What low standards has the UKIP party stooped to that they think this is acceptable and want Mr. Benjamin to represent them? This is from the party that started the whole Brexit avalanche with Mr Farage.

This is a clever and sometimes effective way the right constantly repositions itself to make itself look more reasonable compared to the swivel eyed loons that occupy the even more extreme parties, and the likes of Farage use these extremists like Tommy Robinson as scapegoats to say "oh no those are much too extreme for me / us" etc. So even though they have not moved from their extreme positions they look more acceptable as they are not as extreme as the Looney Tunes in the other party. It is an optical illusion that can work if not exposed and highlighted regularly. It's like Mussolini playing the 'angelic angel' with the ridiculous justification that "we are not as bad as that bloody German bloke with the little moustache who went way over the top!"

Populism can become patriotism can become nationalism can become nationalistic racism which could become a powder keg that we need to keep a close eye on and genuinely understand people's concerns to address them but with facts and reality rather than indulging further the lies and disinformation we saw for example in the referendum campaign.

The hate and vitriol highlighted during and since the EU referendum was directed extremely veraciously towards MPs and particularly female MPs which is horrifying to what lengths people are willing to go to intimidate and frighten people of a different view to theirs. On Twitter we have seen comments from faceless keyboard warriors, probably sitting around in their union Jack Y fronts, such as "Hang traitor MPs", "MPs could do with a course of HIV" etc. Jess Phillips who has suffered horrendous cowardly abuse commented 'I like a challenge.... I didn't expect people to wish I was dead.' The right-wing extremists have traditionally and throughout history thrived on fear and intimidation and the pack mentality and there is no doubt that Brexit opened Pandora's box of hate and it does not seem to be going back in that very same box any time soon. The serious nature of these threats and the reality of the possibility was made clear when the plan by a right-wing individual with links to a banned neo-Nazi group to murder Labour MP Rosie Cooper was discovered and stopped before it could happen. Since 2016 the disgusting behaviour towards MPs has risen and in some quarters is seen as acceptable, and that cannot be right for any functioning democracy. Many MPs, particularly women, have decided not to stand in the 2019 election due to the rise to epidemic proportions of hate and death / rape threats from extremists that have crawled out of the woodwork during and since the 2016 EU referendum vote. We have to ask ourselves was all this really worth it?

Is the Right wing really that dangerous?

Although we have seen a number of small right wing Racist (even though they claim they are patriots not racists) groups protesting at various times they tend to be small, not well funded 'organisations' like the National Front, the English Defence League (EDL) etc. that resemble more of hooligan 'football factories' looking for a fight on Saturday afternoon rather than political movements I am told also by some it is OK as we do not protest like the French etc. as we are not a rebellious society. Now there is historical evidence to prove that with only sporadic violent protests such as the 2011 London riots or Brixton riots in 1981 but they were more about social issues rather than immigration specific (although this is a fine line and one that may overlap) which is where these right-wing groups target their focus.

But we should be very vigilant, and not be laissez-faire about the future risks of such groups as history shows us that such movements can gather speed and mushroom very quickly if the circumstances allow it and the snowball effect can come into play. The German poverty helped lead to the rise of Hitler in the 1930s Germany or in Italy the bizarre (with hindsight) rise of Mussolini's Italy as he could make the Italian trains run on time were examples where at the beginning these people and movements were underestimated!

But on the other hand we should not overemphasise the impact of such small right-wing groups, as some Brexiteers are implying, our parliament should be careful what political decisions, laws or a Brexit deal we strike as the right may decide to riot and burn down cities etc BUT also not underestimate the threat of such a movement if it got organised and well-funded which would give it many more options to influence politics and our society.

We saw in 2019 with the imprisonment of Robert Vidler aged 64 from London for making death threats to MPs he saw as "anti-Brexit", including Nicky Morgan. He was found guilty of five charges of harassment without violence and three counts of sending menacing messages. So we see that it wasn't just short term spat of hate crimes just after the referendum result and then they faded out but these potential nationalists are still there and dangerous trying to influence our democracy through menace which we should be very conscious of and not underestimate as it can come from the most unexpected corners. In Mr. Vidler's case the Deputy chief magistrate Tan Ikram said Vidler had "attempted to stifle [the MPs] legitimate political views" and undermined "the free democratic society in which we live".

History shows us to beware the seemingly harmless eccentric individuals with a small niche following who are very good orators and no matter how frustrating they are with their lies and misinformation appear somewhat amusing they get headlines. There is an excellent book called The Sleepwalkers which is Christopher Clark's account of the prelude to World War 1 and how people / countries can walk unknowingly into a perilous future all of which can grow from insignificant individuals or events that can mushroom out of control. So, when people talk about extreme parties and individuals like Farage and the Brexit party getting anywhere near the levers of power, be very careful what you wish for the law of unexpected consequences! But that is just the start and we can see with Farage and the few thousand blind sheep that hang on his every word as if he was some evangelical Bible basher threatening fire and brimstone.

Is the Brexit Party UKIP repackaged?

The recent emergence of the Brexit party is in itself amazing and we should give Nigel Farage, his rich political backers and team congratulations for that as they achieved what they set out to do, at least in the short term which was to send MEPs to the European Parliament of which they have at the time of writing 29.

We only have to go back to the Multi-Millionaire and anti-EU campaigner James Goldsmith who started the single-issue Referendum Party and got 800,000 votes at the 1997 general election causing close to civil War in the Conservative Party. So, we see a parallel here with very rich people influencing politics sometimes with single issues they have burning inside them. We know UKIP, Leave.EU and Nigel Farage were also heavily financed by Multi-Millionaire Arron Banks and others, and the financing of the Brexit party at the time of writing is to be confirmed as it is not yet clear or the source of all the funds, but Mr. Farage has some very rich friends.

It seems an almost bizarre concept that we vote democratically to send people to an institution they do not believe in and are trying to bring down. It seems almost like training Arsonists to be firemen and once they are in the building, the opposite of what is intended takes place. We only have to look at the fact that most of Nigel Farage's speeches are anti-EU deriding the EU gravy train despite taking that same gravy in the form of a nice salary, pension and expenses, although even then the EU had to take back £35,000 of misappropriation of funds, which is concerning, as well as abusing our fellow partners at every opportunity. Would any business owner, sports club owner, or head teacher leave a person in place that was taking a salary, pension and full expenses facility whilst seeing nothing good in the organisation and constantly slagging off the company, club or school and its leaders. Plus doing little constructive work as shown by Mr. Farage only attending 1 out of 42 meetings when on the common fisheries committee.

On any level this is bizarre bordering on a dereliction of duty and taking money under false pretences. But it is intriguing how it can happen. What do voters think they will achieve by sending Brexit party (and UKIP before them) MEPs to Brussels, and what can be achieved by it apart from bolstering the bank accounts of professional politicians like Mr. Farage, Anne Widdicombe, and now millionaire Richard Tice and Annunziata Rees-Mogg (no elites here then!). Is it just a protest vote and once the cross in the box has been placed they pay no attention to what these politicians do, anyway?

Obviously, the Brexit party did not just appear from nothing it is a reincarnation of Nigel Farage and the UKIP party with many former UKIP donors and members which is why, combined with the referendum Leave vote, they could hit the ground running and could use this data they had already accumulated over the years.

His backers included Catherine Blaiklock, former UKIP party Economics spokesperson and then Brexit party Leader but she was forced to resign as leader in March 2019 when it was disclosed she had made anti-Islamic and racist statements online, which she tried to hide by deleting. But also, UKIP MEPs including West Midlands MEP Jill Seymour and Yorkshire and North Lincolnshire MEP Jane Collins as well as Margot Parker announced they were quitting the party to join Nigel Farage's new Brexit Party so this illusion that it is completely new is a fallacy. This was also highlighted in the 2019 EU Elections when UKIP who had 24 seats won none, but the Brexit party got 29 seats which after Leave winning the Brexit vote is hardly surprising and not exactly a huge leap forward for this right-wing anti-EU party as it simply replaces UKIP on the back of the EU Referendum result.

But it still poses the question, what will they do when they get there? Just make a nuisance of themselves as they do not want to add to the policy debates that is clear. You only have to look at Nigel Farage's poor attendance record including that of not helping support our fishermen on the fisheries committee but still collected his salary thank you very much.

One could have this vision of them propping up the bars, Farage with pint in hand, almost reminiscent of the alcohol laden British tourists on an 18-30 holiday getting totally pissed falling over and being sick in Magaluf whilst the foreigners look on in horror thinking what are these people doing here? The difference is most of them would have been youngsters on their very first lads holiday without Mum & Dad and not so-called serious politicians. Again, one can only emphasise how bizarre this is to any sensible person and is not a good look for the UK or democracy as a whole.

We had the return of the enigmatic Anne Widdecombe wittering on about the ghastly EU and saying the Brexit party should be involved with the Brexit negotiations after their result in the EU elections despite not one seat in Westminster, and then almost immediately says she would not negotiate with them anyway as we have earned our right now not to negotiate and just leave. Yes, I know the irony had not been missed by many. But the vision of her being interviewed after the Brexit party's success still clearly with her extreme views of gay conversion therapy and abortion clear for all to see is frightening. But she would make a good widow Twanky.

I found the following tweet quite amusing from @barnabyEdwards when he wrote:
"Ann Widdecombe has just been elected as a Brexit Party MEP. She's anti-abortion, anti-feminist, anti-LGBT, anti-equality, a racist and someone who advocates female prisoners giving birth in shackles. So, she's pretty much the perfect embodiment of Brexit."

But all jokes aside these are the people that are representing the UK on the international stage which some may find amusing and at school with the kid at the class not wanting to do any work throwing things at the teacher was funny, but I was 13 (OK I still thought it was funny at 16!). But this is fully grown adults that are meant to be intelligent and experts in their field, which just shows in some areas of our society, and conceivably it was always so, the world has gone mad, but we need to make sure that the lunatics DO NOT take over the asylum.

One fears they will be around for a while as they have an ardent as well as extreme following currently with a purpose but after Brexit who knows, they are very well financed with a number of millionaires including Richard Tice involved and one would think that Mr. Arron Banks would not be too far away from this 'project' when he had effectively helped start it off with UKIP. They have a lot of data that they can now use that was collected as Leave.EU which was about a million followers including UKIP members and activists as well as many Conservative members and may be more than that with 4 million UKIP voters at the last general election.

A demonstration that the Brexit party differs from UKIP and more of a power project for Farage is the case that he cannot only be removed by a no-conference vote by board, which HE can appoint! Yes, this is the same guy that screams democracy at every opportunity. We wouldn't be so bold as to say it is hypocritical but rather it is Nigel's toy and he can play with it as he sees fit. It's clear why he would want such set-up as it avoids the hassles he previously had with UKIP when he was more accountable with a national executive committee elected by the membership. As of June 2019, the Brexit party had a lot of registered supporters that had signed up for £25 each but at the time of writing had no formal right to vote on the party's matters, which is very unusual for a political party in our democracy. So much for Nigel the Democrat! The party was originally founded and led by Catherine Blaiklock, but she resigned over having retweeted posts from far-Right groups... repeatedly. Was this an exception to the rule or just a party that will attract such people and attitudes like UKIP did before it? There is concern over how the party is funded with specific criticism given to many donations that came through PayPal of under £500 (a lot at £499?) which are very difficult to trace and do not have to be declared. Sajjad Karim, a conservative MEP asked Nigel Farage to explain these to the European Parliament, but as yet no surprise that has not happened.

The party had only been formed and already Nigel was under pressure to sack one of his EU election candidates John Booker who had shared a screen shot of a chain email suggesting the United States was "cutting its own throat" because it was "not fighting back" against increasing Islamist influence in this country. He also liked other unsavoury Facebook posts. But this indicates the challenge Nigel and his team (even if you do not think they are racist) have as his rhetoric and stance on particular subjects especially immigration attracts such unsavoury individuals, and some blatant racists like UKIP did before the Brexit party. It probably always will as where else do these people go to feel some kind of satisfaction and recognition on a national stage? The BNP and other right-wing crank groups won't do it like a high-profile group funded by multi-millionaires? Nigel claimed he quit UKIP complaining that it had become "obsessed with Islam

371

and Tommy Robinson" – well is Mr. Booker not obsessed with Islam? Perhaps Mr. Robinson stole his thunder and attracted more press and headlines than Nigel and he did not appreciate that.

The Brexit party was and still is at the time of writing a one man show and campaign which has a sophisticated and well-funded digital / social media strategy but as highlighted no members and a very limited manifesto plus none of its candidates were democratically selected. It still offers only one main policy which is a "no-deal Brexit". It relies on empty populist slogans that Mr. Farage, a talented orator, delivers effectively to their core following, but is questionable how effective it is outside their strong anti-EU core. UKIP it is not but a more dangerous reincarnation, perhaps, as it learns from its previous mistakes?

It brought a wry smile to my face as Brexit party merchandise on their website is manufactured in many countries including China and Bangladesh where textile workers get paid 39p per hour! So much for Britain First and supporting the UK workers. As usual it's just disingenuous nonsense.

Does the Brexit party have a long-term future?

Some may look at it as a fad as it has one main policy currently which is BREXIT and so when we leave the EU they should defunct right? Well may be not as a number of their backers (and UKIP before them) do like the notoriety, microphones, cameras, audiences and the feeling of power and are not going to let that go so easily otherwise they sink back into anonymity or flogging insurance door to door! How many had heard of Richard Tice before his Brexit party prominence? Even for rich men with a lot of money it is not enough, and they need that narcissistic boost of non-monetary feelings even if it is a devoted right-wing extremist audience brandishing posters with the protagonists names on them.

We cannot say that all the Brexit party supporters are racists and xenophobes but due to the rhetoric used by the party individuals you can see why those type of individuals would be attracted to such an organisation. We can also see that if people are given the message to people that have suffered under globalisation and have been told that minorities have been given a greater helping hand than them, then the message is for some very seductive. But it is everybody's duty to dispel such myths as they are based on no evidence or fact, rather based on certain urban myths built up over time, not challenged and in some people's minds then becomes 'reality'.

Brexit has a number of advantages that UKIP never had including the fact they have (they hope) learned from the mistakes UKIP made, the momentum of the EU referendum campaign and result plus the new supporters that came out of that exercise, the higher profile, the claim they have left all the 'nutters' behind in their former party, and significant funding that can for example potentially keep Nigel Farage in a house in Chelsea and fly him around in a private jet! Man of the people?

So, we should not make the mistake of comparing them directly to UKIP as they will be much more savvy with their extreme language to not overstep the mark of acceptability in today's society, but some may warn 'beware the wolf in sheep's clothing'.

The Brexit party achieved 32.6% at the recent 2019 EU elections whereas UKIP only achieved 27.5% in 2014 and that having not been around for more than a few months, although one could argue as above it is UKIP repackaged. This performance has also led to a lead in the national opinion poll which UKIP never achieved, although it could be argued that this is due to the chaos in the 2 main parties but even so that is the reality and why they should not be underestimated. The next 6-12 months in the UK's future is unclear and if a general election was to be called and Brexit has not happened, then the Brexit party could make a significant march forward. That is doubtful that will happen as that would sound a death nell for the Conservative party and Prime Minister Boris Johnson. The fact they have performed well in the EU elections could inspire traditional non-voters to vote at the next general election and give them more strength, although they did not win the Peterborough By-Election in June 20e9 and that is ultimately the acid test that they must win constituency by-elections, something Nigel has failed to achieve on 7 occasions.

The Brexit party could have an advantage in that its vote is spread more widely than say remain voters who are more concentrated in metropolitan cities like London. This means the fact that Leave was ahead in 410 of the 650 constituencies could play to their advantages, although we should be clear that despite Brexit being an extremely important political topic people vote for a range of different reasons at a general election plus they will often not change from their traditional party and that the Brexit party will have to contend with.

The big change came when Nigel decided (yes only Nigel, as there is no member democracy as in the other main parties) not to stand against the Conservative held seats and stood down hundreds of candidates, some of whom has paid the party £100 to stand as well as thousands of pounds on campaigning material and were every angry. The rumour circling was that Nigel had allegedly done a deal with the Tories and he would get a peerage, and so as usual just thought of Nigel. Whether this is true only time will tell. But the election dynamic had changed especially for parties such as the Liberal Democrats.

We should though bear in mind that they are still a new party and will have those growing pains of keeping the message consistent as up to now it has been the Nigel Farage show but that will have to change and this means internal organisation, control and discipline to avoid the in-fighting or very extreme influences that dogged the UKIP party. Will the in-fighting begin as they grow from the 'baby' stage? How will Nigel react to others stealing some (i.e. HIS) limelight?

The question will be whether there is a ceiling to their following for such a right-wing party with no reasonable policies and that their popularity fades away as Brexit is done and as a protest party they are not perceived to be fit for government or even a coalition government. After all who would or could work with this type of egotistical individual and his inflammatory views as well as the influence from his rich donors pulling a lot of the strings behind the scenes? There was always talk of the 'Purple ceiling' for UKIP and the Brexit party must find a way to break through that but even if they do, they must win constituency elections where the issues will include transport, health, NHS, the economy, investment in social services, and Tax policy, etc. Will the Brexit party be able to rise to the occasion when they currently have looked like one man's vanity project who has shown on numerous occasions the lack of intellectual rigour to debate complex subjects without basic empty slogans to appeal to the populist vote?

If it is to go with a more Thatcherite look how will they keep those Labour supporters of the Northern Labour heartlands and therein lies their conflict that cannot be addressed with simple slogans like 'Out mean Out' or 'Brexit means Brexit'. It literally announced a 'plan' to save British Steel turning the private company into what they call a 'National Strategic Corporation' supported by what they called 'patient state capital'. Now one does not want to go into great details about this here, mainly as this policy lacked real detail, but it is very interventionist with the state bailing out a failing company owned by a private equity group. So, it seems akin to Jeremy Corbyn's very left-wing interventionist policies, so where do they stand? You can see the contradiction and their dilemma in the real world, but also would voters really want their hard-earned tax used to bail out failing private companies and how much would be needed and for how long? It was again a populist slogan justified as saving British jobs without a modicum of a plan (recognise that somewhere?) but does Farage look like the saviour of the socialist left? Of course not, but it got him a few headlines for a day or so, and we know he is a media whore.

It may rise like a phoenix out of the UKIP flames, but it may also after a few years remain a protest party blaming everyone for everything and sink into obscurity, but with Mr. Farage and co. the ride is sure to be interesting.

It is clear the Brexit party like UKIP is an English focused party with St. George flags often prevalent at rallies etc. with it being much more popular in England than other parts of the UK such as Scotland where UKIP only received only 1.6% of the 2015 general election. Identity politics and the rise of 'English identity' in England was clearly on the rise and has played a role in the Brexit party's popularity and UKIP before it.

How will 'taking back control' as we have heard them so often say make a positive difference to the poor and less well off or those that have not seen their wages rise during the years of austerity etc. what is Nigel and co. tangibly going to offer them and their families, especially if we see after a no-deal Brexit inflation rises, job losses occur, and less investment into the UK, etc?

Nigel Farage's party thrives, as he does, on protest as UKIP did before telling anyone that will listen how they have been betrayed by the establishment, the government, the elites, the Remoaners, the EU, the Civil service as well as many others but can that continue infinitum as he needs people to blame and will have to keep creating new Bogeymen to stay credible. He is himself a professional elite politician but has done well to paint himself to his supporters as something completely different but at some stage people will realise the emperor has no clothes. That may take some time as he is very well funded by his multi-millionaire friends but where does he go next if we leave the EU as his ego will not allow him to slide off into obscurity as he adores the cameras, microphone and limelight, and a slot on LBC show will not satisfy that ego for long.

Even when in the European Parliament the Brexit party MEPs are like a bunch of irreverent school children (although still taking their salaries, pensions, and expenses of course!) adding no value but using speeches for incoherent rants from the likes of Anne Widdecombe which are embarrassing to any British citizen that we should be tainted with the same brush. Farage hardly turns up for work, or the Brexit Party MEPs very rudely and disrespectfully turn their back on the invited orchestra that played Beethoven's ode to thee at the opening of the parliament. This was probably those young people's proudest moment and to be subjected to that is utterly unacceptable from anyone let alone professional politicians and the Brexit party's treatment of that young orchestra tells us more about them than they could ever say and how can we take such people seriously?

David Bull the Brexit party MEP for Ipswich gives an example of the calibre of people you will see representing the Brexit party when having been elected as an MEP he complained in a video as to how far his place of work was! It was Strasbourg where the MEPs sit by the way.
He said "Good morning. It is Monday morning, and this is the beginning of my trip to Strasbourg. So, it's eight hours and as you can see here, it's the first of the many trains. 'So, this is Ipswich to London Liverpool Street, then after that I have to go from London Liverpool Street to Kings Cross. From Kings Cross I then have to go to Paris. From Paris I then have to change stations. I then have to go from Paris to Strasbourg and I will arrive at something like twenty to seven tonight. 'I left home at eight o'clock this morning, having got in at midnight and I'm going to have to do this repeatedly. For some reason the parliament seems to be in a very inaccessible place" (Author "what the middle of Europe and not Ipswich?!").

I am sure you will ask yourself the same thing 'didn't he check the journey time before accepting the job or even realise where his place of work would actually be?
James Melville tweeted: 'I suppose the lesson that David needs to learn is not to apply for a job if he is then going to complain about the location of the job despite knowing that he would be based here when he applied for the job.'

Another asked: 'Are you actually saying it's insane you have to travel to the office to do your job?

In an interview with the BBC, he was asked 'Did you not look up how you might get to the European Parliament in advance before whining on Twitter?' to which Bull responded: 'Weirdly it didn't really cross my mind.' BBC presenter Emma Barnett then asked: 'So you take a job without knowing how to get there or what you'll be paid?' Bull added: 'To be honest, yes, because the principle was far more important than what I was being paid.'

Theoretically, this individual who does not appear the sharpest knife in the drawer could be voting on very important strategic issues, although on reflection you wouldn't put it past this man getting lost quite regularly getting their late not taking part in debates but still remembering to fill in his expenses claim. Farcical.

To read more please go to and watch the video even if it is for the comedic value of Mr. bull:
https://metro.co.uk/2019/07/02/brexit-party-mep-complains-journey-strasbourg-first-day-10102774/

Chapter 26
The Politics of Personality

Despite there being many anti-EU 'personalities' that played roles both positive and negative in the run up to the EU Referendum and the 3 years since including Iain Duncan Smith, Michael Gove, Bill Cash, Jacob Rees-Mogg, Norman Tebbit and others that due to time and not the focus of this book could not be included in this section but felt some special cases should be made for certain high profile and influential individuals, as they did play major roles, and 3 years on are either in the government or like Farage still pressuring the Conservative government and influencing policy as they try to counter the Brexit Party attacks as well as trying not to lose their Remain voters to the reinvigorated Liberal Democrats.

Personalities and influence

- Nigel Farage
- Boris Johnson
- Arron Banks
- Dominic Cummings
- John Redwood

Nigel Farage

For someone that is not an MP in the houses of Parliament, has failed in 7 previous UK Westminster elections, hates the EU and tells anyone that will listen to leave BUT still takes his salary, expenses and pension as an MEP (not sure what the dictionary definition of hypocrite is, but perhaps this could be used as an example) he gets a lot of air time and has sway with largely the older right wing former UKIP voters and the Press. It does obviously help that you have a Multi-Millionaire friend and former donor to UKIP with International connections in Arron Banks, but still sell yourself as a man of the people. In the press's defence he is always good for a one liner or controversial statement that will help sell papers and get Internet hits, although rarely is he pushed on an intellectual level. If he was, it would reveal lack of depth and detail with any strategy or plan having more holes in it than a Swiss cheese, but that's OK with him as they are not a fully-fledged member of the EU!

He has been very successful as portraying himself as this cheeky chappy down the pub man of the people but there may be a more calculated side to Farage who is only interested in getting what he wants at any cost. We remember him shortly after the referendum result when he claimed Churchillian like (well not quite) that the result was for 'ordinary, decent people' which obviously inferred presumably that the 48% were not 'ordinary, decent people' (who just happened to disagree with him). He even claimed that Brexit had been achieved 'without a shot being fired' which when considering what happened to Jo Cox can only be described as disgusting and crass. But that is what happens when Nigel Farage gets wrapped up in Nigel Farage. Despite what happened to Jo Cox he did not let the Cox family off the hook so easily claiming in the December of that year that Brendan, Jo's widower, associated with extremists, without any basis whatsoever.

Such bizarre attacks on distinguished people as President Obama saying 'That Obama creature - a loathsome individual who couldn't stand our country' as well as attacks on his fellow MEP colleagues are plainly embarrassing as a British subject but seem par for the course now. Whilst on the other extreme he will suck up to Donald Trump for dear life like a new-born baby on its mother's nipple as he sees that as getting more exposure airtime and perhaps influence. The American after dinner speaking circuit is also very lucrative.

This looks like a man that would say anything for a few headlines, a couple more minutes in front of the microphone to get some warped message across to the wider world.

It is surprising that people do not look at Nigel Farage with the issue of trust foremost in their minds, but many seem to be captivated almost mesmerised by his effective rhetoric. Having analysed his history one would have thought that people would be horrified by his lies, exaggeration and lack of perceived integrity or trust as we see the following bullet points of Nigel Farage's history:

- Telling UKIP supporters that our beloved state funded NHS should move towards and insurance-based system run by private companies (which only benefits the rich, as we see in the USA). So, a vote for UKIP (and perhaps now the Brexit Party) is a vote for privatisation of the NHS.

- He suggested benefit claimants should be made to clear up litter after six months.

- He also commented there was a big problem with employee rights and protections such as maternity leave for small firms.

- He lied about Turkey joining the EU as soon as 2020.

- He popularised the £350 million a week (he used the figure £50 million a day), but then distanced himself from this number AFTER the referendum result, but not during the referendum campaign itself (make of that what you will!).

- He said on LBC Radio that if Brexit was a disaster, he would go and live abroad (an option the poorer in our society would not have).

- He was docked £35,000 from his MEP salary for misspending taxpayer funded EU money!

- He only turned up to 1 of 42 meetings of the European Parliament Fisheries Committee (Greenpeace research) missing a number of key votes, one of which was for giving higher quotas to smaller, sustainable fishing fleets in coastal communities such as in the UK.

- He claimed the free movement 'has meant the free movement of Kalashnikov rifles with no evidence at all and obviously aimed to scare people and blame EU immigration.

This shows his real lack of willingness to speak for the groups he claims to stand for, rather than looking for cameras and microphones to satisfy his ego.

We know he loves the publicity and limelight but he has done some strange things to get such publicity which included going on George Galloway's Sputnik programme on Russia today, the television channel funded by the Putin regime, which would not normally be in line with Farage's politics, although we start to go back into the realms of 'did Russia affect the EU Referendum vote with their influence and money spent on Social Media?

This is the man people vote for, although the UK electorate have rejected him 7 times in his desire to be an MP at Westminster, where he was under much more pressure to genuinely exhibit some policies.

Farage like most populist groups today and throughout history offer excuses or people to blame but no plans or solutions. They by default need people to blame e.g. foreigners, immigrants, politicians etc. to increase the temperature of the political discourse creating an inflammatory air of anger that they can fan those flames to create genuine discontent no matter on what basis it is created.

One must be honest and say that Nigel has pulled British politics to the hard-nationalist right which was obvious during the EU referendum and he is the most successful demagogue in recent memory, and despite all his shortcomings people flock to his speeches which from a psychological point of view is fascinating. Let's just summarise in a bit more detail than the above bullet points.

He says that Turkey would join the EU as soon as 2020 this is a fabrication as they are nowhere near (and have wanted to join for over 20 years), saying its 75 million citizens would have unfettered access to live, work and claim benefits in the UK, the racist dog-whistle politics of his notorious racist "Breaking Point" poster, and he denies Brexit would cause any problems for the Irish border. He never disowned the lie that the EU costs us £350 million a week (and in fact used the figure of £50 million a day to make popular this lie) although straight after the result he stated he would not have used it but said nothing at the time. Less than a fortnight after the referendum vote, Farage resigned as UKIP leader (AGAIN!) leaving others with the impossible task of fulfilling his promise to stop following EU laws and end free movement of EU citizens, while not tanking the economy. By spring 2017 Farage was even telling callers to his LBC radio show that if Brexit was a disaster he'd "go and live abroad", and he has made a career out of criticising the Brussels "gravy train" – but is not afraid of abusing it and in 2018 was docked over £35,000 from his MEP salary for misspending taxpayer-funded EU money. Farage has also proven unwilling to speak up for the very groups he claims to stand for such as local fishing communities, which he claims to champion as during three years on the European Parliament's Fisheries Committee. Farage attended only one of 42 meetings including missing several key votes, including one on giving higher quotas to smaller, sustainable fishing fleets in coastal communities (what was he doing that was more important instead?!). He's on record in 2012 suggesting the NHS should be privatised (yes privatised!) along the lines of an "insurance-based system" which would mean those that can't pay would suffer. He also described increases to maternity pay as "foolish" in 2010! [28]

The interesting thing about Nigel during the EU referendum campaign is that Vote Leave preferred to keep Nigel out of the spotlight, especially for their activities, wherever they could as it seemed when his profile and that of UKIP rose the support for leaving the EU shrank. The reason for this was clear, and some referred to as the 'Farage paradox' in that Nigel is obviously a magnet for the hardcore Brexiteers, confirmed Eurosceptics et al. but with those undecideds or less extreme individuals he turned them off for various reasons. Douglas Carswell described it as his "angry Nativism". This could also be seen the way Mr. Farage attacks the likes of the BBC as they highlight some of his shortcomings or the hypocrisy of his position on some issues by calling them "the enemy" or "blatant bias" which does not reflect well on the UK politics with such attacks on an independent media service. But at the same time, it is not surprising as Mr. Farage has a list as long of his arm of people and organisations he chooses to blame for the UK not having left the EU yet and takes a leaf out of Donald Trump's book by denigrating anyone he deems hostile to him or his position.

When the leader of UKIP he even suggested that immigrants with AIDS should not be treated by the NHS, which means basically leaving them to suffer. At the time of writing we are still looking for Nigel's heart! What kind of society would we be or what kind of politician would suggest such uncaring things if it wasn't but to get votes and support from every right-wing crank group in Europe or even across the pond!

What a record and this man-of-the-people charade very well cultivated in recent years, means nobody knows what Nigel Farage believes as it is all about him and he has got so far having no policies or conviction. He has almost reached the stage where he knows he does not need them as a few empty slogans repeated will work on a certain part of society that will not question his real incentives or ability to deliver and will still wave flags and cheer "Nigel, Nigel". Remember at one stage when Nigel was keen on a public vote on the terms of our departure from the EU? But he's weaselled out of that too, saying victory for his Brexit Party should reduce the chance of a confirmatory Vote. What changed his mind? Is he worried that the public have seen through his fabrications to the almighty mess at Brexit's heart? One thing you can trust him to do is to try to pull the wool over voters' eyes in the campaign ahead, the sad thing is he is very good at it and resembles the con men on London's Oxford Street running the 'find the lady three-card trick' to take money from unsuspecting tourists and naïve people, who only knew what had happened once it was too late.

Upon Leave winning the Referendum Nigel with Arron Banks went for Breakfast at the Ritz with Telegraph owner Frederick Barclay, Banks claiming 'he is a big UKIP supporter', but is this Nigel Farage a man that claims he is not a part of the 'political elite' and portrays himself as a man of the people? But does this look like a man of the people eating breakfast at the Ritz with Multi-Millionaires? Do you think he ordered beans on toast?

He then announces he is standing down as UKIP leader implying his job is done but in reality he no longer wants to be held accountable for the complexities that now faced the government from a simple IN OUT question and could sit on the side-lines grinning at the chaos he had help instigate. At the time he said he wanted 'to get his life back' but then 2 years later he is back involved. Did he really want his life back of is he just one of the political elite, a political Junky if you like, that just cannot keep away from the cameras and microphones i.e. the narcissist inside him is the stronger side of his personality. His attitude and that of Johnson also not having a plan or a clue about the way forward caused anger in many parts of the country. Irvine Welsh the author of the book that was made into a film Trainspotting and a social commentator tweeted 'Johnson and Farage – a couple of Jakeys [Scottish slang for hard core alcoholic] who wake up from a binge having shat the bed, then sneak out the doss house by the back door' – not a pleasant image!

In July 2019 he then hires a 'journalist' that focused on Breitbart's anti-immigrant Europe coverage including interviews with Tommy Robinson or attacks on Angela Merkel and Sadiq Khan often simply taking The Mail online articles and exaggerating them for inflammatory effect with the concentration on Muslims, crime and immigration. So, with the appointment of such pleasant individuals we can see Mr. Farage's priority and focus, so clearly the Leopard does not change his spots and would not like to live next door to Romanians!

Just an example of how we know Mr. Farage will say one thing and do another and lacks any conviction apart from himself was after he claimed he would boycott and never ever go on the BBC again having been grilled on the Andrew Marr show claiming he was "treated like a war criminal" (when to be fair to Marr he was just trying to get some clear answers out of the man) which resulted in a heated debate. But no quicker than he was offered to be in front of another BBC camera and / or microphone he was, surprise surprise, back again! Within a few days he was on BBC Breakfast and later that day the BBCs Radio 4's Today programme, then a few days later it was South East Today, and a week later on BBC Radio 4s Any Questions! Where were his mighty principles? I think we know the answer to that and really Mr. Farage is interested in Mr. Farage and given any opportunity to spout his propaganda in front of a camera or microphone to promote himself he will be there of that you can be sure.

Boris Johnson, the Brexiteer and Leave campaigner

Everybody seems to agree Boris is an enigma as (apparently) an intelligent man that does and says dumb things but who is Boris Johnson? A charlatan? Liar? or just someone with a desperate cynical ambition to be PM? Well as we know as of 24th July 2019 he amazingly achieved the latter by becoming Prime Minister.

His actions and 'dithering' whilst deciding which side to come out during the EU referendum was telling as it made Boris look like the opportunist, deciding to back the Leave side as it better placed him, in his opinion and that of his advisers, to become PM, which seems to have proved true. Plus, it must be said his type of hyper hyperbole would be much more suited to shouting 'Sovereignty', 'Freedom', and other such empty slogans as opposed to stating the IMF says we are better remaining in, etc. Also, he had written so many disparaging headlines about the EU over the years (including the infamous bendy bananas he concocted) it would be difficult for him to go down that route without all these stories being thrown back at him. Perhaps also the chance of battling with David Cameron, who had made PM before him, may have added a little spice to the game? Although now he must negotiate with the EU as PM which should be eventful.

We know he wrote those two contradictory articles regarding his position on the EU, which in itself was bizarre as it showed mixed feelings that he could write a positive article about remaining, but then suddenly once he took a position

385

he was extremely vociferous in that position and very negative in his oratory about the EU and the other side. If this does not look like opportunism and self-interest, what does? Boris had written probably hundreds of thousands of words and made hundreds of speeches over the years and although he had written scare stories about Brussels to earn money basically, I could find nowhere where he had advocated withdrawal from the EU.

It was always questioned whether he really was a 'Leaver' rather than a 'Remainer' and only chose Leave as he saw it as a much better political move for him to become Prime minister and by competing against David Cameron. This opinion was enhanced when the Times Newspaper announced that he had actually written those two articles, not just the one justifying Leave but also a 'Remain' article which is very strange for someone that claimed he was now very much an avid Leaver. He tried in vain to explain it away, but these doubts have remained ever since that he really is not a conviction politician but rather a chancer and opportunist interested in Boris Johnson and nobody else.

Even his friend David Cameron in March 2016 during the referendum campaign accused Boris of 'simply making it up' for suggesting the UK could have a Canada-style trade deal with the EU, not really understanding the difference in the economies or the importance of services to our economy which the EU trade deal with Canada does not include, as well as the importance of the Irish border which may come back to haunt him. These accusations of 'making it up' seem like a regular occurrence with Mr. Johnson whether it be from his wives, colleagues or journalists.

But sometimes his remarks lack those of a statesman (who would become Foreign secretary and now PM) and were epitomised by his comments in May 2016 saying, 'the EU is pursuing the same super state as Hitler, using different methods'. Although it must be said that it was actually Michael Gove that brought the infamous Nazi leader's name into the conversation about the EU before Boris when accusing the EU of fuelling the rise of 'Hitler worshippers' in Europe.

But despite his shortcomings and obvious economy with the truth both to his family and the electorate he   is popular and amusing and more intelligent than he may sometimes portray. It's feasible the fact that he sleeps around, makes mistakes and has a bit if a common touch (well as far as an Etonian can) makes him one of the boys and can reach out to some voters traditional Conservative leaders such as Teresa May never could?

What is never quite clear with Boris is how intelligent and informed he really is, as many of his supporters would have us believe as on numerous occasions he has seemed wanting on saying the right thing, attention to detail, poor grasp of the facts, or expressing himself coherently and has an ability to just bat difficult questions away without ever answering them. In fact, he is a master of this now. We could see this in his speech in Dartford, Kent on 11th March 2016 where he said '.... can strike a deal, as the Canadians have done, based on trade and getting rid of Tariffs', without apparently appreciating that deal took 5 years from 2009 to 2014 and did not come into effect 2 years after that – so almost 7 years later! Also, the Canadian deal does not include Services which is 80% of our economy so in practice not a practical solution. But 4 days later Boris was putting forward 'associate membership' of the EU like Turkey which is as a matter of fact in a customs union with the EU which Boris also claimed we needed to be clear of. So, this unstructured fuzzy thinking was very light on detail should have sounded alarm bells but as we have seen some people are so desperate for Brexit none of that seemed to matter.

Boris Johnson is indeed the British Prime Minister (yes I know from hapless Foreign secretary to saboteur on the sidelines to PM!). As I write this, I have to check that statement again as I find it so hard to believe on many levels but even his ex-Boss at the Daily Telegraph, Simon Heffer, said on CNN he (Mr. Johnson) would be the man most deficient in probity ever to hold the post! Mr. Heffer is not on his own as Mr Johnson's former Editor Max Hastings wrote in The Guardian that Johnson cared about nothing other than his own "fame and gratification" and shows he is absolutely unfit for the premiership. But sometimes one can be a lucky PM when "events dear boy events" work in your favour.

This is a guy who has been sacked twice for lying both as a journalist and in November 2004 by leader of the Conservative party Michael Howard when tabloids revealed that since 2000 Johnson had been having an affair with Spectator columnist Petronella Wyatt, resulting in two terminated pregnancies. Johnson initially called the claims "piffle". But after the allegations were proven, Howard asked Johnson to resign as vice-chairman and shadow arts minister for publicly lying, but when Johnson refused Howard had to sack him. But this does show the hutzpah (or in London we would say 'front') of the man that even when banged to rights guilty he shows no shame or remorse and decides to try to brush it off! Is this a sign of things to come in the top job?

Johnson, it's claimed by his supporters is a "one nation Conservative", but his first announcement of a proposed policy should he become Prime Minister was reducing tax for those earning more than £50,000 (that obviously includes him and his mates), which is not a one nation Tory and indicates a lack of understanding of what those lower-paid workers have to go through trying to make ends meet. But this is a guy that is known for the following also:

- Called black people piccaninnies with "watermelon smiles".

- Referred to homosexuals as "tank-topped bum boys".

- Unable to deny the role he played in planning to have a journalist beaten up (Eddie Mair BBC interview).

- declared that if equal marriage was permissible, why not a union "between three men, as well as two men, or indeed three men and a dog".

- Accused of attempting to blackmail the head of a national media organisation by his former boss (www.dailymail.co.uk 10th October 2012).

- He edited the Spectator when it published an article indicating blacks have lower IQs than whites.

- He boasted for "sticking up for bankers" more than anyone else after the financial crisis (www.iNews.co.uk 22nd June 2019).

- He refused to apologise for Libyan dead bodies remark about cleaning the dead bodies from Libya to turn it into a tourist resort.

- He lies in his newspaper columns and has been forced to publicly apologise (Guardian 12th April 2019).

- and then compared Muslim women to bank robbers and letterboxes.

- He was caught out repeatedly for lying throughout the Tory Leadership campaign (www.mirror.co.uk 22nd July 2019)

Even colleagues that have worked with him are not positive such as Amber Rudd when she commented "You can't trust him to take you home at the end of the evening," - was she echoing what other colleagues think and that he is a liability and has no eye for detail or cannot concentrate on any complex big issues. Since being voted in as Prime Minister by the conservative membership (only circa. 0.14% of the British population).

So how does it get to the stage where this clearly floored individual who will probably say anything at all to get elected in can be seriously considered by colleagues and then a conservative membership? Basically, the Conservative party with the rise of Corbyn and now Farage and the Brexit party are desperate and see Johnson as the solution as he is popular. Many of his MP colleagues had a campaign called ABB (Anybody But Boris) but now they face their potentially dire general election result 'desperate times call for desperate measures' which is where we arrive at PM Boris Johnson, as farcical as that sounds.

What can we expect from a Boris Johnson government? Probably due to his history nobody knows but with strong supporters like the also popular Jacob Rees-Mogg, despite being a strong opponent of equality and LGBTQ rights as well as a medieval stance on abortion we may see it attracting unpleasant, sinister supporters resulting in some very unpleasant policies. If Boris's life is anything to go by "Chaos"! The age-old adage of "Be careful what you wish for" comes to mind. He will make innumerable unfunded promises that may be undeliverable or some simply fantasies just to get elected, with many of the timescales 5 years + so he is not help responsible for delivering anything.. He was offering funding for schools, police, fibre optic coverage for the whole country, tax cuts for the better off, reductions in National Insurance for the less well-off, and even hinting at a Metro system for Leeds, which was obviously his start of a general election campaign rather than a PM focused on Brexit.

Let's hope he is not as bad as he has the potential to be, for all our sakes.

Arron Banks

Mr Banks is apparently a very successful Insurance Multi-Millionaire (perhaps only a multi-millionaire as his money sits in many offshore accounts and shell companies so it is difficult to know exactly what he is worth) who came to prominence as the largest donor and founder of the anti-EU UK Independence

Party (UKIP) and Leave.EU, one of the main campaign organisations campaigning to have the UK leave the EU. He was before that a donor to the Conservative party but when in an interview William Hague said he had not heard of Arron Banks, Mr. Banks allegedly took his money elsewhere in a huff.

His £8 million ($11 million) donation to the Leave.EU campaign sent shock waves through the political world when it was announced as it was the largest political donation ever made in in the UK, and for a one off cause which gave the Leave campaign an amazing shot in the arm and a lot of power to influence, and influence they did.

But controversy followed as Mr. Banks could not clearly demonstrate where the money came from saying some of it came from insurance companies, he owned but when pushed on The Andrew Marr show he cited a company that was in fact a non-trading shell company. It may well turn out to be legitimate, but his explanation was not clear at all and left one with the impression that it all sounded very "Dodgy" and he may be hiding something. The British Electoral commission felt the same and referred it to the National Crime Agency who can go further to investigate, and this is where it is at the time of writing. But we probably won't know the truth until after we leave the EU (if at all) so the damage would have been done.

Indeed, Mr Banks was questioned about the Leave campaign's alleged irregularities in the referendum campaign and his answer was so dismissive it was a frightening reflection on his attitude towards our democracy when he said '(We) pushed the boundary of everything, right to the edge.... no one cares!' Oh yes, they do Mr. Banks - we care, and democracy cares.

As revealed in the Panama papers Mr. Banks has a very complicated and opaque organisation of numerous companies including companies based in The Isle Of Man, The Virgin Islands and Gibraltar making it almost impossible to see where his money comes from and where it goes, which works to his advantage as it is secretive and 'tax efficient'. Maybe this is where Mr. Bank's dislike of the EU is borne i.e. it is not an ideological campaign but rather a pragmatic one as the EU clamps down on such company constitutions and offshore tax hideaways which would not be good for such people utilising such facilities and if the UK left the EU government would not have the clout or the will to carry out such threats. He could in fact be like many multi-millionaires and Russian Oligarchs throwing a lot of money at a problem with the aim of saving much more down the line. The EU is simply trying to get rich people to pay their fair share of tax to the benefit of the many and not allow very rich people, because they are rich, to use such grey areas to avoid paying tax to the relevant authorities. after all it is these tax receipts that our government uses to pave the roads, pay for the streetlights and numerous other things these people use also.

The UK is known internationally as the place for "opaque money" with it reported that over a third of billionaires use the UK for such purposes, but many of the same billionaires make donations to UK political parties (and they are not doing this out of the kindness of their hearts) so we can see a clear conflict of interest here and that does raise concerns. The Business Insider publication claimed on 10th November 2019 '9 Russian donors named in a suppressed intelligence report'. The EU is moving towards changing such ways of billionaires moving their money beyond the reach of the state, but the British government is reticent, so do you think the billionaires would like the UK to be inside or outside the EU?

Unfortunately, the UK has become a place where the transparency of money and its origins or destinations has become very opaque and is widely accepted. We have become complacent about it, and many continue to lobby to keep the rules that favour keeping them as they are currently.

Mr. Banks is one of those associated with an irony of Brexit that if it is indeed such money from multi-millionaires and Billionaires that has influenced and will help the UK leave the EU it will be to their benefit as the EU has (since 2016) already started slowly enacting new laws to go after such tax avoidance and create greater clarity. But the UK when it leaves may well be exempt. Job done! On reflection a sad indictment on the UK and the aim of greater equality, improved social services, and a better society as a whole.

Dominic Cummings

Perhaps not as well-known as the other personalities highlighted here but Cummings was crucial to the Leave win and some even claim that without him they would not have won and that definitely has legitimacy. He came a bit more to prominence after the Leave win and as a result of the 2018 TV Drama 'Brexit – The uncivil war' where he was played by no other than Mr. "Sherlock Holmes" Benedict Cumberbatch. Well worth a watch if you have not seen it already.

Cummings is a British political adviser and strategist who served as the Campaign Director of Vote Leave and was a former special adviser to Michael Gove. He graduated with a first-class Degree at Oxford University, married Mary Wakefield, the former deputy editor of The Spectator, and is the daughter of Sir

Humphry Wakefield, of Chillingham Castle in Northumberland. Dominic had politics running through his veins and is very well connected with an obsession with Otto Von Bismarck.

Probably borderline genius he is not the easiest of people and is known for his odd character and blunt style plus he does not suffer fools gladly. This was something that was clearly needed during the referendum campaign as he was surrounded by or came in contact with a lot of fools interested in personal gain and notoriety rather than winning the campaign which was Cummings' ONLY focus. David Cameron criticised Cummings as a "career psychopath", but he knew how effective he was in the right role and position. [33] Cummings also stated in public and was filmed saying that many Conservatives do not care about normal people!

He really came into his own in this campaign as this book will show but he had experience of Europe and referendums when he was campaign Director at Business for Sterling, which helped to keep the UK out of the Euro, which proved a good decision, largely driven by Labour Chancellor of the Exchequer Gordon Brown. He was also convinced John Prescott to stop the idea of a North-East regional assembly when he ran the campaign for NO and achieved an amazing 78% of the vote. This was a lesser known Referendum but clearly he had an amazing understanding of knowing what the key issues were and how to get the right result for his 'Team'. He had that required Euroscepticism, could organise effectively, and knew how to WIN.

He knew people in market towns hated London, hated so-called Elites and thought more money should go to the NHS, they hated bankers and did not like too much for foreigners. But that said he knew how to cut through all that and focus on the emotive issues and from the above it was for him immigration, taking back control, and the NHS, and where possible linking them together, which he did very well.

His BLOG is very interesting albeit very long posts but it is clear he believes human beings are flawed and need 'leading' which is probably why he works in the way he does by making things very simple and clear such as "take back control", "Get Brexit done" etc. A powerful but simple empty slogan is worth a thousand words in his world (apart from his Blog that is).

What was revealed that Cummings had never mentioned that he and his family received 235,000 Euros in subsidies for a farm he and his family own as exposed in The Observer newspaper resulting in charges of hypocrisy, especially as he had attacked agricultural subsidies in his Blog claiming they raise prices for the poor to subsidise rich farmers while damaging agriculture in Africa. He may try to portray himself as the working-class hero from the North, but the fact he went to a £30,000 a year Durham school, and his Father In Law is the baronet Sir Humphrey Wakefield that does not really wash, and in some ways has sold out.

To get a real feel for and a handle on Dominic Cummings focus and win at all costs attitude it is when he declared to Johnson and Gove that if 'you want to win this [referendum], you have to hit Cameron and Osbourne over the head with a baseball bat with immigration written all over it'.[45]

John Redwood

Mr. Redwood (Conservative MP for the Tory safe seat of Wokingham) has made a career of being an anti-EU proponent for decades and you may be hard pushed to remember him for anything else. He was infamous as one of John Major's "Bastards" making life very difficult for the Prime Minister at the time. Nothing like loyalty to your leaders.

He appears one of them that this anti-EU stance has become an almost obsessed crusade and once the referendum was announced he was like a kid in a sweet shop, and could drive his unbalanced negative version of our relationship with the EU and would get more of a platform to exude his opinions, that he did not have before the referendum and the EU stood front and centre of British politics. He was literally in 'Brexitacy'!

Mr. Redwood also works on the side as a chief global strategist for Charles Stanley reportedly earning £180,000 per year for this job (not bad for part time!). But despite constantly claiming to the media and the voters that the UK would be an excellent place once we leave the European Union he wrote an article in the Financial Times on the 5th November 2017 advising investors to 'Look further afield' due to the state of the UK economy, and also compared the US and Japan's approach and future preferable to the UK! This obviously on the surface looks like hypocrisy and does not reflect well on what he was saying to his constituents, Leave voters and other parties that will be directly affected by all the negative effects of Brexit.

The expert Forbes commentator Francis Coppola even highlighted the issue of Mr. Redwood's piece writing that the MP had "advocated a course of action by the UK government that he knows would seriously damage the EU economy". Coppola continued and was pulling no punches: "to protect his job as an investment manager, he warned his wealthy clients to get their money out before disaster hits. To me, this smacks of disaster capitalism. Engineer a crash while ensuring your own interests are protected, and then clean up when it hits. This is despicable behaviour by a lawmaker."

This position of Mr. Redwood highlighted one of the real problems with Brexit in that the main high profile proponents of Brexit including Mr. Redwood, Boris Johnson, Nigel Farage, Arron Banks, Michael Gove, and Jacob Rees-Mogg are very well off individuals that can easily handle a huge downturn in our economy as they can move their wealth or already have so much money that they have a comfortable cash balance not to notice it. BUT the less well-off could very well suffer with a turn down in the economy or even a recession. Such developments as higher priced food or increases in taxes or council Tax for example can hit the poor very very hard. Yes, the aforementioned 'rich men' seem oblivious to this or at least do not acknowledge it and almost see Brexit as a jolly amusing debating game at Oxford or Cambridge where the act of winning is the only thing that counts. But why did the public not see this? Was their emotion and fear of immigrants so great that it trumped any of the hypocrisy we have seen from these Gentlemen?

The others?

There are many more we could have listed but wanted to just give you a taste of the leave cheerleaders in this Brexit web of lies and deceit and how many attempted to, and to a great extent succeeded, in deceiving the public with these myths and misinformation and as soon as the project was completed they all scuttled away not having to be held to account or deliver the mess they had created.

The exception being Boris Johnson who is now in the 'hot seat' and will struggle to blag his way through this one, although with Boris who knows. But it should be entertaining if not frightening as we all get aboard the 'Bojo Express'. Hopefully not to hell in a handcart!

You may literally be hard pushed to find someone that got so much wrong about our leaving the EU than David Davis despite being Brexit secretary at a crucial time in the Teresa May government. See the section 'Government and broken promises' for quotes from DD and the reality that ensued. Frightening how wrong someone can be but shows no remorse or shame in the way he has potentially negatively affected millions of lives – welcome to the sordid side of British politics.

Hypocrites, tricksters or opportunists?

Many of the major people backing Brexit and galvanising the Leave vote using their high profiles and political as well as economic influence in their own private or business lives appear to recommend other actions or preferences. One only needs to look at former Chancellor of the Exchequer Nigel Lawson who secured French residency as quickly as possible before Brexit but by promoting Brexit would stop other British subjects having their free movement throughout the EU as we currently have. Many examples highlighted a split in the country as regards who will probably be hit by a bad Brexit i.e. the poor who could see higher food prices and job losses, but the likes of Mr Redwood will not be dramatically affected who has a £180,000 second job, as well as his £80,0000 MP salary and expense account.

Jacob Rees-Mogg's company began to advise on investing outside the UK and set up new funds in Ireland, i.e. within the EU, as his team saw that location as the better future for those funds.

Sir James Dyson an avid Leave campaigner after the referendum result decided to move his company headquarters from the UK to Singapore despite singing the praises of the UK and being better off outside the EU. I am sure it was a coincidence that Singapore had recently signed a free trade agreement with the EU to potentially make imports into the EU easier than the UK if we do not sign a free trade agreement with the EU. One must put Dyson's anti-EU sentiment into context in that it lost a major legal battle with the European Union over the regulation of vacuum cleaners and Dyson trying to scrap EU energy labelling rules. The European Court of Justice heard his case and found against Dyson, which will obviously not increase its love of the EU and left a better taste in the company's mouth.

Some of those MPs such as John Redwood or Jacob Rees-Mogg have been obsessing about the EU for decades and if you consider these 2 individuals and take Europe and the EU away, what have they achieved? What will they be remembered for outside their disdain for the European Union? JRM perhaps for lounging around on the Green benches in Westminster in a very disrespectful act or implying if the poor people of Grenfell tower had used their "common sense" and ignored the fire brigade's advice like he would have done they may have survived! On what planet did JRM believe it was appropriate to insult dead people? Perhaps these two individuals and a number of other MPs would have served their party and the country better if, rather than constantly pushing a distorted and often incorrect image of the EU and its impact on the UK, they had concentrated on more important issues to the public like Health, the environment, inequality in the country, policing, security, etc. But instead they have built careers in very safe affluent constituencies on half truths about the European Union as if it was the evil Emperor Ming in a Flash Gordon film.

After almost 3 years since the Referendum result Teresa May stated publicly that she would stand down once the withdrawal agreement is signed and ratified (although many in her party questioned this as she had gone back on other public statements and timescales) which let loose the foxes in the chicken pen as they begin to position themselves with their colleagues and the ultimate decision makers, the Conservative Party membership. This resulted in it being very difficult to know really what those interested in becoming the next leader of the Conservative party actually thought or believed as they were playing to the future gallery.

A good example of this was Jeremy Hunt who voted remain and is not what one could call an extreme ideologue like say the likes of Mark Francois and some others in the European Research Group (ERG) but was calling for an immediate no-deal Brexit in March 2019. Had he genuinely changed his critical thinking and beliefs 180 degrees or was he more probably playing to the stronger right wing of his party and pro-Brexit membership in his attempt to win the Conservative leadership contest? With an average age thought to be getting on for 60 in the Conservative party membership whoever is pitching to them will be walking a fine line as he / she needs something that the members, many comfortably retired, believe in and want whilst painting a picture for the wider electorate of a new vision of conservatism that appeals to and offers something to the younger generations and attacking poverty, homelessness, food banks, etc. That was a challenge when 75% of the Tory membership are behind a no-deal

Brexit which most economists forecast would make the UK poorer which would hit the generations more as they have longer to endure any forthcoming downturns or recessions and need jobs and money.

Well that is where we were with the last two in the leadership competition, Jeremy Hunt and Boris Johnson, having made so many spending promises and tax cuts it literally became the 'conservative fibbing competition' with Mr Johnson prevailing having told the biggest Whoppers and the 160,000 conservative members lapping it up. But then that is an art of his so we should not be surprised? I challenge you to put forward someone that would beat Boris Johnson in a fibbing competition. Bernie Madoff doesn't count as he has already been convicted!

Are issues of food banks, lack of skills, lack of training, lack of higher qualifications for specific skills we need the fault of the EU or quite simply down to consecutive UK governments and their policies or lack of focused policies and results in these areas and others?

The people against the Elites!

This was the narrative pushed by the Leave campaign which was confusing when you had posh Etonians Jacob Rees-Mogg, Boris Johnson, and Michael Gove leading various leave campaigns but it seemed that the most famous posh boys of David Cameron and George Osborne trumped the others and once this narrative had been set, it would be difficult to shift. But for example, the London Boroughs of Lambeth and Hackney returned the highest remain majorities in the country at over 70%. Is Hackney and Lambeth elite? Was that the voice of the Elite? For readers that may not have been to either London borough believe me it is not. Boris was not organising a Bullingdon club jolly day out to either of these areas, with Windsor being higher up the 'elite scale'. Also, every area in Scotland voted leave – are they Elite? Does he really care about the 'ordinary people'? Could you see Nigel Farage running a charity (obviously not a foreign based charity!) doing great work behind the scenes?

Clearly, this narrative was effective and rich people like Nigel Farage used this at every opportunity although he was the very embodiment of the elite beginning as Dulwich College educated and then a City Trader and then someone that only did politics and was desperate to push himself in front of every microphone or TV camera he could. Was he really representing the people?

An example of Nigel being there shoulder to shoulder with the people was when he organised his "March to Leave" from Sunderland to London a total of 277 miles imploring people to join him and show the Elites what the UK really thought. Well they did tell them when only 350 signed up. Yes, signed up as the poor supporters had to pay £50 each for the privilege, whilst Nigel can fly around the world in private jets! It was a disaster. But the most revealing aspect was when Mr. Farage revealed that he would not walk the whole route but only the first small part of it (for photo opportunities on the bus of course) as he had to be in Brussels (presumably to pick up his salary cheque and expenses) which showed where his priorities lay. Let the people walk in the rain in the UK and Mr. Farage will sit comfortably in Brussels adding no value but being rude to our partners, which is about all he ever does there. But his supporters think this is acceptable, so low have our expectations of our politicians slumped.

Despite all the bluster and rhetoric, he churned out during the campaign and the amazing vision of Brexit and how once out the UK will return to the sunny pleasant lands he had promised once it was won, he backtracked very quickly. He claimed on Good Morning TV that he personally would not have made the claim made on the big red bus despite not saying anything at the time (for obvious reasons) as he knew it could not be delivered. But also tweeted on 29th May 2018 "I never promised it would be a huge success. "Brexit" – This tells you more about a charlatan when you read back their own words to them. The thing about Mr. Farage is that he genuinely does not care what you say about him, as long as you are talking about him. He lives by the adage any publicity is good publicity. I am not sure he does have a political philosophy but rather, as he has been rejected by the electorate 7 times, he simply looks for a vehicle to promote himself as an agitator to the system. UKIP served this purpose and now his new Brexit party does the same, as long as another personality in the party does not steal his thunder. It is the Nigel show, and nobody should compete with him, just finance him!

It was an effective trick used by most of the Brexiteers by discrediting the case for staying in the EU by manipulating the public's distrust of politicians plus discredit the credibility of experts by branding anyone pro-European as elitist. Of course, when one thinks about it it is not credible or accurate especially when coming from political elites and career politicians such as Jacob Rees-Mogg and Nigel Farage. David Davis tried this angle when claiming he was a political outsider from the back benches, but then became Brexit Minister (OK he achieved nothing), so what is he then if not a career politician in the government?

Chapter 27
The Government & Broken Promises

11 Broken promises?

There have been so many broken promises (and cynics may say lies) from government and as I started to compile these, I felt that I could not do it justice as well as the Guardian did in an excellent piece on this written by Jon Henley and Dan Roberts, **on** Wed 28 Mar 2018 [7]. Please see the amazing and also very disappointing performance of our government in their efforts to achieve a good Brexit deal, where Jon and Dan revealed 11 promises that were broken and the actual reality of the situation and what transpired.

Promise 1

Exit will be easy and have no downsides

"Brexit will be easy, and have no downsides There will be no downside to Brexit, only a considerable upside"

David Davis, 10 October 2016

"The day after we vote to leave, we hold all the cards and we can choose the path we want."

Michael Gove, 9 April 2016

"Getting out of the EU can be quick and easy – the UK holds most of the cards."

John Redwood, July 17, 2016

"The free trade agreement that we will have to do with the European Union should be one of the easiest in human history."

Liam Fox, 20 July 2017

The Reality

David Davis now says: "nobody has ever pretended this will be easy. I have always said this negotiation will be tough, complex and at times confrontational."

Promise 2

Trade talks would take place in parallel with divorce talks

"Trade talks would take place in parallel with divorce talks. How on earth do you resolve the issue of the border with Northern Ireland and the Republic of Ireland unless you know what our general borders policy is, what the customs agreement is, what our trade agreement is? It's wholly illogical... That'll be the row of the summer

David Davis, 14 May 2017

"Most of the EU states are very sympathetic to our view."

David Davis, 15 May 2017

"We have to establish the ground rules. The first crisis or argument is going to be over the question of sequencing"

David Davis, 21 May 2017

The Reality

Davis caved in on the first day of talks on 19 June 2017

Promise 3

"The UK did not need a transition deal and would not be subject to EU rules or budgets during one. We're not really interested in a transition deal, but we'll consider one to be kind to the EU."

David Davis, 15 November 2016

"The idea that we'll do a transitional arrangement where you're still in, paying money, still with free movement of people – that we'll do the long-term deal in slow motion... That is plainly not what we're after."

David Davis, 15 March 2016

"We made it clear that control of our own borders was one of the elements we wanted in the referendum, and unregulated free movement [during transition] would seem to me not to keep faith with that decision."

Liam Fox, 30 July 2016

The Reality

The UK will have to abide by all EU rules and regulations including those agreed by members states during the 21-month transition

Article 123 – Institutional Arrangements

During the transition period, where draft Union acts identify or refer directly to specific Member state authorities, procedures, or documents, the United Kingdom shall be consulted by the Union on such drafts with a view to ensuring the proper implementation and application of that act by and in the United Kingdom.

Promise 4

The transition period will not be a problem

"The transition serves merely to implement the final trade deal, which would be agreed by Brexit day. I believe that we can get a free trade and customs agreement concluded before March 2019 . "

David Davis, 18 January 2017

"The point of the implementation period is to put in place the practical changes necessary to move to the future partnership, and for that you need to know what the future partnership is going to be."

Theresa May, 23 October 2017

The Reality

"The transition period will be used to negotiate (as much as possible) of the future relationship, not to implement a relationship that is already agreed."

Guidelines - 23 March 2018

5.   Against this background, the European Council sets out the following guidelines with a view to the opening of negotiations on the overall understanding of the framework for the future relationship, that will be elaborated in a political declaration accompanying and referred to in the Withdrawal Agreement.

Many EU capitals believe even the 21-month transition period will not be anywhere near long enough to conclude a comprehensive free trade agreement and will have to be extended.

Promise 5

The transition would be short but open-ended

"The transition would be short but open-ended. The period's duration should be determined simply by how long it will take to prepare and implement the new processes and new systems that will underpin the future partnership."

Government transition paper, 21 February 2018

"These considerations point to an implementation period of around two years."

Theresa May, 22 September 2017

The Reality

"The period is fixed at 21 months, with no easy way to extend it. This merely postpones the regulatory cliff edge business is desperate to avoid until December 2020. Even this measure of stability is uncertain, since the transition period could be rescinded if there is not wider agreement this autumn."

Promise 6

The UK won't owe any money

"The UK would owe no money to the EU after it left in March 2019. The last time we went through line by line and challenged quite a lot of the legal basis of these things, and we'll continue to do that... [Of rumours of a £40 billion bill:] They sort of made that up."

David Davis, 25 September 2017

"Because we will no longer be members of the single market, we will not be required to pay huge sums into the EU budget."

Theresa May, 17 January 2017

"The sums I have seen that they propose to demand from this country seem to me to be extortionate and I think that 'go whistle' is an entirely appropriate expression."

Boris Johnson, 11 July 2017

The Reality

UK told EU in November 2017 that it was ready to honour its share of all financial commitments made while it was a member of the bloc, estimated at €40 billion to €45 billion, through the transition period.

Chapter 2 – The UK's contribution to and participation in the Union budget

Article 128 – The UK's contribution to and participation in the implementation of the Union budgets for the years 2019 and 2020.

For the years 2019 and 2020, in accordance with Part Four, the United Kingdom shall contribute to and participate in the implementation of the Union budgets.

It has since become clear payments will continue until about 2064, and indefinitely if the UK wants to continue to be part of EU agencies and programmes.

Promise 7

"A raft of new trade deals would be ready on 29 March 2019. Within two years, before the negotiation with the EU is likely to be complete, and therefore before anything material has changed, we can negotiate a free trade area massively larger than the EU... The new trade agreements will come into force at the point of exit, but they will be fully negotiated."

David Davis, 14 July 2016

The Reality

Britain has won the right to negotiate deals with third countries during the transition period (not before) but they cannot be implemented until after December 2020.

4.   Notwithstanding paragraph 3, during the transition period, the United Kingdom may negotiate, sign and ratify international agreements entered into in its own capacity in the areas of exclusive competence of the union, provided those agreements do not enter into force or apply during the transition period, unless so authorised by the Union.

New deals will anyway take a long time to negotiate, especially since few countries are likely to want to sign them until they know the state of the UK's final relationship with the EU. And while the EU will ask third countries with which it has trade deals to keep Britain in them, there is no certainty they will.

Promise 8

A high-tech customs solution would make frictionless borders simple

"A high-tech customs solution would make frictionless borders simple. The UK is currently implementing a new customs declaration service, which will replace the existing HMRC customs system. This is a high-priority project within government and HMRC is on track to deliver by January 2019."

Department for Exiting the EU, 15 August 2017

"I am confident that using the most up-to-date technology, we can get a non-visible border operational along the border between Northern Ireland and Ireland."

David Davis, 5 September 2017

The Reality

Theresa May now concedes customs arrangements are difficult and will take time to set up. May told the Commons liaison committee on 27 March 2018: "I think it is fair to say that, as we get into the detail and as we look at these arrangements, then what becomes clear is that sometimes the timetables that have originally been set are not the timetables that are necessary when you actually start to look at the detail and when you delve into what it really is that you want to be able to achieve."

Promise 9

Arriving after that date would be subject to a different immigration regime

"Free movement would come to an end on 29 March 2019; any EU citizens arriving after that date would be subject to a different immigration regime. It is a simple matter of fact that the four key principles of the European Union include free movement – we won't be a member of the European Union when we leave."

Brandon Lewis, 27 July 2017

"Free movement will end in March 2019."

Government spokesperson, July 31, 2017

"I'm clear that there is a difference between those people who come prior to us leaving and those who will come when they know the UK is no longer a member."

Theresa May, 1 February 2017

The Reality

Free movement continues, the only difference being a registration system for newcomers.

Author: 'The settled / pre-settled status and Freedom of Movement are in truth compatible. In most, if not all. Other EU 27 countries there is a requirement for registration before you can settle! The UK [Government] just chose not to enforce this because it would cost too much money to administer, plus we needed the workers, anyway. So, this was never an EU issue, but rather a decision by our democratically elected UK government!

Article 9 – Personal Scope

Without prejudice to Title III, this part shall apply to the following persons:

Union Citizens who exercised their right to reside in the UK in accordance with Union law before the end of the transition period and continue to reside thereafter;

Even May's commitment that arrivals after Brexit day would be treated differently was abandoned in the negotiations. EU citizens arriving in Britain before the end of the transition period will be treated as before.

Promise 10

"There would be no role for the European court of justice in Britain after Brexit day. The simple truth is we are leaving. We are going to be outside the reach of the European court."

David Davis, 14 May 2017

"The authority of EU law in this country has ended forever... We are not leaving only to return to the jurisdiction of the ECJ. That's not going to happen."

Theresa May, 5 October 2016

The Reality

The ECJ will have full jurisdiction during the transition period and the ECJ interpretation of relevant civil rights laws are likely to hold thereafter

Article 126 – Supervision and enforcement

During the transition period, the institutions, bodies, offices and agencies of the Union shall have the powers conferred upon them by Union law in relation to the UK and natural and legal persons residing or established in the UK. In particular, the Court of Justice of the European Union shall have jurisdiction as provided for in the treaties.

In addition, the transition agreement makes clear that Britain will be "consulted" but is expected to ensure the "proper implementation and application" of all new draft EU rules and regulations during transition.

Promise 11

Britain will take back control of its fisheries after Brexit
"Britain will take back control of its fisheries after Brexit. Leaving the EU means we will take back full control of our territorial waters and for the first time in 50 years will be able to grant fishing access for other countries on our terms."
Department of Environment, Food and Rural Affairs, 3 August 2017

"The UK will regain control over our domestic fisheries management rules and access to our waters."
Theresa May, 3 March 2017

The Reality

The EU will have continued access to UK fishing waters throughout the transition period and has demanded reciprocal access afterwards too as a condition of any future trade deal.

Article 125 – Specific arrangements relating to fishing opportunities

As regards the fixing of fishing opportunities within the meaning of Article 43(3) TFEU for any period falling within the transition period, the UK shall be consulted in respect of the fishing opportunities related to the UK, including in the context of the preparation of relevant international consultations and negotiations.

Article written by Jon Henley and Dan Roberts for the Guardian Newspaper on Wed 28 Mar 2018 [7]

But we should not expect politicians to be unconditionally bound by any "promise" or "commitment" as conditions can change and sometimes dramatically and logic says as circumstances change then decisions may have to change. This idea that you have to honour your promise whatever makes no sense and is often used by those where the promise is politically to their advantage to exploit it. It is the same in your personal life as well, for example, if I promise to take you to a concert at Wembley at 7pm but the concert is cancelled (i.e. circumstances have changed) would you be happy that I honoured the promise but still took you to Wembley despite there being no concert? Of course, not.

Also, it may well be that the aforementioned promises were well intentioned, and they genuinely believed them but were simply incompetent and did not really have a clue what they were talking about. David Davis clearly has the charm and chat and has probably over-used those characteristics to further his career but appears to lack any intellectual rigour. So, when it came to Brexit he turned up to probably one of the most important meetings of his life with just a pen totally unprepared expecting to 'do a Davis' and bluff his way through. But he was met with professionals and not Blaggers and was way out of his depth, although like Boris it is never his fault. The quotations above for promises made, clearly show it would be difficult to find anyone that has spoken so much nonsense about Brexit and got so much wrong. But there is a common trait with many of these Brexiteer politicians that even when talking absolute delusional nonsense they do it with an unbelievable confidence and aplomb that many people will believe them if they do not do a little 'heavy lifting' and background work to then realise the emperor literally has no clothes.

Apart from the above other such promises were made by the likes of Boris Johnson, Priti Patel, Gisela Stewart, Dominic Raab, and Vote Leave, all of which have not come to fruition or look extremely unlikely at the time of writing including: The union with Scotland will be stronger; stronger border controls, new Australian points based immigration system in place by 2020; no controls on the Northern Irish border with the European Union, a system that will not discriminate against Irish citizens but will discriminate against EU citizens of which the Irish are also EU citizens, immigration will be cut, no damage to trade with the EU, no short-term economic disruption, scrapping VAT on fuel bills, more money in our pockets, and more money for scientists, and farmers! It seems a lot of people will be very disappointed when we eventually leave and a lot of this will not happen.

The Leave campaign and its pack of lies during and since the referendum

Below is only a few of those distortions with others covered throughout this book which seep into many areas of British life including social, trade, economics, and other areas.

■   Leaving the EU would save the UK £8 Billion - this was refuted by the Institute of Fiscal Studies stating Brexit would mean spending less on public services or taxing more or borrowing more.

■   The UK has no power to stop becoming a part of an EU army – David Cameron made it clear the UK had a "rock solid veto" on EU defence and foreign policy, which was crystal clear.

■   the UK cannot stop overall EU spending from going up – David Cameron made it quite clear the budget was set in stone and would need the agreement of ALL members to increase it.

- the UK had given up its ability to veto EU Treaties – David Cameron made it clear there was nothing in the renegotiation that relinquishes the UK's veto.

- the UK's EU rebate was at risk – Cameron made it clear he had a veto on changes to the veto.

- The UK is liable for future Eurozone bailouts – Cameron made it quite clear his EU renegotiation meant the UK is categorically not liable!

- A vote for the "easiest Deal in history" became a "vote for no deal at all"!

- "No short term hit to living standards" became "people knew there would be a short-term cost!" (Jacob Rees-Mogg claimed that could be 50 years!

The Vote Leave campaign literature said quite specifically said there would be a deal and leaving with a deal would be a stable calm transition with no risks attached. It was quite explicit which can only lead one to the assumption that there is no mandate for a no-deal Brexit, and to say anything else would be disingenuous and re-writing history.

Boris Johnson, the new Prime minister!

As history of the individual and his duplicitous nature tells us that there will be a lot of misinformation and careful evasion which will come from the top down (assisted by his advisers) and he is the best at it, and shows no shame and often no sense of morals or willingness to accept, own up to, and apologise to those affected by is indiscretions.

At the end of July 2019, newly in position as Chancellor, Sajid Javid was setting out his plans for an extra £2.1 Billion (on top of the £4 Billion his predecessor Philip Hammond set aside for just such an eventuality) of spending for preparations for a no-deal Exit from the European Union. So instead of a Brexit dividend as promised we are faced with a huge cost exercise i.e. money that could have been spent on helping your families with money to the NHS or social services. Who honestly voted for that? Linked to what people voted for I refer you to the £100 million that will be allocated to advertising of the Government's plans for no deal, but why do we need such a huge amount of money for such an exercise when we were told "everybody knew what they voted for"? If they knew, and that was what they are getting, please Mr. Johnson spend the £100 million on value-added services such as Doctors, police or Research & Development etc. Perhaps it is to try to remind people what they actually voted for, even though a lot of that is never going to happen? Staying in the EU could avoid NHS staff shortages, more money for the NHS, quicker access to medicines, and Brits get free healthcare across the EU currently. Plus, outside the EU the risk of the NHS having to pay more for US manufactured drugs becomes a real possibility as an investigation by Chanel 5s Dispatches uncovered in 2019, and meeting between UK and US government representatives has implied. A freedom of Information request by Labour party resulted in a redacted (black pen covering up 'sensitive information) document. But why is it so secret?

The strange thing at the beginning of Mr. Johnson's tenure at PM was that he appeared to be more focused on campaigning for an election (which he obviously hopes will give him a majority he currently does not have) rather than focusing on getting a deal with the European Union, the most important political act in decades. We understand why he is doing that, but it demonstrated lack of political judgement and clarity, or possibly avoiding something that was too difficult for him and he knew he was not going to get which he promised to all his supporters upon taking office?

The number of committees were rapidly put together upon Mr. Johnson being voted in as head of the Conservative party and by default Prime Minister which appeared like headless chickens running around trying to give the impression of progress but was in reality undirected activities with little strategy or plan (does that ring a bell?). We were told he has a "War Cabinet which shows how desperate it has become and what a mess the Leave vote has put us in. There is also an Exit Strategy Committee, the Daily operations Committee" and finally the Exit and Trade Committee which bodes the question what do all these groups do or is it just an exercise in making people feel important by giving them positions on these committees and surely one committee focused on the critical factors where the focus should be. But obviously that cannot be sold as well as we have a lot of groups running around. It does have the fingerprints of Dominic Cummings on it that as the arch expert of deception and creating certain impressions (e.g. millions of Turks are coming to the UK) that are just simply not true.

We should not forget that Mr. Johnson has no mandate from the people or even for no deal he was pursuing and was only voted into office by less than 160,000 Conservative party members, 97% of whom are white, 71% are male and 44% are over the age of 65 - not exactly representative is it?

Mr. Johnson and the Leave campaign campaigned on the European Communities Act would not be repealed until after the British Parliament saw the details of the Free Trade Agreement, which he then deviated from in August 2019, adding again to the growing expectation that he cannot be trusted no matter what he says, and led to 21 rebel MPs voting with their conscience and out of principle against the government in September 2019 including Antoinette Sandbach MP, Churchill's Grandson Nicholas Soames MP, and father of the house Kenneth Clarke MP. This led to the unprecedented action of the PM removing the whip from all of them in a purge and effectively killing the one nation Tory ideal the party had championed for decades. The irony of Mr Johnson's decision is that many of his cabinet were serial rebels including repeatedly voting against Teresa May's deal, but he throws others out of the party at the first sign of dissent. That is irony personified.

A Downing Street source was quoted as stating "the daily meetings show that we are serious about a no-deal [Brexit]" and "... people should not get carried away by suggesting Cobra had been "convened" to tackle a crisis". Yes, you heard correctly a "crisis" and that coming from the heart of the government that is threatening a no-deal Brexit. So, they have basically set up a crisis committee to deal with a crisis THEY have created!

Even after the Brexit result and Boris having campaigned vigorously for Leave his lack of understanding became clear when referring to the leaving the UK in a no-deal Brexit where he believed we could remain in a full trade relationship with the rest of the EU, without transgressing any WTO rules, which is just simply untrue. Now on this occasion I am willing to give Mr. Johnson a pass as to whether he was lying again, as on this occasion it appeared ignorance rather than malice.

One of the issues was although saying a no-deal Brexit is acceptable to the Johnson government, its incoherence on what no deal meant for freedom of movement for example made many feel, understandably, insecure. I was confronted by a Brexiteer that Mr. Johnson's fabrications were years ago, but then I had to point out that The Telegraph newspaper was forced to correct a false

416

Brexit claim made my Mr. Johnson in only January 2019 in a column he wrote for the Newspaper. How the Editor did not correct this is disappointing, and it took a complaint from a member of the public to IPSO to have a correction put forward as there was no evidence for the claim Mr. Johnson made that a no-deal Brexit was the most popular option among the British public. Yes, he made something up again!

But the pressure from Downing Street for promoting a No-deal Brexit as a good choice means MPs are often found wanting. For example, on the Politics Live show MP Andrea Jenkyns said the UK could leave the EU with no deal and trade on WTO rules like the rest of the world. Presenter Jo Coburn then asked her, "who else does that then?" To which Ms Jenkyns could not answer, she didn't have a clue. The fact that she didn't know was not the real point here but rather she is disingenuously promoting something to us that she plainly does not understand herself. Maybe she was just swallowing the regurgitating the Downing Street standard lines. But this type of rhetoric is dangerous as it is giving the public yet again poor information on which to make informed decisions. Just for info. Those countries are North Korea, Kazakhstan, Venezuela, Russia, and Cuba!

Since taking office he lost his first 6 votes, prorogued (suspended) Parliament longer than planned, withdrew the whip from 21 MPs and was found by a Scottish court to have misled the Monarch as to the true reason for proroguing parliament which is unprecedented, as he claimed to be heading for a no-deal Brexit in September 2019. So, his start has not been great by any measure and the appearance of not being able to carry parliament with him leading to the effort to try to silence it. Rather than the executive being held to account and showing the country exactly how they intend to take the country he tries to bypass our legislature.

In Johnson's cabinet there is also a hypocrisy now that they back the Prime Minister's decision to prorogue parliament, which is not illegal (unless he misled the Monarch?), based on what they said previously. Matt Hancock for example said it would "disrespect the war dead and goes against everything those men who waded onto those beaches fought & died for, and I will not have it", and Amber Rudd branded it a "ridiculous suggestion" and although she did resign her post, it was not for this reason, but rather because 21 Conservative colleagues had the whip removed after voting against the government on stopping a no-deal Brexit. Even Chancellor Sajid Javid said "You don't deliver on democracy by trashing democracy... we are not selecting a dictator of our country". All very clear in their position but turned 180 degrees, still they had probably not reckoned with the real Boris Johnson and Dominic Cummings?

We have seen Boris Johnson lose his first 7 votes in the House of commons as he has no majority plus he has been found guilty of acting unlawfully when communicating his intention to prorogue parliament to the Queen, so this does not bode well especially with Mr. Johnson's history of distortions and deception. But also, David Davis suggested in September 2019 that the government might have a legal strategy to avoid extending Britain's EU membership beyond 31st October, despite the so-called Benn Act of parliament to avoid a no deal. This was and is very worrying that a government would consider riding roughshod over its own parliament as that starts to become a Dictatorship and as we know they tend not to end well!

One thing we will have to get used to is Boris's rhetoric boosted by Dominic Cummings behind the scenes which within a few days of taking office included "turbo charging the economy", "rocket boosters", "gangbusters" etc. which is just a way of papering over the cracks with claims we should be more positive and not be so negative (which is code for realistic!) as if this is going to magically get us out of this hole that he has been very instrumental in creating. Try telling the workers at Honda to think more positively about losing their job or the family trying to make ends meet that their shopping and many other items will be going up in price to make them poorer etc. It is clear it is just a smoke screen whilst behind the scenes he and his team try to think of a way out of this mess. Even his team have been whipped into espousing the same baseless positivity with Rishi Sunak, the new chief secretary to the treasury saying in August 2019 "there is strong growth" whilst growth went backwards, and we crept towards a potential recession. Is this more lies or incompetence? These lies are becoming an epidemic as the whole cabinet are taking part, it is not just Boris anymore, and that should concern us all.

One advantage Mr. Johnson has is that his main opponent will be the Labour Party's Jeremy Corbyn whose ratings are at an all-time low and only seems to appeal to his left wing following and cannot reach out strongly to the middle ground like Tony Blair had achieved from 1997 to 2007 which insulates Mr. Johnson's vote to a certain extent. The unknowns may be how the 'rise' of the Brexit party and resurgence of the Lib Dems will impact the make-up of parliament in 2020.

Chapter 28
Personal Experiences of Myself & Others

When is an idiot not an idiot or just idiotic?

Now I may be called out on this section highlighting how ridiculous (probably better word than stupid, but I thought the title of this section may get your attention. Some reasons or ideas for voting leave really were ridiculous and often had nothing to do with the EU or its institutions. These are real life I have personally witnessed and not like Leave parrot politicians saying everyone voted leave for the same reasons when they know that that is untrue and never could be the case of 17.4 million people all voting for exactly the same thing for the same reason. But this will demonstrate with just a few examples how bizarre some attitudes were and how effectively due to such reasoning the EU referendum (and referendums in general) are basically floored as very rarely are the facts or probable future implications fully understood and emotion plays a major and unhelpful role which is not good for making logical well thought through strategic long-term decisions.

Some of the most foolish reasons for voting to Leave include people believing we cannot use our own 3 pin plugs due to the EU even though we are already still using them, or some genuinely believe the bendy bananas story invented by Boris Johnson when a journalist, etc. But a friend of mine voted Leave

419

because her ex-husband ("Arsehole" as she called him) lived in Gibraltar and due to the Spanish claim etc. she thought Brexit may shaft him and that was all the reason she needed to put her cross in the OUT 'shaft your ex-Husband box'!

A neighbour of mine, a Russian lady (married to a Brit and eligible to vote), was working at Gatwick but couldn't get a management job and felt other Eastern Europeans and for some reason people from Mauritius were getting the management jobs so she felt voting Leave would help her personal circumstance. Nothing to do with Sovereignty, independence, and all the other disingenuous reasons given for thinking if we have fewer foreigners coming into the UK it would be better for them. When gently pushed on how she thought leaving would actually help her position when those skilled people with qualifications would probably come any way and we need immigrants to do a lot of the jobs she looked almost embarrassed and did agree it was a bit of a ludicrous reason. The Mauritius angle was obviously just bizarre, but nevertheless it was a personal decision to her. I am sure millions of people had their own 'Mauritius' or 'shaft your husband' that had nothing to the with the pooling of sovereignty or joint laws for the betterment of the people in those member states, and again show the fragile nature of a referendum as they often cover up very complex in-depth issues which normal people do not understand and do not have the time to learn as they are getting on with their lives and making a living. That is why we elect MPs in a parliamentary democracy and employ specialists and Civil Servants to make the right decisions for us as a country as a whole.

But how do we deal with such concerns that are genuinely held? This is very difficult especially when we have so called intelligent MPs such as Jacob Reece Mogg et al. being economical with the facts to present a disfigured image of the EU or the right wing Eurosceptic newspapers constantly feeding the public with blatant nonsense about the EU but we must try to educate people and shake them from their entrenched positions and basically deal with nonsense by highlighting it is nonsense with well thought through logical arguments including observable reality where possible. And hopefully even if they do not admit to you there and then they will go away and consider what has been explained and adjust their position accordingly. Yes 30 years of Press drip feeding disinformation will be tough to counter, but we have to start somewhere and call out BS for what it is, just that, Bullshit.

When you push Leavers as to where they got the information from to make an informed decision to leave I often heard "I made my own decisions influenced by nobody" which obviously cannot be true as we all get our information or knowledge from somewhere whether it be friends, family, the Library, Google, Wikipedia, crazy Facebook groups, disingenuous lying politicians (or honest politicians, yes there are some), the bloke down the pub that just shouts louder than anyone else or the aforementioned newspapers. The trick is to understand and decipher the ramblings of a know it all drunk in the pub or the biased political agenda of a newspaper and that is down to us. But people are lazy and do not want to do the heavy lifting and work to educate themselves to try to understand such issues they are voting on and prefer dramatic inflammatory headlines. Perhaps from some weird Facebook group they know nothing about but that somehow appeared on their time line (by the way it did not appear there by chance, it was the algorithm that felt that was what you were interested in, such as if you had googled 'why are there too many immigrants in Britain or 'Is Britain breaking at the seams because of immigrants', 'help me defend Brexit' etc. So begins the echo chamber!

One person[IA] told me that Eastern European immigrants commit more crime that the indigenous population and that was why he voted Leave (although he used different reasons at different times when it suited) and included a link on Facebook to a badly written article in one of the online daily news media outlets but there was no empirical evidence making it clear national from these countries commit such crimes and I cannot think of any reason why that should be the case. If they wanted to commit crime, why not stay at home and do it there rather than travelling thousands of miles to do this in the UK? Again, such stories are fuelled by discrimination, not nipped in the bud and urban myths result.

One of the issues that has clearly grown in recent years is that fragmentary trust where individuals such as strong Brexiteers will only believe information that comes from their 'tribe' and not from others no matter how strong the evidence or arguments which exacerbates these echo chambers that people struggle to escape from. Clearly, personalised online searches extend this where people often only see a version of the world that one agrees with or reflects one's perspective of the world.

But aside from that as highlighted in the Press section of this book well known editors and proprietors such as Rupert Murdoch, Conrad Black, Paul Dacre, Richard Desmond and the Barclay brothers had been working on a very anti-EU rhetoric and misinformation for decades and that came home to roost in the referendum and of course those newspapers revelled in the result as a sign that they had done their job, which in fact they had. But we should all be concerned that they can say whatever they like about the EU whether it is factual or not and nothing happens. If a celebrity takes out a defamation case against a newspaper they can get large pay outs, so they have to be careful there, but the EU? Who cares, and I would argue the misinformation, lies and defamation of the EU as a campaign has much more far-reaching consequences and we are now experiencing, even though we haven't even left yet. The worst may be yet to come.

Even looking at some Brexiteer MPs we see quite easily a level of ignorance and lack of awareness that is astounding. David Davis admitted he didn't need to be intelligent to do his job (probably stating the obvious as he literally got the job!), Dominic Raab admitted he "hadn't quite understood" how important the Dover-Calais was to trade of goods into and out of the UK. I walk my dog in Folkestone and we see the number of ships going back and forth so unless they are empty my Shi Tzu Honey knows how busy and therefore important this trading link is! Even Karen Bradley the Northern Ireland secretary said she "did not understand" people in Northern Ireland voted for different parties based on their religious affiliation! Where had this woman been? This is incompetence after incompetence

Perhaps as a colleague of mine said to me "calling people idiots even if what they are saying is idiotic, can sound rude so why don't we just call them foolish as it softens the blow?" Good point but for some reason the saying 'A rose is a rose by any other name' to mind, but maybe he is right and let's say "foolish".

"WE believe in Democracy."

After the Referendum we heard so many times from hard-line Brexiteers calling themselves the champions of our parliamentary democracy which they say is so much better and democratic than the EU system. But then we saw them rally against the Speaker of the House of Commons, John Bercow's decision to give MPs the opportunity to exercise that sovereignty. We hear empty slogans like "The Will of the People" etc. but having seen reactions from Brexiteers since Article 50 had been triggered and their unhappiness with the decisions of Teresa May and the progress of legislation through parliament it appears, they like our democracy as long as they get what they want! So, it is not the vehicle they like but rather the end result and having listened to the anti-EU democracy arguments for almost 3 years it smacks of hypocrisy. The leader of the House of Commons Jacob Rees-Mogg was heavily criticised by fellow MPs, who accused him of showing contempt for parliament and democracy as he slouched almost reclining flat on the green benches during a debate in September 2019. This highlighted an unparalleled arrogance from someone who is now a representative of the government that acted like the crusader for democracy, when all it appeared was that he wanted a result NOT democracy, as that was a secondary concern to a man obsessed with leaving the EU.

Also, the veiled threats that if they do not get the result "they" feel they deserve people will take to the streets borders on rebellious which seems bizarre when so many Remainers have been called traitors. But it is clearly a deliberate tactic from Brexiteers when they refer to "The People" which is basically the angry right-wing nationalists who have been intimidating and threatening (with their behaviour) pro European MPs, but this is not the average man or woman of the United Kingdom. When they believe in the will of our sovereign parliamentary system and not the EU why would they think OUR parliament would kowtow to an angry mob? The answer is they do not, but they want to spread fear and doubt, which again is hypocritical when Brexiteers have spent 3 years talking about the Remainers Project Fear, and now they generate their own Fear Project on many levels.

We were told they would revolt if we extended again in 2019 and if we did not leave on 1st November 2019, but where were they? There was nothing despite the second extension. But it was an Internet generated fear by keyboard warriors that were too lazy to get up and revolt but also, more importantly, their lives were OK as a full member of the European Union and therefore they were not desperate to leave really. Otherwise they would have been out there on the streets. I have many passionate, really passionate Brexiteer friends and contacts who have never been on one march but are happy to share and comment on any anti EU post on Facebook. Why? Because it's easy and they can do it whilst sitting on their arse! Welcome to Social Media world.

Democracy is a powerful force, but it is not perfect, and the referendum was a prime example of that but Winston Churchill's quote about democracy "Many forms of Government have been tried and will be tried in this world of sin and woe. No one pretends that **democracy** is perfect or all-wise. Indeed, it has been said that **democracy** is the worst form of Government except all those other forms that have been tried from time to time." But Democracy is not one day in 2016 year but rather a process and when the possibility of a second referendum (on the actual negotiated deal) or the so called "People's Vote" was suggested Brexiteers were up in arms that it was a disgrace as we had voted already, and it was undemocratic etc. Undemocratic? How can more democracy be less democracy, especially if it is on something specific i.e. a final withdrawal deal rather than an ideal, that was as we now know based on many lies, deceptions and untruths? Now it is clear why Leavers would not want another vote, as they may lose next time, despite many of them claiming they would win again but with a larger majority. What this reveals is that democracy takes a clear backseat to the end result and the focus on Leaving the EU at any cost and if democracy was the victim of that focus then so be it. Like many of the Brexiteer claims and arguments once the onion is peeled back it reveals some quite unsavoury feelings and, in this case, it is that democracy is not sacred, and secondary to other more important concerns of Brexiteers.

When there were rumours of Russian money having been used to influence the Referendum result, there was no serious questions posed by Brexiteers or any outcry from Leave politicians as they were so happy with the result. Democracy is hailed from the rooftops when it serves their cause but when something as serious as a foreign power having potentially influenced a critical vote democracy suddenly comes a poor second to the result. Even if it was not Russian money the largest ever political donation in the UK by Arron Banks to the Leave campaign had at the time of writing not been satisfactorily explained as to its origins. Mr Banks was on the Andrew Marr show (4th November 2018) to explain where the money came from but through a complex company structure it was not at all clear and he failed to show for example 'look here is the money in XYZ bank account and it was transferred into this bank account on this date' etc. but that did not happen and certainly gave the impression of being shady even if it was not. So Mr. Bank's intention to explain and put the matter to bed backfired and threw up more questions than answers and raised the profile of this potentially illegal donation and its origins. This is now being investigated by the criminal authorities as even if this money was not Russian money and did in fact come directly from Mr. Banks or one of his companies, if they were in the Cayman Islands or the Channel Islands for tax reasons this would still be illegal as these are foreign territories for such donations.

But even if found guilty he will receive a fine which as a multi-millionaire he will easily pay but the damage that that donation has done cannot be rectified as regards the referendum result. Is that the Democracy that Leavers so often praise or is this an abused of the rules knowing the penalties relative to the result are pitiful?

Surely, truth and lies are an important part of democracy also, otherwise how do citizens make informed decisions? If someone voted leave based on the expectation that the NHS would receive an extra £350 million more per week, you would have felt lied to and may very well have made a different decision if that lie was not espoused or was clearly highlighted as a lie and undeliverable. This is where some justification for a People's Vote originates, the lies, biases and misinformation meaning the first referendum was epistemically (of or relating to knowledge or knowing) compromised and would hope that based on what we had seen and learned from the first referendum a second would be fairer. Democracy is and should be a learning system and not a few weeks of lies to deceive the public and therefore it is entirely reasonable to change our mind when we learn from events as many have done in the years following the 2016 EU referendum. In any shop if you are sold a product under false pretences you can take it back, but should such a deceitful and fabricated referendum result be any different? Where are the controls or the moral fibre to stop such things happening or if they do to reverse them?

President Obama highlighted this issue of democracy when criticised by Brexiteers for commenting before the EU Referendum saying, 'I am offering my opinion, and in DEMOCRACIES everybody should want more information, not less, and you shouldn't be afraid to hear an argument being made.'

Did Bernard Jenkin, a Director or Vote Leave, have democracy first in his mind when trying to silence Mark Carney from commenting on the risks of Brexit as the Bank Of England saw them knowing an impartial and non-political BOE is a very important part of our democracy? It was almost like he was trying to stop debate as he did not like the message. Mark Carney to his credit responded that all his interventions had related to the Bank's 'statutory responsibilities', which included a duty to assess the implications of Brexit on the Bank's 'core objectives'.

In July 2019 with Prime minister Johnson confirming a no-deal Brexit will be achieved on 31st October "Do or Die" and not ruling out closing parliament to achieve that if required many people were very worried about this attack on our parliamentary democracy. Michael Heseltine (Former deputy Prime Minister) and Betty Boothroyd (former Labour MP and speaker of the House of Commons) wrote an excellent article in the Sunday times on August the 11th 2019 extolling their horror at Mr. Johnson's dismissive attitude to Parliament if he cannot get his way. These were some of their thoughts in that piece: [43]

- Boris Johnson wants to bypass both people and parliament to force a scorched earth Brexit on the UK.

- He wants to inflict on us the most grotesque act of national self-harm committed in peacetime by a British government.

- He wants to do this despite knowing he does not have a majority in neither the House Of Commons nor the country for no deal.

- Let's be clear: he has absolutely no mandate to take the UK out of the EU on no deal. This vicious form of Brexit was dismissed by him and a host of prominent Leave campaigners in 2016 as "Project Fear".

- Neither of us (Heseltine and Boothroyd) imagines that a prime minister of the UK would set out so deliberately to rip the heart out of our democracy and subvert our parliament.

- For now, it is essential to reaffirm the principle of democracy in which the legislature can, must and will rein in an executive that is lurching out of control.

Brexiteers like to lecture Remainers about the importance of democracy but then the silence is deafening when Boris Johnson or Dominic Raab refused to rule out closing parliament to force through their personal chosen political path. Some people spoke out like Amber Rudd who commented "we are not like Stuart kings", referring to Charles 1s attempts to dismiss Parliament leading to civil war and the bloodshed that followed. But many Brexiteers were silent on this horrific possibility and was this really what Mr. Johnson and Mr. Raab really wanted? Rory Stewart Member of Parliament for Penrith and The Border since 2010 and Conservative leadership contender in 2019 described this eventuality from the PM as "illegal... unconstitutional and it would be undemocratic". Clearly, he is correct to be outraged for someone to achieve Brexit by the back door, and if it happens do we have to throw our hands up and concede 'The lunatics have literally taken over the asylum'?

Democracy was probably the most misunderstood and abused word during and since the referendum campaign by both sides, each using its own personal definition and ignoring or dismissing the other side's use of the terminology. All this seemed to highlight was that democracy did not start and end

426

on one day in 2016, it is a complex and complicated issue where again people could not even come together to admit or accept the other side's opinion and view of British democracy.

The People's vote - Can there be Too much Democracy?

I admit the title 'Peoples Vote' is not great as we could simply call it the confirmatory referendum on the deal but it is not as catchy and does not role of the tongue so the intention was good and seemed with Parliament not being able to decide or even the Government cabinet between them as to the definite course of action, it seems a good idea to pass it back to the people.

Now I understand why Leavers / Brexiteers would not want that (unless of course they had changed their mind after all the chaos and more accurate information we now have) as they had, to their surprise, gained their victory and they could not stomach the result going the other way and do not wish to take that risk.

But some arguments against a confirmatory Vote were plainly laughable such as "if you win then let's have a best of three" which treats it like a game of football in the streets using jumpers for goalposts and not a critical juncture in the UK's history and constitution when we would literally be voting on a deal that had been negotiated and agreed by our independent sovereign government (remember that?). Or the "a second referendum would be undemocratic" which is bizarre in the extreme that more democracy can be called less democracy! If still alive I am sure George Orwell would have had something to say about the language of dictators and fascists when the information and the true picture are now much clearer for a more informed decision to be made.

I am sure Orwell would have agreed that it is extremely worrying when MPs voted for by the people, assuming they are balanced reasonable people, are claiming and calling people traitors and saboteurs as they have a different opinion as they are basically intimidating MPs in order to influence the democratic process, that same democratic process that Leavers wanted so much and wanted to brought back from Brussels. Now they have it and we see the result. Was it really democracy they wanted or just the "Result"?

Rather than a second referendum people would rather watch food and medicine having to be stockpiled, business having no clue what comes next or how

427

to plan for it or watching the Prime Minister basically blackmailing MPs from both the leave and remain wings of Parliament to agree to her or his withdrawal deals. What is becoming clearer every day is that nobody knew what Brexit meant or its implications as there was no small print on the ballot paper telling us what we were ultimately voting for as "Leave means Leave" was and still is an empty useless slogan and means nothing. Some don't care, but some of us do as we know the implications could be serious for our children, our children's children and the less fortunate in our society.

Seems quite democratic to go back to the people and basically say you know that Brexit we promised you, well it doesn't actually exist and as it doesn't really exist, we want to make sure that it is now what you want so we are going to give you another vote with a lot more true information and an actual deal for you to vote on. Surely that is sensible and democratic, particularly as much of what was promised is now not going to be delivered? Could you imagine if you had an injury to your leg and go to hospital and sign a consent form before the operation stating they may have to amputate the leg due to the infection. Afterwards you wake up with no leg and the Doctor says we didn't have to cut the leg off, but we thought as you have consented we would do it anyway, even though you will be worse off. It is the same with Brexit and clearly doesn't work by simply saying well we voted so we cannot change even if we will be worse off.

How can more democracy be less democracy and if people genuinely still feel the same, when we have a deal they can still vote the same way but from a stronger more informed position. Surely, that cannot be a bad thing, unless you are 'Leave at any cost', preferred the ignorance and lies of the 2016 referendum, or know that others have learned so Leave cannot win second time around.

Did Leavers really want Democracy or a simple OUT result?

Brexiteers constantly commented on how we must uphold British democracy and not be dictated to by the EU or the European Court of Justice as our democracy and laws should be recognised and adhered to and not undermined but then on the other hand choose to ignore the illegalities of the deliberate overspending of Vote Leave when they broke electoral law, because presumably that is different as they were so focused on getting the result they wanted. But on the surface this appears like hypocrisy i.e. "I want British laws and democracy to be adhered to and respected, but only if it is in my interest!" Clearly, the retort is that the Government spent £9 million on a pro-remain leaflet sent to all households but this deliberately ignores our legal systems for political expediency and the fact that the Government initiated, and parliament voted to give them a referendum and was mandated to put the government's position forward. Obviously some will shout "Double Standards" here but the Law is the Law, British law the same laws Leavers wanted to be obeyed and adhered to. Double standards? Hypocrisy? I will let you be the judge!

The Prevention of War in Europe

I was amazed how little a role this played in the debate and felt that the Remain camp missed a massive trick as this was the original idea and foundation of the EU and we have not had a European war between EU countries since. So why did it not seem important to campaigners and citizens? Was it the case that only a few people were old enough to remember and experience a war first hand (excluding military personnel that may have served in Iraq, Northern Ireland, The Falklands etc.) that we have become so comfortable that we no longer think there will ever be a war in Europe ever again or at least in their lifetime.

One of the problems we face is that the current political generation as no serious experience of bad times and is very cavalier about precipitating events they cannot control but feel somehow they might exploit (even if they cannot say how!) and this reflects so many Brexiteers. We only have to go back to the pre-First world war era when very few believed or even considered that a very long period of European peace and equilibrium could actually be shattered in months, and this is how quickly these things can materialise.

It could be that the public felt that we are the strongest military power in Europe and therefore if something did escalate, we would have no problem dealing with that?

It looks like not many people at all considered this and important factor or advantage of the EU for various reasons, so it just became a non-issue, but history teaches us to be very cautious and extremely vigilant when it comes to outbreaks of war. The first world war came out of nowhere in 1914 with an obscure Serb dissident shooting the Arch-Duke Ferdinand in Sarajevo. What did that have to do with us? Well quite a lot it turns out, and the rest is literally history.

But many thought we had learned our lesson and such a world war would never happen again. But only 21 years later Hitler and the Nazis were on the March and we all know how that ended with the entire world effectively losing. So why so complacent now? Is Russia not a threat? Iran or North Korea not a threat to world peace? We are stronger in an EU political and economic unit rather than on our own, that is indisputable, despite some macho imperialistic rhetoric coming out of the mouths of Brexiteers.

We should accept that due to the success of the EU there have been no wars between member states ever (fact!) which has allowed NATO and the UK military to better focus on and help keep the UK and other regions safe. If European countries are not waging war on each other, as they have in the past, it can better focus on those, more critical regions and better deploy resources.

The "Condescension complex" (or Patronising Paradox)

This is basically where Remainers were pointing out to tell Leavers the weaknesses or misinformation in their arguments or the information they had been fed but rather than countering with facts or logic to prove their arguments they fire back with you are condescending or patronising or even you are calling them stupid, even though what they were saying was stupid. This effectively closes down the argument for them and means they do not have to defend their position they put forward. An example of this is when they claim a no-deal scenario will be no problem at all but when you highlight issues of the Irish border, trucks stacked up at Dover, potential for stockpiling or even worse lack of critical drugs etc. they claim you are condescending and implying they did not know what they voted for. Even though these examples above were never mentioned as risks during the referendum campaigns.

The interesting development in the 3 years since the referendum was more Leavers, rather than Remainers, that kept saying "you say we did not know what we were voting for" almost as if there was a subconscious or even conscious questioning of themselves whether they were indeed gullible to vote in the way they did. Remember a stupid decision does not make people stupid. This attitude seemed to take place when they realised that reality had reared its ugly head to confront them and many things they were promised or told would be easy are clearly not. There has definitely been a change in the Leaver / Brexiteer psyche which has gone from jubilation and preparation to the sunny uplands of the promised land they were promised to other emotions including anger, frustration, confusion, aggression, and hate to name but a few. Reality has turned out to not be the place they had hoped for, expected or were promised. But they seemed to attack Remainers for highlighting this rather than the pied pipers they followed and believed.

This 'complex' can create more extreme reactions and an example of this I witnessed myself was with the argument: *"we have too many immigrants in this country"* but one counters with "but we have the lowest unemployment for decades, the highest Employment for decades plus we have many vacancies to fill, so how can we have too many immigrants?" The extreme fallout of this encounter was an angry response of "You are now calling me a racist!" Now we cover racism in another part of the book, but you can see how poor arguments or poor 'beliefs' lack logic or substance can result in an extreme response and anger, with people like Nigel Farage fuelling such extremism, where frustration with many aspects of their lives can be exploited. This could very easily lead to violence. [The death of] Jo Cox, MP comes to mind.

But where people have these strong views and air them quite freely we have to ask ourselves and society why do they think that way? Do they genuinely believe we have too many, in which case they are wrong and need somehow to be educated or convinced that this cannot be the case, or they do know we need more immigrants to help drive our economy and choose to ignore this and so what do they have against immigrants if they know we need them? Does this make them racists or are they simply frightened individuals that cannot handle or work with multiculturalism, or perhaps they do not understand the diverse cultures we now welcome in the UK in this more global world, which is where these prejudices formulate themselves?

The interesting dynamic to this is that it is often big strong sometimes aggressive men appearing brave on the right-wing marches in their groups following the likes of Tommy Robinson who are the most outspoken talking about the tough great British brave lions draped in Union Jacks, etc. But is it these people that are actually inside the most frightened of the developments in the UK and in reality the bravado and bravery (rather like some football fan hooligan groups) they demonstrate in their gangs that maybe masks frustrated poorly educated individuals that feel society has left them behind and they are simply looking for a way to protest and immigrants are an easy target being visible and by default a small minority and easy to abuse? Does it make them feel good and even powerful for a short period of time? This may be over thinking the issues for some, as some simply do not like foreigners or anything new and different and will

431

act out their fears accordingly.

One Brexiteer (and he will not be the only one) told me his reason (a rather old fashioned nationalistic one) for voting Leave was "The right to live in a country controlled entirely by people who live in that country", and he did not believe immigrants should vote unless they had been in the country for many years, but unable to clarify how many years. So basically, a two-tier system.
To which I replied "So basically you feel it is acceptable for people to lose their jobs, costs to rise, the pound to plummet, have not a clue about future trade, go from the largest trading block in the world to nothing (i.e. from the premier league to the third division through choice!), for British citizens to lose their freedom of movement rights, stockpile medicines and products as if going back to the war, and reduce many of our standards etc. all for some abstract idea of sovereignty (that we never lost!) and rule-making none of which you can name?

I actually asked him which EU law he would change tomorrow, that would improve the UK, but he couldn't name one. As he couldn't name one and felt a bit stupid when that was apparently his 'true' reason for voting Leave he then went off on some other rant / tangent. Getting aggressive and rude implying condescension again.

When you look at it like that it looks pretty dumb I am sure you would agree. But Was that his real reason or is immigration hiding away under the surface somewhere bubbling away but he lacked the courage to say that? Perhaps its their fear of political correctness, that makes it very difficult to get honest replies from Brexiteers for some reason?

Apparently it is condescending if we question why people voted leave when they say they all voted for the same thing and one questions that. But when you break it down for Brexiteers by saying many people voted leave for different reasons, many of which will not be satisfactorily addressed by leaving the EU they get angry and tend to shout "we just want out" without thinking the consequences through.

So, we have to ask ourselves how many of those reasons for leaving would genuinely be improved or addressed by leaving the EU, as some of them could be worsened. Would any of the following be improved by Brexit? Suffered at the hands of Globalisation? Too many immigrants? End austerity? Foodbanks? Homelessness? Lack of investment in the NHS? Lack of investment in mental health? I fear these people may be greatly disappointed.

Chapter 29
Recent Developments & The Future?

Before and After

When one looks back and analyses what was said and how this changed over time, you realise how much bullshit (and in Street terms it was exactly that, no matter how some like to flower it up!) was spouted to get the result required, but how it changed once reality set in and the vote was won.

It was amusing how Project Fear transformed into 'the people knew what they were voting for' or claims that living standards would not be hit transforms into 'people knew there would be a short term cost', which came about largely because it was genuinely starting to happen and the liars could not hide so they updated the message. Remember Rees-Mogg told us short term could be 50 years! Very remiss of him he forgot to mention that minor point during the campaign do you not think?

Remember the Leave campaign talked of many ways of leaving such as the Norway solutions (which is a member of the EEA like Lichtenstein and Iceland) mainly because Brexiteers could not decide on the best way to leave or even have a framework or plan. But now 3+ years after the result suddenly that didn't happen, and the vote was always to leave the customs union and single market no matter what the cost or even without any deal whatsoever, again whatever the cost. So desperate have they become, since the Leave campaign told us we would get a great deal from the EU as they would be desperate, and it would be a vote for the easiest deal in history. How things have changed.

Nobody can deny that what was promised is nowhere even close to the unsatisfactory position we found ourselves in after the referendum and has endured ever since up until the time of writing and the foreseeable future. We can therefore only conclude that the big swindle succeeded but has now backfired and the firefighting, recriminations and excuses are rapidly afoot.

Observations since the Referendum result

Despite all the chaos, the clear issues with making Brexit happen as well as the costs to the UK including job losses that have already taken place there appears to be little regret or buyer's remorse that Leavers have made the wrong vote and decision, which should intrigue us and one of the reasons it would be good to have a second referendum would be to see just how much reality would make people change their mind. But talking to people it seems like it is a mixture of genuinely not understanding the negative impacts of a no-deal Brexit, the pride of not being able to change their mind as people had been telling them before, during and after the referendum what a bad and nonsensical decision leave was. Also, this powerful irrational fear of immigration and immigrants, especially amongst the older generations was still palpable and even though some felt that immigration would not be reduced because we need the workers, they felt there is a much better chance of dramatically reducing the number of immigrants if we leave the EU. Even if that is not the case in practice. It is not based on any facts or evidence but rather hope and faith, similar to a religious person still believing that Jesus did walk on water even though everything you have learnt and know tells you that is not physically possible, realistic, and there is zero evidence. It is amazing to listen to and witness this, albeit obviously very saddening at the same time.

One of the most disappointing developments immediately after the referendum was the increase in racial abuse where some felt due to the Leave result that they could tell foreigners to go home, some of whom had lived in the UK for 20+ years, and some people now try to tell you the referendum was not about

434

immigration! As a British person such behaviour is embarrassing and reprehensible but when one reflects on some of the speeches, posters and rhetoric from the likes of Nigel Farage et al. who claimed, for example, that the Referendum "had been won without a single bullet being fired" despite poor Joe Cox, a mother and the MP for Batley and Spen having been shot and stabbed when assassinated by a right-wing extremist shouting "Britain First" as he carried out his disgusting act. If you do not find that disgusting there is probably something amiss.

Had the result and such rhetoric been understood by a number of people as a green light to abuse the people they had been told are the root cause of many of their problems? As we have cited in this book, the numbers of reported hate crimes (doesn't obviously include the unreported!) spiked after the EU referendum result which is covered elsewhere in the book.

What will happen with Boris and Brexit?

When I first wrote this section. Johnson was not PM but rather sniffing around number 10 like an Tom cat looking to urinate on the doorstep to make his mark. Well he is now inside but arrives in this position with background of jettisoned jobs, principles and relationships. Ha had a reputation of only caring about what is in Boris Johnson's interest which concerned many now he had been given the number one job.

As usual with Boris Johnson as PM who knows but it will be a roller coaster with a general election now set for 12th December 2019. He is clearly someone that is inconsistent, economical with the truth, doesn't seem to know what he will do himself next, is often poorly briefed, makes promises he cannot keep, and has shown many examples of simply saying whatever he thinks will get him what he wants. It is quite amazing with someone of his history of gaffs, lies and cavalier use of the English language was even being considered for such a position let alone achieving it. That is privilege and connections for you. But how will Brexit and Prime Minister Johnson develop?

I remember around 18 months ago saying at least we couldn't get a Donald Trump character as Prime Minister in the UK – shit how wrong was I! A YouGov poll in June 2019 even found 59% would not buy a used car from Boris

Johnson! Now this may sound funny at first glance but that is how far we have sunk that 59% of people polled and probably of the country based on his history think our next PM is Del Boy from Only Fools and Horses.

He has so far made, so many promises including more money for this and more money for that whilst also cutting tax for anyone earning more than £50,000 which obviously includes him, the other MPs and his mates (later withdrawn before the election), so those at the bottom that have suffered most from austerity and globalisation that voted for Leave to hopefully improve their lives will be greatly disappointed. Left behind again? Many people say he is intelligent, but he does a really good act (if it is an act?) of hiding it well with his bumbling and muddled thinking. But hopefully he and his advisers care about the budget deficit which is expected to be nearly £30 Billion in 2019. Public sector debt is rising in cash terms to around £1.8 Trillion which is more than 5 times its level 20 years ago and more than three times what it had been before the 2008-9 financial crisis and up by nearly £800 billion since the Tories came to power (in coalition) in 2010. But they told us austerity would significantly reduce this.

At the time of writing he has said definitely leaving "deal or no deal", "do or die" on the 31st October but showing a serious lack of understanding of many of the things that would have to be done to achieve that and waffling around his ideas or lack of ideas as to how he is actually going to achieve that. The fact is the timing of 31st October was unrealistic due to the timescales and time for negotiation but people were not putting it past Boris to try to get a no-deal Brexit through the Commons just to crash out and then see what happens, as frightening as that sounds. No deal is still on the cards. Even when told it was unrealistic he reiterated his "would rather die in a ditch" statement, but then what happened? Yes, he requested an extension leaving his political opponents asking, "where was the ditch?"

Therefore, this is the shortest section of the book because who the really knows when it comes to Boris Johnson, Dominic Cummings and the crew when they do not know themselves. His pantomime insistence that everything will be fine just as long as we think positive and have lots of energy. OMG that is his plan! It is reminiscent of a sales conference I attended once and the speaker said (and I encourage all of you to do this) take the cup on your desk and think really positive and focus so hard like you have never focused or felt so positive before and convince yourself the colour of the cup is going to change. Please try harder and harder and think more positive than ever before as Boris wants you to. What happened? Clearly nothing and this was the message of the speaker that no matter how positive you think nothing will change until someone takes action and that is where his problems start, as Boris has no clue what those actions are. But he is happy in that ignorance as he now has the top job. It's all about the top job for Bojo! Basically, he has blagged his way into it with positive thought energy and his Etonian contacts, but little else.

In September 2019 Johnson and his team said they were confident of getting a deal with the EU but put in no concrete changes compared to Teresa May's deal and when pushed he resembled a graduate that had not done the requisite work and is trying to bluff his way through the exam with limited knowledge of the curriculum. His team claim they are trying "turbo charging" negotiations and had made steps forward although the EU seemed completely unaware of this and reports of Dominic Cummings privately admitting the negotiations in Brussels are a "sham" added to the fears that Mr. Johnson and his cabinet have no intention of realistically trying to get a deal. It should be noted that he only got a deal as he took Teresa May's deal he voted against twice made a couple of minor changes and moved the backstop into the Irish Sea (effectively creating a 'Front stop') which Mrs May had rejected as it treats Northern Ireland differently. The union has changed, but Boris doesn't care about that as it is just collateral damage for his political ambition.

It could also be argued that some of the cabinet, based on some of their comments, still do not appreciate or understand the huge complexities of Brexit which is concerning. There has been a movement of Conservative principles or thinking of country first as the Chancellor Sajid Javid ditched fiscal prudence in pre-election 'gifts' to the public and a war chest for advertising and preparations for Brexit. So, Brexit has hit the public finances already.

In October 2019 it was being questioned whether Boris Johnson genuinely understood the critical issues of withdrawing from the EU especially when he put forward his solution for the Irish border. The reason the EU could not accept it was because it would basically impose a new customs border in Ireland that would be both intrusive and unenforceable. It would give a veto over every aspect of Northern Ireland's future to the DUP, making a fragile peace settlement hostage to a party that rejected the Good Friday Agreement.[61] Maybe it was never a genuine offer and was just aimed to move blame for the blocking of a deal to the EU, who knows as Mr. Johnson's relationship with the truth is infamous?

One of the concerns with Boris Johnson being PM is that our constitution is based on precedence and norms with most of our checks and balances based on decency and people acting fairly and rationally and not for their own political gains even when willing to be economical with the truth. That does not bode well for the country when this system faces a serial proven deceiver in Mr. Johnson, and we should all be very concerned about that.

We have seen indications of the future with the drip feeding of poisonous announcements from Priti Patel's home office that will have direct impact on people's lives, but they just don't think it will be them. Mrs Patel in an interview even claimed poverty was not the governments fault and not just their responsibility! This is surely a dereliction of duty or even compassion from someone that had only been in the job 5 minutes! Does she even care? The Conservative government slipped out a Press Release on the first day of the Labour Party's conference in 2019 saying they would only fund health care for Brits in the EU for six months (including cancer treatment) with a no deal Brexit, or 12 months if people had just started treatment! We should not forget that a part of what we pay into the EU as part of our membership is paying for such services in the EU 27 countries to better support our British nationals abroad. This truly is playing politics with people's lives and is a real problem as the creep of nastiness back into the Conservative party could be significant and lasting.

We should not take rights (workers' rights, human rights etc.) for granted otherwise a government can soon make them privileges which they give us and therefore can take away. Brexit reduces freedoms such as our freedom of movement across 28 countries for example and with the lack of guarantees from this latest government towards our EU citizens that have been contributing for many years to our economy and social services, etc. is very concerning. If you want to see how a country / Government will treat its citizens see how it treats its foreign workers / visitors as if this is very poor then we are just one step away from how then the government will deal with its people in future if it wants. This has been seen numerous times in history especially 1930s Germany where it began with foreigners such as the Jewish community but rapidly spread to the terrorising of German citizens as well.

What happens when we leave?

It should be highlighted very strongly here that no country has ever done this before anywhere in the world and there is a very good reason for that notably they normally, like the UK, have a good free trade deal and working relationships. This future is totally unknown, and the risks are vast (many unknown yet), so vast

438

that the risk never equals the reward as many would now say with Brexit and the UK.

Under pressure to produce something of 'substance' Vote Leave produced this document (http://voteleavetakecontrol.org/briefing_newdeal.html) to try to show what they think 'Leave' looks like. This document could actually be changed and updated as any online document can but when I printed it out on 7th February 2019 at 17.20 it had some interesting aspects. Firstly, it was still claiming we are sending £350 million per week to Brussels when this has been totally disproven on numerous occasions and even Nigel Farage has abandoned that figure. This does sound warning bells to the credibility, honesty and accuracy of this document and therefore the Vote Leave organisation as a whole but let us investigate a bit further. It says we will have a 'UK-EU treaty based on free trade and friendly cooperation' which is pie in the sky and the EU has already shown that we cannot have the same benefits without paying a 'membership' fee. They claim we will take back control of our migration policy without highlighting what that will cost us or the fact the part of our immigration we control is larger than the EU immigration and that EU immigration has dropped since the referendum campaign.

We will regain our seat on international bodies' (e.g. WTO) implying we will have more influence on our own as a part of 60 million people than as a part of the EU with 500 million and the largest free trade block in the world, which is obviously nonsense. 'We will build a new European Institutional architecture that enables all countries, whether in or out of the Euro, to trade freely and cooperate in a friendly way' which again is just fanciful and makes literally no sense, and bodes one question who is believing and not questioning such claims? 'We will negotiate a new UK-EU Treaty and end the legal supremacy of EU law and the European court before 2020' which will mean we have a worse deal as how can we get the same or better if outside the EU, plus the ECJ is not a problem? You just ask any normal man / woman on the street what it is and how it negatively affects their life! But it is now December 2019, and nothing has happened.

The document also refers back to Jacques Delors and the 1980s as a simple diversion as it is irrelevant to today's situation and ignores that standardisation helps transparency and keeps the cost of trade down for EU AND UK companies. It claims, 'every Prime Minister' has tried to oppose something and they have failed.' Without any examples and failing to mention Maggie Thatcher achieving the UK rebate (or UK correction) from the EU. This is a financial mechanism that reduces the United Kingdom's contribution to the EU budget in effect since 1985. ... Although the rebate is not set in the EU treaties, it is negotiated as part of the Multi-annual Financial Framework (MFF) every seven years and must be unanimously agreed. It claims we are stopping skilled labour coming into the UK but again no evidence or examples whatsoever and why would we stop the skilled labour coming in and supporting our economy? It seemed to deliberately avoid mentioning any details of the WTO despite that now seeming to be the leave preferred position (forgetting their unrealistic requests from a free trades deal) mentioning it only once. But this makes sense as if you go into any details you have to look at the fact that the WTO also has hundreds of rules and regulations that we have to adhere to which flies in the face that we are fully independent and can do what we like as this sovereign power.

It states 'In many areas we will continue existing arrangements at least for a while' which shows that the rules cannot be so bad as they would like to imply and avoids the complexities of what will follow afterwards which is quite deliberate as they do not know. The final claim that is confusing is when it states, 'The great advantage of a 'Leave' vote is it gives Britain wider options. It is the best move regardless of how the EU responds' – this is just madness and cannot be true simply because 44% of our trade is with the EU and how they react WILL have an impact as every action has a reaction, and this unfortunately summed up the impression of a document that promised so much and was Vote Leave's opportunity to be factual, focused and exhibit a detailed plan. It was meant to be their 'Bible', but it ended up being their 'Beano comic'.

Even after the campaigns had finished and 3 years after Leave had won the referendum, Eurosceptic arguments and debates so many of the Brexiteer arguments seemed to have or need people or organisations to blame which included Remainers (or Remoaners or Remainiacs as they detrimentally like to refer to them), the EU in general (no specifics), Jeremy Corbyn, Jean-Claude Juncker, Tony Blair, Mark Carney and the Bank Of England, the BBC, David Cameron, George Osborne, The European Commission, the European Parliament, The Lib Dems, Chuka Umunna, Nicola Sturgeon, and the CBI to name but a few. The fact that often scapegoats are needed tends to indicate that the arguments for Brexit are weak or were based on misinformation or are just incorrect, otherwise why would you need to blame people and make the arguments personal rather than just simply explaining and clarifying the clear and detailed way forward for a better United Kingdom outside the EU?

Leavers – Will you genuinely get what you wanted?

As someone that voted Remain I make no secret of the disappointment that we lost the vote. But I feel that maybe it could be the Leavers that end up being most disappointed as they may not get very much of what they voted for and were told it would all be "very easy" by David Davis et al. Now it is very difficult to know exactly why people voted to Leave and to list them all would be a challenge just demonstrating there is no such thing as the "will of the people" as some claim. But let's for a moment look at some of the major reasons we know people voted to Leave.

- Reason 1 – Immigration

  o   We need immigration in this country to help drive our economy as we do not have the skills or people to do specific jobs so whether or not this is controlled via Visas (which is expensive to manage), they are already here many of whom will stay here, and more will come. The non-EU immigration is controlled as you know but the numbers of this is higher than the EU, therefore so-called control is not a guarantee of reducing numbers. What Leavers may see over time is less Polish accents (especially as many Poles are returning home as the Polish economy is doing very well currently) but replaced by more African, Indian and Pakistani faces. Was that what Leavers voted for or expected?

- Reason 2 – Return of sovereignty

  o   As the UK always was sovereign, they will notice limited change, and actually one must question whether they genuinely wanted sovereignty or whether sovereignty was ever a true issue (maybe code for immigration?) as once our independent sovereign parliament was discussing the plans to leave the EU and it wasn't going as Leavers wanted the verbal attacks and abuse of our MPs such as Anna Soubry took place. So how can you call for bringing back the sovereignty you

441

feel you have lost but then attack it as it is not giving you what you want? Was it more about getting what Leavers wanted i.e. out of the EU and sovereignty was a suitable label to hide behind with the fear of feeling or being called racist if the main thrust was stopping immigration? Perhaps they didn't actually understand what sovereignty meant and just repeated it parrot fashion.

■　　　Reason 3 – Not having Laws set by the European Court of Justice (ECJ)

o　　What I found amusing by this argument was that laws ARE NOT set in the ECJ. European Union law is the system of laws operating within the member states of the European Union. The EU has political institutions and social and economic policies. According to its Court of Justice, the EU represents "a new legal order of international law". The EU's legal foundations are the Treaty of the European Union and the Treaty on the Functioning of the European Union, unanimously agreed by the governments of 28 member states.

For full disclosure the ECJ's specific focus is to ensure that "the law is observed" "in the interpretation and application" of the Treaties of the European Union. To achieve this, it:

■　　　reviews the legality of actions taken by the EU's institutions;

■　　　enforces compliance by member states with their obligations under the Treaties; and

■　　　interprets European Union law.

But that inaccuracy aside whenever I asked someone that spoke of this or claimed it was a reason for leaving (plus those I heard on Radio Phone-ins like LBC interviews etc.) "What laws would you change that were set by the EU?" I get a blank look or a retort of that isn't the point, it's a point of principle! This point of principle seems strange when they do not know what laws are made by the EU or negatively impact their lives but it's a principle? When speaking or communicating with them it appeared, they had indeed been impacted by the constant Eurosceptic press over the years as it had sunk into their Psyche and therefore influenced their opinion or vision of the EU. If it was not this then maybe they are just anti-EU, Anti-foreigner, Racist, or maybe all of the above? But in their 'defence' maybe they probably don't even know it? Otherwise there is no logic or reason in their opposition to the ECJ.

In every Free Trade Agreement or other international agreement there is an arbitration mechanism for obvious reasons. Within the EU the arbitration mechanism for all issues is the ECJ, but even with the Canada EU FTA there is a supra-national arbitration mechanism, and there will be one in every single Free Trade Agreement the UK agrees and signs.

The nonsense about laws made by bureaucrats is just that nonsense and does not stand up to scrutiny as harmonisation of laws, standards, and regulations benefit all Europeans by providing a level and consistent environment for business, life, and work for all across the 28 countries.

The cost of Brexit?

The treasury has said in the past that leaving the EU could lead to a drop in tax revenue of between £38 and £66 billion each year compared to if we remain in the EU, which was based on the expectation that the economy will grow less compared to if we remain in the EU, as if people get paid less money and UK based companies make less profits they pay less in taxes, etc. That large figure of £66 billion is about a half of what we spend on the whole of the NHS which is significant and even if it was on the smaller side, it would still be a significant loss to our economy and our public services with no tangible benefit.

Before and after the referendum the Treasury and the Bank Of England are accused of Fake News or Project Fear etc, admittedly from Brexiteers with a vested interest but the BoE's job is to forecast probable and possible outcomes of any significant development or event that could affect the UK economy, which is exactly what it did. Yes, the numbers are huge and very concerning but they are based on some form of logic where clearly the risks of additional costs, reduced growth, reducing our business with our largest trading partner across the channel, and other negative effects on our economy are there with no tangible benefits with no free trade deals etc. so they are effectively just doing their job.

As stated the level of costs will only be defined over time but we should not accept the defence of Brexiteers of 'you haven't got a crystal ball so do not know exactly what will happen'. This is obviously true but as in life one makes informed calculated decisions to help optimise, the chances of success and not blind choices based on emotion on emotion and no idea of costs, impacts, implications or any other logical thought process. Otherwise that is plain dumb. Yes, people do take such decisions and often they do not end well, but they are personal decisions that only really impact themselves and not 60 million people including their children and their children's children.

The fact is even before we have left and not saved a penny the EU referendum result has already cost us Billions (as of 2019) with no discernible benefit. These costs include but are not limited to:

■   Offering a multi-million-pound contract to a ferry company with no ships, which was then cancelled but led to Eurotunnel receiving 33 Million in compensation because of Chris Grayling's department not tendering the contract correctly. Total cost of this farcical exercise was £50 million to UK taxpayers!

■   A study by Standard & Poors in March 2019 found Brexit had cost the UK economy £66 Billion or around £1,000 for every person in the country. This was due to slashing of business investment and around 3% has been wiped off GDP which it estimates is about £550 million of economic growth per week, a sharp drop in the pound reduced people's purchasing power which reduced household spending. Despite the weaker pound the UK enjoyed no significant increase in overseas sales, the analysis found.

■   Costs rose due to the devaluation of Sterling.

■   A Goldman Sachs report found a similar picture to S & P estimating the chaotic exit from the EU has cost the economy about 600 million pounds per week since the 2016 referendum.

The claims from some Brexiteers that a no-deal Brexit will cost us nothing and we can simply leave is nonsense and they know that or should do. Part of the divorce will have to be paid which at the time of writing was estimated at £33 Billion but with another extension this could reduce, a reduction in economic output will cost the country, £1.5 billion was allocated by the Chancellor Philip Hammond for Brexit preparations, then new Chancellor Sajid Javid promised another £2.1 Billion in 2019, cost of cancelled ferry contracts, and the cost of employing more extra customs officers at the HMRC will have an impact the irony of which is that if we don't have enough suitable skilled British people more immigrants will have to be employed! Introducing a points-based immigration system will also add additional costs to allow the same number of immigrants into the country. It is addressing a problem that does not exist and will not give some Brexiteers what they wanted, i.e. less immigrants.

The true cost of Brexit will only become clear at least 10 Years from now and will be very difficult to nail down as there will be so many variables, what-if and maybes, results looked at relevant to other countries, etc. But the fact remains that it was a very emotive decision with no plan or real concrete ideas of how the future outside the EU was going to create a better country for our citizens, which should be the bottom line of any government decisions or huge constitutional change as leaving the EU is. Clearly, ardent Brexiteers will say it was the right decision whatever happens to the UK. One thing is clear Billions of extra costs means Billions less for the NHS, social services and schools.

Other Possible Costs and inconveniences post Brexit

Roaming Fees

The EU with its block power puts pressure on the Mobile phone providers to reduce the horrendous costs they were charging when people were using their mobile devices in other countries. The EU legislation now means you are charged the same fee as if you were at home, but as Mrs. May said the UK would be leaving the EU's "Digital Single Market" meaning we will no longer be covered by these rules, therefore an additional cost to UK citizens. Dominic Raab in September 2018 stated that Vodafone and Three have "publicly said that they wouldn't introduce any roaming fees for the UK consumers travelling on the continent", but that was not correct as Vodafone had at the time NOT ruled it out! So Mr. Raab, a Leaver, not exactly being accurate again. But the bottom line is no advantage in this area to leaving the EU apart from potentially added cost.

New Driving Licenses

If we leave the EU without a deal or driving licences are not included in any deal UK citizens may need an International Driving Permit (IDP) alongside their driving licence to drive in the EU. This will probably not be a high cost, but it is an additional cost / inconvenience / paperwork and the time for applying and waiting for the permit etc.

Cost to families

Mark Carney at the Bank Of England stated on 22 May 2018 that since the referendum families "real household incomes are about £900 per household lower than we forecast in May 2016 which is a lot of money. The question is why and what drove the difference. Some of it (and we can't be absolute about it) is arguably ascribed to Brexit". But when questioned Mr. Carney confirmed that some of this change could be due to Brexit. But we have not even left yet or suffered the medium- or longer-term detrimental effects of Brexit. So worse could be on its way.

Obviously Brexiteers do not think any of this will happen, and that we will do lots more trade with the Commonwealth and the continent of Africa, but as highlighted elsewhere in this book they do not offer the riches some Brexiteers would have you believe. Some Brexiteers I spoke to almost used this as a smoke screen to justify their position and either did not believe that or didn't actually know very much at all about potential UK trade with Africa or the commonwealth.

Chapter 30
The Winners?

What have the Leavers won?

There was a question 3 years after the referendum I asked many Leavers "What have you won?" and they genuinely struggled to articulate this without empty slogans such as 'Leave means Leave', 'sovereignty' and 'independence'. The economic advantages of continuing membership of the EU are clear to most and the experts back that up and the obvious and potentially extreme disruption and inherent costs of Brexit make it look on the surface as a foolish decision to Leave. But that is with the benefit of hindsight as we now know and have experienced a lot since the referendum that has highlighted many issues and information that have enlightened the debate with many. Unfortunately, with the referendum being what it was one could claim it is too little too late, especially when one considers the 20 years of lies and exaggeration from the British Press.

Many commentators and experts believe that Brexit will be damaging for the UK at least short term and a number of economists say medium term as many of our companies and industries would have to restructure and that does not happen overnight. But the question is what is short-term? What is medium term? This can mean different things to different people. Jacob Rees-Mogg stated in a Channel 4 interview that the benefits of Brexit could take 50 years to be evident.

Yes 50 years – aren't you pleased you voted to Leave now? More immediately experts are saying Brexit will have a damaging effect on the British economy, some of which are dire indeed, and this implies that the Rees-Mogg obsession with the EU for decades has made him decide it is Leave 'at any cost'. This dogmatic 'at any cost' frame of mind means he appears he does not want to or is incapable of changing his mind in the face of expert predictions and forecasts.

The UK has spent Billions, yes Billions, on Brexit with no obvious, tangible discernible benefits and many downsides so there are no winners in this exercise in national absurdity, based on lies and invention that reached another level made possible by a very biased press as we have shown and Social Media and the Internet to speed up and take those lies and distortions around the country and the world very quickly and so fast we could no longer control it, if we ever could any way! The only guarantee is that it is going to cost the UK Billions in the short to medium term which is less money for the NHS and social services.

What voters did not vote for!

We heard and still do hear a lot about what Leave voters voted for, although this does seem to turn into basically "OUT" without any concern for what that really means and the implications for the UK economy, jobs, society and ultimately our people, especially the poorer people in our society. Many of the things Leavers were promised and consequently voted for will not come to pass so they will be ultimately disappointed but many things that could come to pass, especially with a no-deal Brexit, that they did not vote for which include the following:

Shortages of critical imported medicines, people losing their jobs as outside the Single European Market some companies cannot compete and / or function if they need a frictionless supply system. These results in loss of a company's corporation Tax, VAT contributions, national Insurance and job creation, as well as the employee's tax and National Insurance contributions and wages they spend on the high street or in our economy. Plus, they will then claim unemployment benefits to support themselves and their families, creating a further strain on the exchequer's purse strings! The risks to food supplies etc. will also be a concern both in terms of sourcing quality of food from outside the EU and the rising costs of that food, but also some types of fresh food supply could decrease.

Bank of England governor Mark Carney claimed food prices could rise between 5-10 percent if there was a disorderly Brexit in December 2018, where he told MPs on the Treasury Committee: "In the most extreme scenario, your shopping bill goes up 10 percent." The reason this is the case is that 28% of the UK's food for consumers comes from EU (source = www.gov.co.uk) and even more so 79% of food imported to UK by supermarkets comes from the EU (Source British Retail Consortium / Defra). We have not left yet but the principle remains.

Former Salisbury's CEO and food Director at Marks & Spencer Justin King stated there will be "gaps on the shelves within a week" if there is no deal in place, which is largely because "30-40% of our produce at that time of the year is coming from the European Union." The issue is also highlighted by Minette batters, who farms in Wiltshire, says the country is producing only enough food to be self-sufficient for 61% of the year. She says that the UK needs to grow more in case supplies are affected by a no-deal Brexit.

Who voted for that? Would anyone today realistically and sensibly put their hand up for that? No, they didn't, but it is not their fault as people did not and still do not to a great degree understand the workings of international trade or the EU (apart from may be the very bias nonsense our right wing press asserts, and we cover in a separate part of the book) or how it impacts on their everyday lives. But we should hold those to account that do understand the EU but still attempt to misinform and use inflammatory for their own personal gains such as Nigel Farage or Boris Johnson.

It is possible that at the end of 2019 and the impending threat of a no-deal exit from the EU the employment numbers may start to be affected after many years of great developments as a member of the EU. In August 2019 the UK unemployment rate moved up to 37,000 or 3.9% with the number of vacancies falling which may indicate the Brexit effect will hit the UK more than it has done so far, with the global slow down also playing a role.

Did people honestly vote for their country scampering around making desperate preparations for exiting the EU reminiscent of pre-war conditions? This has included stockpiling products, foodstuffs and medicines, at considerable costs, including buying up or at least renting many industrial fridges to be able to store the aforementioned medications. How have Brexiteers put the 6th world's largest economy in that position? We should be ashamed that we have put our people and citizens in such an unenviable position.

Why no second referendum?

Many of you will know this as "The People's Vote". I understand why people called it this as they wanted to differentiate it from the Referendum of 2016 but effectively it is and would be a second referendum or confirmatory referendum on an actual deal. But the difference, and it is a clear difference, is that we would genuinely be voting for a specific deal, e.g. Boris Johnson's deal. If one is voting for something specific, then that specific deal can be analysed and dissected much more accurately than the original idealistic picture painted by the Leave campaigns, which are now clearly proving to have no resemblance to reality. On reflection this would have been a better plan and idea from Cameron originally, but this was not the case, and parliament even enacted Article 50 also without a plan, so it is no surprise that chaos and confusion has ensued in the proceeding 3 years.

Even Dominic Cummings, the arch architect of the Leave result, wrote a BLOG suggesting himself that there could be a second referendum after an 'OUT' vote, in which the public could give their views on any subsequent deal with Brussels. The clear problem after the first disaster and its many weaknesses becoming apparent is that parliament would struggle to agree on its form including what question and how many questions etc. although this is possible if there was the political bravery and will to do it, but this is unlikely. Yet many would say that now that people are realising what Brexit REALLY means they deserve the chance to say whether they still want it. Is that not true democracy, and why would a democracy be frightened of that?

Some polls suggested that Brexit voters would still support a no-deal Brexit in a second referendum, but this is easy when asked about a hypothetical situation. People are not stupid and if they were faced with such a genuine decision that would become law many would probably vote to remain now they now know they and their families will probably lose out economically and their livelihoods could suffer considerably. Clearly, a minority would want Brexit whatever the outcomes but that is more of a dogmatic position rather than a more considered logical position, but their vote counts the same as everybody else's of course.

Yes it would resurrect bitter arguments and infuriate leavers, who would see it as a rematch of the contest they had already won (although as posed in this book already 'What would they have won?'), but with almost 4 years of water under the proverbial bridge since the 2016 vote it may be more important than ever to check that voters are really in favour of what appears to being done in their name.

At the time of writing polls showed public support and there is just about a majority for it in parliament, when they cannot seem to agree on anything else! Unless Brexiteers are afraid of the result going against them, surely it makes sense that with all these facts highlighted in this book were predominantly unknown or ignored in 2016 and now with all these new facts and information the people should be allowed to make a more informed decision.

There are so many things in Boris Johnson's withdrawal agreement that was never even mentioned during the referendum campaigns, so it would seem sensible to put it back to the people for clarity as to was that really what they wanted with all this new information? Did anyone tell the voters there would be £39 Billion to pay when we leave? Or that there would be a separate status for Northern Ireland post Brexit? Or that there would be a border down the Irish Sea? Did anyone tell us that? I think not so a confirmatory vote would make sense. We have found ourselves in a culture war created or at least revealed by the referendum vote and to clear the air and be clear what the people want, a confirmatory vote would be the best and fairest choice.

Chapter 31
The End?

Brexit – will it actually happen?

If I knew that for sure including when and how I would play the lottery numbers immediately but unfortunately nobody does or can know. My feeling is it will happen despite the negatives and downsides as no MP or political party would have the courage to revoke Article 50 for political reasons. At their Political conference in Bournemouth in 2019 the Liberal Democrats did indeed pass a policy to revoke Article 50, but this is easy when you know you are not going to win a majority in parliament. The question is not 'if' but 'when and how' i.e. how hard or soft the Brexit will be. A no-deal Brexit could still happen although the so-called Hilary Benn bill (European Union (Withdrawal) (No. 2) Act 2019) makes this more unlikely as we have now extended until 31st January 2020 but if a FTA with the EU is not agreed we are back at the point of a no deal which was never mentioned in 2016.

If one considers that electoral laws were broken, numerous lies the Leave campaigns told, the public now appearing to have learned from the last 3 years since the vote including those myths and growing support for remaining in the EU due to the obvious risks they see to them and their families, as well as the potential use of Russian and foreign funds. Plus, if you want a free and fair election not unfairly influenced, one would logically say Brexit should not happen. But political pressure says it will. No deal is clearly the worst of all scenarios (which nobody was pushing for or even discussed in any depth at the referendum vote) as we become an outsider after being a senior member of 40+ years of the largest free trade area in the world and all the economic and legal arrangements, regulations and regulatory bodies that are included in that tightly organised Pan European body. But Boris' deal is not much better than Teresa May's just offering different coloured unicorns.

How far people are willing to go to win?

The clear line between good and bad and what is acceptable has been torn up and many now have had their moral compass thrown into disarray and will accept almost anything and almost believe anything to get their desired result, and that should concern us all going forward. We have now seen with Farage and his Brexit party as they have had a taste of anything goes and I do not have to be accountable for anything so why not do it again?

This theory of the perfect storm has a lot of credibility when one considers the limited reforms of the EU despite calls from various corners of the EU which would add to its democratic legitimacy. This led to its difficulty in handling such crises as the debt crisis of 2010-11 especially with the vastly different economies within the EU with Germany at one end and Greece at the other extreme all inside one umbrella currency of the EURO and one monetary policy. This inflexibility saw Greece suffer considerably at the hands of Germany who had to bail Greece out, but at a price! But the Greeks had no other realistic option but to accept the conditions of this effective refinancing. It should be added here that the Greeks were their own worst enemy creating a lot of the issues they had, one of which was the lack of efficient tax collecting systems with unrecorded cash transactions quite normal in Greece at the time to avoid paying tax.

There is always a chance of the land of milk and honey that the Brexiteers describe and crave but it is all about risk and reward backed a sensible, honest fact-based decision. We may well thrive, but it could take 50 years to find out as Jacob Rees-Mogg intimated but on the other hand we may find ourselves isolated with no close allies or partners with a smaller economy, higher unemployment, and the many challenges associated with that. We were doing very well as a member of the EU, potentially forced to tax more and it will be the young and the poor that may be picking up the tab or paying the price of the greatest act of self-harm to the country's future.

The remain campaign was accused of Project Fear which seemed to work but I found it ironic when most of the Leave campaign was based around fear i.e. Immigration and free movement, millions of Turks coming to the UK very soon etc. and it could look on the surface as if Remains' Project Fear did not work, but in reality it was clear that Leave's project fear was much more believable and effective even if based on fabrication. The controlled the narrative of the 'Fear factor' and Remain basically got 'Out-Feared', although it looked like many people 'wanted' to believe the lies.

One thing that is incredible is that 3+ years after the referendum result and despite all the chaos, the proven lies, no solution, the Government's own Yellowhammer report of the probable issues and risks, the fact that Leavers were promised things that are clearly not going to happen etc., there is still no buyer's remorse that they were sold unicorns over and over again. Clearly a lot of people still believe things are going to be so much better without any shred of evidence or indications that that will in fact be the case others don't seem to care as they think they have won, that's it! Exhibiting blind faith like a Jesuit priest who does not need proof or evidence but has a strong enough 'belief' is difficult to get one's logical head around it, but this is where many Brexiteers now find themselves. Although it was very much old versus young in 2016, we saw when the "Graffiti Grandma" came to fame when pictured chalking on a school wall "Brexit based on lies, Reject it" as she saw what a disaster it was becoming and she justified it by explaining that her generation had "fouled up the prospects of younger people", saying she is doing it "for her Grandchildren". She gets it, but why do many of the older generations not?

Hopefully people will see this book as one of concern, disbelief and to a certain extent embarrassment and disgust as a British citizen as to what political individuals like Nigel Farage, Boris Johnson et al. are willing to go to for power and influence no matter who they harm or abuse in that aim. Plus, the fact that the public let them! But also, a book of hope and belief that we are a caring charitable and understanding country with individuals like myself that have been very lucky and privileged to have been born here and not in Syria or Afghanistan for example. Plus, the hope that truth and logic will shine through the lies and misinformation that we have seen so people can learn and understand the realities of the country and the world which would give them a completely different impression of that world and not lead to fear and discrimination. Sooner or later our children and their children will be more integrated and understanding of foreign voices, people and cultures and will judge a person for what they are not the stereotype that their parents or their grandparents may have shown which helped block integration and happiness.

Maybe that is naïve of me but if you do not believe that what do we have left?

The whole Brexit debate after about 2 years got to the stage that the referendum took place and therefore justifies the referendum and we got dragged down the road of we have to honour the result no matter how dangerous and short sighted it appears. Many people, for various reasons including vested interest, literally stopped discussing whether or not it is a good idea and logical reasoning ceased, and we arrived at a place where we were having conversations such as:

Q. "why did we want Brexit?"
A. "Well we voted for it?

Q. But why did we vote for it?
A. "Because we wanted Brexit? etc.

And so it went around in circles, with many people not able to or not willing to stop and say hold on this does not seem like a good idea now we know so much of what we heard in 2016 was deceit and many of the implications we were told was 'fake news' are now coming home to roost!

Even once we leave many Brexiteers will not admit to things being worse than they would have been as they are entrenched and as it would indeed be very difficult to accurately calculate the opportunity cost of all those opportunities, we would have missed or lost if we had still been in the EU. These are opportunity costs not to the older generations that overwhelmingly voted leave but rather the younger generations that have been pushed backwards through no fault of their own. Some Brexiteers will have the answer of "see we survived" as if that was the aim and as if that was acceptable and justified their short-sighted decision.

The fear must be that the UK is like a teenage child that had a strop in 2016 and is too proud to admit it and change and is threatening to leave home packs his bags, leaves, his mate won't let him sleep on his sofa as planned and then he thinks 'Shit, what do I do now?!' As like Brexit little thought was put into where he was going, how he will get there or even what will happen when he knows where he is going! The result being insecurity, chaos, confusion and probably a lot of blame focused on the messengers and not the deceivers.

Did 17.4 million people try to commit suicide without knowing it? Why were people willing to enact a decision of such self-harm, or did most even know? The willingness to accept that the country and its citizens could very well be poorer for no obvious reason is not a logical position to take or justify but many have, indicating that the anti-EU sentiment was so ingrained nothing was going to budge it.

Going back to the initial introduction of this book and after all the investigations, research and conversations I have had what is my conclusion to the following question I set myself and others. Was it a sensible and logical decision and how based on what we know could anyone answer in the affirmative?

Q. Were the arguments in favour of Brexit sound and certain enough to justify the risk we are taking and exposing our children and our children's children to?

The Obituary is left for David Cameron, the ex-Prime minister, that took us out of Europe, by mistake and that is probably all he will ever be remembered for, and it all looked so good for him at one stage. So well done David, but that is what happens when you lack courage and take what you thought was the path of least resistance to fend off UKIP and please the anti-EU right wing of your party. Perhaps a bit more courage, conviction and a real vision for the UK would have been more appropriate. Was this Mr. Cameron's 'Darkest political hour'?

The world we now live in is changing rapidly and in not many years at all The 3 major world powers both economically and politically will be China, USA and probably India and they will be way ahead of the country in 4ht place with the difference being stark. So, for us to tear ourselves away from the largest trading and political block of countries to go it alone with some sense of illusionary power, based on many older citizens still dreaming of empire and having watched too many war films is very disturbing and doing our grandchildren a massive disservice.

Government research report Project Yellowhammer (July 2019)

Having mentioned this a few times in the book but only in passing it was felt it should be highlighted as an important document as it showed the Government's own research showing the risks of a no-deal Brexit, which was then dismissed by the new Boris Johnson administration as the absolute worst-case scenario (which it was not) they changed the title of the expert document and then said they would be having their own (presumably more favourable) research carried out, as they obviously did not like the conclusions as it went against their painting of a problem free exit from the EU and looking to reintroduce unicorns once again to the British Leave psyche.

Just touching on some of the issues that the experts who compiled this report highlighted were critical delays at channel ports, the negative impact of border checks (could be substantial delays in Gibraltar for example), supply chain delays and issues, effect on food and fresh water supplies, impact on law and order, disruption of UK financial services, legal implications for transferring data from inside and outside the EU, disruption to fuel supplies (borders, traffic blockages and customer panic creating shortages), the lack of clarity on the Irish border question, energy supplies, the Gibraltar question, the rights of British citizens in the 27 EU states, post Brexit plans, potential protest and policing concerns, implications to the change in fishing rights, the disproportionate effect on the poorer British citizens, and the impacts on the UK social services from many angles.

So, you can see the critical strategic areas the Government research covers and revealed real concerns about a smooth transition going forward and although the Johnson government play it down with words like "bumps in the road" "challenges" etc. they know the issues and risks faced but as a part of this "simply think positive" rhetoric they are hiding this from the public at large. Especially as they have an election to win at either the end 2019 or beginning of 2020.

It actually took the government some time to release the results of this report for obvious reasons, but this coincides with the fact that in October 2019 nobody is selling a hugely positive great future without any issues when we leave the EU as they can't.

After the above was eventually released Doug Bannister the relatively new CEO of the port of Dover was agreeing with the Government's positive line saying, "they are ready for a no-deal disruption". It is a difficult position for Mr. Bannister to walk the political tightrope and was spinning it as best he could. But also, in this interview for Bloomberg he highlighted some interesting points. This included that he expects some disruption and added he still has no clarity on the rules of the game, some things are unknowable until Brexit happens, drivers French import papers may not be in order, freight could be prevented coming over to the UK if the holding area in Calais is exceeded, no idea whether unprepared lorries exceed the capacity for the system to handle that, if two minutes is added to the normal time it takes to process each truck traffic would back up by 17 miles, nobody can predict how long disruptions will last, preparing sites across southeast England will not be ready. He stated quite clearly "Whether it will be successful or not, we need to see on the day." See on the day? That's a bit bloody late, but that is project reality!

Now when someone says they are ready for a no-deal Brexit but then reels off a number of unknowns, concerns and other issues that describes an institution that is NOT ready, no matter how the CEO tries to spin it for the media and the government. How can something definitely be ready when there are so many unknowns! Basically, they do not have a clue.

Why not Revoke and Stay?

Now I personally do not think this will happen, but I have posed the question to a number of Brexiteers and I pose it to you now. Clearly, the other initial responses were 'excitable' to say the least shouting things such as "Democracy" "17.4 million" "treason" etc. but then they calm down and I posed some questions / thoughts to them asking:

■ Q. If we remained with the Status quo you seem to be doing OK right, and that wouldn't change right? Most confirmed in the affirmative.

■ Do you think your life or that of your family or friends would be negatively affected if we stay? Again, most reply no not really.

■　Q. How do you think your life or that of your family and friends will be positively be affected when we leave? With this they struggle often replying with anecdotal stories of immigration (some fabricated) or an abstract idea of sovereignty, etc.

■　Q. So why again honestly did you decide to vote Leave, and do you think those things you voted for will be delivered or in fact positively change your life or that of your friends and family?

I get mostly blank faces or lack of cohesive responses online (except "I told you before Chris", but they hadn't for obvious reasons to avoid justifying their lack of reasoning) as a wave of reality brushes across them and the benefits they realise are minuscule if any, the disadvantages growing and risky, plus what they were promised and what will be delivered are worlds apart! Many resort to an empty "nobody knows what will happen in the future" which is a cop out and covered in the 'Crystal Ball argument' in this book.

So, when one puts it to them like that the reasonable, sensible individuals see the light and have to admit that they were sold a dud and as regards the Brexit argument as a whole we have proved "the emperor genuinely has no clothes". For that reason, one has to feel sorry (and not angry) for those people as they have been conned big time (although a very good well-funded swindle) and although they attack and abuse the messengers (as opposed to the charlatans that lied to them) like a pack of wolves, sometimes it is often out of embarrassment or fear of standing alone against their own tribe.

These are often intelligent people so they must see the reality now (even if they did not in 2016) and would most probably vote Remain at a second referendum but would not admit this publicly or on Social Media for fear of being ridiculed, abused, attacked or 'ostracised' from the passionate Brexiteer tribe where the extreme elements of such a tribe would go for them, and that is uncomfortable for everyone. The other possibility of having said so much in favour of a particular Leave position and then realising over time it was false, having the courage to admit to that mistake takes a lot of doing, especially in public or on social media for the reasons cited above.

459

Just imagine hypothetically if we did revoke tomorrow very few people can say it will negatively affect them (so no problems there) and no longer swallowing up Government's time and our money which must be a good thing. The Government could then call an election and the winner then concentrates on critical issues that do directly affect people's everyday lives such as reform of the NHS, modernising the UK economy in a rapidly developing global world, focus on high quality job creation and training the right skills for the future, improving education, achieve restructuring of social services to create a more joined up service with hospitals, and building more housing. But Brexit is a choice to neglect everything else that affects people's daily lives, and that is in nobody's interest. Who cares about our society as a whole? Multimillionaires and Billionaires will benefit from Brexit in many ways, but the everyday man and women will not, and they could pay a heavy price.

One would hope sense would prevail if a second referendum took place sometime in the future or a vote on re-joining, but it was clear that Brexiteers seriously struggled to reasonably justify leaving and any realistic tangible advantages it would bring apart from "we voted for it". Consequently, one has to conclude remaining was and still is the logical sensible answer and revoking of Article 50 would be the best decision for the country, unfortunately it will not happen I fear.

Chapter 32
Summary and Conclusion

Summary and conclusion

It will be clear to you from the facts, logic and observable reality cited in this book that the leave decision in 2016 was not a good decision at all for the UK and very much based on emotion, false information, and good old fashioned lies exaggerated by politicians with vested interests and money as well as Social Media.

Was the Brexiteer mantra as Samuel Beckett so famously cited and is often used by sporting teams these days "fail, fail again, fail better"? It may be a good mantra for sports teams but not when you are playing with people's lives as if it is some jolly hockey sticks game at Eton and the poorer, less fortunate in our society get poorer as a result of a jolly good debating game at the dispatch box by Boris Johnson and his rich friends. If this all goes pear shaped Johnson goes back to his £80K plus expenses MP job and £250,000 a year columnist job, plus highly paid speaking engagements. So, he will be alright whereas the Nissan production worker may lose his / her job with little else in the area to replace those jobs. Welcome to Brexit and the real world.

461

In any logical or sensible thought process we must agree that the EU referendum was greatly flawed and the process since the vote a total embarrassing chaotic mess and the saying 'Led by donkeys' definitely comes to mind. How did we get to a point where a plummeting pound, loss of jobs, increasing costs, and an impending recession are perceived to be a success? Even the government minister Michael Gove in August 2019 was suggesting the idea of closing down British banks the day after Brexit to prevent financial chaos! Yes, such an action for something exhorted by Brexiteers to be a good thing for the UK does seem bizarre. When did our country and part of the population enter the twilight zone?

It became clear that no UK institution is immune to the Brexit 'virus' with even the queen getting dragged into proceedings with Boris Johnson and his unlawful proroguing government with the Prime Minister also being accused of lying, not for the first time of course! This will hopefully have the impact of politicians having to deliver on promises they have made in that they will be forced to deliver them as if not they will make even more wild and wonderful promises without any intention of delivering on them in the future. Who can blame them when they know Brexiteer politicians have spun a huge web of lies with little or no comeback? Brexit released a poison not seen in British politics or society in recent years but was it the cause or was it the catalyst that just let the poison loose that was there dormant all the time waiting for the right opportunity to rear its ugly head?

Do you remember many people before the referendum campaigns mentioning or even complaining about the EU, apart from anti-EU politicians or political odd balls like Nigel Farage as it kept them relevant? Certainly, research shows that in 2015 and even 2016 it was not really on people's radar of concerns with many other items much more important. It was quite clear that politicians led the UK public into this anti-EU chaos and subsequent rise in hate crimes and not the other way around. But do Leavers really think 'violence' is a price worth paying to leave an organisation that many before June 2016 did not think negatively affected their lives, and still cannot to this day? Maybe if the Press keeps telling us we are on the brink of violence as they did if we did not leave on October 31st, 2019 (which amounted to nothing) it becomes a self-fulfilling prophecy and they create a tinderbox that could ignite at any time?

Did the referendum just crystallise all those divisive subjects including globalisation and the feeling of being left behind the UK economic development, the perceived 'Haves' versus the 'Have Nots' and therefore inequality, immigration, stretched public services, austerity and how a lot of people felt they were negatively affected by these resulting issues rather than purely a judgement solely about the EU and our position in the club. But became also a protest vote to how people had seen their lives developing. Even those that voted Leave surely voted for a smooth and orderly exit to still maintain where possible a special relationship with the EU, but no deal would achieve exactly the opposite of that and a clear act of self-harm for the UK. Those that felt they have been left behind by acts of government such as austerity will be very disappointed in the leave vote as it could make their plight worse than they had hoped if the country becomes poorer and the economy smaller over the next few years.

What have we learnt about people and their group think, sticking together, and echo chambers? Brexit did not create prejudices but revealed many that were clearly bubbling under the surface which bordered on racist without people realising they were in fact racist. Those subconscious biases, sometimes quite extreme, rose to the surface and the wave of anti-foreigner sentiment that Brexit brought with it allowed people to feel justified, especially as a part of a large group, to air those feelings and exercise actions that would normally be felt unacceptable.

The emergence of a hierarchy of immigrants was initially surprising but then on reflection not, as it has always been there but has moved over time where once the Irish got this hate speech and xenophobic attitudes but then it moved to the Blacks, and then to the Indians and Pakistanis (all grouped into the "Paki" group), and most recently it was the Eastern Europeans but even within that Group some Brits had their own hierarchy with Polish being better than Bulgarians and Romanians for example. But like the Paki example above areas of certain towns like Chatham in Kent are referred to as "Little Kosovo" with many locals thinking those immigrants are all from Kosovo in that area. This then linked to the EU referendum becoming a focus of dislike and hate. But even when one pointed out that Kosovo is not even in the EU it did not matter as it was just a focus of superiority and the apparent way "they" (i.e. the Kosovans) live. No thought of poverty and the fact they may not be able to live anywhere else or have to live 6 to a house to pay the bills, etc. On the other hand, it is these people that are apparently taking all, the well-paid British jobs! You can see the hypocrisy. But I found examples of people voting leave because of "little Kosovo".

Cameron made a number of mistakes but perhaps his biggest and that of his team was that of Hubris and thinking he would just go out there and charm the electorate and win the vote. He didn't, the vote was lost, and chaos ensued. Most people did not understand how the EU worked or the value it added as it was not a priority for them as they carried on with their lives and saw very few areas where it negatively affected them or their families. The referendum basically offered on a plate anyone that was discontent with their lives a chance to vent their spleen and their unhappiness about almost anything they chose. This allowed them to easily blame politicians, immigrants or the EU and felt they were in a group of people that felt the same. When combined with the extremists that were willing to fuel that discontent with ever increasing false inflammatory stories which could easily be spread via the Internet the snowball became unstoppable.

Most Brexiteers, well at least the honest ones, accept that leaving the customs union and single market (if they even knew what that was) is very likely to have a significant negative effects on the British economy in the short term, as it has to adjust to new trading rules and regulations as well as the new reality post Brexit. But even if Brexit leads to economic crisis, many Brexiteers will claim it has nothing to do with the leave vote but will as usual blame other outside forces such as "foreigners", "Politicians", "Remainers for not thinking positively enough", or the good old 'global economy' who all conspired to make the project fail and the economy shrink, even though it was flawed in the first place with no solid base, plan or strategy.

We have seen that many of the promises of utopia from prominent Brexiteer politicians but also that many of those promises used to win the referendum were then broken or recoiled including Michael Gove now admitting that EU trawlers will continue to operate in UK waters, or David Davis now admitting immigration may rise from time to time. Did they say this during the referendum campaigns? If not, why not? They must have either been ignorant of that reality or deceitful to the electorate! Remember Michael Gove's pledge Brexit would see VAT on energy and fuel slashed? These people should be held accountable for such statements they could never deliver, as this disproportionately affects the poorer in our society.

We found that following the referendum vote, prices increased more in product groups where imports account for a higher proportion of consumer expenditure which has had an impact on household costs. The 1.7% increase in inflation implies that by June 2017, the Brexit vote was costing the average household £7.74 per week through higher prices which is circa. £404 per year, but this is expected to rise especially with a no deal Brexit should that happen.

We should all be committed to our representative democracy and the rule of law where we are all supporters of a pluralistic society which is a diverse one where the people in it believe all kinds of different things and tolerate each other's beliefs, even when they don't match their own. We should see the rich variety of attitudes and cultures as a good thing and our society should be about engagement, openness, and consensus which are attributes that should define our political processes. Unfortunately, during and since the EU referendum we have not seen people punished for constant lies whether it be the false statements and deceit of the leave campaigns or the unlawful act of a Prime Minister and that should change and never happen again. We must learn from this but my concern is there are limited powers / sanctions to stop well financed individuals or parties saying and doing whatever they to influence our politics such as and not being held responsible for those actions, misinformation or fabrication of lies, and I fear it will happen again very soon at the next general election.

The British economy in the last 3 years has been resilient but the signs of job losses, lack of investment, and uncertainty are clear and that combined with the forthcoming global slowdown could lead to a UK recession and falling living standards and rising inequality could be extremely dangerous for the country in such polarised times. Job losses and rising prices have already started but could much worse when we leave actually the EU.

The Leave campaign was a deception and elaborate con trick perpetrated by those who will reap the few benefits of a Brexit, if the UK leaves the EU, basking in isolation on the world stage. If the myths and obsessed self-interest of the Brexiteers can be defeated, the future of the UK could still be as a full partner with its European friends and allies in the EU, but that is very doubtful now. If not we should all beware the 'long tail effect' of Brexit to the British economy where only after some time, as we experienced with austerity, will the true negative effects be felt by the British citizens, especially the poorer in our society.

It was quite clear there was a lot of identity politics before, during and after the referendum result which was focused on the state of being 'English' not necessarily 'British'. This was clear in the result when pollsters found 80% of people who voted Leave saw themselves as English but 80% of Remain voters saw themselves as 'British' and was clear on Facebook posts and social media where the St George's cross flag emoji was very prevalent. For some Brexit has become an unchangeable almost holy doctrine that has to be delivered at any cost even if the price is a catastrophic no-deal Brexit. This irrationality is embedded in a rabid fear that it may not happen so as long as the UK leaves they can sing from the rooftops that they had won, even though it may be staring them in the face that we could all lose. That no longer counts in their eyes – emotion had taken over from facts, critical thinking and logic.

The right-wing press went into overdrive when they went after the Remain campaign, and especially Cameron and Osbourne which was due to its continued extreme position on Brexit and its anti-EU stance. But perhaps they also saw it as a chance to kick the posh boys for their role in the Levison [enquiry] process which curtailed their powers and held them to account and they did not like it. That way they could kill two birds with one stone with the ferocious onslaught and possibly even saw it as a belated act of revenge? We should not forget that Lord Levison in his 2013 report into the ethics of the British press stated there was "clear evidence of misreporting of European issues"!

As you can appreciate in my Brexit journey with the research carried out and the number of people spoken to, interviewed or communicated with I have experienced all sorts of attitudes, aggression and passions, some logical some less so. One of the most interesting and recent positions is the fact that few Brexiteers can or are willing to justify their decision to vote leave with any facts, logic or sensible dialogue in the face of the chaos they saw. Well apart from "we voted for it" that is, which is a huge cop out of course. But it went further in that many claimed they were not influenced by the Bus, the racist posters, the many lies, the promise of reduced number of immigrants, Facebook or social media posts, or that they were even influenced by the British press. Obviously, I then asked where they then got their information from or developed their attitudes to vote leave? This flummoxed them as they could not say, either through embarrassment that they had been hoodwinked, or still do not understand the EU and the issues involved. Possibly some just 'hoped' there would be fewer foreigners in the UK and they were willing to take that risk? So, the dishonesty sadly seemed to have been passed on from the usual suspects covered in this book to the everyday leave voter who could not verbalise why they voted leave or perhaps why they still think they will get what they voted for or what they were promised. This crystallised Brexit in just a few conversations and it was difficult to know if we should be angry at such developments or pity the individuals that had been manoeuvred into such positions without even knowing it.

A number of inaccurate and mutually incompatible statements with no sensible destination or solution post-Brexit helped create the chaos that ensued. We saw this when Boris Johnson as Prime Minister claimed that a no-deal Brexit will not be a catastrophe but at the same time needed to keep no deal on the table as a threat to the EU that it could be a catastrophe! Does he not see this hypocrisy, or does he even care, preferring a soundbite, a cheap joke, or offensive language in a speech or a Telegraph column. Is he the ultimate charlatan?

Some still believe one of the Brexiteer deceptions was when Michael Gove said "we hold all the cards" i.e. Britain had more leverage than the EU. Clearly, this was nonsense, exposed very quickly and many times subsequently where a bloc of 27 countries working closely together to protect their combined interest. They were in a stronger position than an isolationist state not quite knowing exactly what it wanted apart from having its cake and eating it, which was never going to happen.

How will the constituents' lives of deprived areas in the North such as Boston and Skegness that voted heavily for leave be improved via exiting the European Union? We cannot and should not blame everyday people that did not understand the impact of a leave vote on Sterling (or inflation) or how that would affect them, or the job losses it would cause etc. as they were just getting on with their lives when they are expected to make a complex far reaching decision. But we <u>can</u> blame those prominent Brexiteers that sold them that unicorn vision of the future that was never possible and was more linked to their own discriminatory prejudices and vested interests.

Brexiteers say "we will survive and get on with it" as if that is OK in accepting a worse situation than we had as a member of the EU. If they moved to a new house in an area that they then disliked and was worse than where they lived previously, would they take the same stance or would they, if they could, move back to where they lived previously so their lives did not get worse i.e. change their mind? The answer is clear, so why is Brexit different?

Nick Clegg wrote in the conclusion to his book 'How to stop Brexit' that people did in fact know what they were voting for with the reasoning, in my opinion, to avoid saying people made stupid decisions and staying politically correct. But just because they did not genuinely know what they voted for does not automatically make them stupid, rather the issues were way too complex and opaque for a normal person that is not going to read treaties, reports, or delve into political TV and radio programmes to make an informed decision because that is not normal behaviour, or a priority for people more interested in running their own lives. But they were suddenly faced with a decision to make having seen anti-Eu headlines from an Eurosceptic Press and a torrent of lies and fabrications from leave campaigners that seemed convincing. How could they have been expected to make an accurate informed decision? This is why we have a parliament and MPs who are paid to look at and analyse in depth and make decisions on such issues based on what they see as the best outcome for their constituents and the country as a whole. My experience of talking to leavers about the EU referendum after they had voted was that they did not know about or understand the EU, how it worked or what value it added to the United Kingdom. They may have not known what the single market or customs union were, they did not know about the working time directive to help protect workers was an EU initiative / law, or it was the UK government that decided not to limit the number of EU immigrants etc. and why should they? But they were then pressured by the Government in 2016 to choose sides, make a decision upon which they had limited knowledge or information with emotions riding high and faced with an extremely disingenuous press.

When asking leavers about the influence of the Eurosceptic press, the big red bus promise, the racist posters of 'Syrians' streaming into the UK, fears spread about Turks coming to the UK, or right-wing Facebook posts influencing people etc. they all claimed that none of those things influenced them or determined their decision. But when faced with the supplementary question of "where did you get your information then" the often-repeated reply was "I just made up my own mind". But how? Where did the information come from? This then stops them in their tracks and the reality dawns on them that they <u>were</u> in fact influenced by these inputs whether or not they were conscious of it.

Unless something drastically changes in the negotiation of the withdrawal agreement or more accurately the subsequent Free Trade Agreement negotiations, the deal we achieve will almost definitely be worse than the deal we have currently. Why is that? Well, the EU had already given us a number of concessions such as opt-outs from the Euro, the borderless Schengen Zone and home affairs policy, as well as a £4.9 Billion annual budget rebate. So, when Brexiteers say the EU needs to be more flexible the above plus what David Cameron negotiated such as an official exemption from "ever closer union", a four-year ban on in-work benefits for EU migrants (actionable for seven years), and greater safeguards for the City of London. Clearly this shows how flexible the EU has been towards the UK resulting in the UK having the best deal of any EU member state or associated country including the likes of Norway, etc. Boris Johnson's current deal is very close to Mrs. May's deal (some say worse) but praised by his followers as an amazing deal followed by the moronic "Get Brexit Done" etc. But when all is said and done it will be worse than the deal we have now. It really is as simple as that and I understand people will not care and are obsessed with leaving the EU, but we should not be under any illusion it will be a worse deal than the UK already possesses.

In reality nobody has won anything, it is, and always will be, a losing game all round with many victims, especially the poor which have been impacted by the 15% devaluation of the pound since the referendum (as of August 2019) and any other further devaluation of the Pound when we leave will hit them even more. It is now clear to everyone apart from the most irrational ardent Brexiteers that the promises made to voters of an easy Brexit with increased fairness and increased prosperity for the country is dead and impossible to deliver, and we were rarely

469

hearing such claims anymore, which speaks volumes.

We have been sold a fantasy of national liberation, but if people truly still believe that, there is little hope of sensible dialogue as one cannot free oneself from imaginary oppression. This is why the Brexiteer list of people to blame for their own lack of a plan or progression has grown out of all proportions partly in desperation but also as a smokescreen to paper over the cracks of a very bad idea, badly planned and so poorly executed it is remarkable that some of these people are still in front of microphones and television campaigns. But that is the hutzpah of some of these people like Boris Johnson with skins like Rhinos and willing to say anything to anyone for their own benefit no matter how many other people suffer.

Project reality replaced project fear when one considers there was in fact an emergency budget albeit it in another guise (Sajid Javid adds another £2.1 Billion, on top of what had been spent already, to help with preparations for exiting the EU, now calling it "planning"), Sterling has plunged, Jobs have been lost or companies' moving them now and more planned, plus supply chains have been disrupted. Certainly, these are events that have happened or are continuing to happen so Leavers are in fact still lying to the public telling them everything is OK and will be fine! As David Cameron put in his memoirs of 2019, he felt it was not project Fear but project CLEAR (i.e. better off in and worse off out) and felt justified in his concerns about leaving the EU as we now see in 2019.

But a no-deal Brexit is going to cost a lot more than that £2.1 Billion as that is really just a first down payment and not a one off but some of the privileged 1% that have instigated and driven Brexit may get their wish of a gig economy with very low tax (maybe even zero if the tax havens and loopholes can be maintained without the pressure of the EU to reform or close them down?) resulting in a rapid race to the bottom where public services could suffer significantly.

As we have highlighted there are numerous floors in the Brexiteer arguments for Brexit, many of which are now quite obvious and even the intention to roll over international trade agreements that were negotiated via the EU but one of the 'selling points' of Brexiteers was we can do so much better on our own. The two things obviously do not add up.

470

Even these so called 'new' trade deals do not get anywhere near the value of the free trade we already enjoy with the European Union. Estimates by the treasury and National Institute of Economic and Social Research (NIESR) calculated that signing trade deals with all the English-speaking countries, as well as the so-called BRICS emerging market economies, would only increase GDP by less than 0.2-0.4% by 2030! But also such a revered Trade agreement with the USA could result in major increases in the costs of the drugs purchased by the NHS from US Pharma giants, many negative developments for our farmers, food safety standards as well as many other areas as that major economy will squeeze the UK for many compromises.

Even as late as October 2019 and after Boris Johnson claiming he had secured a great historic deal the NIESR found that deal would leave the UK £70 Billion worse off by 2029 than if it had remained in the EU. It concluded that GDP would be 3.5% lower in 10 years' time under Boris's deal. Some extreme Brexiteers even claim his deal is not in fact Brexit as the UK will still be subject to the rulings made by judges on the European Court of Justice despite leaving the European Union. It gives the ECJ the final say on the meaning of any EU law in the treaty and lays down a new framework for the relationship between Parliament, the courts and the EU institutions that could have big ramifications for the British constitution. In the Withdrawal Agreement Bill (WAB) it provides what it calls a "conduit pipe" for some EU laws to flow directly into UK law.

Although he claimed a great success we should be clear he got a deal because he backtracked massively and essentially accepted a proposal for a "Northern Ireland-only backstop" that the EU proposed back in February 2018 which Britain rejected. This was a significant concession, because Mr. Johnson had previously categorically rejected any customs border in the Irish Sea. But his deal apart from that significant concession is still very similar to Teresa May's deal and even retained a typo from the original, which referred in section E on terrorism to "violent extremis [sic]." That says it all!

One thing to add as regards Boris's deal is we should also not forget he betrayed Northern Ireland and his partners the DUP to get that deal. Nobody is safe with Boris who seem happy to betray anyone to get what he wants. Also, it DOES NOT rule out a no deal Brexit as some have claimed. All he needs to do is fail to present a FTA to parliament in 2020, the transition then lapses, and then we have no deal. Parliament will not be able to stop it. But even with a deal, with an election many Brexit questions will still need to be answered, and the implications are stark. But as stated any deal Boris or anyone else reached would be far inferior to the UK's current terms which includes full membership with an array of opt-outs. In truth the UK is going to give up the best deal any EU member state has ever had. Why compare Johnson's deal to May's deal when the real comparison is an inferior deal to the better deal we currently have, which has been lost over time?

Brexit was the creation of Millionaires, Billionaires and Press Barons etc. wanting to avoid tax and to them it was never about immigration or other topics discussed in this book. Brexit will allow this new world of offshore money and tax avoidance schemes we have read about to continue unabated and countries like the UK will lose out and money that could have been put to good causes and social activities in the UK will remain in bank accounts in the Cayman Islands, etc. If you look at it in the cold light of day Brexit is great for anyone exploiting offshore tax havens, as the European Union were catching up with them and attempting to close down such avenues they were abusing. Also, the fact that in the UK foreign money can easily become domestic and assets hidden with connections concealed should make us all very uneasy and concerned about the future influence of such people on our society, political parties and our democracy.

A worrying aspect of the referendum and the aftermath was the amount of hostility towards professional expert organisations such as the World Bank, International Monetary Fund (IMF) and the Bank Of England which questions the role of experts and specific expertise. A more visceral politics has replaced important areas of evidence and fact or at least informed prediction and forecast where people preferred to believe the lies of Nigel Farage, Vote Leave, Leave.EU etc despite them not being experts in anything. But they were in the same 'tribe', so the echo Chamber affect continues as certain individuals no longer believe anything said outside their 'Belief Gang' which stunts learning and lateral thinking but also exacerbates group think in an extreme way. UK Politics appears no longer about who gets what (which always needs compromise) but now more about questions of identity (which do not include compromise) creating a more US style of politics, with all its ugly side. We have unfortunately entered and may never return from this post truth world of UK politics, which when combined by a desperate desire to return to some imaginary bygone age does not bode well.

The paradox of the EU referendum was that it took a vote to leave to shock millions of Britons into realising how much they liked the EU and how much value it did indeed add to their lives and that of their children moving forward. It has become clear that since the referendum the UK has the largest and most enthusiastic Pro EU movement of all 28 EU countries, as the other countries take the EU for granted (as we did) and it is only since we voted to leave that reality has hit and we see the real advantages the EU adds to our country and the complications and issues of leaving.

Some feel that the UK cutting itself adrift from the EU will be an absolute disaster becoming a lonely isolationist country declining into some mediocre irrelevance. But that is not the point rather the UK will be poorer short / medium term (even Jacob Rees-Mogg agrees to that, although he feels it could be 50 years for us to reap the rewards!) with no guarantee or plan of how the future will make the UK better or wealthier which is how it will help to benefit our citizens of course.

Clearly, Brexit has reshaped our electoral politics, and conceivably for ever but it will also have an impact on our politicians to deliver on promises they've made with so many lies, and untruths being told during and since the EU referendum campaigns. Remainer and Leaver are now political identities like liberal or conservative etc. Which could shape Britain long after Brexit with a potential chasm between the 'young' and the 'old' solidifying. These definitions may take on a life of their own with a Remainer being an open minded individual looking to cooperate across borders, but Leaver could become associated with closed minded individuals that cling to their own 'type' and traditions, in an isolationist manner which creates a wedge between these two groups for ever.

Looking back to the run up to the referendum campaign and the campaign itself the country almost found itself in a perfect storm where a number of various groups and beliefs had the opportunity to make protest votes and were not as focused on the EU as Leavers would have us believe. Some of those groups were:

■   The so called 'have nots' that felt globalisation had passed them by and they wanted to show their dissatisfaction.

■   Anti-government attitudes to give the government a kick (some not thinking Leave would necessarily win) or even more specific give posh Eton boys Cameron and Osbourne a kick up the backside.

■   Some of the Labour heartlands that had suffered from de-industrialisation and blamed the government and /or the EU, believing immigrants were taking their jobs.

■   Those that genuinely believed that 1 million + Turks could / would come to the UK if we stayed in the EU.

■   Those that honestly believed the distortions of charismatic Leave campaigners such as Nigel Farage, Boris Johnson, et al.

■   Plus, a number of others!

Whatever happens the ultimate outcome of Brexit achieving a satisfactory conclusion that does not send the UK backwards will be a massive challenge and makes one ask oneself how or why we even got here. It is purely very poor political judgement beginning with David Cameron at the top of the list which will negatively impact other policies future governments want to implement and carry out. A report suggested that the long-awaited review of building and safety regulations (after the Grenfell tragedy) had been delayed, with one reason cited as civil servants being taken off or 'redirected' to other projects / issues one of which was Brexit. So, we can see how Brexit seeps into the most unusual corners of our political, social and economic fabric with a clear negative knock on effect and the law of unintended consequences rearing its ugly head again.

The aspect of the pressure on Civil servants in Whitehall due to Brexit has been real and stark. In June 2018 it emerged that the cabinet secretary planned to redeploy 750 policy experts from across Whitehall to key Brexit departments, which is on the back of the Civil service numbers being cut from 480,000 down to 406,000 full-time staff. Clearly, something has to give, and Brexit is now directly and negatively impacting many other areas of our country including important social services, and others. These hidden costs are significant.

This is a political crisis, but most British people don't have a clue what a crisis really is which is what a successful European Union and 70 years of peace and economic growth in Europe does for a nations people, and their feeling of comfort and security. But as highlighted in this book that can be shattered very quickly.

The few people that read through this book draft before publication noted there are few reasons for Brexit in the positive sense, which on reflection is true. But we have addressed most of the Brexiteer arguments having analysed and dissected them and the conclusion was that it is very difficult to see how, and these arguments stand up to scrutiny when balanced against what the UK will lose. I won't repeat arguments highlighted elsewhere in this book but if we look at just a couple which are those that want to stop or seriously curtail immigration. The facts are we need the workers and have the lowest unemployment and highest employment for decades plus hundreds of thousands of vacancies to be filled. Then we have the multi-millionaires, billionaires and their friends that do not want the EU to stop or limit the use of tax havens so they can still avoid paying their fair share of tax but they are less than 1% of the population and this is obviously not good for the majority of the country.

There does not seem like any good outcomes of Brexit for anyone (maybe Nigel Farage and his band of 'agent provocateurs', and those with offshore bank accounts?) and only bad, risky and costly outcomes for everyone, just some may be worse and more costly than others. But despite the visible issues with Brexit some are so entrenched in their beliefs they cannot get out from the promises they made to millions of people and so the exaggerations, half-truths, fabrications and plain lies continue in an attempt to get Brexit over the line and then everybody can suffer afterwards. As the song goes "suicide is painless", well Brexit is not, especially for the less fortunate in our society.

Linked to the ultimate outcome of Brexit and the future relationship with the EU some Brexiteers will claim it is a success no matter what the outcome, and without what the economists call a 'counter-factual', i.e. something to compare it against it will be difficult to contradict that. If the country gets poorer as forecasted they can and will claim other outside influences such as global economy slowdowns, trade wars or even comparisons with the Greek or Sudanese economic growth over the same period which any sensible person knows are ridiculous comparisons But it wouldn't be the first time in the last 3+ years!

There was never a clear official manifesto for Brexit which lead us to this position where even Brexiteers cannot agree on what "IT" is or should be in practice and we then have to fall back on empty slogans, media stunts and innumerable fabrications to constantly mislead the public, and that should never have been the case. We even experienced in October 2019 where Boris Johnson's cabinet coming out just repeating the empty slogan "Get Brexit done" (which like "Brexit means Brexit" means nothing!), clearly fed by Dominic Cummings as he thinks it will resonate, but gets us not one step closer to a solution, but the government ministers like Lemmings just repeat the slogan parrot fashion. The issue seems to be that after 3 years we can clearly see that Brexit was only ever a campaign born out of protest and despondency but accelerated by unrealistic pie in the sky promises by charlatans and was never going to be anything near Government policy as the Brexiteers implied.

The £100 million spent by the Government on "Get Ready for Brexit" adverts to apparently help prepare people and companies for Brexit were totally useless and completely wasted money, as they helped in no way whatsoever. I used them personally for my company and the result was "please read these 32 documents". Yes 32 for something that nobody knows when it will happen or what will actually happen when it does take place! But it got worse as even some of those documents were useless. I look back at these and it is clear they were simply publicly funded government propaganda. There is supposed to be a ministerial code governing taxpayer-funded communications, but these seem to me to break every rule in that regard. Perhaps we just have to accept and look forward to more of the same with Prime Minister Boris Johnson, where the PM treats the country like some banana republic which began with the attempt to prorogue Parliament, later found to be unlawful.

The following example from a contact (ER) on his frustration and realisation that Brexit has been a no-win exercise for all concerned with no winners, but a religious devotion for some that "IT" had to happen, regardless of the cost. (PS – ER is not her Majesty, so let me make that clear before you read her, I mean his, concerns!)

(ER): I've learned a few things from this episode:

1) We should never have been offered the referendum. Despite what everyone says, no-one truly understood the magnitude of this. You wouldn't invite 10 unqualified people to look at a house you wanted to buy and base your decision on 6 of them saying 'yeah go for it'. Leaving the EU is far more complex than that.

2) Brexiteers are not worth arguing with. It's very similar to arguing about religion vs science. There is no (zero) evidence that leaving is a good thing, but they will not budge. It's pointless trying.

3) The newspapers and media have been slowly drip feeding the negativity for over 30 years and they did it to make money.

4) Not one politician gives a flying fuck about us. Any Brexiteer that thinks Johnson is acting in our best interests is deluded. I'm sad for the state of my country but there is no amount of evidence that will encourage a sensible solution.

This is just the feeling of a normal person who has tried to understand and research the Brexit issues and implications and was clearly distressed as to where our country had been dragged kicking and screaming. There appears no magic that will keep leave voters happy that will not harm the UK or diminish its standing in the world as it isolates itself. This was the poison chalice that each government since the referendum has been presented, although it must be said Mrs May and Mr Johnson gladly accepted that as the price for fulfilling their political ambitions. The saying "Be careful what you wish for" comes to mind.

Despite the EU referendum being a question of a multiple of very complex interwoven issues, laws, and trading relationships that needed considering and weighing up to arrive at the pros and cons in quite some detail and finally reach a logical well thought through conclusion. Unfortunately, many people did not consider it that way. They were more focused on one specific item that weighed on their mind such as immigrants, and freedom and that one aspect dominated their decision. So, it was dictated by one, often emotional, element and not a balanced choice resulting in a vote that would be better for the country and the individual's family as a whole, and this demonstrated the stark issue with the referendum concept for such a critical constitutional issue of change.

You should ask yourself whether the no deal chaos that could result was something you wanted for your children, family and friends as my answer is a definitive "NO". But if your answer is "yes it will be fine", you should ask yourself the following supplementary question:

"How will my life or that of my children, friends and family improve upon leaving the European Unions?" that is the crux of this issue.

In the same way everybody should look at Brexit and ask themselves am I and my family a winner or a loser, and certainly so far with rising costs, job losses, and a very uncertain future with no obvious tangible benefits of Brexit the answer is unfortunately crystal clear. We could all be losers. With so much water under the bridge, so many lies uncovered, many changes already made to what people expected and a deal nobody envisaged or spoke of it seems only logical and sensible to put the decision back to the people on a specific deal and not the various fantasies peddled by many individuals with various ideals or vested interests. A confirmatory vote on the final deal is only fair and logical for the country.

Chapter 33
Final Thought

This book has been very difficult to write, especially as it was my first both from a time / commitment point of view but also having been hounded on Social Media from many Brexiteers who did not like my points, the facts, the logic or even the revelation of reality that sometimes burst their leave bubble. I had 'friends' unfriend or block me (which is fine and their prerogative) on the basis of when I politely disassembled or proved their arguments to be false they did not take to kindly to that. Sometimes retorting with cries of "BULLSHIT"[1A] or "TWAT"[1L] etc. but then not being able to qualify why they felt it was BS, other than it was not what they believed. Simple truths like countering their claims that we had too many immigrants with "we have the highest employment and lowest unemployment for decades and lots of vacancies to fill" did not go down too well or even register as that was not what they had been fed or wanted to believe. They told me mass immigration had been going on for years but when I asked which of those they would send home I was faced with either "none of them" which made no sense if we had indeed had too many immigrants for years, or complete silence. Sometimes it was "the illegal ones" which I politely pointed out was not the fault of or an issue that leaving the EU would rectify. The look of the realisation on their faces that they had been fed these anti-EU and anti-immigrant lies for years was palpable.

If one sticks to one's principles of treating everyone the same and not to discriminate based on colour, race, ethnicity, where they came from, or their political / religious status which then backed up by facts, logic and observable reality, then one can't go far wrong. Just don't expect certain people to agree with you.

Having finished this book I had to add a story told by an older gentleman (who was openly a Brexiteer) at a boxing event in Kent that the "French police were ferrying illegal immigrants across the English channel and then letting them loose so the British coastguards would then pick them up in English waters where they would get housed and given lots of benefits!" I was flabbergasted at something so bizarre and asked where he got that from, and he said it was in all the papers and on the TV! I missed that massive story of French police corruption as I am sure you did also. But could you imagine if such actions were rife and the story true what a truly International diplomatic incident that would have been? Clearly it was not corruption on an industrial scale but this individual and the 2 Gentlemen next to him nodded in agreement, even though they had not heard that particular story before! It appears on researching this rumour originated from a guy that phoned LBC radio claiming this was true, but no evidence was shown for such a claim.

But again, a common thread throughout this book is where do many of these stories originate which then grow into huge urban myths and the story grows legs? This story was followed by anecdotal stories of Romanians walking into job centres who just "gave up and presented them with benefits", as if there are no rules and it was like someone asking for sweets at the school tuck shop! This then leads one to the question as to 'how it is even possible to convince or even discuss such fabrications with people' that believe such stories? The problem is that they want to believe such stories.

As many told me "you will not change my mind no matter what you say or write" which is obviously their prerogative but that was never the intention. I put forward many facts, points, and highlighted real-life situations that clearly disproved what they had been told or believed, but in this post-truth political world it was completely wasted. Many were and still are entrenched in their anti-immigrant and / or anti-EU positions and are comfortable in those positions. Unfortunately, they struggled to justify them with any facts or logic and replace that with emotion and anger to show this country is going downhill and looking for scapegoats to blame it on, even if they are not the root cause of any perceived issues they may feel.

Ultimately, nobody but themselves can pull them out of an imaginary discriminatory bubble they have created around themselves based on illusions, misinformation, fabrications that they have been drip fed for years. The worrying thing that hit me like a freight train was that after all my conversations, communications and research people really truly believe so many of these lies as it fits their already predetermined picture of the world and they were unmovable. It does make one think how or what are they teaching their children to believe going forward? Is it facts, logic and observable reality or fiction, untruths and fabrications to create a vicious circle from which those children will find it very difficult to escape from and open their minds.

In essence there will be many reasons people voted leave some simple and others may be more complex and the reasons for the Leave vote are also numerous but as you have seen in this book, they probably include the years of Eurosceptic propaganda from the Brexit press including powerful owners and editors including Rupert Murdoch and Paul Dacre. This combined with useless leadership of the Labour party throughout the campaign, the lack of understanding of the public opinion especially in the Northern heartlands by the conservative dominated Stronger In campaign. Undiluted and unabashed deception and untruths by the Leave campaigns worked, as well as a more focused and organised Vote Leave campaign, plus Arron Banks' money including a willingness to 'push the boundaries'.

Remain underestimated the feeling of being left behind and suffering many average people in the UK felt and their need to blame someone as well as kick someone with their vote was poignant, and Cameron's avoidance of blue on blue attacks whilst Gove, Johnson and Priti Patel did exactly that creating more confusion and havoc. Cameron was unwilling to change tack when the 'project fear' was not working and naively underestimated how many Conservatives would go against him such as those above putting party before country, and the final nail in the coffin was the Leave campaigns willingness to go as far as needed to win and were not there to make an academic discussion about Brexit – they were there to WIN, whatever the cost!

It does bode one question how we got where we are and why people were happy for this self-induced chaos to prevail despite no natural disaster, epidemic or war?

The Brexit story could over time prove to be one about winners and losers but those that thought they had won may very likely find they have in fact lost like many of us as well. But the Brexit debate and arguments will not end in 2019 or even 2020 as they will rumble on and on with further analysis and recriminations as the UK attempts to optimise its relationship with the EU and the rest of the world from a position of weakness compared to when it was a full member of the EU with influence and strong voting powers.

How exactly will this play out over the next decade nobody knows, but it is a high-risk game backed up by little logic and the stakes for the UK, its children and its children's children are high. Once we take everything into account 2 things are clear:

1. **The referendum should never have been called for such an ultra-complex issue with a simple In or OUT option.**

2. **The risks of leaving especially with no deal cannot be justified in any logical sense as there was never a plan or any real idea of what the probable outcome would be, and it has cost the UK Billions to even prepare for a potential disaster and that shows a lack of judgement on the part of many people.**

When finishing this book, the most frustrating and confusing thought I am left with is the people to this day still believe so many of the lies and fabrications about the EU and the referendum despite having had it explained and proved to them many were and still are false. But they seem to want to believe the fabrications no matter how far-fetched or exaggerated they are! It is saddening and can only be compared to a religious cult where sense, logic and observable reality are ignored!

This book finishes with the United Kingdom having still not left the European Union on the 31st October 2019 as the Prime Minister had promised (as Teresa May had promised for the 30th March 2019) and now extended until 30th January 2020, so let us see what the future holds and whether the chaos continues.

482

But it is clear Brexit will not end in January 2020 but will drag on for months and years with the aftermath potentially creating much more chaos than we have witnessed to this day. Free movement and fishing rights will be back on the table when the Free Trade Agreement is negotiated, with Leavers being disappointed in these areas also.

Let's cross our fingers (what a ridiculous thought when talking about the future of our country!) for the UK and hope we do not reach the worst-case scenario many fear. Good luck everyone but let me finish with the words of the late Jo Cox MP who said it better than I ever could when she stated in her maiden speech in the house of commons in 2015.

"We are far more united and have far more in common with each other than things that divide us"

RIP Jo Cox

Chapter 34
Glossary & Key Names:

Glossary and Key names

AggregateIQ - Data analytics company based in Victoria, British Columbia, Canada. Worked for Mercer-funded Pacs that supported the Trump campaign. Robert Mercer owns AggregateIQ's IP. Paid £3.9m by Vote Leave to "micro-target" voters on social media during referendum campaign. Outside British jurisdiction.

Arron Banks - Bristol businessman. Co-founder of Leave.EU who owns data company and insurance firms. Single biggest donor to Leave campaign of £7.5m.

Article 50 - The formal mechanism for exiting the EU: the clause in the 2007 Lisbon treaty that allows any member state "to withdraw from the union in accordance with its own constitutional requirements". The two-year article 50 negotiations, which among other things must settle citizens' rights, the question of the Irish border and the UK's exit bill, are in effect the divorce talks.

BeLeave - Youth Leave campaign set up by 23-year-old student. Given £625,000 by Vote Leave & £50,000 by another donor. Spent it with AggregateIQ.

Cambridge Analytica - Data analytics company formed in 2014. Robert Mercer owns 90%. SCL owns 10%. Carried out major digital targeting campaigns for Donald Trump campaign, Ted Cruz's nomination campaign and multiple other US Republican campaigns – mostly funded by Mercer. Gave Nigel Farage's Leave.EU "help" during referendum.

Canada-plus deal - A free trade agreement identical to the EU's deal with Canada (Ceta) would abolish almost all tariffs on goods and reduce some – though by no means all – non-tariff barriers through mutual recognition of selected standards. But it would not cover some sectors, such as food or chemicals, that are important to the UK, nor many services, which account for 80% of the UK's economy. In a Canada-plus deal, the UK would therefore be looking for more mutual recognition of standards in sectors that matter to it, and a greatly enhanced services component.

Canada plus, or SuperCanada - Leading Brexiteers David Davis and Boris Johnson have outlined greatly improved Canada-style free trade agreements they believe the UK can negotiate with the EU. Johnson's "SuperCanada" plan would include zero tariffs and zero quotas on all imports and exports; cover services as well as goods; ensure full mutual recognition of regulations and standards; and rely on technology to keep supply chains smooth. Many trade experts doubt such a deal is achievable, and if it were it could take decades (the basic EU-Canada Ceta deal took seven years).

Christopher Wylie - Canadian who first brought data expertise and micro-targeting to Cambridge Analytica; recruited AggregateIQ.

Customs union - EU members - plus Turkey, Andorra, Monaco and San Marino - trade without customs duties, taxes or tariffs between themselves, and charge the same tariffs on imports from outside the EU. Customs union members cannot negotiate their own trade deals outside the EU, which is why leaving it – while hopefully negotiating a bespoke arrangement – has been one of the government's Brexit goals.

DUP - Democratic Unionist Party of Northern Ireland. Spent £32,750 with AggregrateIQ.

EEA / EFTA - The European Economic Area is made up of the EU's single market (see below), plus three European Free Trade Association members - Iceland, Liechtenstein and Norway. They trade freely with the single market in exchange for accepting its rules. Switzerland is in EFTA but not the EEA. Bilateral accords give it special access to the single market. The four EFTA countries are not in the customs union and can negotiate trade deals with third countries such as China.

Ethnicity - the fact or state of belonging to a social group that has a common national or cultural tradition or an ethnic group; a social group that shares a common and distinctive culture, religion, and / or language.

European council / European commission - The European council, headed by Donald Tusk, is the gathering of heads of state or government that sets the bloc's priorities and strategic goals. The commission, headed by Jean-Claude Juncker, is often called the EU's civil service but is more than that. Its 28 member-appointed commissioners formally initiate EU legislation.

European court of justice (ECJ) - The Luxembourg-based ECJ rules on disputes over EU treaties and legislation. Cases can be brought by governments, EU institutions, companies or citizens. Leaving the ECJ's jurisdiction has been one of the government's requirements for Brexit.

European Research Group. ... Defined by its opposition to the UK's membership of the European Union, the **ERG** is an IPSA-funded pooled service within the formal IPSA Scheme of MPs' Business Costs and Expenses and is one of two such publicly funded pooled services maintained for Conservative MPs.

Frictionless trade - A Theresa May mantra, "frictionless trade" would require a "bespoke arrangement" with the EU creating a "new free trade area" for goods and a "combined customs territory" that together would protect supply chains and just-in-time delivery with a bare minimum of customs and regulatory controls. The EU sees frictionless trade as something that can only come with being in the single market, so is incompatible with the UK's plan to leave both. The term does not appear in the withdrawal agreement.

Great repeal bill - A piece of legislation that will transpose, at a stroke, all existing EU legislation affecting the UK into domestic UK law to avoid a legal black hole and prevent disruption the day after the UK leaves. The British parliament is then meant to "amend, repeal and improve" each law as necessary – a gargantuan task.

Gross Domestic Product (GDP) - The Gross Domestic Product measures the value of economic activity within a country. Strictly defined, GDP is the sum of the market values, or prices, of all final goods and services produced in an economy during a period of time.

Hard Brexit - A hard Brexit would take the UK out of the EU's single market and customs union and end its obligations to respect the four freedoms, make big EU budget payments and accept the jurisdiction of the ECJ - what Brexiters mean by "taking back control" of the UK's borders, laws and money. It would mean a return of trade tariffs, depending on what, if any FTA was agreed.

ISDS - Investor-state dispute settlement (ISDS) or investment court system (ICS) is a system through which investors can sue nation states for alleged discriminatory practices. ISDS is an instrument of public international law and provisions are contained in a number of bilateral investment treaties, in certain international trade treaties, such as NAFTA (chapter 11), and the proposed TPP (chapter 9) and CETA (sections 3 and 4) agreements. ISDS is also found in international investment agreements, such as the Energy Charter Treaty. If an investor from one country (the "home state") invests in another country (the "host state"), both of which have agreed to ISDS, and the host state violates the rights granted to the investor under the treaty, then that investor may bring the matter before an arbitral tribunal.

National Debt and Deficit – A budget deficit is the difference between what the federal government spends (called **outlays**) and what it takes in (called **revenue** or **receipts**). The **national debt**, also known as the public debt, is the result of the federal government borrowing money to cover years and years of budget deficits.

Neo Liberal - relating to or denoting a modified form of liberalism (the holding of liberal views one of the basic ones being tolerance) tending to favour free-market capitalism.

Nigel Farage - Former UKIP leader. Leader of Leave.EU, and close friend of Arron Banks.

Norway model - See EEA/EFTA and soft Brexit. This would see the UK out of the EU and customs union (so able to negotiate independent free trade agreements with third countries) but with enhanced access to the single market and selected EU programmes. But it would entail continued financial payments and acceptance of the core principles and legislation of the single market, with no participation in EU decision-making, so is seen by Brexiteers as a betrayal of the referendum vote.

One Nation Conservatives (Tories) - One nation conservatism is a paternalistic form of British political conservatism. It advocates the preservation of established institutions and traditional principles within a political democracy, in combination with social and economic programmes designed to benefit the ordinary person. According to this political philosophy, society should be allowed to develop in an organic way, rather than being engineered. It argues that members of society have obligations towards each other and particularly emphasises paternalism, meaning that those who are privileged and wealthy pass on their benefits. It argues that this elite should work to reconcile the interests of all classes, labour as well as management, instead of identifying the good of society solely with the interests of the business class.

Pluralistic society – A pluralistic society is a diverse one, where the people in it believe all kinds of different things and tolerate each other's beliefs even when they don't match their own.

Purdah – is the civil service term for the time between the formal start of the election campaign and the announcement of the results. Civil servants are given official guidance by the Cabinet Office on the rules they must follow in relation to Government business during this time. For civil servants prohibited from making EU pronouncements or releasing information in four-week run-up to poll.

Race - the fact or condition of belonging to a racial division or group; the qualities or characteristics associated with this, or a group of people sharing the same culture, history, language, etc.; an ethnic group.

Single market - The EU's single market is more than a free-trade area. It aims to remove not just the fiscal barriers to trade (tariffs) but also the physical and technical barriers (borders and divergent product standards) by allowing the freest possible movement of goods, capital, services and people. In essence, it is about treating the EU as a single trading territory.

Soft Brexit - A soft Brexit, which not officially defined, would keep the UK in either the single market or the customs union or both. It could be achieved along the lines of the Norway model - see EEA/EFTA - or via an FTA, but would require concessions on free movement, ECJ jurisdiction and budget payments. Brexiteers do not consider a soft Brexit as really leaving the EU.

Transition period - A period designed to bridge the gap between the end of article 50 talks, when the UK leaves the EU, and the start of a future FTA. The two sides have agreed to a transition period - the UK calls it an "implementation phase" - to avoid the cliff edge outlined above that will end on 31 December 2020, although this may be extended by one or two years.

Withdrawal agreement - The 599-page agreement published in mid-November that will regulate the UK's formal divorce from the EU. It addresses points such as the transition period; the financial settlement ("divorce bill") to cover the UK's past and ongoing commitments to the bloc; the rights of EU citizens in the UK and British nationals on the continent, and (most controversially) how to ensure there will be no hard border on the island of Ireland after Brexit.

WTO terms - Without an FTA, trade between the UK and the EU would happen under the rules of the 164-member World Trade Organisation, of which the UK is an independent member (although it applies the EU tariff schedule). After Brexit, the UK could set its own import tariffs providing they are no higher than its current (EU) schedule, which might in some circumstances be beneficial. But UK exports to the EU would be subject to the EU's schedule, which for many product categories would prove punitive. Trading on WTO terms would also raise big practical and logistical problems around things such as product approval and customs checks.

Vassalage - A position of subordination or submission (as to a political power).

Chapter 35
References:

References

(1) Blake, Aaron (January 22, 2017). "Kellyanne Conway says Donald Trump's team has 'alternative facts.' Which pretty much says it all". The Washington Post. Retrieved January 22, 2017.

(2) Guilty men by Cato the Younger. P.156.

(3) https://www.bbc.co.uk/news/av/uk-40667879/eu-trade-deal-easiest-in-human-history

(4) https://www.buzzfeed.com/alexspence/heres-a-leaked-whatsapp-

chat-showing-tory-leavers-confusion

(5) EUR-Lex. Laws include regulations (directly applicable to all EU member states) and directives (rules to be incorporated into individual member states existing national laws) - but exclude decisions.

(6) https://tompride.wordpress.com/2017/12/05/see-20-years-of-fake-news-about-eu-by-uk-press-vote-for-your-favourite-here/

(7) https://www.theguardian.com/politics/ng-interactive/2018/mar/28/11-brexit-promises-leavers-quietly-dropped

(8) Britain Post Brexit, Peter McGarrick, p.182

(9) Guilty Men, by "Cato the younger" p.22

(10)   Guilty Men, by "Cato the younger" p.44

(11)   https://www.kcl.ac.uk/sspp/policy-institute/news/newsrecords/2017/new-data-driven-analysis-of-how-the-uk-media-covered-the-eu-referendum-campaign

(12)   https://www.kcl.ac.uk/sspp/policy-institute/CMCP/UK-media-coverage-of-the-2016-EU-Referendum-campaign.pdf

(13)   https://dominiccummings.com/2015/06/23/on-the-referendum-6-exit-plans-and-a-second-referendum/

(14)   Brexit fears leave daffodils in the ground, Tommy

Stubbington, The Sunday Times 31st March 2019.

(15)   https://en.wikipedia.org/wiki/Developed_country

(16)   https://www.bbc.co.uk/news/business-45633592

(17)

https://en.wikipedia.org/wiki/Government_spending_in_the_United_

Kingdom

(18)   https://www.gov.uk/government/consultations/fisheries-

white-paper-sustainable-fisheries-for-future-generations/sustainable-

fisheries-for-future-generations-consultation-document#setting-our-

course

(19)   https://www.doverport.co.uk/about/performance/

(20)   Leave versus Remain: the digital battle, Dr. Andrew Mullen,

senior lecturer in International Relations and politics at Northumbria

University.

(21)   https://www.thelondoneconomic.com/news/rationalist-destroys-leavers-with-list-of-all-eu-laws-that-have-been-forced-on-us-against-our-will/22/01/

(22)   https://kclpure.kcl.ac.uk/portal/files/109250771/UK_media_coverage_of_the_2016_EU_Referendum_campaign.pdf

(23)   https://kclpure.kcl.ac.uk/portal/files/109250771/UK_media_coverage_of_the_2016_EU_Referendum_campaign.pdf - Page 65.

(24)   https://www.dailymail.co.uk/news/article-3611697/Record-number-jobless-EU-migrants-Britain-Hammer-blow-PM-270-000-EU-nationals-came-year.html

(25)
https://www.newstatesman.com/politics/economy/2019/01/why-uk-cannot-see-brexit-utterly-utterly-stupid

(26)   https://fullfact.org/europe/irish-backstop/

(27)   https://www.greenpeace.org.uk/press-releases/farages-voting-record-on-fishing-makes-mockery-of-new-election-poster/

(28)   https://infacts.org/farage-wants-voters-to-trust-him-thats-rich/

(29)   https://www.economist.com/britain/2019/05/09/how-is-brexit-affecting-fdi-into-britain

(30)

https://www.newstatesman.com/politics/staggers/2019/05/why-are-we-governed-incompetents

(31)   Guilty men by Cato the Younger. P.156.

(32)   https://ukandeu.ac.uk/wp-content/uploads/2018/12/What-would-trading-on-WTO-terms-mean-Long-Guide.pdf

(33)   Mason, Rowena (18 June 2014). "PM backs Michael Gove but suggests former aide was a 'career psychopath'". The Guardian. Retrieved 1 July 2016.

(34)   https://www.economist.com/bagehots-notebook/2016/01/21/an-interview-with-dominic-cummings

(35)   All Out War – The full story of Brexit p.115 – Tim Shipmen

(36)   All Out War – The full story of Brexit p.201 – Tim Shipmen

(37)   Coalition: The inside Story of the Conservative-Liberal Democrat Coalition Government – David Laws, p.244

(38)   Brexit: Battle for Britain, BBC2, 8 August 2016.

(39)   https://www.theguardian.com/politics/2019/apr/09/loss-of-eu-doctors-is-a-disaster-for-the-nhs

(40)   Racism unleashed: incident by incident – the grim litany of post Brexit hate crime – The Independent, 28 July 2016.

(41)   https://www.independent.co.uk/news/uk/politics/racism-unleashed-brexit-eu-referendum-post-referendum-racism-true-scale-of-post-eu-referendum-a7149836.html

(42)   How to be right, James O'Brien p.73.

(43)   Sunday times on August the 11th 2019
https://www.telegraph.co.uk/news/2016/06/06/eu-rules-stopped-britain-deporting-murders-rapists-and-violent-c/

(44)   Financial Times, 18 December 2016

(45)   'David Cameron: Brexit vote ended a "poisoning" of UK politics', Guardian 26th April 2017

(46)   https://blogs.lse.ac.uk/brexit/2019/04/05/britains-

wartime-generation-are-almost-as-pro-eu-as-millennials/

(47)   Professor Jonathan Portes https://ukandeu.ac.uk/weather-is-not-climate-forecasting-the-impacts-of-brexit/

(48)   https://www.gov.uk/government/publications/hm-treasury-analysis-the-long-term-economic-impact-of-eu- membership-and-the-alternatives

(49)   Swati Dhingra 'UK economic policy'

https://ukandeu.ac.uk/wp-content/uploads/2017/05/Red-Yellow-and-Blue- Brexit-The-Manifestos-Uncovered.pdf

(50)   Jonathan Portes, 24th November 2016

https://ukandeu.ac.uk/brexit-migration-and-the-uk-economy/

(51)   https://unherd.com/2019/08/the-roots-of-our-brexit-divisions/ - Diane Purkiss is a professor at Oxford University. Her book, The English Civil War: A People's History, published by HarperCollins.

(52)   Source BES: https://www.britishelectionstudy.com/bes-findings/what-mattered-most-to-you-when-deciding- how-to-vote-in-the-eu-referendum/#.XZi7l0ZKiUl

(53)   https://www.dailymail.co.uk/news/article-3903436/Enemies-people-Fury-touch-judges-defied-17-4m-Brexit-voters-trigger-constitutional-crisis.html

(54)   https://www.bbc.co.uk/news/uk-46618532

(55)   https://www.bbc.co.uk/news/uk-politics-47488047

(56)   https://trade.ec.europa.eu/tradehelp/everything-arms

(57)
https://www.theguardian.com/politics/2019/mar/13/brexit-tariffs-on-87-of-uk-imports-cut-to-zero-in-temporary-no-deal-plan

(58)   https://www.bbc.co.uk/news/uk-england-46788530

(59)   "Tackling the under-supply of housing in England" by

Wendy Wilson & Cassie Barton

(60)

https://www.theguardian.com/commentisfree/2019/oct/08/boris-johnson-deal-reality-election-brexit - Raphael Behr.

(61)   https://blogs.spectator.co.uk/2017/01/dominic-cummings-brexit-referendum-won/ - Dominic Cummings.

(62)   https://www.bbc.co.uk/news/magazine-36619342 - Jon Kelly, BBC News Magazine

(63)   https://www.ucl.ac.uk/economics/about-department/fiscal-effects-immigration-uk - Christian Dustmann and Tommaso Frattini, University College London.

Resources / Further reading

1.   Breinlich, H., E. Leromain, D. Novy and T. Sampson (2017) 'The Consequences of the Brexit Vote for UK Inflation and Living Standards: First Evidence', CEP Technical Report.

2.   http://www.cbi.org.uk/insight-and-analysis/our-global-future/factsheets/factsheet-2-benefits-of-eu-membership-outweigh-costs/

3.   https://www.euractiv.com/section/uk-europe/linksdossier/europe-a-la-carte-the-whats-and-whys-behind-uk-opt-outs/

4.   https://brexit853.wordpress.com/2016/09/27/powers-that-the-uk-has-failed-to-use-to-control-eu-freedom-of-movement-directive/

5.   HM Treasury (2016) 'The Long-term Economic Impact of EU Membership and the Alternatives', HMSO

6.   http://www.fullfact.org

7.   https://en.wikipedia.org/wiki/Brexit_withdrawal_agreement

8.   https://smallbusinessprices.co.uk/remain-eu/

9.   https://www.gq-magazine.co.uk/article/list-of-brexit-lies

10.   https://www.gov.uk/government/publications/withdrawal-agreement-and-political-declaration

11.   The Brexit Vote, Inflation and UK Living Standards - Holger Breinlich, Elsa Leromain, Dennis Novy and Thomas Sampson –

12.   http://cep.lse.ac.uk/pubs/download/brexit11.pdf

13.   Clarke, S., I. Serwicka, and L.A. Winters (2017) 'Will Brexit Raise the Cost of Living?', National Institute Economic Review 242(1): R37-50.

14.   https://www.gov.uk/guidance/help-and-support-for-traders-if-the-uk-leaves-the-eu-with-no-deal

15.   http://www.brexitshambles.com/a-thought-provoking-expose-shining-a-light-on-how-in-allowing-brexits-cheats-and-liars-to-avoid-punitive-justice-our-democracy-has-been-left-in-jeopardy/

Bibliography

(also further suggested reading that gives much more detail of certain subjects and sections of this book)

- The elephant in the room? The Free Movement of Services and Brexit – Gavin Barrett.

- 9 Lessons in Brexit – Ivan Rogers

- A short History of Brexit – Kevin O'Rourke

- Breaking Point: the UK referendum on the EU and its aftermath – Gary Gibbon (Hause curiosities 2016)

- Brexit – The impact of 'Brexit' on the United Kingdom, my Ebook publishing house.

- Brexit – the road to freedom – Will Podmore

- Brexit – the tip of the populist iceberg? – N.J. Paquet

- Brexit - What the Hell Happens Now? Ian Dunt.

- Brexit – why Britain voted to leave the European Union. Harold D Clarke, Matthew Goodwin, and Paul Whitely.

- Brexit and British politics – Geoffrey Evans and Anand Menon (polity books)

- Brexit and the British, who are we now – Stephen Green

- Brexit without the Bullshit – Gavin Esler

- Britain Post Brexit, A practical guide to moving on – Peter McGarrick

- Fall Out: A year of political mayhem – Tim Shipman

- For the record – David Cameron

- Guilty Men (Brexit Edition) by Cato The Younger

- Heroic Failure, Brexit and the politics of pain – Fintan O'Toole

- How to be right ... in a world gone wrong – James O'Brien

- National Populism: The revolt against Liberal Democracy (Penguin)

- The Bad Boys of Brexit: Tales of Mischief, Mayhem & Guerrilla Warfare in the EU Referendum Campaign - Arron Banks / Ed. Isabel Oakeshott

- The Brexit Club: The inside story of the leave campaign's

shock victory (Biteback, 2016)

- The history of the European Union – Richard T. Griffiths

- The lies we were told – Simon Wren-Lewis

- The Story of Brexit – A Ladybird Book

- The strange death of Europe – Douglas Murray

- Unleashing Demons – Craig Oliver

- Well you did ask: Why the UK voted to leave the EU - Michael Ashcroft and Kevin Culwick

- Why we lost the Brexit vote - Daniel Korski (Politico 2016)

- WTF – Robert Preston

- How to stop Brexit – Nick Clegg

Chapter 36
About the Author

About the author

Christopher is a small business owner importing from many countries worldwide with a global customer base so has seen the trials, tribulations and challenges of international trade first-hand, including the advantages of the EU single market giving him a great insight to the EU and International trade but not having the restrictions of being a journalist or specialist advisers in the Westminster bubble.

He graduated in 1992 with a BA Hons. (2.1) in European Business and a German Degree (Diplom Betriebswirt) from the Fachhochschule Trier in 1994.

Christopher grew up in and around London but lived in Germany for a number of years leaning fluent German so has experienced the advantages of a multicultural experience in both the UK and Germany, as well as the advantages of free movement within EU member states. Having also played semi-professional Table Tennis in Germany and representing the England team at the European championships in 1984 he now concentrates on his business and coaching the next generation of junior Table Tennis players.

He now lives in South East England near London with his family and Shi Tzu dog Honey (starring above).

Chapter 37
APPENDICES:

APPENDIX 1

The Quick-Fire replies to Brexiteer arguments / reasoning

1.	"We have too many immigrants" / "We need to stop Immigration"	But the UK has the highest employment and lowest unemployment for decades with over 100,000+ vacancies still to fill, so does not have too many, plus the UK lacks enough people with certain skills such as Doctors, vets etc. so we need these people!
2.	"We need to take back sovereignty"	The UK never lost it (it's a fallacy) and could always make our own decisions as we have by invoking Article 50, including vote to Leave the EU. But the UK pooled sovereignty for the UK's benefit and that of its citizens which led to economic growth in recent decades!
3.	"We are losing our identity"	The UK or its citizens do not have 1 identity with a highly mixed vibrant mix of identities and cultures creating a rich and interesting country. You can do anything you want now as you could before as regards this ideal of 'identity'. What part of YOUR identity do you feel you are losing?

4.	"I voted Leave as there are too many Eastern European criminals and rapists being let in	There is no empirical evidence that any one nationality is more likely to commit crime than another, with crime more directly linked to poverty than a specific race. Don't believe the lies that become urban myths and then truth in some people's eyes. Poverty and lack of opportunity is a more likely reason for crime and remaining inside the EU will give our young people, more options mot less!
5.	"The speed and numbers are too high for us as a country to handle"	We need the people and their skills for our dynamic developing economy, but 4consecutive governments failed to build and invest in affordable housing and some infrastructure, which linked to austerity cuts has led to a bottleneck when it comes to housing etc., but any government can address that fairly quickly if it wants to. Build affordable housing and infrastructure and initial issue solved!

6.	Will we be able to give loans to struggling industries (e.g. Steel Works) without having to ask permission from the EU commission?	CB: We do not want to introduce a socialist re-nationalisation of industries which seems a retrograde step into 1970s Labour industrial policies or giving money to private companies like Greybull Capital LLP which is a private investment company that specialises in medium-to long-term investments in UK companies and owned British steel that was no longer economically viable. So effectively the idea would be to give a private investment company UK taxpayers money which is counterintuitive and not a good long-term idea. The rules are there to protect all the EU from unfair subsidisation etc. in an attempt to create a level playing field!
7.	We gain more control (instead of losing it) over taxation such as VAT which can help those on low incomes.	The EU rule is no less than 15% on VAT, so the UK government is choosing to keep VAT at 20% but could reduce it to 15% tomorrow. In summary the EU is not a problem here, as nobody or sensible economist is recommending going below 15% on VAT. Other taxes like income tax, capital gains tax etc. is all UK decisions to lots of flexibility on fiscal policy!

8.	We just needed to be tougher in the negotiations	The UK government was very robust in trying to achieve the best deal for the UK, but we have to be realistic and admit that in the face of 27 other member states, and we are the ones leaving and they are in a stronger negotiating position. The government achieved stopping free movement of workers, UK fishing rights, no ECJ ruling, No more sending larger sums to Brussels etc. so they have achieved a lot for those that no longer wanted such influences by the EU!
9.	"We must carry out the 'WILL OF THE PEOPLE'"	There is no such thing as "The People" as if everyone is exactly the same and as only 37% of the electorate voted Leave (so 63% did not!) the MPs and our parliament should be governing for the whole of the country and not a minority. The country is split, Parliament is split so a compromise deal must be found!

10.	"EU Migrants are Benefit Scroungers"	There is no empirical evidence that EU Migrants come here just to collect benefits and they are not literally allowed by EU law to receive benefits in the first 3 months as they must prove they are looking for work, and can be returned home if they have not got a job or prove how they can support themselves without an income. Just look at how low benefits are to see how ludicrous such an argument is!
11.	"Charity begins at home"	This is a harsh and selfish view of the world where we use only 0.7% of our GDP for International aid, i.e. to help people dying or starving in the most remote parts of the world or who are in war torn countries suffering great hardship. People should not forget their privilege for having been born in the UK by pure luck, and not having done anything to receive that privilege!

12.	"The German Car makers will tell the EU and Angela Merkel to give us a great deal!"	Cleary, this is not true and has still not happened 3 years since the referendum which is because it was nonsense and the German automotive industry does not have as much influence as Brexiteers tried to have us believe!
13.	"We can trade with the rest of the world when we leave!"	We can already do this a full member of the EU. Also trading on WTO rules will cost us so much more money and therefore make the UK poorer when it already has 50+ trade deals with other countries as a full member of the EU. There is no massive advantage to achieve and many complications that will come with those new trade deals!
14.	"We want to Take back control of our Trade"	We never lost control of our trade and it was an untruth from the Leave campaigns. In fact, potential trade deals with the USA could lead to greater restrictions and loss of control from such a larger country who wishes to lower our food standards and animal welfare as well as privatise more parts of the NHS to introduce their powerful Pharma industry into the UK healthcare systems!

15.	"Why should Germany, France etc. have input in our laws?"	Isolationism is long dead with positive cooperation for the common good as countries work together. No EU decisions are made without UK input, and often have strong Vetoes available, such as new members like Turkey joining to prevent such developments!
16.	"Churchill would never have allowed us to be swallowed up by Europe!"	The UK is not swallowed up by the EU (if you disagree please explain how?) and Churchill knew the benefits of Europe working as closely as possible together after what he had witnessed in WW! And WW2! He said Britain should promote *"every practical step which the nations of Europe may take to reduce the barriers which divide them and to nourish their common interests and their common welfare."* Winston Churchill, News of the World 1938.

17.	"It's our money argument"	The money we send to the EU as a part of our cooperation programme with them is a very good investment as we receive some of that money back, have rebates which other countries do not have, and the benefits and economic growth from free trade we achieve far outweigh what we pay in!
18.	"I hate the EU Laws and regulations imposed upon us!"	If Only 4,514 out of 34,105 laws have been influenced by the EU, of which just 72 of them we accepted which we did not necessarily agree with, and that is the process of cooperation and compromise! Which of those 72 laws that we did not agree with do you not like? Which ones would you change and how?

19.	"You do not know what will happen in the future"	This is the "crystal ball" argument used by people with no obvious, realistic and logical reasons for leaving based on facts, but ignore that the status quo is a much safer bet than the no deal "no idea" future for the UK and all the risks, costs and unknowns that it brings with it. Just jumping into the dark is not an option and nobody would, for example, move to a new house in that way!
20.	"It will be alright eventually"	This is an unacceptable argument again by people with no reasonable realistic and logical arguments for leaving and offer just a 'wait and see argument', which is no argument and Jacob Rees-Mogg even suggested it may be 50 years before we reap the benefits of Brexit Our children do not have 50 years to wait!
21.	The "we just need to be stronger" argument	This lacks and tangible logical arguments and smells of old imperialistic views of when Britain had a huge powerful empire which it no longer does and so the argument is no longer valid, and we have to cooperate and compromise with our partners, rather than thinking we can just ram through our own plans and countries will just accept it!

22.	We can "Abolish all Tariffs" argument	Abolishing tariffs could detrimentally expose domestic manufacturers, auto manufacturers, and sectors such as farming. So, in many years the UK could no longer be competitive in strategic areas, and business could go bust!
23.	"Job Losses and Depreciation of Sterling is Project Fear"	The 12% drop in Sterling which would increase the cost of imports happened straight after the Leave result in 2016. Also, in July 2019 Sterling took another tumble in light of soon to be Prime Minister Boris Johnson claimed he will take the UK out of the European Union on 31st October "Do or die". This is project reality and means increased costs for UK citizens disproportionately affecting the poorest in or society!
24.	"It's OK we are preparing for a no-deal Brexit"	It is not OK as even if we are preparing the pain will still be significant and affect all citizens in the UK whether they want it or not. Imagine preparing to burn you hand, it will still hurt like hell when you genuinely burn your hand! Also, it is impossible to prepare 100% and unforeseen issues will create issues and delays etc. with no significant benefits for our country!

25.	"We voted to Leave but still have high employment and low unemployment!"	That is because this was achieved as a full member of the EU and the advantages it brings to the UK trade and economy, plus we have not even left yet and so the negative and serious impacts on employment and inward investment etc. which will lead to a reduction in jobs and opportunities are still to come!
26.	"They need us more than we need them!"	They do not and that has become clear especially as the UK exports to the EU is 13% of our total economy but the EU exports to the UK amount to only 3% of their total economy. 27 countries losing one of their most important trading partners is much less important to them than it is to the UK losing its 27 closest trading partners!
27.	"It's not all about money"	It is never just about money, but the argument is wrong in that the more money a government has due to the success of its economy the more it can spend on the NHS, Social services, capital investments and other ways to improve UK society as a whole. Money makes this possible and the single market helps the UK government do this and the UK citizens would benefit accordingly!

APPENDIX 2

The Quick Fire overview of potential issues of a no-deal Brexit many of which have been covered through the book earlier, some that will hit earlier than others that may take longer to seep into the UK economy and affect the social fabric of the country.

Delays in food and product shipments due to border delays and the end to frictionless EU trade

Legal chaos with such rules and regulations ceasing to be operational including moving of controlled chemicals such as Mercury etc.

Unrest and potential return to violence in Ireland with a potential border and the impact on the Good Friday agreement and fear of a return to the old days of terrorism and violence.

Trucks may not be allowed into the EU after the planned grace period as there are only 4,000 permits for an estimated 40,000 lorries.

Issue with Fee travel such as international travel permits, pets needing blood tests, expensive use of credit / banking cards and the loss of the important EHIC (European Health Insurance cards creating issues for many.

Issues with travel insurance such as travel for those with kidney dialysis requirements as the insurance will be much too expensive for them to travel.

Worries of EU citizens who deliver such critical services to our country and fellow citizens about the lack of guarantees of protecting their rights after a no-deal Brexit with many already having had issues and complications such as proving their eligibility despite having lived in the country for 20+ years! We all remember the Windrush generation cock ups, so it is understandable they have concerns and cannot rely on the competence of the home office and civil service.

Our students wanting to study abroad could be very disappointed as the UK will no longer be a member of the EU's popular **Erasmus system** plus UK educational activities across the UK would lose Erasmus funding. We basically lose access and the benefits of an excellent pan-European organisation that has offered many opportunities they may never have received.

Uncertainty for UK ex-pats living in the other EU states as the EU rejected a blanket deal protecting all the UK ex-pats in the event of a no-deal Brexit although Spain has protected their rights as they are a good income for the country with fairly wealthy UK pensioners retiring to the sun. But other states see it differently.

Linked to the above British citizens **lose that great free movement** including travel, jobs, residence, recognition of qualifications etc. All gone and replaced by the old complicated red tape of the past. Surely a step backwards.

Companies will find it more difficult to **get the right talent** as free movement for work is ended and potential quality employees may go elsewhere with their future's in the UK unsure, the unwelcoming nature of a large part of the UK towards immigrants, and no obvious long-term opportunities to lay down roots in the UK.

The public finances could be seriously hit if the economy shrinks, companies make less profits due to restricted trade with the EU the UK's largest trading partner, and therefore less taxes paid. Higher unemployment also means less taxes and higher strain on the public purse.

Jobs Lost – linked to the above the CBI warned that with a no-deal Brexit unemployment could rise to 7.5% which would be disastrous and could hit those areas most that voted heavily to Leave. Did they understand the consequences?

Reduced investment – as international companies look for easy access into the EU and avoid the uncertainty the UK economy now brings as well as the concern over the lack of or difficulty in attracting the right talent going forward. Many companies including BMW, Airbus, Panasonic, Honda and Nissan plus many more have either cut jobs, threatened to cut jobs or move factories / operations or cut planned investments and move those elsewhere.

Linked to the above companies, especially those suppliers and sub-suppliers to those major manufacturers that may move operations **companies could go bust** generating yet more unemployment.

The risk of a recession has heightened the risk of recession from a strong economy pre-2016 EU referendum result and although the global slow downplays a big role, but Brexit has a had a major impact with a slowdown of the economy and uncertainty everywhere. According to the

OBR (Office of Budget responsibility) due to customs delays, loss of trade agreements and barriers to services companies would contract by 2% in 2020.

Sterling has tumbled and could tumble yet further signalling the markets lack of confidence in the UK and its currency but also creating higher costs of imported products and more pressure on inflation that should not be underestimated.

Lost Bilateral agreements – The UK has around 400 "relevant" such agreements unrelated to trade which the UK has, via the EU, with other countries including in strategic areas such as aviation, and nuclear cooperation but also on other areas such as judicial cooperation or professional qualifications

We will **lose very good trade deals with other non-EU countries** with some of the major ones in Japan and Turkey stating those deals will not be rolled over, so the UK will face tariffs and quotas that will limit trade between the UK and those countries and they may find trading with the EU will be a lot simpler.

Tariffs on UK imports as the UK will probably be put on goods from the EU like other non-EU countries which could expose many industries to higher costs which increases the cost of living to the UK citizens with no benefits.

Issues with supply chains and border blockages etc. that need frictionless trade due to the nature of those products could cause all sorts of issues including companies having to make temporary shutdowns especially in the event of a no-deal Brexit. Goods specifically at risk could be medicines, fresh fruit and similar products for obvious reasons, or even essential imports such as chemicals used to purify water.

APPENDIX 3

Quick Fire guide to the advantages of being a member of the EU, which is by no means an exhaustive list but gives a good overview of some of the things UK citizens could lose out on.

1	Being a part of the strongest trading block in the world so the USA and China pay attention to our values of tolerance, openness and shared values of the EU 27 so we cannot be bullied in trade talks.
2	Freedom of movement for our citizens throughout the whole of the EU.
3	Improved consumer rights protecting UK consumers against unscrupulous companies.
4	Tariff-free trade within the EU lowering costs of trade for the UK
5	Closer political and economic Cooperation = less chance of European wars as in the past – jaw jaw is better than war war!
6	The UK enjoys an opt out from the single currency and maintains full control of its borders as a non-member of the Schengen area, giving the UK advantages other EU states do not have.
7	Cheaper food and alcohol imports from the EU states in continental Europe

8	3.1 million jobs in the UK are directly linked to exports to the EU and could be negatively affected post Brexit.
9	EU competition laws protect consumers by combating monopolistic business practices that could negatively affect UK citizens.
10	Membership of the world's largest trading bloc with over 500 million consumers, representing 23% of global GDP has helped the UK economy thrive in a very erratic global world.
11	The abolition of non-tariff barriers (quotas, subsidies, administrative rules etc.) among members has helped UK service companies compete on an even playing field and with 80% of the UK economy being services this is critical.
12	The EU accounts for 44% of all UK exports of goods and services so is critical and being outside the single market / customs union could be very damaging.
13	The EU accounts for 53% of all UK imports of goods and services so is critical and being outside the single market / customs union could be very damaging.

14	The ability for UK citizens to retire in any EU member state with Pension transferability making the whole process and control much easier.
15	Foreign Direct Investment (FDI) into the UK from outside the EU has doubled since the creation of the EU Single Market but once the UK is outside the European Union this amount will be thrown into doubt.
16	Foreign Direct Investment (FDI) from the EU accounts for 47% of the UK's stock of inward worth over $1.2 trillion, but once outside the EU this will probably reduce as we forgo the advantages of being inside the single market and the benefits that brings.
17	The right of UK citizens to receive emergency healthcare in any member state (EHIC card) which can be lifesaving and absolutely critical to UK citizens.
18	The abolition of mobile telephone roaming charges saving UK citizens hundreds of thousands of pounds.
19	Cheaper air travel due to EU competition laws saving UK consumers millions of pounds.

20	EU cross-country coordination offers greater protection from terrorists, paedophiles, people traffickers and cyber-crime etc. rather than being an isolationist island with limited access to European databases that can help uncover and stop such criminal activities.
21	The right to work no more than 48 hours a week without paid overtime, reducing the chances of unscrupulous employers exploiting workers.
22	Free movement of labour has helped address shortages of unskilled workers including fruit picking, catering, social services etc.
23	Free movement of labour has helped UK firms plug skills gaps including translators, doctors, plumbers, Vets, nurses etc.
24	Strict controls on the operations of Multinational Corporations (MNCs) in the EU help to ensure high standards of transparency including business practices to help protect consumers and UK citizens.
25	The mutual recognition of professional qualifications has helped facilitate the free movement of engineers, teachers and doctors across the whole of the EU which has proved very beneficial to UK workers and professionals.

26	The UK receives around £730 million a year in EU funding for research and development which add real value to the UK economy both short and long term including important patents.
27	Improvements in air quality (significant reductions in sulphur dioxide and nitrogen oxides) as a result of EU legislation has led to a healthier environment for UK citizens.
28	Improvements in the quality of beaches and bathing water was a necessity which UK citizens now benefit from.
29	No time-consuming border checks for travellers (apart from in the UK) saving UK citizens a lot of time and inconvenience.
30	The right to reside in any EU member state has given UK citizens (estimated at almost 1 million) great freedom and flexibility whether it be living with a partner in Munich or retiring to the Costa Del Sol in Spain.
31	Structural funding for areas of the UK hit by industrial decline including South Wales and Yorkshire which was sadly lacking from UK governments.

32	Financial support for over 3,000 small and medium enterprises (SMEs) in the UK from the EU giving opportunities and lifelines to many.
33	Cornwall for example receives up to £750 million per year from the EU Social Fund (ESF) allowing it to make some significant regional developments in that deprived area.
34	Access to the EU Single Market has helped attract major investment into the UK from outside the EU, which may dry up once the UK is outside the EU and investors need that internal market access.
35	EU funding for infrastructure projects in the UK including £122 million for the "Midlands engine" project for example, and this is just one example.
36	Europe-wide patent and copyright protection proving very beneficial to many UK companies and inventors.
37	With Trump in the White House the UK's strongest natural allies are France, Germany and our other West European neighbours
38	As a member of the EU the UK maintains a say in the shaping of the rules governing its trade with its European partners, whereas when we leave we will not but will probably still have to meet those standards for UK companies to be able to sell into the European Union.

39	The EU provides an effective counterweight to the global power of the US, Russia and China, which the UK could not do on its own.
40	A ban on growth hormones and other harmful food additives to help protect UK and EU citizens Europe wide.
41	Improved food labelling which was lacking and especially with the issues of food allergies etc. this is an important qualitative development.
42	The European common arrest warrant gives the UK the ability to follow, trace and capture fleeing criminals, which as a non-EU state may prove more complicated.
43	Equality - Equal pay between men and women enshrined in European law since 1957 and has become a major principle in its dealings and is at the forefront of equality legislation.
44	EU consumer protection laws concerning transparency and product guarantees of quality and safety for the benefit of UK citizens.
45	EU rules governing health and safety at work are very strict to protect UK workers against employers cutting corners or not adhering to acceptable health & safety legislation to help protect their employees and workers.

46	Minimum guaranteed maternity leave of 14 weeks for pregnant women to protect UK mothers the flexibility and security of being able to tend to their new-borns without the pressure from some UK employers to return ASAP.
47	Common EU greenhouse gas emissions targets (19% reduction from 1990 to 2015) to become a leader in the environmental standards, targets and expectations which will help protect our future generations against the destruction of the planet.
48	The EU has played a leading role in combating global warming (Paris 2015 climate change conference) and leading the way in helping to protect the planet for the future generations.
49	The freedom to work in 28 countries without visa and immigration restrictions has opened up so many opportunities for UK citizens and their children as opposed to being an isolationist island limiting opportunities.
50	Strict safety standards for cars, buses and trucks has improved many aspects of safety including road deaths etc. Standard were raised and maintained.
51	British banks and insurance companies have been able to operate freely across the EU, which has benefited the powerful UK banking and insurance industries which will come in question once the UK leaves the EU.

52	No paperwork or customs for UK exports throughout the single market saving UK companies time, resource and money making them more efficient and profitable leading to more tax receipts from those companies flo0wing into the Treasury's coffers.
53	EU Support for rural areas under the European Agricultural Fund for Regional Development (EAFRD) helping numerous UK farms and agricultural businesses as a strategic part of a country being able to support itself.
54	EU anti-discrimination laws governing age, religion and sexual orientation helping reduce discrimination and increasing fairness to UK citizens and across the EU.
55	Cooperation in the peaceful use of nuclear energy as a member of Euratom is a very important and strategic partnership / operation the UK may be locked out of once we leave the European Union.
56	Membership of the European Medicines Agency (EMA) which monitors the quality and safety of medicines which has now moved its base in London to Amsterdam due to the threat of Brexit which led to job losses, reduced influence and potentially longer approval times for UK drugs and medicines.
57	Strict ban on animal testing in the cosmetics industry raising the standards and acceptability in animal welfare and testing processes etc.

58	Giving UK parents' Rights to a minimum 18 weeks of parental leave after childbirth giving parents greater flexibility and choice after the birth of their child.
59	EU standards on the quality of drinking water to the benefit of UK citizens and their children.
60	Protection of endangered species and habitats (EU Natura 2000 network), a major step forward to protecting many species on our planet that were dying out for various reasons.
61	The freedom to study in 28 countries (many EU universities teach courses in English and charge lower fees than in the UK) giving UK citizens greater options and opportunities to study in the EU but also to save money compared to just studying in the UK.
62	Consular protection from any EU embassy outside the EU, which can be critical if you cannot find or are not near the UK consulate in that country.
63	The Erasmus programme of university exchanges benefits around 16,000 UK students a year, but once we are outside the EU they will probably not qualify for this support programme and so limiting their options.

APPENDIX 4 - Lies or Just Misinformation?

1.   £40 Billion Divorce Bill for commitments already made will not be paid?

        a.   "OK we didn't know about that but why didn't the Brexiteer experts (Rees-Mogg, Boris, David Davis etc.) mention it, now we know there will be a 'divorce' bill?!"

2.   The big red Bus and £350 million per week extra for the NHS?

        a.   "OK we are not genuinely getting that, and it was made up and the only talk of a huge increase in NHS spending is via a tax increase"

3.   David Davis said it would be the easiest deal to complete?

        a.   "OK let's face it, it is a nightmare and the statement was totally false and was always going to be!"

4.   We will be better off outside the EU?

        a.   "OK in reality most informed commentary and experts say we will be poorer as a country due to higher costs of trade, no guarantees in improved trade agreements etc. Which leads to less company profits which will lead to less tax receipts for our government to spend on public services etc.

5.   Immigration will be dramatically cut?

        a.   "OK, I thought they weren't drain on our economy, but it looks like that will not happen as nobody seems to be guaranteeing that anymore and stats show we really need these workers for many jobs and figures show they contribute positively to our economy! More immigrants come from outside the EU so if the government really wanted to cut immigration they could. It isn't happening and people have been conned.

6.   Five million more migrants could enter Britain by 2030 if Turkey and four other applicant countries join the EU?

    a.   "OK I see now that it was all made up as a part of project fear by Farage and his friends, but it was convincing at the time, especially that poster of the Syrian refugees!" But people bought into that fear factor and Lie as Farage knew it was nonsense.

7.   'The UK loses out because other members favour a highly regulated and protectionist economy' – Jacob Rees-Mogg

    a.   "Ok That claim that the UK is constantly being overruled by other EU countries is false. Research by UK in a changing Europe shows that the UK has been in a minority on 57 legislative acts at the European Council since 1999, when the decisions were made public. Since then it has been in the majority on 2,474 acts and abstained on 70 occasions. Very disappointing as I trusted JRM but he is just a posh con artist!"

8.   No short-term economic disruption "After we Vote Leave, there won't be a sudden change that disrupts the economy."

    a.   "OK now all the major Brexiteers are saying there will be significant disruption and not sure for how long and Rees Mogg says it could be 50 years before we reap the benefits of Brexit! Very disappointing and many feel hugely misled"

9.   We'll get brand new trade deals all over the world, "We would immediately be able to start negotiating new trade deals... which could enter into force immediately after the UK leaves the EU" – Chris Grayling

    a.   "OK that has proved to be totally false and will Leave is with no significant trade deals which makes us poorer, and all countries in the world are looking to be a part of Strong trading blocks to make them more competitive. It feels like we have been lied to and will go backwards."

10.   There'll be no damage to trade with the EU, "There is a European free trade zone from Iceland to the Russian border and we will be part of it... Britain will have access to the Single Market after we vote leave... The idea that our trade will suffer because we stop imposing terrible rules such as the Clinical Trial Directive is silly." Vote Leave

> a.   "OK this has proved to be totally inaccurate and we are desperately searching for / almost grovelling for a deal with the EU and on the verge of crashing out with no deal! Now I ask who exactly was Vote Leave?"

11.   With a new system in place by 2020, "By the next general election, we will create a genuine Australian-style points-based immigration system." – Michael Gove, Boris Johnson, Priti Patel and Gisela Stuart.

> a.   "OK this sounds great in theory, but we have a similar system already and more people are coming in under this system than EU immigrants, and now with the Polish economy doing well there are less Polish now than there was in 2016! A points-based system cost millions to set up and manage that, money which could be sent elsewhere in the economy. But also, a points-based system which stop who? The Doctors? The Nurses? The care workers? The cleaners? The fruit pickers? The factory workers? The builders? We need them all, so it is a nonsense argument which cost millions to allow the same people to do the same jobs!

Contact the Author

For anyone wishing to contact the author for any reason including to disagree with any of the content enclosed in this book please email Christopher at BrexitWhatHappened@gmail.com, and he will endeavour to reply to all enquiries, points or even any critique offered about this book.

Thank You in advance for your communication and for reading my Brexit journey.

Christopher Bartram